Explaining the Cosmos

OXFORD STUDIES IN LATE ANTIQUITY

Series Editor
Ralph Mathisen

Late Antiquity has unified what in the past were disparate disciplinary, chronological, and geographical areas of study. Welcoming a wide array of methodological approaches, this book series provides a venue for the finest new scholarship on the period, ranging from the later Roman Empire to the Byzantine, Sasanid, early Islamic, and early Carolingian worlds.

The Arabic Hermes:
From Pagan Sage to Prophet of Science
Kevin van Bladel

Two Romes:
Rome and Constantinople in Late Antiquity
Edited by Lucy Grig and Gavin Kelly

Disciplining Christians:
Correction and Community in Augustine's Letters
Jennifer V. Ebbeler

History and Identity in the Late Antique Near East
Edited by Philip Wood

Explaining the Cosmos:
Creation and Cultural Interaction in Late-Antique Gaza
Michael W. Champion

Explaining the Cosmos

Creation and Cultural Interaction in Late-Antique Gaza

Michael W. Champion

OXFORD
UNIVERSITY PRESS

OXFORD
UNIVERSITY PRESS

Oxford University Press is a department of the University of Oxford.
It furthers the University's objective of excellence in research, scholarship,
and education by publishing worldwide.

Oxford New York
Auckland Cape Town Dar es Salaam Hong Kong Karachi
Kuala Lumpur Madrid Melbourne Mexico City Nairobi
New Delhi Shanghai Taipei Toronto

With offices in
Argentina Austria Brazil Chile Czech Republic France Greece
Guatemala Hungary Italy Japan Poland Portugal Singapore
South Korea Switzerland Thailand Turkey Ukraine Vietnam

Published in the United States of America by
Oxford University Press
198 Madison Avenue, New York, NY 10016

Library of Congress Cataloging-in-Publication Data

Champion, Michael W. Explaining the cosmos : creation and cultural interaction
in late-antique Gaza / Michael W. Champion.
pages cm.—(Oxford studies in late antiquity)
Includes bibliographical references and index.
ISBN 978–0–19–933748–4
1. Creation—History of doctrines—Early church, ca. 30-600. 2. Gaza—Intellectual life.
3. Aeneas, of Gaza, active 5th century. 4. Zacharias, Bishop of Mytilene 5. Procopius. I. Title.
BS680.C69C43
2014231.7'65—dc232013018112

1 3 5 7 9 8 6 4 2
Printed in the United States of America
on acid-free paper

Contents

Preface

In one of his letters, Aeneas of Gaza claimed that 'the Academy and the Lyceum are among us'. Three thinkers associated with Gaza—Aeneas, Procopius, and Zacharias—provide a case study for the appropriation, adaptation, and transformation of classical philosophy in Christian late antiquity, as well as for cultural transitions more generally in the city. The three Gazans mix in a range of social groups in the city and beyond and are interesting for the history of ideas in their own right, for the reception of Neoplatonic ideas, especially those of Proclus, and for the light they cast on later debates between thinkers such as Philoponus and Simplicius.

Aeneas' dialogue and that of Zacharias is self-consciously Platonic and both thinkers, along with Procopius in his *Commentary on Genesis*, respond to the contemporary Neoplatonic claim, put cogently by Proclus in the fifth century, that the world is eternal. This would undermine the Christian belief that God will ultimately bring in a new creation and make the cosmos perfect. The Gazans do not match the philosophical sophistication of Philoponus, although they do on occasions offer arguments that might give Neoplatonists pause for thought. Their arguments are more often governed by Christian problems, and they set out a version of the divine plan of salvation that moves their thought from physics to ethics and on to soteriology. Analysis of the dialogues simultaneously yields rich information about the cultural dynamics of the Gazan schools, on relationships between Christians and Neoplatonists in the schools, and on interactions between the schools and local monasteries. The book therefore maps the local cultures that constituted educated elite society in Gaza. My emphasis on local cultures aims to counteract the tendency to talk of Christianity as a unified monolith and goes beyond approaches which pluralize Christianity in terms of different doctrinal readings or 'heresies'. It also provides a model of cultural groups as heterogeneous and open, moving away from paradigms of cultural analysis that privilege conflict in explaining cultural identity formation.

Throughout, my aim is that intellectual history will support cultural analysis and exploration of power dynamics, and that cultural problems encoded in their texts will help to situate the Gazans' ideas. As such, the book is an attempt to bring intellectual and cultural history closely together. The book is inherently interdisciplinary. Scholars of early Christianity will recognize many of the Christian arguments, scholars of ancient philosophy will recall the main outline of the Neoplatonic debates, and scholars of late-antique history will find familiar cultural traces left by the texts, although the Gazans provide surprises in all these areas. Putting these different disciplines in closer dialogue with each other is intended to enrich each.

It is a pleasure to acknowledge the many scholars who have helped me along the way. The book began its life as a London doctorate, and much of the research was completed in London, supported by a King's College London Research Studentship, in the libraries of the Institute for Classical Studies, Warburg Institute, and British Library. I am very grateful to staff there and at the Dalton-McCaughey Library in Melbourne. My Ph.D. supervisors Peter Adamson, Judith Herrin, and Charlotte Roueché all provided critical advice and encouragement in shaping the present volume. My examiners, Isabella Sandwell and Richard Sorabji, both offered copious suggestions for improvement and greatly helped refine my ideas, as did the two anonymous readers for the Press. In Melbourne, the example and advice of the late Eric Osborn was very influential, and I have learned much from discussion with David Runia and Roger Scott (who supervised my earlier work on creation and Zacharias). I have enjoyed the support of colleagues at the University of Western Australia as I have drafted this book. I also benefit greatly from the support and criticism of family and friends and happily record my deep gratitude to Gaye, Neil, Benita, Matthew, Miranda, Philippa, Martin, and Hilary. A final word of thanks to my wife Sarah Gador-Whyte, for her love, intelligent criticism, and practical help, and to Samuel, who will one day learn what all the fuss was about.

St George's College, University of Western Australia
May 2013

Abbreviations

Journal titles are abbreviated in accordance with *l'année philologique*.

Titles of classical historical and literary texts and standard reference works are abbreviated in accordance with the *Oxford Classical Dictionary*, 4th edition, ed. Simon Hornblower and Anthony Spawforth (Oxford, 2012).

Works of ancient philosophy are abbreviated in accordance with the series *The Ancient Commentators on Aristotle*, ed. Richard Sorabji (London and Ithaca, NY), for which see *The Philosophy of the Commentators 200–600 AD*, Volume 1 (New York, 2005), 415f.

Citation systems for Greek texts usually follow those used in the *TLG*. For full bibliographic details of ancient sources, see the bibliography.

In addition, the following abbreviations or citation conventions are employed:

For citing Aeneas' and Zacharias' dialogues, line numbers in Minniti-Colonna's editions are used without noting the title (*Theophrastus* or *Ammonius*), unless this leads to ambiguity. See Aeneas, *Teofrasto*, ed. M. Minniti-Colonna (Naples, 1958); Zacharias, *Ammonio. Introduzione, Testo Critico, Traduzione, Commentario* (Naples, 1973).

Procopius' commentary is referred to without title where this is unambiguous. In this context, (37A) refers to Procopius' commentary, PG 87.1, column 37A.

ACO	*Acta conciliorum oecumenicorum*. Edited under the direction of the Bayerische Akademie der Wissenschaften (Berlin, 1984–).
CAG	*Commentaria in Aristotelem Graeca*. Edited under the direction of the Deutsche Akademie der Wissenschaften zu Berlin, 23 vols. (Berlin, 1882–1909).
CPGV X.10	Hierocles' *Commentary on the Pythagorean Golden Verses*, Chapter X and section 10 of the text edited by

	F. G. Köhler, *Hierocles in aureum Pythagoreorum carmen commentarius* (Stuttgart, 1974).
CSCO	*Corpus scriptorum christianorum orientalium*
Prov.	214.3.172a Photius' *Bibliotheca* codex 214 (where a summary of Hierocles' *De Providentia* is found), paragraph 3 in Schibli's translation, section 172a in Henry's edition of the *Bibliotheca*. See *Bibliothèque*, ed. R. Henry (Paris, 1959– : vol. 3 for codex 214, 1962; vol. 7 for codex 251, 1974); H. Schibli, *Hierocles of Alexandria* (Oxford, 2002), for translations of this work, and for *CPGV*.
Q&A	600 Letter 600 in the collection *Barsanuphe et Jean de Gaza* SC 426–27, 450–51, 468 (Paris, 1997–).
SC	Sources chretiénnes.
VSev	*Life of Severus*. Other Lives are abbreviated analogously.

Explaining the Cosmos

Introduction

EUXITHEUS ...*Come, tell me, do you still have people among you who display the mysteries of philosophy, as Hierocles, our teacher, did? And do fine and noble young men, such as my contemporary Protagoras the Lycian, who was pre-eminent in virtue and character, still attend a school?*
EGYPTUS *There were noble things long ago, but now they have departed and are destroyed. This man does not want to learn, enlisted into the [group of] students; that man who pretends to give instruction does not have the knowledge to teach. The theatre and the hippodrome flourish, while philosophy and the Muses fall into terrible neglect.*

—(Aeneas, *Theophrastus*)

A. You seem to me sufficiently initiated into the mysteries of philosophy, and not an uncultured man, uninitiated in his soul about either such sacred rites or such oral teachings. In addition, you also want to be a public figure.... But tell me, sir, how is the interpreter of the doctrines of Plato and Aristotle, who has left Athens, but came from [Proclus], the philosopher who is especially deficient in philosophy and wisdom? [This philosopher] now boasts that he is wise in the city of Alexander, and professes to make others wise harmoniously...
B You seem to me to be inquiring about Ammonius, dear sir. With such words you are accustomed to jeer at him.
A. ...Mortal fear holds me in agony in case he fill the young men with his idle talk. For that man craftily corrupts the young men's souls, renouncing both God and the truth as he does.

—(Zacharias, *Ammonius*)

Just like a teacher of children, [God] introduced the first elements to them, knowing that once they had learned them, other teachers would come, who would teach and transmit the more perfect knowledge.

—(Procopius, *Commentary on Genesis*)

These works by Aeneas, Zacharias, and Procopius, thinkers associated with Gazan rhetorical schools from the late fifth century, appear to tell standard stories. Aeneas esteems ancient knowledge, including the Neoplatonism of Hierocles (fl. 440). The *Theophrastus* is the earliest of the three works, written after 484 and before c. 490, when Zacharias began composing his work with a copy of Aeneas' dialogue on his desk. The dialogue sets itself clearly in the Platonic tradition by recalling Plato's Protagoras, the 'wisest of his generation' (σοφωτάτῳ μὲν δήπου τῶν γε νῦν) (*Prot.* 309d). Aeneas uses classical clichés to bemoan the fact that the sacred mysteries of classical philosophy are being taught badly to apathetic youth. Classical knowledge defines a virtuous public life, but the signs of demise are apparent as Philosophia's charges frequent the theatre and hippodrome instead of her school. In his *Ammonius*, Zacharias considers some of the same themes, and elsewhere similarly claims Platonic lineage, setting his dialogues in a place suitable for philosophy (*Ammonius* 47 ff.; cf. *Phaedr.* 227a–229b). But Zacharias ridicules Philosophia, who is characterized as a threat. Those who want to be Christian citizens may be corrupted by her, particularly by her representative in Alexandria, Ammonius (435/445–517/526), or still worse, by Proclus (411–485) and his successors in Athens. For Zacharias, Christian identity is constructed by emphasizing conflict and difference. In the third extract, Procopius, Zacharias' contemporary who was probably writing in the early years of the sixth century, has left philosophy behind, basing his work on divine revelation. The world has moved from paganism to Christianity, from the classical world to the early medieval era, from governors to bishops, from students to disciples.

Yet such a neat picture of progressive departure from the classical world through a process of cultural and intellectual conflict is much too simple. Interactions between diverse groups in the Gazan schools and wider cultural trends at the turn of the sixth century make for a richer picture of cultural and intellectual collaboration, and for appropriation and adaptation of ideas, beliefs, and practices. At Gaza in the late sixth century, we are fortunate to have a diverse range of evidence from rhetorical and philosophical schools, monasteries, and the archaeological record, alongside philosophical, theological, rhetorical, and poetic writings, and much comparative material from other late-antique cities, which allow us to construct a picture of a society undergoing a process of transition.[1] This book aims to elucidate this transition by exploring the writings of Aeneas, Zacharias, and Procopius on the subject of the creation and eternity of the world. Through an analysis of how these writers seek to effect change in their local cultures, I aim to explain the distinctive features of late-antique Gazan society and intellectual culture. Throughout, I offer a dual focus on cultural history sensitive to ideas and on intellectual history as culturally situated ideas. Cultural and intellectual history are richer if practised together, so while Part One (Chapters 2–3) focuses on cultural history and Part Two (Chapters 4–6) emphasizes intellectual problems, I aim to enrich both by placing them in dialogue.

The intellectual contributions of the three Gazans within the history of ideas are significant and their writings have been largely overlooked.[2] Their dialogues

1. For a broad view of Christianization from Constantine to Justinian, see Trombley (1993). For Gaza particularly, see Van Dam (1985).

2. This is an appropriate time to provide a detailed analysis of these works, as an English translation of Aeneas of Gaza, *Theophrastus* with Zacharias of Mytilene *Ammonius* has recently appeared in

cast new light on a long-running and influential late-antique philosophical debate about the creation and eternity of the world. Earlier in the fifth century, the Neoplatonic philosopher Proclus of Athens had published his *Eighteen Arguments on the Eternity of the World*. His magisterial *Commentary on Plato's Timaeus*, with its five pages for every lemma of Plato's original, also brought questions about the creation and eternity of the world to new prominence in late-antique philosophy. Such questions had long been debated, and much of Proclus' work is an analysis and synthesis of earlier opinions. But his works gave the problem new philosophical precision and intellectual momentum. Whether or not Proclus was himself motivated to write these works because of impertinent Christians in the Athenian schools, his works were a major stimulus, directly and indirectly, for the later treatment of the topic by pagan and Christian philosophers in the fifth- and sixth-century schools.[3] The intellectual background to the Gazans' contribution (within Neoplatonism and Christianity) is the subject of Chapter 4.

The three Gazans contribute to an intermediary stage in the debate, responding in part to Proclus as well as considering problems generated from within Christianity. The creation debates thus place Gaza on the intellectual map of late antiquity, demonstrating that Gaza was well integrated into networks of late-antique education without being itself a major centre of Neoplatonic thought. The distinctiveness of the Gazans' intellectual contribution therefore helps to identify unique aspects of Gazan society (Chapters 5 and 6). Gazan thinkers contributed in distinctive ways to debates more commonly associated with Alexandria and Athens. The Gazan debates are also significant for the history of ideas partly because of the framework they provide for the later more narrowly Neoplatonic arguments in the sixth century. In this episode, John Philoponus' Christian-Neoplatonist treatise against Proclus' *Eighteen Arguments*, published in the year Justinian closed the Academy in Athens, was attacked by the Neoplatonist Simplicius as well as in the idiosyncratic contributions of the Egyptian merchant and monk, Cosmas Indicopleustes. Chapter 7 concludes the book with an analysis of the distinctiveness of the Gazan contribution when compared to these later debates.

The Gazans use Neoplatonic categories to argue that only the persons of the Trinity can be coeternal, and they reject the Neoplatonic idea that the world is

the Ancient Commentators on Aristotle series (Gertz, Dillon, and Russell 2012). I have consulted this translation against my original translations of the texts.

3. For the question of stimulus for Proclus' views, see the contrasting positions of Saffrey (1975) and Lang and Macro (2001), with the judicious review of Baltzly (2002).

eternal (and central Neoplatonic concepts of creation by emanation and return) in the process. A key element for all the thinkers analysed in the debate is how to use the doctrine of creation to elucidate the question of divine and human freedom, and so to explore the related problem of evil. For each thinker, physics moves to ethics, and eschatology becomes the foundation of soteriology. The emphasis on eschatology expands the Neoplatonic focus on arguments about the temporal finitude or infinity of the world from the beginning to considerations of a possible end-point of the universe. Neoplatonists and Christians differ in how they configure these categories, but a common concern about explaining and understanding evil emerges from the debate and may be taken as characteristic of late-antique thought.

These arguments, and their relation to earlier and later debates between Christians and Neoplatonists, are the subject of the second part of this book. In the first part, I set the Gazan writings in their broader cultural context and ask how they sought to reconfigure their local cultures through their respective writings. In Chapter 2, I sketch the contours of the local cultures which gave Gazan society its distinctive characteristics at the turn of the sixth century, and I explore ways in which these local cultures formed their identities in creative interactions. The creation and maintenance of power imbalances between these groups through the construction of difference is just one component of their social interactions. The porous boundaries of the monasteries, rhetorical schools, and their members' religious and philosophical affiliations are evidence for more dynamic ways in which the local cultures formed their identities. This theme of dynamic and fluid identity formation continues in Chapter 3, where I examine how Aeneas, Zacharias, and Procopius perceived their local cultures and outline their attempts to make others accept their worldview. Since ideas are always culturally situated and not mere epiphenomena of power relations or material conditions, exploring the logic of the Christian and Neoplatonic arguments helps to define what was distinctive about different groups within the Gazan schools, and thus to characterize more precisely late-antique Gazan society as a whole. Thus, the chapters on the intellectual history of the creation debates in the second half of the book add finer details to the construction of cultures analysed in Part One.

In setting the works of Aeneas, Procopius, and Zacharias at the heart of my analysis, I do not claim that their works are strikingly original (although they have unique and original contributions to make). But unlike the eccentric geniuses who are often the subject of histories of ideas, they can be taken as representative of generally accepted norms of thought and practice among their contemporaries in educated Gazan society. When they seek to reconfigure power relations in their local cultures, we should read them as identifying real cultural problems that exercised the attention of a range of Christian thinkers in the Gazan schools. And when they engage with Neoplatonic ideas and seek to rebut them, we can assume that the intellectual problems they identify, and the argument strategies they employ, were more generally relevant in Gazan society.

In the remainder of this introduction I set out briefly the methods and analytical categories by which I interpret the texts. A continuing, if largely subterranean, argument of the book is that cultural and intellectual history can best illumine and support each other through the method of elucidation of problems set out below. I also contribute to recent studies which move beyond a paradigm of conflict in reconstructing late-antique culture. The chapter concludes with short biographical introductions to Aeneas, Zacharias, and Procopius.

1.1 Culture and Ideas, Conflict and Identity

A central analytical category throughout this book is the concept of a 'local culture'. By this I mean a social group within a society, which shares many of the assumptions, beliefs, and practices of the society as a whole, and hence its members accept allegiance to that society, but which also shares a set of characteristics which give it a distinctive identity and may sometimes bring it into tension with the general society or other local cultures. Such a culture is a complex of shared symbols and practices which is contingent on the actions of agents, changeable and time-dependent, interactive and non-discrete, and heterogeneous and contested.[4] It is always richly steeped in time—events leave their mark on the trajectory of people's lives, and structures of meaning are created and changed as people perform meaningful acts in meaningful lives. Societies are not totalizing but are instead made up of many different local cultures, themselves the product of internal disagreements and negotiations and external interactions. Culture is a product of internal coherences, disagreements, and negotiations. It does consolidate groups, but it may also provide the means for its own subversion.[5] The particular historical setting of Gaza, and the experiences of each of the thinkers I analyse, as well as how they seek to use the resources available to them—intellectual, geographical, institutional, economic, and symbolic—are central to my argument. On the side of intellectual history, this emphasis on local cultures helps to produce a more refined account of differences within Christianity which does not reduce to the identification of doctrinal conflict or heresy hunting. It counteracts the tendency to characterize Christianity as a unified monolith. Similarly

4. This view of culture is consistent with that offered by Sewell (2005), 10. For Sewell, culture is fateful, contingent, complex, eventful, and heterogeneous.

5. Compare e.g. Geertz (1975) with Geertz (1983).

in the case of cultural history, I paint a picture of tensions and exchanges within and between distinct and overlapping local cultures, and thereby reconstruct some culturally binding shared assumptions in Gazan society, considered as a complex of overlapping local cultures.

A performance metaphor may usefully encapsulate much of this conceptualization of culture and identity. The metaphor takes seriously agency, temporal and spatial setting, the symbols people can employ, the particular, historically contingent material and institutional situations in which they are placed, and the actions they perform. The concept of culture I work with accounts for the virtuosity and improvisations of the performers (agency), the sets they have (the institutions and built environment of Gaza, Alexandria, and Berytus), the props they use (material resources), the languages they can speak (predominantly Greek), the dialogues they participate in (different local communities such as the monks, the students, the lay public, the philosophers) and the audiences they address (Christians of various types, Neoplatonists).[6]

In providing a detailed description of the characteristics of different local cultures and the ways in which they interacted, I offer an account of how individuals and groups go about forming their ideas and identities. Personal and cultural beliefs and identity are not simply the sum of attempts to differentiate oneself or one's local culture from another. Such a model, like its related sister-model of cultural and intellectual interaction as conflict which has also been popular in late-antique studies, requires modification. Individuals and local cultures do try to distinguish themselves intellectually and socially from others by emphasizing real and imagined differences or conflicts, but my claim is that both individuals and groups are more heterogeneous, open, and inconsistent than such models assume, so that conflict or the construction of difference is too blunt a model by which to seek to understand cultural and interpersonal interactions and the personal and social changes these interactions bring about. Sandwell has recently argued that 'discourse [of any sort is] particularly suited to constructing identities because of [its] use of clear-cut categories and contrasting oppositions to create meaning and structure', yet few authors always make their categories perfectly clear and meaning and structure can be created through means other than contrasts.[7] The openness of texts is partly an index of the heterogeneity of the cultures by which they are generated, to say nothing of the complexities, inconsistencies, and fallibility of their

6. This metaphor values the linguistic model for culture while allowing for symbolic systems which are not merely linguistically mediated. This metaphor, if read as implying a unified cultural plot, rather than one that shows thin coherence, would be misleading, but performances may be improvised. Dougherty and Kurke (2003), 8 rightly emphasize narrative and thin coherence.

7. Sandwell (2007),13.

authors. Intellectual and cultural formation is as much about appropriating and adapting valued characteristics of other people and groups as it is about marking boundaries between people and cultures.

Of course, there are many individuals and groups within society which are aggressive in defining themselves through conflict with others. And many of the sources available to us for the study of late antiquity may easily be interpreted as fitting this more clear-cut model. Sandwell helpfully argues that some discourses seek to become totalizing, thus acting as an ideology which sets 'its agenda and masks the fact that its representation both has an agenda and that there could be other representations and agendas'.[8] A 'fluid' approach to religious identity, which understands religion mainly as a support for valued social practices or civic life and otherwise minimizes its importance in many public settings, has raised the ire of some types of Christians in all ages, and at times their corresponding totalization of religious identity in the face of such apparent accommodation with the surrounding culture may indeed amount to 'ideological and rule-bound impositions of religious identity'.[9]

In the case of late-antique Gaza, Aeneas, Procopius, and Zacharias all seek to construct exclusive religious allegiances and this construction is achieved partly by constructing a discursive conflict between themselves and others in the schools. Some of their least appealing arguments are designed to marginalize their opponents by painting pagan religion as politically subversive. In these arguments, the Gazans invoke and help to strengthen increasing imperial suppression of religious difference. Yet other voices speak through these apparently aggressive texts. While the Gazans thus partly construct their arguments and preferred religious identity though conflict and opposition, we also find them quietly borrowing and adapting ideas or proudly claiming other identities they share with their non-Christian neighbours. Careful examination of their works reveals elements of Gazan society more open to difference and supports a model which takes conflict as just one element in the construction of ideas and associated cultural practices and personal identities.

The method of elucidation of problems, which seeks to interrogate and explain the cultural and intellectual problems faced by a historical actor is expansive enough to account for culture as I have conceptualized it and moves beyond models of identity construction based on ideological construction of difference. Elucidation of problems asks: 'What problems are particular people trying to

8. Perkins (1995), 2 in Sandwell (2007), 27–28. I would include ideology in the category of discourse.

9. Sandwell (2007), 20 argues that this is true of John Chrysostom, as, in the pagan case, for the emperor Julian. See also ibid. 22, drawing on Wöhrle (1995), 76–82.

solve through this particular act?'[10] An advantage of this method is that it is equally useful for 'cultural' and 'intellectual' histories. It provides mechanisms for 'historians of ideas' to 'learn to think the thoughts of others, as a philosopher must learn to think his own',[11] based on the principle that understanding thinkers means thinking 'as they thought and [seeing] things in their way'.[12] While 'cultural' historians have not used it explicitly, the method is appropriate, since it is consistent with a rich understanding of the concept of culture. Elucidation of problems allows so-called intellectual historians to reconstruct symbols and practices employed by thinkers in their arguments. Analogously, cultural historians can use the method to analyse how symbols and practices are applied in other domains of social action. Hence, this method can be useful for helping intellectual and cultural historians work together profitably. The application of a method of elucidation of problems is designed to facilitate careful attention both to the standards of rationality which govern the arguments as well as to the social and cultural conventions and practices which give them shape.

1.2 Introducing Aeneas, Zacharias, and Procopius

It remains to introduce Aeneas, Zacharias, and Procopius. Given that I am largely concerned with cultural specificity, my use of the adjective 'Gazan' to describe three thinkers with considerably different associations with the city requires explanation. We hear of 'Gaza schools' (rhetorical or monastic) and 'Gazan monasticism', and we read that Aeneas, Zacharias, and Procopius are 'Gazan thinkers'.[13] Each of these labels elides differences. Browning has drawn attention to stylistic differences between Aeneas and Procopius; each thinker writes different sorts of works; each spends different amounts of time in Gaza.[14] Each studied in Gaza, but while Aeneas and Procopius made their homes there,

10. Passmore (1965) defined this method from the perspective of the history of philosophy. He set the method against 'doxographic' history, which hunts sources without providing a framework for understanding the new synthesis, retrospective history, which writes the history of philosophy from some privileged moment (for instance, the early church councils) and so omits material which is not relevant to the privileged idea, and polemic history, which seeks to prove that an idea was right or wrong, and so often misses complexity or, like retrospective history, is guilty of conceptual parochialism. Problematic elucidation shows how sources are used, sets the ideas in their own context, and identifies what the thinker thought was logical, thus incorporating the best elements of the other methods while escaping their pitfalls. See also Levine (2005); Osler (2002); Watson (2002).

11. Edwards (2002), 114.

12. Skinner (1988a), 252.

13. See most recently the treatment of Bitton-Ashkelony and Kofsky (2006); Kofsky and Bitton-Ashkelony (2004).

14. Browning (1963).

Zacharias only briefly returned to his birthplace, Gaza's port-town, after studying in Alexandria and Berytus, before making his career elsewhere. The geographical label also masks diversity: Gaza can be used to refer to the town of Gaza as well as its port-town, Maiuma, which had significantly different social profiles.[15] What is the value of the term?

Despite these difficulties, describing the three thinkers as 'Gazan' captures something of the complexity and specificity of their experiences. Apart from particular disputes (e.g. about church governance) between Gaza and Maiuma, the word 'Γάζα' in the ancient sources can refer to an amalgam of these localities. Zacharias, born in Maiuma, can describe a fellow student 'Thomas the Sophist, who loves Christ in everything, and who is, like me, from Gaza' (*VSev* PO 2.1 23,18–24,1). The interactions between urban, semi-urban, semi-rural, and port-town 'Gazans' help to create the 'Gazan' culture I analyse and elucidate. So one may examine the influence of different local cultures within Gaza, without doing away with the usefulness of the term to describe the sum total of local cultures in this area of Palestina Prima. Thus this difficulty about how to use the term 'Gaza' is an example of the difficulty of conceptualizing culture as, on the one hand, the broad and loosely bound conceptual schemes and practices which unite a society at a macro level, and, on the other hand, as the symbols and practices which bind groups within the wider society at the local level.[16]

Aeneas, a leading Gazan sophist, was the earliest of the three.[17] Born in the first third of the fifth century, he probably did not live to see the sixth. Aeneas may have studied under the Neoplatonic philosopher Hierocles of Alexandria; his dialogue is evidence that he knew Hierocles' works. Zacharias provides evidence for Aeneas' reputation as a philosopher, and also connects him to the monastic communities in Gaza.[18] There was a productive overlap between the monasteries and the schools, which makes late-antique Gaza distinctive (see further Chapter 2).

Zacharias describes Aeneas as 'the grand and wise Christian sophist from the town of Gaza' (*VSev* PO 2.1 90), yet goes on to speak of Aeneas' philosophical interests. As in earlier generations, sophists in Gaza were more than rhetorical teachers; they had wider theological and philosophical interests.[19] According

15. For territorial definitions of Gaza, see di Segni (2004). For the geographical spread of the monasteries, see Hirshfeld (2004). For the distinction between Gaza and Maiuma in the historical sources, and their respective religious profile, see e.g. Eusebius *Hist. eccl.* 4.38; Sozomen *Hist. eccl.* 5.3, 9–10, 15.

16. For this distinction, see Sewell (2005), chapter 2.

17. For modern analyses of Aeneas' dating and life, see Aujoulat (1986); Segonds (1989); Seitz (1892); Sikorski (1909); Wacht (1969).

18. The suggestion that Aeneas may have been Bishop of Gaza, based on an eponymous figure listed in Choricius, *Laud. Marc. II* 8 is dubious. Cf. Ashkenazi (2004), 200.

19. On the continuing tradition of philosophical and rhetorical sophists, see the forthcoming volume edited by Ryan Fowler, *Plato in the Third Sophistic*.

to Zacharias' admiring, hagiographic account of Abba Isaiah, a leading Gazan figure in the non-Chalcedonian camp, Aeneas' expertise in philosophy was surpassed by the untrained holy man's. Zacharias has Aeneas explain that

> Often, if I came across some problem in a certain place concerning a word from Plato, Aristotle, or Plotinus, and I could not find a solution to it among those who teach and interpret their opinions, I would ask [Abba Isaiah] to make their intention and purpose clear to me as to what they wanted to say, and he would illumine and reveal the meaning and purpose of the passage, and he would not only redress its error but also restore the truth of Christian teaching. (*VIs* 8; my translation from the Latin)

From Procopius we learn nothing of Aeneas' philosophical accomplishments, but he does praise Aeneas' legal expertise (Procopius of Gaza, *Ep.* 82; cf. Aeneas, *Ep.* 3).[20]

Epiphanius 5 (*PLRE* II), a student of Aeneas and addressee of two letters from him (*Epp* 12, 23), wrote an epigram in praise of his teacher (Εἰς Αἰνείαν τὸν Γαζαῖον), which heralds Aeneas in conventional if inflated terms as being 'the most eminent of rhetors in the Attic art'. Aeneas 'excelled both his contemporaries and forefathers in more holy speeches'. Gaza, claims Epiphanius, should take to heart the fact that it was fortunate enough to count such a father among its citizens.[21] These testimonia point to a figure who was socially influential and educated in philosophy, theology, and rhetoric.

Aeneas' extant oeuvre comprises a set of twenty-five letters and the dialogue which is of central interest to this study, the *Theophrastus*.[22] The *Theophrastus* was written after 484 and before Zacharias' dialogue (489/90) (on Zacharias' dating, see further below).[23] Aeneas' letters provide a window into his contexts and those of his correspondents, who include presbyters, rhetoricians, officials, and other intellectuals, and provide useful detail about the social characteristics of Gaza in this period.

Aeneas' dialogue has three characters: Theophrastus, a Greek philosopher, Euxitheus, a Christian who has studied philosophy, and Egyptus, a Christian who plays only a small part in the dialogue. Adverse winds blow Euxitheus' ship off course and he cannot continue his journey, so he settles

20. See Wacht (1969), 16 n. 19.

21. *Anth Gr*, App, *Epigrammata demonstrativa* 176.

22. Aeneas (1962); Aeneas (1958). A projected and still required second edition of the *Theophrastus* never transpired.

23. For dating, see Wacht (1969), 18 n. 17. See also Aujoulat (1986); Segonds (1989), 83.

down to a philosophical conversation with the Greek traveller and philosopher Theophrastus and Euxitheus' associate, Egyptus, on topics including the pre-existence and immortality of the soul, the creation of the cosmos, and the resurrection of bodies. The limited previous scholarship on the dialogue focuses on sources (Christian and philosophical) or, more recently, on what the dialogue may suggest about power conflicts in late-antique schools.[24]

The dialogue form chosen by Aeneas and, later, by Zacharias presents several challenges of interpretation to which we will return. The dialogue genre may reflect social and intellectual conflict and collaboration. The extent to which the dialogues aim to perform or allow real intellectual and cultural polysemy is an open question. Aeneas' choice of dialogue form may be seen as creating a space in which different local cultures can find their voice, yet the author carefully controls what the different characters are allowed to say in the dialogue, and we may often suspect that the genre is being used ideologically, to control what can be imagined in Aeneas' desired society. Analysing these tendencies reveals some of Aeneas' most deeply held commitments, but a concern for providing an intellectually compelling account of Christian doctrine makes such power discourse analyses of the dialogue insufficient. The dialogue also reveals a genuine knowledge about, and positive evaluation of, philosophical argument. Aeneas wants to persuade his philosophically inclined audience partly on the basis of argument, even though his dialogue also functions to disempower them in various ways.

Zacharias Scholasticus (or Zachariah Rhetor) (c. 465–post 536) was perhaps some twenty to thirty years younger than Aeneas, whom he describes as 'a great teacher'. Aeneas' dialogue provides an intellectual model for Zacharias' *Ammonius*.[25] He died some time after attending the Council of Constantinople in 536.[26] Zacharias studied rhetoric under Sopater 3 (*PLRE* II) and philosophy under Ammonius in Alexandria before undertaking legal studies in Berytus. While in Alexandria, he witnessed and recounted the turmoil which arose from Pagan–Christian tensions in the schools (*VSev*). In Berytus, he was a member of the so-called *philoponoi*, a group of students who performed various

24. See Aujoulat (1986, 1987); Gallicet (1978); Wacht (1969); Watts (2005).

25. Some recent authors refer to Zacharias as 'Pseudo-Zacharias'. See, for example, Haarer (2006); Maas (2005). This arises from debate about whether the Zacharias whose church history is preserved in Evagrius' *Historia Ecclesiastica*, identified by Evagrius as Zacharias ῥήτωρ (*Hist. eccl.* 2.2), is the same person as the bishop of Mitylene and/or Procopius' brother Zacharias. Frend argues against the grain in modern scholarship for non-identity: Frend (1972), 202f. For the consensus that the writer of the history is the writer of the biographies, see Allen (1980), 471; Honigmann (1953), 194ff. Haarer (2006), 268f. judiciously gathers the arguments and provides further literature. I will refer to Zacharias, not Pseudo-Zacharias.

26. Honigmann (1953), 194ff.

charitable works, and sought to preserve Christian orthodoxy in the school, which Zacharias in his *Life of Severus* depicts as potentially spiritually dangerous.[27] After working as an advocate (*scholasticus*) in Constantinople, he was made (Chalcedonian) bishop of Mitylene.[28] This appointment should caution against reading Zacharias as a strongly committed non-Chalcedonian, although political pressure to change ecclesiastical allegiance could be strong. A letter from the non-Chalcedonian Patriarch Severus, written when he was exiled in around 519–521, may refer to our Zacharias, and states that 'those without [i.e. the Chalcedonians] are at peace with you'.[29] If so, there is evidence that Zacharias, despite his friendship with Severus, had moved to the Chalcedonian camp by the early years of the reign of Justin and Justinian. Zacharias' dialogue, the work of most relevance to this study, shows no signs of non-Chalcedonian emphasis.

Zacharias is variously referred to in the manuscripts as 'Zacharias Scholasticus', 'Zacharias Rhetor', and 'Zacharias, bishop of Mitylene'.[30] Honigmann's case that these figures should also be identified with the Zacharias who was an imperial official and a brother of Procopius of Gaza is circumstantial, but persuasive.[31] If the identification of Zacharias Scholasticus, author of the *Ammonius* and future bishop of Mitylene with Zacharias the brother of Procopius is accepted, it places all three Gazan thinkers in an elite stratum of society with strong connections to the imperial court.[32]

27. For the *philoponoi*, see Miller (1985); Watts (2006), 213–19, 251–58.

28. This seems certain, despite Schwartz's emphatic belief to the contrary, cited in Honigmann (1953), 195: 'Ihn mit dem Bischof von Mitylene zu identifizieren, der auf der scharf chalcedonischen Synoden von 536 eine aktive Rolle übernehmen musste, ist platterdings unmöglich' (It is completely impossible to identify him with the Bishop of Mitylene, who must have played an active role in the strongly Chalcedonian Synod of 536). Honigmann uses striking resemblances between passages in the *VSev* and the *Antirrhesis*. The former is ascribed in the MSS to Zacharias Scholasticus; the latter is explicitly attributed to 'Zacharias, Bishop of Mitylene who was formerly a Scholasticus'. See Honigmann (1953), 197–98, 200–201. For the identification of the figure known in the MSS as Zacharias Rhetor with the figure known as Zacharias Scholasticus, see Honigmann (1953), 197–99.

29. Brooks (1916), PO XII, 269–78, Severus of Antioch, Ep. XXXIV. The letter is cited and discussed in Honigmann (1953), 202–4.

30. See above, note 25.

31. The names of Procopius' brothers are found in Procopius' correspondence, and Severus' letter mentions the names of all these brothers, names one, correctly, as a presbyter, and gives instructions to a 'Zacharias Scholasticus'. Honigmann (1953), 202; Rist (1998, 2003). *PLRE II* lists two different Zachariases. This paragraph is indebted to Honigmann's study, 201–4. Procopius wrote thirteen letters to his brother Zacharias, a 'rhetor' (*Ep.* 52) individually: *Epp* 20, 51–52, 58, 69, 80–83, 85, 93, 152, 161. There are also thirteen letters addressed to his brothers Philippus and Zacharias jointly: *Epp* 57, 73, 79, 84, 96–97, 105, 108–10, 143–44, 148. Procopius also wrote nine letters solely to Philippus (6–7, 10, 15, 19, 86, 92, 135, 157) and one letter solely to Victor (74).

32. Rist (2003) argues that our Zacharias had 'gute Kontakte zum kaiserlichen Hof' and that his elevation to the episcopate was probably a reward for his imperial service.

Zacharias wrote church history, biography, and dogmatic works.[33] All his writings may be interpreted as polemics, and his lives of key non-Chalcedonian figures are responsible for much of the scholarship which emphasizes religious and social conflict in this period. The biographies justify their heroes against Chalcedonian attack, the ecclesiastical history takes sides on doctrinal disputes, and the titles of the works against the Manichees (Ἀντίρρησις; *Capita adversos Manichaeos*) set the tone for works which conform to the 'anathema' genre.[34] Yet while Zacharias' dialogue resonates with this general enjoyment of polemic and disputation, it also reveals cultural complexity which a focus on conflict misses. Zacharias was a writer who identified problems and tenaciously tried to solve them. This fact, together with the uncertainty surrounding his biography, makes elucidation of problems useful for entering his thought-world, and opens avenues by which to explore cultural adaptations and appropriations.

His dialogue, the *Ammonius*, is the focus of this book.[35] It depicts a Christian teacher strengthening the faith of an Alexandrian student 'slipping towards paganism'. Zacharias achieves the goal of educating the student by recounting a series of mini-dialogues he claims to have had with Ammonius and the Neoplatonist iatrosophist Gessius (fl. late fifth century). The mini-dialogues investigate creation, resurrection, the eternity of the cosmos and matter, the forms, and the Trinity. The dialogue ends, like the *Theophrastus*, in prayer: the student's faith is renewed by Zacharias' teaching. Recent theories positing a mid-sixth-century date for sections of the dialogue are unconvincing.[36] It seems most likely that it should be dated to around 490.[37] Particularly, the idea that

33. See Rist (1998). The life of Severus is extant in Syriac. The lives of Isaiah and Peter the Iberian are much less securely preserved. The (Syriac version of the) *Life of Isaiah* is fragmentary. The *Life of Peter* is both fragmentary and disputed. The Syriac fragment is included in a manuscript among a series of texts by John Rufus concerning Peter. Horn concludes that 'the existence [of a *Life of Peter* by Zacharias] . . . still remains merely a matter of hypothesis' from the Syriac evidence. See Horn (2006), 46. The Georgian version of the *Life* claims to be a translation of a Syriac life written by Zacharias. Despite this, Honigmann believed the life to be a revision of John Rufus' *Vita Petri Iberi*. This view was countered by Lang in an article negatively evaluated by Devros, who supported Honigmann's position. See Devros (1950); Honigmann (1953); Lang (1951). Horn concludes that the Georgian version is not good evidence for a life of Peter by Zacharias either. I therefore exclude this text as a resource for Zacharias' ideas, despite the common implicit acceptance of the *Life* as a work by Zacharias in some other recent writers, such as Watts (2007). See further Horn (2006), 47–49.

34. For the anti-Manichean works, see Lieu (1983).

35. His non-Chalcedonian histories have received detailed attention but do not touch on the doctrine of creation. Hence, I merely use them where appropriate in forming a picture of Gazan social history in Chapter 2, below. For Zacharias' non-Chalcedonian biographies and church histories, see Watts (2007); Zacharias (1977); Zacharias (1919–1921).

36. Watts (2005c). The conclusions of this article are incorporated into his recent book, Watts (2006), 228.

37. For which, see Bardy (1950), col. 3677; Segonds (1989), 89; Wacht (1969), 18 n. 17.

the dialogue was revised to include a prominent sixth-century pagan doctor after Ammonius' death seem to fail, given that Gessius is elsewhere described as a doctor who flourished under the emperor Zeno (Damascius, *VIs*). The dialogue's intellectual debt to Aeneas of Gaza is marked, explained by the recent influence of that thinker and the Gazan milieu, although it also inscribes Zacharias' Alexandrian experiences.

The questions about the genuine openness of Aeneas' dialogue also apply to Zacharias'. In this regard, it is important that Zacharias moves the philosophical conversations from the traditional *locus philosophicus* of a shady outdoor setting as in the *Phaedrus* ultimately to the confines of a great church, although a literary allusion at the end of the dialogue returns us to the *Phaedrus*. Zacharias' attempt to use the dialogue form to limit social difference is explored in Chapter 3. Like Aeneas, he displays direct knowledge of his Neoplatonic opponents, and like all three Gazans he also seeks to solve intra-Christian problems in his dialogue. A central intellectual problem the dialogue explores is how to think about the freedom of God and humans as part of a more general argument about how the first principle of being is also the first principle of goodness. This emphasis, as in Aeneas before him, makes the debate about the creation and eternity of the world also a debate about ethics. The dialogue also introduces a new concept of eternity which makes a significant difference to how Christians think about the eternity of the world. As for Aeneas, this new concept is partly motivated by Trinitarian considerations.[38]

Finally, we come to Procopius of Gaza (c. 465–528). He wrote a large corpus of letters which helps to provide us with biographical detail and rich information about Gazan culture.[39] Two of his brothers, Philippus and Zacharias (whether ours or not), were at some stage lawyers and officials in the imperial court at Constantinople. Procopius won a rhetorical contest in Alexandria in his youth and began teaching rhetoric by his early twenties after turning down offers of employment in Antioch, Berytus, Caesarea, and Tyre (Choricius, *Fun. or. in Proc.* 12, 15). He is best known for his panegyric for Anastasius and his large corpus of letters. Through this correspondence, we are provided with a picture of a man deeply involved in civic affairs. We see him writing letters of preferment and reference for students and teachers; he contributes to the political life of Gaza, including organizing imperial embassies and mediating disputes; he is in demand as a sophist, both for civic occasions in Gaza and for teaching in urban centres, including Antioch and Caesarea. He wrote a variety of works, including

38. See further Chapter 6.

39. Procopius (1963). See now the recent Italian edition and translation of his letters, with several highly informative introductory chapters, edited by Amato (2010a).

a Metaphrasis of Homer,[40] speeches (ekphrasis,[41] panegyric,[42] monody), letters,[43] and exegetical works.[44] He may have written philosophical works against Proclus, although these are either lost, or fragmentary and disputed.[45]

Some categorize these works by dividing them into obviously and dubiously Christian texts, making Procopius appear somewhat schizophrenic.[46] The Christian Procopius, author of the exegetical works (the philosophical ones are generally left out of this picture), displayed no great knowledge of classical authors, whereas the non-Christian Procopius, sophist and rhetor worthy of the Atticism he aspired to, was thoroughly steeped in the classics, including Homer, Hesiod, Thucydides, Herodotus, Isocrates, Demosthenes, Plato, Aristotle, Euripides, and many others.[47] This marked difference in sources used in various works has led to suggestions that Procopius was either converted late, or else that we have two 'Procopiuses'.[48] Generic differences, where different source materials are expected because different writers are taken as authoritative for different subjects and occasions, provide a more promising solution to the variety and particularity of Procopius' use of earlier writers.[49]

Aly long ago suggested that the letters may have been written to be sent but were then used as teaching materials, and closer attention to the cultural context of the rhetorical schools helpfully moves beyond generic or religious categorizations of Procopius' works.[50] The Panegyric may have been presented at a public occasion and was written to fulfil Procopius' duty as a public rhetor, a duty which fell to teachers of rhetoric. The *ekphraseis* similarly function as rhetorical exercises. Ter Haar Romeny has suggested that the commentaries, which are largely geared towards basic biblical literacy, also fulfil an educational function in the rhetorical schools, and his philosophical interests are also plausibly generated in the school context.[51]

40. Brinkmann (1908) discusses the tradition, based largely on Photios' comments in his article on Choricius (Cod. 160). Brinkmann also finds parallels for the 'τόπος περὶ φιλοψυχίας'. See also Rabe (1908).

41. Procopius (1963).

42. Procopius (2005).

43. Massa Positano (1962), Letters 1–166; Procopius (1963). For additions to this corpus, see Maltese (1984); Westerink (1967).

44. Procopius (1983); Procopius and John (1978a); Procopius and John (1978b).

45. Des Places (1971), 46–47; Westerink (1942).

46. Ter Haar Romeny (2007), 189.

47. For a fuller list, see ibid. 177–78.

48. Kennedy (1983), 171.

49. As recognized by Ter Haar Romeny (2007).

50. 'Prokopios' *RE* XXIII.1, 265–66.

51. Ter Haar Romeny (2007), 190.

I focus on Procopius' *Commentary on Genesis*, particularly its preface, and the *Refutatio*. Significant problems of interpretation encircle both these works. In the case of the *Commentary*, it is clear that Procopius used a catena, drawing on it systematically to furnish his work.[52] The originality of his contribution is thus called into question, although Procopius had independent access to earlier sources and the section relating to chapter one of Genesis, which is most relevant for this book, is also most independent of the earlier tradition.[53] In addition, the process of collating, editing, merging, and summarizing earlier sources can introduce a new logic, one in which distinctive Gazan concerns may be heard.

Procopius' rebuttal of Proclus' philosophy was called into question when fragments of it were discovered to be identical to a later, twelfth-century treatise by Nicholas of Methone. Yet a plausible case for authenticity, while insecure, remains possible.[54] I use the fragments as traces of sixth-century views with care strictly to limit the conclusions drawn from them. To underline the continuing uncertainty of attribution, I label the author of the relevant fragment 'Procopius(?)'.

Procopius' biblical commentary places him very firmly within an intra-Christian context, yet commentary was the dominant mode of intellectual endeavours in the rhetorical, philosophical, and medical schools of late antiquity, so Procopius may be seen as valuing contemporary models of scholarship while simultaneously using his commentary to construct a Christian chain of authority. The early part of his commentary seems directed against a philosophically aware audience. The extent of his engagement with Neoplatonism in particular is contested, but his engagement with many of the problems which exercised Neoplatonists, albeit within a Christian theological frame, makes his treatment a good introduction to relevant problems in Aeneas' and Zacharias' dialogues, and it is therefore analysed first.

All three Gazans have cultural and intellectual problems to solve. They are concerned with establishing their own power and demonstrating the truth of their arguments. Their various works are partly generated by cultural problems

52. Petit (1996), 244; Petit (1991); Ter Haar Romeny (2007). I refer the reader to these works for more complete discussion and merely set out the relevant conclusions here. See also Devreese (1928 and 1959); Nautin in Origen, Guéraud, and Nautin (1979), 83–86, 93–95.

53. See further Petit (1996), 244f; Petit (1991), 329–33. This question about originality voices a peculiarly modern anxiety which Procopius did not share. On originality in late antiquity, see Littlewood (1995).

54. For arguments *pro* and *contra*, see most recently Amato (2010b), with new arguments for authenticity, and the contributions of Stiglmayer (1899); Russos (1893); Aly (1957); des Places (1971); Westerink (1942); Whittaker (1975).

in and beyond the Gazan schools and by intellectual challenges from contemporary Neoplatonists, philosophically inclined Christians, those who would attempt to reject philosophy entirely, and from local monks. While intellectual and cultural problems cannot ultimately be disentangled, for the purposes of clarity of analysis it is useful to separate them initially. Intellectual challenges to the Gazans are explored in Part Two. In Part One, I use the texts as case studies of cultural problems. A key cultural problem is how to limit the power of pagan religion in the schools and more widely in a culture still largely shaped by the classical world without thereby losing the valued social status which attached to classical learning and which supported the Gazan rhetorical schools. To begin to see how the Gazans went about solving this cultural problem, and the strategies they used to shape their local cultures, we must first gain a clearer picture of the constituent local cultures of Gazan society and the sources available for its study.

PART I

Creating Gazan Cultures

2

Late-Antique Gaza

Teachers, Monks, and Philosophers

The Gaza which emerges from this chapter was formed through diverse interactions between people involved in multiple often partially overlapping local cultures. These various interactions, in philosophical, theological, legal, educational, religious, governmental, and business contexts, make possible creative use of diverse ideas and are occasions of potential competition between thought systems and associated modes of life. Gaza's rhetorical schools and monasteries were the key institutions in and through which Aeneas, Zacharias, and Procopius lived. While many of the processes, structures, and ideas of late-antique education strengthened social bonds and had the potential to collapse difference, education was not homogeneous and could therefore also generate creative tensions. Diversity, interaction, and competition in the schools can be seen within Neoplatonism, between different groups of Christians, between Christians and Neoplatonists, and also in the Gazan monasteries. Gazan society at the turn of the sixth century displayed the dynamism as well as the conflict born of claims to power associated with periods of cultural and intellectual transition.

2.1 Social and Material Contours of Late-Antique Gaza

The sources for the history of the late-antique city of Gaza are rich. While geopolitical conflicts have hindered study of the material culture of the ancient city, recent archaeological work has shed brighter light on Gaza's economic strength, material culture, and religious diversity.[1] We are particularly fortunate in literary sources. Gaza is mentioned briefly in the fifth-century church historians Sozomen and Socrates, where it is described as a pagan stronghold. For the period just following the three Gazans, the speeches of Procopius' student

1. Archaeological finds are collected and discussed in Ovadiah (1969), 197; Ovadiah (1982); Sadek (1999), especially 62–64, 66f.; Saliou (2005b). Ovadiah (1969), 197 dates a Jewish synagogue to A.D. 508. A dye works, dating from the early to mid-fifth century, yields evidence of trade between Gaza and Greece, Italy, Sinaï, and Negev. In Saliou's volume, see especially Ballet (2005); Dixneuf (2005); Elter and Hassoune (2005).

Choricius provide a wealth of information, and speeches in praise of Procopius (a funeral oration) and Procopius' contemporaries (various panegyrics) may be used to reconstruct the Gaza they helped to shape.[2] The letters of two Gazan holy men, Barsanuphius and John, who lived in a monastery close to Gaza at Thawatha, provide a valuable account of Gazan social and religious history around the middle of the sixth century.[3] At the other chronological end of this study, the letters of St Jerome offer a fleeting perspective on Gaza in the early fifth century, and his *Life of Hilarion* offers an account of the origins of Gazan monasticism.[4] The most complete source for Gazan social history in the period immediately preceding the main focus of this study is Mark the Deacon's *Life of Porphyry*. At first sight, this looks like a crucial source for a study of the interactions between Christians and pagans in and around Gaza. Its vivid narrative is replete with temple destructions, the mechanics of imperial support for Christianization, including the use of the imperial army to support Christian efforts, and networks of imperial and episcopal patronage which aided the church's mission.[5] It appears to record the extent of Christianization in Gaza in the living memory of the three Gazans. Yet strong doubt has recently been cast on its trustworthiness.[6] These doubts may be overstated, but it is prudent to use the text only together with other sources to offer a probable account of Gaza in the generations immediately preceding Aeneas, Zacharias, and Procopius.

As an important centre for the trade of luxury and everyday items, late-antique Gaza was economically prosperous. As in earlier centuries, it derived much of its economic and strategic power from its position as a bridge between Syria, Palestine, Egypt, and the Mediterranean.[7] It was located on the coast at the node of a number of busy Roman roads. Many Roman emperors travelled through Gaza in military campaigns or tours of the eastern provinces. None of this is to say that Gaza counted among the most prosperous and strategically important

2. Litsas (1980); Mayerson (1986); Rabinowitz (1949). More recent studies on Choricius may be consulted in Saliou (2005b).

3. See Hevelone-Harper (2005). See also Binns (1994), 21, 201; Chitty (1977); Barsanuphius and John the Old Man of Gaza (1997–2002). See also Bitton-Ashkelony and Kofsky (2006).

4. Elter and Hassoune (2005); Jerome (2007); Maraval (2004).

5. Mark the Deacon (1913).

6. For relevant literature pro and contra, see MacMullen (1997), 39; MacMullen (1984), 86–89; Peeters (1941), 65–100; Rubin (1998); Trombley (1993), vol. 1, 246–82; Childers (2006).

7. See also Flusin's preface in Saliou (2005b), ix. For more detailed accounts, see Downey (1963); Glucker (1987); Saliou (2005b). For the slightly later period, see Bitton-Ashkelony and Kofsky (2004, 2006). For recent work on material culture, see Ballet (2005); Dixneuf (2005). The ceramic finds are evidence for trade between Palestine and Egypt and further afield. Gaza's main trade in late antiquity was in wine. See Avi-Yonah (1958). For the parallel case of Constantinople, see Harrison and Hayes (1986); Hayes (1992). See also Reynolds (2005).

cities in late antiquity, yet neither was it a rural backwater. Flusin's evaluation, that Gaza could not rival the main urban centres of the empire, but was nevertheless above average, seems safe.[8] Choricius recognized the value for trade and commerce of Gaza's position between earth and sea in his second oration to Bishop Marcianus (Choricius, *Marcion II*, 2). Gaza's pleasant location also made it attractive for tourists and its festivals gave the city a further means of advertising its educational establishments and building their reputations. Gaza also benefited, according to Choricius, from civic benefactions from the (Gazan-born) governor of Caesarea (Choricius, *Panegyric for Stephanus*, 53–56, 60–62). Stephanus sent his son to be educated in Gaza, and repaired Gaza's fortifications, the roof of its basilica, and its theatre; he also provided a new public baths and water supply, as well as the church of St Sergius.[9]

Gaza's location meant that it was well-placed to benefit from Palestine's increasing prosperity in the fourth to seventh centuries.[10] Reasons for the increase in economic strength in Palestine include immigration, stabilization after second- and third-century conflicts, agricultural production, increase in Christian tourism to holy sites, and expanded imperial and ecclesial investment in the province. The leaders of the monastic communities around Gaza themselves travelled to Jerusalem on pilgrimage and the Gazan monasteries gained income from pilgrims using Gaza as a staging-post.[11] Analogous Palestinian centres such as the (admittedly larger) city of Caesarea provide ample evidence for the increasing prosperity of the provinces of Palestine.[12] Caesarea shows a substantial increase in building work beginning in the fourth century; a late fourth-century city wall enclosed two to three times the earlier built-up area of Caesarea. Caesarea housed a major library and had a strong history of rhetorical education which could support the rhetorical schools in Gaza. Likewise, proximity to Alexandria and a network of relationships which extended to Athens exposed the three thinkers to the best of contemporary rhetoric and philosophy.

The archaeological picture of Caesarea's continued economic strength suggests that Procopius' and Choricius' statements should be read partly in the light

8. 'Gaza ne peut certes rivaliser avec les grands centres comme Constantinople, Antioche ou Alexandrie, mais elle est plus importante et plus active que la plupart des cités de l'Empire.' See Flusin (2005), x.

9. Stephanus may also appear in Procopius, *Ep.* 134, but see Hollum (1986), 236 n. 23. See also Mayerson (1986), 270.

10. For economic growth in the region in late antiquity, see Kennedy (2000), 601–7.

11. For the monasteries around Gaza, see di Segni (2004); Elter and Hassoune (2005); Hirshfeld (2004); Neyt (2004); Regnault (2004).

12. For recent archaeological work at Caesarea, see Raban and Holum (1996). See especially the survey in the introduction ('Caesarea and recent scholarship') by Holum and Raban, xxix–xxxi. See also Raban, Artzy, Goodman, and Gal (2009).

of intercity rivalry between the two Palestinian centres.[13] Choricius provides glimpses of the strength of such intercity rivalry in the sphere of education when he claims that Antioch, Berytus, Tyre, and Caesarea all vied for Procopius' rhetorical services (Choricius *Fun or. in Proc.* 12). According to Choricius, Caesarea used force, flattery, and bribery in its vain attempt to prise Procopius from his native city. Such methods were apparently not uncommon; they were simply the normal allurements used to build up a city's educational establishments.[14] Such rivalry is itself a possible explanation for the rising prominence of the Gazan schools, as they sought to surpass Caesarea's pagan schools, which had recently been built up by figures such as Acacius, Libanius, and Orion.

As in Caesarea, Alexandria, and other late-antique urban centres, Gaza's educational establishments contributed materially to their city's economic strength. This supported the intellectual pursuits of the three Gazans; in turn, they contributed to the economic prosperity of their city by making Gaza an attractive centre of education for the elite. Choricius' Gaza, with its light breezes, extravagant festivals, and its elegant buildings and temperate citizens, was a prime location to send one's child to begin his rhetorical education.[15] The monasteries around Gaza may also have attracted pilgrims and other tourists to the region. The 'frequent festivals' which Choricius describes provided the perfect opportunity for orators to display their abilities: visitors to the city for its festivals went to hear public rhetorical performances (*Laud. Marc. I*, 83–94). Downey helpfully interprets this description as a contribution to the strength of education in fifth-century Gaza.[16]

Like many urban centres in late antiquity, Gazan society included citizens with diverse religious affiliations, and there was substantial interaction between different religious groups. Those to which Aeneas, Procopius, and Zacharias refer are Jews, Christians, and pagans.[17] The evidence from Gaza confirms

13. See Sivan (2008), 311–13 for the difficulty of reconciling archaeology with literary evidence, especially given the conflicting archaeological traces: only 15% of late-antique Caesarea is now excavated.

14. 'The city of Caesarea outstripped the enchantment of both [Antioch and Tyre], employing force, threats and bribery with much gold to entice him, and as many wiles as the lover of students always used as bait' (Choricius *Fun or. in Proc.* 12).

15. Choricius' *Laud. Marc. I* draws on Homer's description of Alcinous' garden in *Od.* VII, 112ff. to paint a picture of Gaza's epic prosperity.

16. Downey (1958), 315.

17. Other religious groups existed in the city, although the main evidence is for these three groups, and comparisons from other Palestinian centres would be necessary to expand the picture. See further Lehmann and Holum (2000) for Samaritan inscriptions from Caesarea. For the Samaritan revolt in Caesarea, see Kennedy (2000), 598. For this conflict, and further discussion of religious diversity in Caesarea, see Sivan (2008), 302–17, and Palestine more generally, passim. For the Alexandrian case, see Haas (1997), chapters 4–6.

Bowersock's model of exchange and interaction between citizens with different religious allegiances:

> The ethnic and cultural communities with their broad range of religious observances and their local roots were integral parts of a larger Palestinian world. These communities did not exist with walls around them to keep them from associating with each other. Quite the contrary. Among educated persons bilingualism was common and trilingualism was not unknown. The communities enriched each other, and sometimes converted each other.[18]

The phenomenon of multiple linguistic attainment is also seen in religion and philosophy. Christians like Aeneas, Procopius, and Zacharias understood the language of Neoplatonism, and used it to support their own beliefs while seeking to convert its more fluent speakers to their own first language, Christianity. John and Barsanuphius witness to such interactions in the sixth century. They tolerate Christians pressing grapes for their Jewish neighbours and allow business transactions with pagans (*Q&A* 686; 777).[19] The two holy men were comparatively undisturbed by interactions between monks and pagans or Jews, directing their stricter opprobrium against interactions with heretics.[20] This may suggest a weakening of the pagan and Jewish communities in the sixth century, in comparison (particularly in the case of the pagans) with the preceding century. Justinian's laws against pagans of 529 had a marked effect on religious allegiance in Palestine, so the high level of contact suggested by Barsanuphius and John should if anything be magnified for the preceding period.[21]

The correspondence from the Old Men in the monasteries points to inter-religious interaction in late-antique Gaza (e.g. *Q&A* 775–76). One lay correspondent (φιλόχριστος) asks:

> If a Jew or a Pagan invites me to his holy day for a meal or sends me meat from his festival, should I accept or not?
>
> [Ἐὰν ἰουδαῖος ἢ ἐθνικὸς καλέσῃ με ἐν τῇ ἑορτῇ αὐτοῦ εἰς ἄριστον, ἢ καὶ ξένιά μοι πέμψῃ, καταδέξωμαι ἢ οὔ] (*Q&A* 775)

18. Bowersock (1998), 45. Bowersock is quoted in Hevelone-Harper (2005), 81, whose discussion of different religious communities in sixth-century Gaza (79–89) informs the following paragraph.

19. For the Jewish community in Gaza, see Ovadiah (1969), 130ff., who cites a Greek inscription from the Gazan synagogue, dating from A.D. 508/139. A central figure, King David playing Orpheus-like to the animals, is identified using Hebrew letters; Ovadiah (1982). See also Ma'oz (1985), who notes that late-antique urban centres display ethnic diversity, where Samaritans, Jews, Christians, and pagans lived together, in contrast to rural villages, which appear somewhat more homogeneous (65).

20. See Hevelone-Harper (2005), 13. For advice about interactions with heretics, see ibid. 83–84, with *Q&A* 732–35, where the Holy Man quotes Titus 3:10.

21. For converts in the wake of 529, see e.g. *Q&A* 821–22. See also ibid. 82.

The Holy Man responds that he should not, since church canons do not allow it, but the layperson tries to find an exception, giving a glimpse of the potential for strong friendships, and perhaps patronage relationships, between Christians and non-Christians:

> What then should I do, and what should I say to him, when he is a great man and my friend, and would be grieved if I refused?
>
> [Τί οὖν; Ὅτε μέγας ἐστὶν ὁ ἄνθρωπος καὶ φίλος μου, καὶ λυπεῖται ἐὰν μὴ δέξωμαι, καὶ τί εἴπω αὐτῷ] (*Q&A* 776)

The Holy Man stands firm, but the letter, together with others which ask about the etiquette of using sorcerers for the purposes of healing (e.g. *Q&A* 753–54), implies continuing religious heterodoxy in Gaza in the late fifth century and the reality of such relationships suggests that religious conflict is too simplistic a model for reconstructing the experiences of late-antique Gazans.[22]

Paganism persisted strongly in the late-antique schools, as Zacharias' *Life of Severus*, Jacob of Sarug's polemic *Homilies* against classical mythology, Rufus' story of the wealthy Egyptian Christian 'caught in the error of pagan philosophers, whose ideas he loved greatly' (*VPet* 72) or the pagan religious polemic of Damascius' sixth-century *Life of Isidore* variously attest.[23] Yet, as the Barsanuphius and John corpus implies, Gazan society more generally was still undergoing the process of Christianization during the fifth century.[24] In the mid-fourth century, only the Church of St Irene had stood within the city walls; this contrasted with many pagan temples (*VPorph* 64). Gaza had enthusiastically welcomed Julian's restoration of paganism, including his renewed attention to city gods (Gregory Nazianzus, *Or.* IV, 868; PG 35 616A). Sozomen's account of Gaza characterizes it as a stronghold of paganism, a city renowned (from the Christian viewpoint) for the heroic exploits of its martyrs (*Hist. eccl.* 5.8–10, 15).

22. Hevelone-Harper's conclusion for the sixth century may be applied to the fifth: 'The citizens of sixth-century Gaza lived in a world governed by multiple value systems.' See ibid. 118.

23. Damascius (1999); Damascius (1967b); Jacob (1935); Olinder (1939) for mainly philological commentary on Jacob's letters; Zacharias (1907). Jacob displays a wide knowledge of classical mythology, as he studies the theatre like a doctor lancing a boil. He summarizes Greek myth 'in order that, when the tongue lances it, and is spattered with it, it may become clean' (*Homily* 5 Moss translation). See Moss (1935).

24. Zacharias' *Life of Isaiah* suggests that pagans in the schools hoped that Illus' revolt against Zeno in 484–488 would mean the rise of paganism more generally. Illus' attempted usurpation sought support among the schools of Alexandria (Damascius *Phil. Hist.* Athanassiadi 77D = *Isid.* fr. 178 Zintzen; Zacharias, *VIs* 10). Damascius praised contemporary pagan political attacks, including repeated assassination attempts (*Phil. Hist.* Athanassiadi 115A = *Isid.* fr 303 Zintzen; cf. Zosimus, *New Hist.* 4.36). On the Isaurian revolts, see Elton (2000), 403f.; Lee (2000), 50; Trombley (1993), vol. 1, chapter 3. For criticism of Trombley's account, particularly his dependence on the *Life of Porphyry*, see the review by Frankfurter (1995).

At the turn of the fifth century, the Gazan *boule* was still controlled by pagan interests, whom the emperor Arcadius (395–408) was loath to challenge for fear of losing revenue (*VPorph* 41). Pagan control of civic institutions may be a reason why Christians in Gaza could not use economic aid for the poor as a way to gain converts. Gazan Christians apparently did not have sufficient wealth or status to provide such support.[25]

Gaza's port-town, Maiuma, had become Christian before Gaza itself (Sozomen *Hist. eccl.* 2.5; Eusebius *Vita Const.* 4.38), and the picture of Gaza as a pagan stronghold at the end of the fourth century, sketched in Mark the Deacon's *Life of Porphyry*, is over-painted to glorify the *Life*'s hero. Nevertheless, with Porphyry, a wealthy bishop, who was also politically minded, well-connected, and religiously militant, Gazan Christians gained an advocate who was able to advance their interests effectively. Porphyry was, however, unsuccessful in his aim of uniting the urban and port-towns under one see, and Maiuma retained its own bishop into the sixth century (Sozomen *Hist. eccl.* 5.3).[26] Yet in urban Gaza, Porphyry's own wealth, booty from temple destruction, and possibly patronage from the Empress Eudoxia, seem to have laid the foundations for the growth of the Christian community in Gaza during the fifth century. The destruction of the Marneion temple (A.D. 402) and the building of a great church on the temple site were powerful physical demonstrations of the defeat of paganism and the institutional strength of the Gazan Christian community.[27] Replacing temples with churches irrevocably altered the built environment and ostentatiously displayed Christian power. However, the new Christian churches were built with materials from the original pagan buildings.[28] This may be read partly as a colonization of pagan physical objects and a simultaneous desacralization of them.[29] Yet it might also be interpreted as an architectural analogue of the intellectual engagement between the three Gazans and their Neoplatonist contemporaries. Just as in the intellectual debates, so the new churches contain

25. For an extended analysis of this dynamic, see Brown (1992).

26. For the dispute over episcopal jurisdiction, see Sivan (2008), 337.

27. Cf. the destruction of the main temple in Caesarea around 400, for which see Tsafir (1998), 206ff. Tsafir sees Christian caution as accounting for a delay of one hundred years between the fall of the temple and the building of a new church. He speaks of Christians 'daring' to use pagan materials (206, 207) and the possible 'offence or danger' attached to using a pagan site for a Christian purpose (208). More prosaic explanations, which do not take mere conflict as the base unit of analysis, remain possible. See Hanson (1978) for the practice of destroying and rebuilding, rather than simply appropriating old temples for Christian use.

28. Marinescu (1996).

29. See Caseau (2001); Cormack (1990a, b); Saradi (1994).

within them supporting material from a different community, reconfigured into a new construction.

Despite Porphyry's episcopate, Christians probably remained a large minority in Gaza at the start of the fifth century.[30] Aeneas, Procopius, and Zacharias would have heard stories of a world where Christianity did not enjoy its contemporary status. The texts help to strengthen Christian conversion efforts in Gaza by consolidating Christian religious allegiance in the schools, where conversion either way—from paganism to Christianity and from Christianity to paganism—was still possible. Aeneas' dialogue ends in the conversion of a Platonist, Zacharias' steadies the faith of a Christian 'slipping towards paganism', and Procopius' commentary makes authoritative biblical interpretations available.

The Gazan church had various institutional interests in the Gazan schools. There was structural interaction between the church and the schools through the local Gazan monasteries (see further 2.3 below). There may well have been close structural connections between the see of Gaza and the schools.[31] After Procopius' death, Marcianus, the bishop of Gaza, took over the management of Procopius' 'school' on a temporary basis (Choricius, *Fun. or. in Proc.* 50). As Peter Brown has argued, 'many Christian bishops owed their prestige in society at large to the fact that they had once been rhetors'.[32] Classical education remained essential for officials managing church business and for negotiating an advantageous position for ecclesial interests with local and imperial authorities. Furthermore, the theological disputes of the day used concepts developed and refined in the schools of rhetoric and philosophy. So while Gazan schools seem to have been institutionally separate from the church, the links between the two bodies were close. Such ties go part of the way towards explaining the Gazans' interest in upholding Christianity within the schools and the high value they continue to place on classical rhetoric and philosophy, even when they disagree with its conclusions.

The archaeological and literary sources for Gaza thus provide glimpses of a city with a rich variety of interactions between different ethnicities, regions, and intellectual and religious systems and institutions. The rhetorical schools contributed strongly to the city's elite culture.

30. Trombley's attempt to determine precise figures based on Porphyry's account is overly optimistic. See Trombley (1993), 227. The figures are questionable partly because there is no clear definition in Porphyry about what counts as a Christian, and because the numbers may be inflated to glorify the protagonist.

31. For a general discussion focusing on the sixth century, see Ashkenazi (2004).

32. Brown (1992), 75.

2.2 Gazan Rhetorical Schools within Late-Antique Education

Vössing rightly cautions against assuming strong institutional bonds between the various groups of teachers and students in Gaza, given the centrality of the teacher–student relationship in late-antique rhetorical education. There is no simple analogy with modern 'schools', where the teacher–student relation depends on the existence of an institution such as a physical school, university, or library.[33] Yet whatever their degree of institutional cohesion—and Aeneas, Procopius, and Zacharias moved in similar social circles—the Gazan school or schools shared structural characteristics as social institutions of the same kind.[34] A group of students was gathered around a teacher, students studied similar subjects, education gained at Gaza was recognizable as a school education in other cities and membership of a Gazan school implied entrance into a set of social networks shared by the educated elite in the later empire. As such, the different groupings which constituted Gazan education may be analysed together.

The culture of the Gazan schools may partly be constructed from the Gazan's own writings, but it is also useful to compare them to similar institutions in other late-antique cities. Alexandria is particularly relevant, although Caesarea and Athens were also important for the Gazans. Renault and Szbat have shown that many teachers associated with Gaza studied in Alexandria.[35] This common experience in Alexandria, which Procopius calls 'the common mother of words' (*Ep.* 119), suggests that many aspects of the culture of the Gazan schools were shared with the Alexandrians.

Until recently, our understanding of late-antique schools has been almost exclusively based on literary sources. Archaeological discoveries at Kôm el-Dikka in Alexandria now give a fascinating physical insight into Alexandrian education at the turn of the sixth century, which can supplement and refine the extant textual descriptions, and enrich comparison with Gaza.[36] A large educational complex in the heart of the ancient city has been uncovered, located on the main east–west road. Around thirty classrooms have been excavated so far, backed onto a monumental colonnade which borders a large civic square and

33. Vössing (2007), 165: 'Die Kooperation mit irgendeiner Institution war nicht vorgesehen, auch nicht die mit irgendeiner Bibliothek.' For the meaning of the term 'school', see Dillon (2004).

34. The most thorough work on the school remains Seitz (1892). See also Downey (1958).

35. See Renault (2007); Szbat (2007).

36. See Derda, Markiewicz, and Wipszycka (2007). On education in Alexandria, see Watts (2006). For the Christian schools in Alexandria and their relation to Jewish schools and earlier activity, see van den Hoek (1997). See also Eusebius, *Hist. eccl.* 5.10.1,4; 6.3.1–3; 6.15.1.

backs onto a large public baths.[37] The classrooms are about 5.0–5.2 metres wide, and 7.0–17.0 metres long, rectangular or sometimes curved to make a semicircle at the end where a teacher sits on a raised platform, elevated 'especially sophistically and pompously', as Zacharias has it (ἐν ὑψηλῷ τινι βήματι σοφιστικῶς μάλα καὶ σοβαρῶς καθήμενος) (*Ammonius* 98f.).[38] Similar auditoria are also found in libraries and bath complexes elsewhere in the late-Roman world, suggesting the possibility that these buildings could have been used for similar educational purposes.[39] The auditoria in Alexandria also adjoin a theatre, which probably served as a performance space for rhetorical displays.[40] That these classrooms, which date to the end of the fifth and the early sixth centuries, were funded by the civic authorities rather than by imperial gift underscores the importance of education to late-antique cities.[41]

The Alexandrian excavations provide the only tangible evidence for an educational complex of anything like the Constantinopolitan scale elsewhere in the empire.[42] For Constantinople, the Theodosian Code grants public funding for three orators, twenty grammarians (ten each for Greek and Latin), one philosopher, two Roman law teachers, and five Greek sophists (*CTh* XIV,9; XV,1).[43] Hence, the Alexandrian complex, with chairs in philosophy, rhetoric, grammar, and medicine, is significantly smaller than the one envisaged for Constantinople.

Students in this complex could study Greek and Latin grammar, but they were more likely to be studying advanced topics such as medicine, philosophy, or, most commonly, rhetoric. Zacharias' *Life of Severus* gives a vivid picture of life in the Alexandrian schools, as well as in Berytus, where many Alexandrian

37. See Majcherek (2007), 12–16 and McKenzie (2007), who provides maps and axonometric reconstructions, and situates the auditoria in the urban and religious context of the city.

38. Cf. Themistius *Or.* 21.243b = 2.18.5. Libanius also described a teacher positioned as the auditoria confirm: 'The teacher is established in an imposing chair, like judges are. He seems terrifying. He frowns in anger and shows no signs of calming down. The pupil must go forward in fear and trembling to give an artistically conducted demonstration, which he has composed and learnt by heart' (*Chriae* III.7). For this translation and citation, see Majcherek (2007), 39, and 17f. for classroom dimensions.

39. Libanius claims to have taught in the baths (*Or* 1.55).

40. Majcherek (2007), 40f. The theatre was also used by the Green circus faction, as in the parallel case of the theatre in Aphrodisias. See Roueché and Reynolds (1989), IV.34 no. 43. Welch (2007) offers other Aphrodisian parallels, but her argument that the lack of philosopher portraits means that the auditoria were not used by philosophers may be discounted. Damascius writes that the complex was used, in addition to private residences, for philosophical teaching. Further, it is unlikely that the publicly funded chair of philosophy in Alexandria did not use the main civic education complex. See also Cribiore (2007), 147.

41. Bagnall (2007), 5–6 points out that the construction of the educational complex is both particularly Alexandrian and should reshape scholarly understanding of the effectiveness of late-antique government. Cf. Liebeschuetz (2001). For dating, see Haas (2007), 86f.; Majcherek (2007), 29–35.

42. See *CTh* XIV.

43. See Cribiore (2007), 149; Majcherek (2007), 44.

rhetorical students went to study law at the completion of their studies. Zacharias himself studied law in Berytus, after initially rejecting Severus' invitation to continue his studies there, since he 'still needed to study the speeches of the rhetoricians and philosophers more because of the pagans who were so proud and arrogant about those studies, in order to fight them publicly from this point of view as well' (*VSev* PO 2.1 46). This passage suggests that the centralized education complex in Alexandria encouraged and facilitated mingling of students and teachers from different disciplines. Damascius writes that the Alexandrians

> were often eager to be with [the Neoplatonic philosopher Isidore] to hear the words which flowed from his wise mouth. Those who were at the head of the rhetorical schools or of the poets also welcomed frequent intercourse with the philosopher, for although he was unlearned in their subject, through another kind of sharpness in philosophy he added something more careful into their own little disciplines [τεχνύδρια]. . . . At a rhetorical recitation in the theatres he praised the performers a little and was actually quiet with praise, but nevertheless [he praised] fittingly and relevantly. For that reason the whole theatre, so to speak, used his judgement as a rule [to adjudicate] the better and the worse [quality] of the speeches. (*Isid.* 276 = *Phil. Hist.* 106B)

While the diminutive τεχνύδρια and the (rather modern-sounding) claim that philosophy's role is to clear up the conceptual mistakes of the other human sciences stake out ground for philosophy in opposition to rhetoric, the passage is also evidence for interactions between students and teachers from different disciplines. Such mingling between students and teachers in the Alexandrian schools (cf. *CTh* XIV, 9) helps to explain the Gazans' interdisciplinary philosophical interests.

Teachers in other centres could not always guarantee such an ordered and well-resourced educational setting: few urban centres had the wealth which Alexandria could lavish on education, and Dillon's injunction to 'think small' when imagining higher education in late antiquity remains safe in the general case, especially when thinking about specifically philosophical education.[44] There is no definitive evidence that education in Gaza was publicly funded, although the extent of intellectual activity in the city in the fifth and sixth centuries makes it probable that some form of financial incentive was given to the Gazan teachers by the *boule*, either by payment or taxation incentives. The

44. See Dillon (2004), 402. Key centres of education in late antiquity remained substantial in different fields. Berytus seems to have had lecture halls. See *Expositio totius mundi et gentium* XXV and Cribiore (2007), 148. See also Hall (2004), 66f.

evidence for where classes took place in Gaza does not point to one dominant central location as in Alexandria.[45] Procopius writes about holding classes outdoors (*Epp* 81, 87, 91, 124).[46] He records a public reading of a letter in the midst of the city, probably referring to the *agora* (τῇ Γάζῃ μέσῃ πρὸς πάντας ἐλέγετο) (*Ep.* 91).[47] John of Gaza suggests that classes were sometimes held in the public baths (*Description of the Cosmic Panel*) (cf. Libanius *Or.* 1.55). It seems that classes, like orations, probably took place in such public venues, which would have provided excellent material for rhetorical exercises including *ekphrases.*[48] Yet John of Gaza also speaks of a Gazan classroom as a διατριβή (*Anacreonta* 5), which is defined, in the Alexandrian philosopher Elias's sixth-century commentary *in Isagoge* 21.30, as a place not unlike a theatre which is rounded so that one can see the other students. This description clearly recalls the Alexandrian auditoria (see also Aeneas, *Ep.* 2).[49] So there is some evidence that a scaled-down version of the Alexandrian classrooms was used in Gaza. The new interpretation of the theatre in the Kôm el-Dikka complex may also have a bearing on educational practices in Gaza, although the evidence is indirect. Procopius refers to a theatre (θέατρον) in Antioch, when he asks an Antiochean sophist whether many students attend it (*Ep.* 89), while Choricius talks about a public space, perhaps a theatre, for rhetorical displays (πρὸς τὴν ὡραίαν…σκηνή) (*Laud. Arat. et Steph.* 55).[50]

While Gazan education functioned somewhat differently from its larger and richer neighbour, the schools doubtless benefited from Alexandria's public expenditure on education. Alexandrian students were plentiful, and the best students could be confident that they were not removing themselves very far from the main intellectual centre. Furthermore, families who could not afford the best education in Alexandria would see Gaza in a positive light, sufficiently

45. Cribiore (2001), 24ff. for the diversity of locations of teaching in the classical world and beyond.

46. See Renault (2007), 172. Cf. Dio Chrys. 20.9–10, where grammar classes, with flute and dance schools, are held in the streets. Cribiore (2001), 25ff. collates this and similar evidence, including striking murals from Pompeii depicting outdoor grammar classes.

47. Cavallo (2007), 152f.

48. Baths and other public buildings were repositories of classical art which provided material for *ekphraseis*. See Bassett (2004), 51–58, based on Christodorus of Coptos' fifth-century *ekphrasis* of the Constantinian Baths of Zeuxippus in Constantinople. Geiger points to Procopius' *ekphrasis* of the (classically decorated) clock in Gaza and the ubiquity of classical and non-Christian art in late-antique Palestine. See Geiger (1998), 13–14.

49. 'Just as the theatres are rounded for seeing each other, so the diatribai are also rounded, in order that the students can see one another as well as the teacher' [διὰ τοῦτο γὰρ τὰ θέατρα κυκλοτερῆ διὰ τὸ ἀλλήλους βλέπειν, καὶ αἱ διατριβαὶ κυκλοτερεῖς, ἵνα ὁρῶσιν ἀλλήλους καὶ τὸν διδάσκαλον] (Elias *in Isag.* 21,30). For the reference to Elias' description of a διατριβή, see Majcherek (2007), 41. For the common use of the term διατρίβη to describe Alexandrian and other classrooms, see Szbat (2007), 178–81.

50. For the interpretation of Choricius supported here, see Cavallo (2007), 153; Saliou (2005a), 178f.

close to the major centre, with teachers linked into Alexandrian social networks, without the same level of expense that education in Alexandria would have entailed. Gaza's intellectual dependence on Alexandria, as well as its social and geographical proximity, would, on this analysis, make Gaza an attractive option for students who could not gain access to teachers in Alexandria itself.[51]

The late-antique schools in Gaza were a hive of intellectual activity in the late fifth and early sixth century.[52] In addition to the activities of the thinkers who are of chief interest for this study, Zosimus (not to be confused with the historian) wrote commentaries on Lysias and Demosthenes,[53] while John of Gaza composed anacreontic and hexameter ekphrastic poetry in the style of Nonnus, as well as epithalamia.[54] There was a circle of anacreontic poets in Gaza, all contemporaries with John.[55] His *Ekphrasis of the Cosmic Panel* [ἔκφρασις τοῦ κοσμικοῦ πίνακος], a rhetorical description of a wall-painting or mosaic probably in the Baths at Gaza, bears witness to the Gazans' interest in both classical culture in general and the question of creation in particular.[56] Choricius, a pupil of Procopius, is famous for his orations on various themes.[57] Hierius 8 (*PLRE* II), a contemporary of Procopius, moved from Gaza to teach Latin in Antioch along with two Gazan Greek *grammatikoi*, Alypius 6 and Stephanus 8 (*PLRE* II) (Procopius of Gaza, *Ep.* 149). While Greek was the main language studied for rhetorical purposes, Gazan students were also educated in Latin, the language necessary for much imperial administration and law. Timothy of Gaza composed a work on syntax, and like Aeneas, Procopius and Zacharias also displayed scientific and philosophical interests.[58] He had studied under Horapollon, the Alexandrian philosopher who was forced to flee Christian persecution in the

51. Gaza is counted as a 'spiritual colony' of Alexandria in Schmid, Christ, and Stählin (1920), 1028.

52. See Downey (1958); Seitz (1892). See also the relevant entries in *PLRE* II and III and Kaster (1988); Szbat (2007), 212ff. Many Gazan works are now lost; my analysis will focus on Aeneas' letters, since they have not received the attention given to Procopius' corpus.

53. For Zosimus, see Seitz (1892), 27–30; Wilson (1967), 254–55.

54. For John of Gaza, see Friedländer (1969). His poems have recently been edited by Ciccolella in John of Gaza, Ignatios, Leo, Elias, and George (2000). Her comments on the school of Gaza at 118–26 are pertinent. These poets were well aware of contemporary thinking in rhetoric, for which see Amato and Schamp (2005).

55. See Ciccolella (2005), 171f.

56. Alan Cameron has pushed the dating of this work back to before 526. See Alan Cameron (1993).

57. For Choricius, see Ashkenazi (2004); Choricius (1929); Litsas (1980).

58. Timothy's (wholly or partially) extant works are Κανόνες καθολικοὶ περὶ συντάξεως ἐπικῶς and the περὶ ζῴων τετραπόδων θηρίων τῶν παρ' Ἰνδοῖς καὶ Ἄραβι καὶ Αἰγυπτίοις, καὶ ὅσα τρέφει Λιβύη. He also wrote a treatise on exotic birds and snakes (*Suda* T 621). Fragments of *On Animals* are collected by Haupt (1869). The treatise *On Syntax* is edited by Cramer (1835–37). He also wrote a (lost) oration on the Chrysargon tax to Anastasius.

late 480s.[59] Gaza was also the birthplace of Ulpian, a philosopher in Alexandria and Athens, who had been a fellow student of Proclus, and the Neoplatonic philosopher Isidore (Isidorus 2, *PLRE* III). While the thinkers associated with the Gazan schools whose works have come down to us are all recognizably Christian, the avowedly pagan sixth-century philosopher Damascius refers to a certain Antonius (Antonius 3, *PLRE* II), who 'made [Gaza] far more holy than it previously was' [τὴν Γάζαν ἀπέφηνεν ἱερωτέραν πολλῷ μᾶλλον ἢ πρότερον ἦν] and may have been a sophist or possibly an advocate in Gaza in the mid- to late fifth century (Damascius, *Isid.* fr. 186 Zintzen). While Gaza is not noted as a major centre of Neoplatonic intellectual activity, such a reference nevertheless suggests that Neoplatonists formed one recognizable local culture in the Gazan schools and that traditional religious practices were maintained within that culture.

Aeneas, Procopius, and Zacharias benefited from creative exchange with people like these in the Gazan schools. Timothy of Gaza's works suggest an interest in Aristotle, an interest shared by Aeneas and Zacharias; and the references to Isidore, Ulpian, and Antonius also suggest that specialists and interested lay people could be found to discuss matters of contemporary philosophy. Zosimus' literary studies suggest that Procopius' *Commentary* was partly generated by a culture which valued literary criticism and had the resources to support such study. The large number of grammarians and rhetors imply that while specialization was possible in Gaza, the Gazan institutions also prepared students for advanced rhetorical study or science, philosophy and medicine in Alexandria, or courses in law at Berytus.[60] The combined intellectual interests of members of the Gazan schools suggest particularly strong ties to Alexandria, Athens, and Caesarea.

The philosophical interests of members of the Gazan schools particularly suggest contact with Athens and Alexandria. By the time the Gazans enter the stage, Neoplatonism was well established in the major philosophical centres of Athens and Alexandria.[61] Philosophy, as in earlier centuries, largely proceeded

59. See Kaster (1988), 368–70; Wellmann (1927). See also *Suda*, loc. cit. Downey placed Procopius of Caesarea as a student in the Gaza school: Downey (1958), 315; Evans (1972), 31f. It is equally likely that he studied in Caesarea. See Cameron (1985), 4–5. Whether or not Downey is right about Procopius of Caesarea, I contest his characterization of Gaza as a place where it was thought 'more suitable, and also in better taste, to keep Christianity and classical thought quite separate'.

60. The inclusion of grammarians who could teach Latin may be an indication that some Gazan students wanted to continue with legal studies, as Zacharias did, although Latin remained on the grammatical curriculum outside the context of legal studies in late antiquity. On law in Berytus, see Collinet (1925); Hall (2004).

61. See Watts (2006) for an excellent overview of the social context and activities of the schools in Athens and Alexandria.

by way of exegesis, and later Neoplatonists produced commentaries on both Plato and Aristotle.[62] The sense of school identity was strengthened in the process of the construction of such philosophical commentaries, as the views of earlier Neoplatonic philosophers were woven into later works. Students of philosophy were inducted into a largely standardized curriculum, which included study of original works by Plato and Aristotle, often taught through the use of commentaries.[63] Proclus' *Timaeus Commentary* has been likened to an advanced dissertation; students earned their philosophical stripes by writing commentaries.[64] The rich tradition thus contained Platonic and Aristotelian canonical books, an authoritative set of protreptic and interpretive texts (written by the acknowledged 'greats' of Middle and Neoplatonism over a period of some centuries) and a thriving contemporary interpretive community. This community both honoured thinkers of previous generations and sought to add to the tradition which, so the Neoplatonists thought, contained the truth. As in the analogous and overlapping case of Christianity, Neoplatonism had the resources to form a distinctive community and rejuvenate itself with creativity and novelty.

Neoplatonic culture was transmitted to Gaza in three main ways: mediation by overlap of membership, travel, and through the oral culture of the late-antique schools. The implication of Zacharias' *Life of Severus* is that studying at more than one centre was the norm. For those with a philosophical bent, Alexandria-Athens was the obvious pairing. There was significant overlap between Athenian and Alexandrian teachers and students. Proclus began his study in Alexandria before becoming attracted to Iamblichan Neoplatonism and moving to Athens (Marinus, *VProcl* 15). Hierocles studied in Athens with Proclus before moving to Alexandria to teach. Ammonius followed suit, taking the publicly funded chair in philosophy in Alexandria, after student days in Athens. The sixth-century stalwarts of the Athenian school, Damascius and Simplicius, both studied in Alexandria. This exchange between the two major centres of late-antique Neoplatonic philosophy suggests that ideas from Athens would have circulated in Alexandria and vice versa.[65] Proclus' ideas probably reached Gaza though Alexandria, where they would have been well known

62. For commentary in antiquity, see Most (1999). For the development of Platonic commentary on Aristotle, which took a new form from Porphyry onwards, see Karamanolis (2004). For the origins of the tradition of commenting on Plato, see Tarrant (2007), 30–33. Tarrant is now less certain of the early date he gave to the anonymous commentator on the *Theaetetus* in Tarrant (1983).

63. For the curriculum, see Baltzly and Tarrant (2007), 13; Tarrant (2007), 48; Westerink (1990).

64. By Proclus, Tarrant, Baltzly, Runia, and Share (2007–2008), vol. 2, in Runia's introduction, 3 n. 10.

65. See Athanassiadi (1993), 29 for a diagrammatic presentation of this exchange between the two intellectual centres.

among the highly mobile group of students and teachers in the Alexandrian schools. The networks of people like Antonius would have been especially significant for fostering Neoplatonism in Gaza, although other members of the Gazan schools who did not subscribe wholeheartedly to Neoplatonism would also have come into contact with Neoplatonic ideas.

This suggestion is further strengthened by emphasizing the oral nature of instruction in the schools. Much learning was achieved by talking and listening. The oral culture instilled bonds of loyalty between student and teacher and helped to construct intellectual continuity within a school, and between schools separated by large distances. Teaching by conversation transmitted ideas over centuries, even when written philosophies were not available, thus disseminating diverse philosophical ideas. When commentaries on texts are written down, they are often 'from the voice' of a philosopher.[66] In this way, much philosophy in late antiquity originated in the classroom. Proclus' commentaries on Plato, like other contemporary commentaries, arise directly from a teaching context, as do his *Arguments on the Eternity of the World*.[67]

Such philosophical writings give insight into how teaching, oral debate, and the formation of school and doctrinal identity go together. The late-antique Athenian school had only three heads of philosophy in the one hundred years from 385 to 485. Proclus, who was head of the school for forty-five of these years, could remember the teaching of two heads of the school before him. Discussions he had with Plutarch in the 430s could be transmitted orally to students in the 480s. Oral teaching—philosophy as a living conversation—is one key means by which the philosophical tradition was maintained and a diversity of philosophical views remained in living memory. Such oral tradition could augment the doxographies—philosophical collections akin to rhetorical handbooks—which circulated in educational establishments.[68]

The oral, disputation-based culture of the philosophical schools seems to have overflowed the bounds of the philosophical schools into other areas of late-antique education. Teachers of rhetoric were often different from teachers of philosophy, although the philosophical and theological interests of the Gazans suggest that the boundaries were not rigid in late antiquity, just as classical literary figures had wide-ranging interests. Sorabji has argued that teachers of rhetoric and philosophy were the same people in Iamblichus' school, and Bowersock has shown that there was significant overlap in the second sophistic.[69] With such

66. See Richard (1950), 191–222; Sorabji (1987b), 3f.

67. I am not arguing that all philosophical output in late antiquity was generated in a pedagogical context, simply, that this was how a large amount of philosophy began.

68. On ancient doxography, see Mansfeld and Runia (1996).

69. See Bowersock (1969); Sorabji (1990), 10. See also Stanton (1973).

overlap and conflation of categories, discussions and topics from a philosophy class might take on a new life among the wider student population, especially in schools like Horapollon's in Alexandria, where, as we have seen, institutional arrangements facilitated such interaction.[70] Whether or not students of rhetoric also studied philosophy, they had the opportunity to develop friendships with students who had. Furthermore, the same social values which supported the rhetorical schools also supported the philosophical schools, suggesting that we should conceptualize the rhetorical schools and the philosophical schools as sharing a similar cultural space, implying contact between members of the different schools.

Gaza also benefited from proximity to Caesarea, which boasted its own educational accomplishments. Acacius had been an esteemed rival of Libanius in the fourth century (Eunapius, *VSoph*) and an Orion taught in Caesarea in the first half of the fifth century.[71] By far the most important element of Caesarea's attraction as an intellectual centre was its ecclesiastical and episcopal library. This library began on a small scale, designed to service the local church as the area became more Christian between about A.D. 150 and 250.[72] Its collection was significantly expanded when Origen left Alexandria for Caesarea, bringing a substantial library of classical, philosophical, Jewish, and Christian literature with him. Successive priests and bishops preserved and augmented the library, up into the sixth century.[73] Jerome records the renewal of a library at Caesarea in the mid-fourth century, when papyrus volumes were copied onto parchment (Jerome, *Ep.* 34.1; *viris ill.* 75, 113).[74] The library, which included Origen's massive biblical commentaries, was a tremendously useful resource for Christian exegetical and biblical textual scholarship and also included a large number of Greek philosophical works (it is the probable source for Eusebius' citations of many authors whose works would otherwise be lost) as well as being the repository of a large amount of non-canonical Hellenistic-Jewish literature.[75]

The Caesarean library is one possible source for the Greek philosophical material included in the writings of all three Gazans, although given the

70. Note, however, that the time needed to complete the full Neoplatonic curriculum was prohibitive, minimizing the number of people who undertook the full training. For the curriculum, see the texts and scholarship collected in Sorabji (2005), vol. 1, 319–22.

71. This Orion may also have taught in Alexandria circa 420/430. If so, he may have taught Proclus. His identity is very difficult to fix. See Wendel, *RE* XVIII 1083–87. See also Downey (1958), 301f.

72. For this library, see Grafton and Williams (2006).

73. See van den Hoek (1997), 83. For the sixth-century evidence, see the colophon of the sixth-century cod. Coisl 202^2, cited by Swete, Ottley, and Thackeray (1914), 75.

74. See Runia (1996), 480–81, who provides a facsimile of MS Vindobonensis theol. gr. 429 together with discussion.

75. Ibid. 477, and, for the Jewish material, passim.

extent of intellectual activity in Gaza, it is more than likely that Gaza also had its own library and that competition with Caesarea may have helped to sustain and improve Gaza's own collection. Runia has concluded that the library was the main (though not the only) source for the manuscripts of Philo that have come down to us and that it included some works now only extant in fragments. Philo's *Questions on Exodus* is in the latter category. This work is also quoted in the *Catenae* from which Procopius worked, yet he cites it in more detail than the Catenist.[76] This suggests that Procopius and the Catenist independently had access to the *Questions on Exodus* and that they were both dependent on the same source, the copy held in the library of Caesarea. The library was clearly available for interested scholars to visit, and books could be borrowed or copied for use elsewhere.[77]

The foregoing discussion places the Gazan schools firmly within a network of late-antique cities. This network helps to explain the distinctive, if not unique, activities of the Gazan rhetorical schools. Gazan intellectual culture seems remarkably open to connections with the specialities of other centres. Gaza's status as a smaller intellectual centre arguably necessitated this distinctive openness to intellectual currents from elsewhere. Philosophy came to Gaza through Alexandria and Athens, and the religious practices associated at least with Athenian Neoplatonism, and seen to a lesser degree after Ammonius in Alexandria, seem to have entered into the Gazan schools, if Damascius is to be believed. The medical and scientific interests of members of the Gazan schools also point to influence from Alexandria especially. Caesarea, with its extensive library, perhaps provides a further philosophical resource, as well as motivating competition, and is most probably influential in the creation of Christian commentaries in Gaza. The network of influence and interaction between these different centres helps to explain the flourishing and characteristically broad engagement with a variety of ideas in the Gazan schools. Gaza's receptiveness to influences from different cities helps to explain the Gazans' active engagement with Neoplatonism as well as their more open evaluation of non-religious aspects of Neoplatonic culture.

2.3 Gazan Monasteries and the Schools

The Gazan schools existed alongside local monasteries and the distinctive culture of the monastic communities helped to shape the writings of Aeneas,

76. See Runia (1996), 478–82.
77. Ibid. 493.

Zacharias, and Procopius. A recent study has drawn attention to the diversity of monastic communities surrounding Gaza.[78] Monastic foundations of varying types grew up during the fourth to seventh centuries in rings of approximately 15–25 kilometre radius from the city of Gaza, beginning around A.D. 340–390.[79] Thus, to speak of a 'Monastic School', as two recent writers have done, is to point to a high concentration of monastic activity rather than a unified or centrally organized collective, somewhat analogously to the classical schools.[80] The monasteries were typically organized around a mixture of eremitic and cenobitic living.[81] For example, the monastery at Thawatha, where Barsanuphius and John resided, had a central complex, including a church, library, and dining hall, surrounded by caves for individual monks.[82] The *Asceticon*, probably written in a Palestinian monastic setting, sets out the amount of time monks should spend in isolation, and what they should do in common with their brethren.[83]

The first large influx of monks to the Gaza region seems to have been related to the suppression of the Origenist controversy in Egypt in the fourth century.[84] Monks who were sympathetic to Origenist ideas fled from Scetis and settled near Gaza.[85] These links between Gazan monasticism and Egyptian monasticism, including connections with Alexandria, directly parallel the links between the Gazan schools and the Alexandrian rhetorical and philosophical schools.[86] This shared dependence on Alexandria and Egypt assisted in the transmission of ideas between the schools and the monasteries. Direct interaction between

78. Bitton-Ashkelony and Kofsky (2000). See also Bitton-Ashkelony and Kofsky (2006). For Hilarion, see 8–16, and for the later figures, see 18–20 (Zeno), 20–24 (Isaiah), 24–36 (Peter the Iberian), 36–39 (Barsanuphius and John), 39–42 (Seridus), and 42–46 (Dorotheus).

79. See Hirshfeld (2004).

80. See Bitton-Ashkelony and Kofsky (2006).

81. Bitton-Ashkelony and Kofsky (2000) discern a shift between the fifth and the seventh centuries from anchoritic monastic life to cenobitic monasteries.

82. Hevelone-Harper (2005), 34–35; Hirshfeld (2004), 87–88.

83. For the debate about the origin of this text, see Gould (1993), 1–25. Hilarion was buried in Maiuma. See Jerome, *VHil* 146; Sozomen, *Hist. eccl.* 3.14; 5.10. On the *Life*, see Rubenson (2000). See *VHil* 2–3; Sozomen, *Hist. eccl.* 5.15. See also Hägg, Rousseau, and Høgel (2000). The other monk with a claim to being the father of Gazan monasticism is Chariton. See the translation by di Segni (1990b).

84. Rubenson (1999) has argued that Origen's ideas had been a constant in Egyptian monasticism. What changed at the end of the fourth century was episcopal power politics.

85. For the Origenist controversies, see Clark (1992); Guillaumont (1962); Hombergen (2001). These so-called 'Origenist' ideas are explored in the correspondence of Barsanuphius and John (*Q&A* 600–608). They form one intellectual horizon of the creation debates (see below, 6.6). The migration was also probably related to tribal conflict around Scetis.

86. For example, Hilarion, his disciples Hesychas and Epiphanius, and a key figure in the next generation, Silvanus, all studied in Alexandria. For Silvanus, see Sozomen, *Hist. eccl.* 6. 32. For further Alexandrian connections, including those of John Rufus, Severus, Peter the Iberian, and Abba Isaiah, see Zacharias, *VSev* and *VIs*, and John Rufus' *VPet*. For further discussion, see Bitton-Ashkelony and Kofsky (2000), 26, 28f., 43ff.

school members and monks remained possible after the monks had entered their monasteries.[87] As Hevelone-Harper has argued, 'the boundaries between monastery and city appear surprisingly permeable'.[88] Barsanuphius and John provide a picture of strong interaction between monks and urban laity. Lay clients could visit the monastery, host monks who were away from home, and perform services, including legal services, for the monks (see e.g. *Q&A* 620–25, 667–73, 681–82, 712–18, 727–29, 736–42, 749–56, 764–74).[89] Interaction between monks and outsiders caused some tension with monastic ideals and there are strictures against socializing (*Q&A* 173). While monastic travel was often related to ecclesial politics or pilgrimage, we can imagine that their travel helped to keep them in contact with other members of elite late-antique society.[90] The boundaries of the monastery were not so solid as some contemporary monastic theorists might have wished.

Most importantly, many monks were themselves classically trained. Questions asked by a monk interested in Origen's ideas demonstrate that Gazan monks had easy access to patristic works, including those by Origen, Didymus, Evagrius, and his followers (*Q&A* 600), and suggest that a monastic library was one of the communal buildings, at least at Thawatha.[91] Silvanus, a prominent late fourth-century monk, came from an educated circle, which included Marcus the Calligrapher and a certain Zacharias, who is said to have been able to read Hebrew.[92] We have seen that Abba Isaiah, despite professing no formal education, was apparently consulted by Aeneas on matters of Neoplatonic philosophy. John Rufus, known to both Aeneas and Zacharias, if not Procopius, had been educated in law, while Peter the Iberian, whom Rufus counted as a teacher, had received the rhetorical education commonly attained by his elite contemporaries.[93] For the late fifth century, we can identify monks who had been educated in rhetoric or law in Alexandria and Berytus (Zacharias, *VSev* 46–85, 93–103). In addition to Rufus, Severus, the future Patriarch of Antioch,

87. For this paragraph, see Bitton-Ashkelony and Kofsky (2006), chapter 10, especially 200–212.

88. Hevelone-Harper (2005), 5.

89. See Hevelone-Harper (2005), 89–100.

90. See further Bitton-Ashkelony and Kofsky (2006), chapter 1, especially 18–26, 32ff., and chapter 10, especially 200–209. The *Asceticon*, chapters 1 and 3, gives instructions on how a monk should act on his travels. Not all monks were part of elite society but there was significant social-class overlap between monks and schoolmen.

91. Hevelone-Harper (2005), 24–25. Perrone (2004), 133 characterizes the Thawatha monastery as a 'school'. See also Neyt (1974), 57.

92. For Marcus, see *Apophthegmata* PG 65, 293–96; for Zacharias, see Sozomen, *Hist. eccl.* 9.17.

93. The story about Abba Isaiah displays similarities with the *topos* of the unlettered holy man nevertheless being wiser than the wisdom of the world. However, given the educational attainments of his contemporaries, we are justified in reading this story rather more literally than we might otherwise.

entered a Gazan monastery after his education in Alexandria and Berytus. John Rufus' fellow law student, Theodore of Ascalon, joined him as a disciple of Peter the Iberian (Rufus, *VPet* 78). Rufus' *Plerophories* identify *scholasticoi* and sophists who became monks, including Epainetes, Paul, Ammianus, and Serapion (*Plerophories* 13, 14 & 57, 38, 77), as well as a former Alexandrian *scholasticus* who became a Stylite (*Plerophories* 78).[94] In the sixth century, Barsanuphius and John developed a Christian form of question and answer literature, while their disciple Dorotheus displayed intellectual creativity and classical learning in his own writings.[95] This overlap between the members of the monasteries and the classically oriented schools makes it highly plausible that the ideas current in the monastic communities may also have influenced thinkers in the rhetorical schools and vice versa.

According to Watts, cultural interchange between the two groups

> created a unique discourse from the diverse cultural ideas circulating in the Palestinian and Egyptian intellectual world of the later fifth century. This was their own discourse, neither fully sophistic nor fully ascetic, but completely comprehensible to those whose minds were shaped in these seemingly incompatible intellectual environments.[96]

When we turn to the Gazans' arguments about creation, it will become clear that this shared discourse forms one horizon for the Gazans' creation-oriented works. This survey of Gazan monasticism flags some possible influences, including non-Chalcedonian Christianity and forms of Origenism. Particularly, questions concerning the pre-existence of the soul, the origin of the material universe, and the nature of the bodily resurrection, all controversial in the Origenist debates, partly motivate Aeneas, Procopius, and Zacharias when they investigate these problems (see below, 6.6).

2.4 Conclusions

Gaza's economic prosperity made it an attractive location for students and teachers, who came to the schools in part because of their continuing social utility in the later empire, and thereby contributed to their continuing institutional strength. Gaza's geographical proximity to Alexandria and Caesarea greatly influenced its intellectual life. The city's intellectuals and institutions

94. For the material from John Rufus' *Plerophories*, see Watts (2007), 158.

95. Dorotheus' intellectual curiosity was a cause of some concern to Barsanuphius and John. See *Q&A* 308.

96. Watts (2007), 164.

of education mediated different intellectual and cultural stances, just as Gaza, partly by virtue of its location, mediated different cultures of the empire. If its geographic position in relation to the wider empire made it a place of transition and flux, the local geography, with its urban centre imbued with classicism and its immediately surrounding countryside dotted with monasteries, also contributed to the possibility of intellectual transition. Contact between monks and sophists, between the theological ideas circulating in the monasteries and the Neoplatonic and classically literate argumentation of the schools, helped to form the distinctive discourse of each of the Gazans' works. Intellectual life in Gaza, supported by the institutional validation of classical learning in the schools, was able to engage with non-Christian thought worlds. It had at its disposal the tools required for such engagement, including centres of education, a community of scholars, access to books and the possibility of travel to key centres. Gaza at the turn of the sixth century was a city of overlapping local cultures, where the dominant explanatory categories were exchange, interaction, and transformation.

Religious change in Gaza following Porphyry's episcopate provides one useful explanatory context for Aeneas' dialogue. Zacharias' experience of this religious change, as well as his somewhat more dramatic involvement in Christian–pagan struggles in the schools of Alexandria and Berytus, similarly motivated his dialogue. Although Procopius' *Commentary on Genesis* does not have the dialogue form as a marker of Christian–Neoplatonic conflict, his direct refutation of axioms accepted by Neoplatonists, and his concern to consolidate the unified truth which he believed was discovered by patristic authorities, are evidence that this conflict also partly motivated his commentary, while his collection of Christian authorities could be useful both in the monasteries and in the schools. In each case, the Gazans employ and transform classical genres to make contact with the Neoplatonists who provide an important audience within the schools, while simultaneously attempting to marginalize Neoplatonic authority and religious practices.

3

Gazan Culture Performed and Transformed by Aeneas, Zacharias, and Procopius

How did these local cultures affect the lives of the three Gazans, and how did they negotiate their lives within them? I begin by analysing what Aeneas' letters may imply about how they constructed, consolidated, and were constrained by their cultures, before investigating the rhetorical strategies they used in their creation-oriented works to address particular cultural problems.

3.1 Gaza through Aeneas' Letters

Confidence in the social value of classical education and idiom is the dominant tone of Aeneas' letters. Aeneas writes to the wealthy imperial official Encratius urging him to support teachers in the schools (*Ep.* 13).[1] Aeneas' problem is how to finance his activities; his solution is to draw on the discourse of classical learning (*paideia*). This discourse is the effective solution to many social problems, including those posed by letters of reference, business transactions, requests for aid for and from friends and consolatory letters, and it even graces a letter about a new hydraulic device (where the garden of Alcinous and other Homeric references are employed) (e.g. *Ep.* 3, 5–9, 11, 17–20, 25).

Many letters display strong confidence in the intellectual ability of the age. Antioch is described in glowing terms as the 'city of the Muses', where fathers can happily enrol their sons in the expectation of their learning argument and reason (*Ep.* 17). Antioch is resplendent: it exults in its ancient heritage, and its blessing by Calliope, Apollo, and Hermes means that classical glory still exists in Aeneas' age (*Ep.* 17). References to classical mythology, in this letter as in others, should be read as coding social meanings well-removed from pagan religious belief. While educated pagans could partially construct their religious identity through such stories, and their continuing circulation holds open a space for such religiosity, for Aeneas and the growing Christian elite, the stories have a different function. Myth is used because the educated know and enjoy mythical stories; this shared

1. I focus on Aeneas' letters given the detailed treatment Procopius' have received in Amato (2010a); the conclusions reached in that volume are broadly consistent with my conclusions based on the evidence from Aeneas. For Encratius, see *PLRE* II loc. cit. The letter may be evidence for one way in which the Gazan schools financed their activities.

knowledge and enjoyment is part of what binds the educated class, whatever their preferred religious identity, together. So Choricius can praise Marcian, who was bishop of Gaza in the early sixth century, on the basis that 'when you were a young man, you plucked from the poets the finest parts and collected whatever was useful, smiling upon the myths and considering that they had been constructed by the Homeric writers for mere enjoyment' (Choricius, *Laud. Marc. I*, 6). Choricius himself uses Herodotean language in his encomium 'not for his storytelling, but for praising the bishop himself in proportion to his honour' (Choricius, *Laud. Marc. II*, 2). Such a use of classical discourse by Aeneas and Choricius is congruent with what has been identified in another context as 'an encoded model of human relations', where the 'names of gods and heroes serve...as an assertion of the high cultural values to which participants [in the process of gaining *paideia*] aspire'.[2] They are also used to cement valued social relations. This high evaluation of Hellenic intellectual attainments offers cultural support to Aeneas, Procopius, and Zacharias in their engagement with Neoplatonism.

Aeneas writes to his former student Theodorus, praising the excellence of his oratory and claiming some of the glory for himself, since 'the excellence [τὰ καλὰ] of the children may be considered to be that of the father' (*Ep.* 18). In this letter Aeneas continues:

> Congratulations for your excellence of voice, because of which the children of the Athenians consider it worthy to learn to Atticise, not from their fathers, but from the Syrians. They no longer disembark...desiring the Academy, nor wander near the Lyceum, since they consider that the Academy and the Lyceum are among us. I certainly receive sufficient recompense from you.

This echoes the opening of the *Theophrastus*: as in that dialogue, truth has moved from Athens to Syria. The optimistic evaluation of contemporary attainments of classical *paideia* not only gives Aeneas, Procopius, and Zacharias the confidence to engage with Neoplatonism but also drives them to recast it into something new. Scott has identified the sixth-century pattern of claiming allegiance to classical practices and ideologies, while simultaneously acting confidently in novel ways.[3] The use of Neoplatonic arguments by Christians against Neoplatonists in order to make novel intellectual points fits this cultural pattern.

2. Roberts (1989), 335–36, 341. Roberts is quoted in Penella (2005). Where Roberts and Penella focused on myth and epithalamia, I extend the analysis to wider processes of education.

3. See Scott (1990), 72; (1981), 73. I move the optimism Scott identified in Justinian's reign before the 540s back into Anastasius' reign. Haarer has shown the strength of a reign which has previously been somewhat overshadowed in modern assessments by Justinian (taking Justinian's period to include the years of Justin I). See Haarer (2006).

The confidence in the school also points to its continuing social utility, despite the rise of the monasteries explored above. Aeneas' letters testify to the strength of Brown's argument that *paideia* was 'the distinguishing mark of the diffused governing class of the empire, shared alike by the notables of each region and by the personnel of the imperial government... the cultural concomitant of innate good birth and fortunate circumstances'.[4] Such social utility can be seen in letters which recommend excellent students to other teachers or for places in government. These letters employ all the conventions of classical letters of recommendation.[5] Extended classical allusions and references are used to introduce the student to the prospective benefactor, as if to assure the addressee that the student speaks the same language as Aeneas and his friends, and as such really is suitable for employment. So one student, Ponton, is referred to as a 'gymnast', who has learned 'the wrestling matches of the rhetorical arts' and 'leaves as if he were a good athlete, on the way to Olympia, already well-prepared for the contest' and ready to 'take an Olympian victory' (*Ep.* 11). Cultural plots recognizable from the classical world about agonistic performance are explicit in this extended metaphor, which is completed by Aeneas asking his addressee, who is a 'member of the consuls', 'to preside brilliantly at the games and establish prizes not in boxing and wrestling, but in argument and intellectual soundness [σωφροσύνη]' (*Ep.* 11). No less than in the classical world, identity was constructed through conventional metaphors of performance and rhetorical contest.[6] Education was intimately connected with identity formation.[7] One did not go to the schools simply to learn how to perform a speech. Instead, students were introduced into a set of social relationships, practices, customs, and discursive expectations which formed how they lived.

The power of the teachers in the schools was largely a function of their role in shaping acceptable social identities and thereby maintaining the power dynamics of elite society. Aeneas' social standing is also demonstrated by his being called upon to arbitrate legal and business disputes (e.g. *Ep.* 3). In the letters of recommendation, Aeneas' mastery of classical literature and rhetoric made him a gate-keeper, as it were, for high society. He has the power to negotiate futures for his students, just as his students gained power—the possibility of entering elite society—by the learning he imparted to them.

4. Brown (1992), 36–37.

5. Michael Trapp's comments about letters of recommendation apply to Aeneas' letters. See Trapp (2003), 236ff.

6. For rhetoric and contest, see Roisman (2007).

7. For education and identity formation, see Brakke, Satlow, and Weitzman (2005); Kaster (1988); Watts (2005b).

It is clear from Aeneas' letters that the social power of classical discourses persists. The similarity between Aeneas' letters and those of earlier writers from the classical period onwards is partly evidence for the continuing value of these discourses. Yet in Aeneas' case they have been suitably transformed and understood within a dominantly Christian framework. The letters also leave other traces of social transition. They record social violence from which the elite was not insulated and which may point to instability in the midst of wider social changes. Three letters sympathize with people who have suffered robbery, including robbery with violence (*Ep.* 5, 6, 24).[8] Other social transitions may have affected the schools more directly. Aeneas wrote to one friend, a certain Cassus, urging him to stay and teach in the city (*Ep.* 2):

> When Laertes was an old man, he no longer wanted to be king, nor to govern men, but he wanted to be a gardener and care for trees (*Od.* XXIV). You seem to me to emulate this man, for otherwise you would not, having left the city and its inhabitants, and sitting around in the open for such a long time, spend your time talking to plants. But it is necessary not to have remembered Laertes but rather Socrates and his teachings, in which he philosophised most pleasingly and properly that places and plants do not tend to teach anything, but rather the men who are in the cities do (*Phaedr.* 230d). Obeying Socrates instead, and disregarding the fields where the farmers pluck the fruit which is barren of wisdom, be reminded of your familiar schools, in which it is possible to learn and teach a certain wisdom, and indeed the greatest thing: to please one's friends.

Here Aeneas can still draw on classical literature, alluding to Homer and Plato. Yet the letter may suggest that narratives other than those encoding the social value of the schools could claim greater allegiance among elite society. Of course, perhaps Cassus is simply a latter-day Cicero, who has retired to his country estate to engage in the contemplative life. In that case, the letter could not be strong evidence for such social change. But another letter within the corpus suggests an alternative interpretation. Aeneas wrote to the presbyter Dorotheus, urging him to help another man of God (ἱερῶν ἐστιν ὑπηρέτης) on his journey:

> The multitude, it is said, assault the holy places with unwashed feet, just like that bald tinker in Plato (*Rep.* 495e), who, when he was still smelling of smoke and filth, revolted against his mistress.[9] But you are going from

8. When Aeneas writes in one such letter (5) that 'I am grieved to such an extent, by the gods, that I could not speak', the expression 'by the gods' (μὰ τοὺς θεοὺς) should not be read as some sort of crypto-paganism, but rather as Aeneas conforming to the demands of the classical epistolary genre.

9. Plato's bald tinker is newly freed and has only just had a bath before he marries his master's daughter.

a holy place into a holy place, from philosophy into the priesthood. The one who carries this letter is a servant of holy things. So he is yours. He desires peace and since he has learned (I do not know how) that there is a mountain in the desert dedicated to God that is suitable for peace, he is journeying towards it. (*Ep.* 21)

The reference to Plato's *Republic* confirms the (by now familiar) story of a culture where classical allusions are valued and can be expected to be understood. Yet the intertextual allusion is far from straightforward. The Platonic passage comes from a section of the *Republic* where Socrates is arguing about what would happen to Philosophia if philosophers deserted her. He argues that as soon as true philosophers desert her, Philosophia would be taken over by 'second-rate interlopers', who would rush to her 'like a crowd of criminals taking refuge in a temple' (*Rep.* 495c–d).

At one level, then, by contrasting Dorotheus with the great unwashed, Aeneas is praising his friend, hoping thereby to gain his cooperation. Yet the allusion also encodes anxiety. Dorotheus might have gone from one philosophy to another, but there is no comforting claim that classical philosophy and ideology is being augmented by true philosophers in the same way as Aeneas claims the church is. This letter, together with the evidence for mobility between school and monastery given above, may authorize reading Aeneas' anxiety about Cassus leaving education in the city as figuring a more general anxiety about people failing to remain within the immediate sphere of influence of the schools. It can be read as evidence for a desire on Aeneas' part to reinforce the intellectual community and social value of the schools.

In the case of Dorotheus, a presbyter who has left the schools for the church, the new religion seems to be questioning the classical idea that honourable, successful lives should be measured by one's attainment of civic virtues, displayed by exercising power in positions of civic authority.[10] Given that the schools derive much of their prestige from their function as a training ground for specifically civic involvement, this changing evaluation of civic virtue offers a challenge to the late-antique schools.

Such a social situation implies a need for diplomatic use of classical *paideia* in late-antique Gaza. Classical *paideia* can now be a means of estrangement as well as a connector among the educated elite. In Letter Seven, Aeneas writes to the scholasticus Diodorus, praising the excellence of a poet called Herodotus who excels Orpheus, who charmed nature itself with his lyre, and Thamyris, the

10. Brown (1992).

bard who boasted that he could out-sing the Muses (*Il.* 2.594–600). Herodotus' poetry has made peace between Aeneas and Diodorus, who are presented as having had something of a tempestuous friendship (cf. *Ep.* 22). But Herodotus' poetry is explicitly contrasted with the poetry of comedy, which is 'shamelessly in vogue' and causes social disorder. Aeneas begs Diodorus to guard their friendship with sympathy, favour, pleasure, applause, and praise, setting up a 'holier theatre' and 'forbidding comedy to trouble anyone'. Again, we have a hint that not all forms of classical discourse were acceptable in Aeneas' Gaza, and we glimpse, perhaps, an earlier version of the conflict over the Gazan mimes known from Choricius' speech in their defence.[11] The reference to a 'holier theatre' may be read in the light of contemporary debates about whether theatrical productions should be allowed in a Christian Gaza.

In a tantalizing letter to the otherwise unknown Sarapion, Aeneas returns to the imagery of the theatre (*Ep.* 16). Sarapion's letter to Aeneas brings together spectators in a theatre and arouses applause, providing a compelling case for rhetoric in response to a letter from Aeneas in which he had apparently 'confessed a love of rhetoric, hoping to receive a cure' [ἐγὼ τῆς ῥητορικῆς ἐρᾶν πρὸς ὑμᾶς ὡμολόγουν, ἐλπίσας παρ' ὑμῶν εὑρίσκειν τὸ φάρμακον] from Sarapion. Why should a rhetor have to confess a love for rhetoric? And why should he need a cure? Without Aeneas' earlier letter or Sarapion's response, the answers to such questions remain beyond our grasp. But in the rest of the letter, Aeneas demonstrates that Sarapion's response has indeed 'strengthened rather than dissolved' his love of rhetoric. He begins by expressing sympathy for a 'tragic event' which caused him to flood 'the very earth with tears' [αὐτὴν ἐδάκρυσα τὴν γῆν]. The event seems to be conflict within a Christian community, since Aeneas writes that 'we are being destroyed from that source from which we should have been saved' [εἰ γὰρ ὅθεν ἔδει σεσῶσθαι, ἐντεῦθεν ἀπολλύμεθα] in a battle 'begun by the priests, by those whose preaching is peace' [εἰ ἐκ τῶν ἱερέων ὁ πόλεμος ἄρχεται, παρ' οἷς εἰρήνη τὸ κήρυγμα]. In this letter, biblical allusions are mingled with classical ones. The 'gospel of peace' (Isa. 57:2; Rom. 10:15) is closely followed by a nod to Plato's question about whether one can be the best general without having seen a battle (e.g. *Ion* 541a–c). Both references stand within a conventional classical *consolatio*, again affirming the strength of classical culture as a mechanism to bridge distance between correspondents. Yet Aeneas' stated anxiety about classical rhetoric, and his use of biblical allusion is evidence for increased competition between the different discourses which shaped late-antique Gaza.

11. Webb (2008) offers a comprehensive and fascinating treatment.

3.2 Creating Cultures through the Creation Debates

The Gazans' creation-oriented works broadly confirm the account of their local cultures reconstructed from Aeneas' letters, while more precisely identifying particular cultural problems which they attempted to elucidate. Particular social problems which generate their creation-oriented works are Neoplatonism in the schools, the power of Plato and Aristotle within this culture, and the associated religious claims of Neoplatonists. The potential for pagans to gain political power through the connections they form in the schools is also problematic. Faced with such threats, they reinforce the social value of the schools and argue that particular aspects of their classical inheritance (e.g. classical myths, literature, and philosophy) should continue to be one powerful means by which elite society is formed. But the Gazans seek to transform aspects of their classical inheritance which they think threaten to conflict with new cultural assumptions. They endeavour to maintain the social power of already transformed classical plots while making room within them for Christian discourse. In this process of combating unsettling elements of their local culture while seeking to retain a place for aspects of classical discourses, they employ classical genres in new ways, use classical myths to tell Christian stories, incorporate Platonic figures within Christian history, and employ Neoplatonic arguments to undermine Neoplatonists. The Christian identity thus created is intolerant of competing religious truth claims but embraces within Christianity many of the beliefs and practices valued by non-Christian groups in Gaza. The boundaries of Christian identity are defined but the culture the Gazans' seek to construct is heterogeneous and overlaps with several other social groups including Christians who reject philosophy, traditional Neoplatonists, and members of the surrounding monasteries.

The initial section of Aeneas' *Theophrastus* uses rhetorical allusions to Plato's *Phaedrus* (*Theophrastus* ποῖ δὴ καὶ πόθεν, Εὐξίθεε; cf. *Phaedr.* Ὦ φίλε Φαῖδρε, ποῖ δὴ καὶ πόθεν) to set up an atmosphere of openness to Platonic philosophy. The *Phaedrus*, of course, begins with the characters choosing a scenic location for the ensuing dialogue. The characters converse amiably and they find themselves a pleasant position under the shade of a plane tree to embark on their ethical and metaphysical discussions (*Phaedr.* 229a–b). The meeting of friends we remember from the *Phaedrus* is paralleled in Aeneas' dialogue, as old friends from student days in Alexandria are reunited, discuss the state of philosophy in Athens—a Neoplatonic stronghold—and begin to grapple with philosophical problems associated with the question of the pre-existence of the soul. Aeneas' dialogue sets discussions on the banks of the Nile, rather than the

Phaedrus' Ilissus (*Theophrastus* 2.5–6: καὶ ἰδού σοι πάρειμι τὸν Νεῖλον οὐ τὸν Ἰλισόν, τὴν δὲ Φάρον οὐ τὸν Πειραιᾶ θεώμενος; cf. *Phaedr.* 229a), but allusion to the Platonic dialogue helps to create a sense of open conversation between the Christian and pagan philosophical characters at the beginning of Aeneas' dialogue. The Platonic world has been transposed into the late fifth century, and readers can expect fruitful philosophical discussion between the different intellectual systems.

The friendships made in the philosophical schools are binding and lasting. Egyptus gives 'many thanks to the wind' because it 'forced [Euxitheus] to disembark among friends' (2.8–9). Euxitheus similarly speaks positively of Theophrastus as soon as he learns that he is a philosopher: 'already you have made me a lover [ἐραστήν] of Theophrastus' (3.25). Likewise, on being introduced to Euxitheus and told that he 'loves philosophy', Theophrastus exclaims, 'Euxitheus is really my old friend, if indeed he loves philosophy' [Ἦ μάλα μοι παλαιὸς φίλος ὁ Εὐξίθεος, εἴγε φιλοσοφίας ἐραστής] (4.5). Education lends social respectability and is a basis for friendship in Aeneas' section of society. As the analysis of Aeneas' letters suggested, education provides the capabilities, connections, and values which were necessary preconditions for entry into elite society. The dialogue figures this as natural and proper, thus seeking to maintain the social power of classical literacy.

The dialogue also stages Gaza's dependence on Alexandria. Alexandria is imagined by the Gazans as the proper location for philosophical discussion. That Aeneas chose to set his dialogue in Alexandria rather than Gaza suggests that Gaza took a large part of its intellectual identity from Alexandria. Alexandria's geographical position is presented as one reason for its intellectual vitality. The drama opens with the characters gazing 'upon the Nile not the Ilissus, the Lighthouse not the Piraeus' (2.5–6). The invocation of Hierocles, who displayed 'the mysteries of philosophy' to Euxitheus and Egyptus, also draws attention to Alexandria, and rebuttal of Hierocles' philosophy in general terms is also important for the choice of setting.[12]

Yet while it is true that Gaza depended on Alexandria in intellectual matters, this should not be taken to imply that Gaza was Alexandrian *instead of* Athenian in its philosophical outlook.[13] If the reference to Hierocles may imply an arguing

12. On the extent to which the dialogue rebuts Hierocles, see Aujoulat (1987); Goulet (1989); Hadot (2004); Schibli (2002).

13. The extent of philosophical difference between Alexandria and Athens is controversial. For important contributions to this question, see Armstrong (1970); Blumenthal (1993); Blumenthal (1986); Browning (2000); Saffrey (1984); Sheppard (2000); Sorabji (2005); Watts (2005a, 2006). Hadot's arguments appear most promising: there is no such thing as Alexandrian Neoplatonism, if by that one means philosophy substantially different from that practiced in Athens. See also Hadot (1990); Praechter (1990); Verrycken (1990); Westerink (1990).

partner on matters relating to providence, choosing an Athenian philosopher may hint that Proclus' views are under scrutiny in the section of the dialogue relating to creation. Euxitheus has been driven to Alexandria by unfavourable winds, but he had been on his way to Athens, 'where philosophy is especially distinguished', and he believes that his intellectual problems can only be solved by an *Athenian* philosopher. The substantial overlap between Alexandrian and Athenian philosophers throughout late antiquity, and especially in the fifth and sixth centuries, should in any case make us wary of suggesting major doctrinal and cultural differences between the two schools. Where Procopius condemns the errors of the Greeks, it is predominantly Neoplatonism, rather than other Greek philosophical systems, which he has in his sights (PG 87.1, 29Aff.) (see further below, Chapter 5). Zacharias' dialogue is, like Aeneas', set in Alexandria, and combats the Alexandrian Neoplatonists Ammonius and Gessius who both, like Hierocles, had strong connections to Athenian Neoplatonism. Gaza is thus a place which interacts with both Alexandria and Athens, and without minimizing the particular importance of Alexandria, the Gazans' works seem directed more generally against Neoplatonic culture.

Aeneas' dialogue allows us to identify what he considered most troubling as well as what he considered most beneficial in his culture. Theophrastus' extended doxography (5.10ff.) about the fate of the soul after death and whether the soul descends willingly, a key debating topic in the Platonic tradition, sets him up as a traditional Neoplatonist and performs the strength and vitality of the Neoplatonic tradition.[14] It is largely dependent on one of Plotinus' *Enneads* (4.8.1). The doxography begins with the pre-Socratics, and ends with Proclus, listing the opinions of Heraclitus, Empedocles, Plato, Aristotle, Boethus, Numenius, Plotinus, Porphyry, Iamblichus, Syrianus, and Proclus. In this outline of opinions, Aeneas makes Theophrastus recount the traditional, official, Platonic succession, which Neoplatonic philosophers from Alexandria and Athens all claimed in order to establish their own intellectual credentials.[15] As a traditional Neoplatonist with a standard and orthodox Neoplatonic pedigree, Theophrastus stands for Neoplatonism more generally. His victory would be the victory of Neoplatonism; his defeat at the hands of the Christian hero of the dialogue performs the defeat of Neoplatonism in the schools. But there is also a middle ground, where Theophrastus' values are shared by Aeneas.

14. The argument about willing or unwilling descent in *Enn* 4.8.5 generated debate. See e.g. Iamblichus, *On the Soul* 21–30.

15. Hierocles' version of the history of philosophy privileges the same figures.

By bringing the doxography up to Proclus, Aeneas takes account of Neoplatonic history up to his own day (the *Theophrastus* is written within a few years of Proclus' death) and claims that Neoplatonism has contemporary value. The doxography simultaneously demonstrates Aeneas' grasp of the Neoplatonic tradition, and implies that such knowledge is useful for Christians. It also suggests that a Christian and pagan audience in the schools could recognize quotations from Neoplatonism, enjoy such intertextuality and recognize its social value, in a similar way to the use of myth in Aeneas' letters or Choricius' orations.

Within Neoplatonic culture, Plato is taken to be the philosopher *par excellence*; beliefs are true inasmuch as they can be harmonized with (Neoplatonic interpretations of) Plato. While it is difficult to determine Plato's coherent position, since he 'speaks in many different contexts and does not always say the same things' (6.5; cf. Plotinus, *Enn.* 4.8.1), Theophrastus insists that Plato is never inconsistent (6.3ff.). Those who think that Plato contradicts himself 'change words and concepts according to their own fancy' [νοήματα καὶ ὀνόματα ὡς ἂν ἐθέλωσι μετατιθέντες] (8.12). In a typically Neoplatonic passage, Plato himself is taken as the best guide to Plato's thought: 'There has not been, nor might there be in the future, anyone more competent than Plato in clearly interpreting everything which Plato intended' (8.14–15). Any position which finds fault with Plato is confused, shameful, ignorant, contentious, and born of a pernicious desire for originality or innovation (8.11–22). This is an entirely apt characterization of Neoplatonic attitudes towards the relationship between Plato and Aristotle. Two further examples, from Aeneas' probable teacher, Hierocles, may suffice to show Aeneas' understanding of this attitude. For Hierocles, all those who destroy the unanimity of Plato and Aristotle are trivial and dangerous thinkers:

> They have corrupted many of the Platonic accounts, and yet they claim Plato as their teacher, just as is the case with the writings of Aristotle among those who confess to honour his school. Their machinations have no other purpose than to make the Stagirite clash with the son of Ariston. (*Prov.* 214.8.173a)

Photius also quotes Hierocles in a second summary:

> Many of the students of Plato and Aristotle have applied their zeal and attention to show that their teachers clashed with one another concerning the critical points of their doctrines; their contentiousness and daring have driven them to the point of falsifying the writings of their teachers in order better to show that these philosophers fought against each other. (*Prov.* 251.3.461a)

By claiming to be interpreting Plato consistently, Theophrastus adds force to his argument in a culture where Plato's word was given maximum weight. The dialogue thus gives evidence for the continuing authority of Plato in the late-antique schools.

The Neoplatonic culture Aeneas sketches in the opening pages of the *Theophrastus* also draws support from other texts, beyond the standard 'golden chain' of Neoplatonic succession or the authority of Plato. Theophrastus quotes Homer, alludes to mythological stories in Sophocles, Euripides, and Herodotus, refers to Egyptian and Indian religious beliefs, and cites the *Chaldean Oracles* approvingly. Therefore the Neoplatonic culture, which Theophrastus personifies in the dialogue, draws strength from the wider literary culture described above, and which the schools embody. Proclus frequently drew on mythological themes in his philosophical works as well as his hymns; he had undergone rhetorical training before pursuing philosophy. He also reputedly ranked the *Chaldean Oracles* as highly as Plato's *Timaeus* (Marinus, *VProcl* 38).[16] Hierocles seems to have structured his *On Providence* in a historical scheme which harmonizes figures from Homer and the *Chaldean Oracles* down the Platonic chain of succession.

Given that the *Chaldean Oracles* and religious rituals associated with them are highly esteemed by Neoplatonists, especially following Iamblichus, Neoplatonic culture as related by Aeneas also has religious force; indeed, it is thoroughly religious, as a system of thought purporting to explain the world and our place within it and as a set of practices for properly living within the world.[17] This is suggested from the start of Aeneas' work, when Theophrastus begins his doxography by saying that he 'will unfold the secrets of the ancients to [Euxitheus and Egyptus], as if [he] were examining offerings in the temples' [Ἐγώ σοι διανοίγειν ὥσπερ ἐν ἱεροῖς πειράσομαι τὰ τῶν παλαιῶν ἀπόρρητα] (5.11–12). The term used for the ancient sayings, ἀπόρρητα, is the same term used to describe religious mysteries, particularly the beliefs of the Chaldeans (6.8). Neoplatonic religion is also apparent in references to procession and return to the One. This religious colouring of Neoplatonic culture sets Euxitheus on a collision course with Theophrastus, despite their shared enjoyment of elements of classical culture.

The central characteristics of Neoplatonic culture as personified by Theophrastus and constructed by Aeneas' dialogue may be briefly summarized. The culture gives authority to Plato and Aristotle, it values philosophical

16. For Proclus' hymns, see Berg (2001).
17. Fowden (1982) analyses Neoplatonic religiosity.

speculation and the writings of select figures in the Platonic tradition as well as classical literature more generally, and it makes particular polytheistic claims. Taken together with the immediate professions of friendship between all the characters of the dialogue, Theophrastus' strong adherence to these key assumptions and components of Neoplatonism points to a wider culture where Neoplatonism and Christianity were able to coexist peacefully and constructively. This coexistence is partly figured by Aeneas' use of the dialogue form, which allows differing views to be placed creatively alongside each other, and, to some extent, asks the reader to choose between the different views. Certainly, Aeneas sets the scene for his dialogue more positively than Zacharias did in his later dialogue, the *Ammonius*.[18] Theophrastus is praised for his philosophical expertise (3.15ff.), whereas the pagan philosophers in Zacharias' dialogue are ridiculed for pomposity and stupidity (Ammonius: 21, 31, 995ff., 1332f.; Gessius 362ff.). The dialogue form, then, partly models for Aeneas' readers continued positive social interactions with Neoplatonism.

Yet the *Theophrastus* is not simply generated by a culture where Neoplatonism and Christianity lived happily together, and its dialogue form does not simply figure creative exchange: it also embodies tension.[19] The wider religious change following initial Christianization of Gaza is one motivating factor for the *Theophrastus* and similarly for Procopius' and Zacharias' works. The religious composition of the schools in Gaza may be taken as similar to nearby institutions in Alexandria and Berytus. Zacharias provides a vivid description of the religious conflict within those schools in the 480s and early 490s. In Berytus, Zacharias describes the public burning of pagan magical books to preserve orthodoxy (*VSev* 61ff.). In the schools as elsewhere in late-antique Palestine, religious identity was unstable, as demonstrated by Damascius' account of the conversion to paganism of Epiphanius and Euprepius, and by Severus' admission of his initial paganism (Damascius, *Isid.* fr. 100 = *Phil. Hist.* 41; Severus, *Homily* 4.1–6).[20] Zacharias' account of the conversion of Paralius, the subsequent fracas in the Alexandrian schools, and the beating and exile of philosophical

18. Minniti-Colonna (1973).

19. Theophrastus never in fact wins a point, is often ridiculed in a similar manner to Ammonius and Gessius in Zacharias' dialogue, and, like Zacharias' student, he ends up praying to the Christian God. In this action, Aeneas' dialogue actually goes beyond Zacharias', where it is only a student 'slipping towards paganism' who is converted or secured in his wavering faith, not one of the philosophers. Cf. Gallicet (1978); Watts (2005a). I cannot agree with Sivan that the three Gazans soothed the conflicts of Gaza's pagan past with 'enjoyment of art qua art. The education which the city's outstanding educators offered the community bridged the pagan past with the tranquillity of classical pursuits and Christian piety.' See Sivan (2008), 347. On dialogue and 'patterns of sociability in late antiquity', see Lim (2008).

20. For Damascius, see Damascius (1967a, 1999). For Severus, see Garitte (1966).

teachers like Horapollon, Isidore, Heraiscus, and Asclepiodotus, is well known (*VSev* 16ff.).

So the construction of Neoplatonic culture in the early passages of Aeneas' dialogue sets up a series of cultural claims which Aeneas uses his dialogue to explore, moderate, or reject outright. On the question of Plato's and Aristotle's authority and status as standards of truth, Aeneas is firmly at odds with the cultural claims of the Neoplatonism he has constructed. This will not stop him using Plato and Aristotle (see further Chapter 6), but it does undermine the heroic status given to the two classical philosophers within Neoplatonism. Aristotle is something of an embarrassment to the main Christian character in Aeneas' dialogue, Euxitheus:

> I am silent about Aristotle, who through intellectual arrogance denied the immortality of the soul. Each philosopher has destroyed the opinions of the others and proposes philosophical opinions which contradict others and are not internally consistent. (8.6–10)

Similarly, where Theophrastus had been constructed as a perfect Neoplatonist with a coherent philosophical pedigree, whose claims to knowledge were partly based on the strength of the tradition and the authority of its members, Euxitheus largely sees incoherence:

> I would marvel still more, if, now that I have learned this, you might fill me up further with Pythagoras, Plato, the Chaldeans and the Egyptians from ancient times down to the present, given that all together they do not speak consistently about these things, nor are they even individually consistent. To affirm contradictory things is a property of ignorance, not of knowledge. Furthermore, I believe that God was not the one who led the way in that doctrine, or it would seem the same to all, but rather it is some human notion, in which many contradictory things are interwoven. (9.5–10)

Divine and human thought are contrasted; simplicity as a criterion of truth is on the Christian side. Procopius will make strong claims for the Bible as the main criterion of truth for Christians.[21] His collation of the arguments of the Church Fathers may be read as a response to the Neoplatonic claim that their tradition of thinking was more vibrant and coherent. Zacharias similarly undermines the authority of the Neoplatonic tradition represented by Ammonius and Gessius in his dialogue, arguing that Christian revelation, rather than authority within

21. See below, 5.1.

Neoplatonic culture, is the proper criterion of truth. He openly ridicules the idea that Plato and Aristotle agree on the question of the forms, and agrees with Plato against Aristotle that the universe is composed from four elements (1093, 696–715).[22] Furthermore, instead of seeing authority in the antiquity of Neoplatonism as Theophrastus does, Zacharias sees only an empty claim to power:

> It is only right to honour the ancient things, when they also have the truth appearing plainly for [their] time. But whenever the story is false, bewitching the hearer with embellished words and the sweetness of fancy language, then indeed we place Homeric wax in our ears so that we might escape the deadly song of the death-bearing sirens, when we recognise the honey-rimmed cup of poison. (467–73)[23]

In this example, Zacharias explicitly acknowledges that non-Christian authors could discover and teach true doctrines. Yet Homer and Plato himself, who disregards a poem's antiquity in judging its value, are used as pagan heroes to undermine the authority of the Neoplatonic canon. Aeneas' and Zacharias' dialogues seek to strip Neoplatonism of claims to universal value without denying its truth claims *in toto*. This allows their form of Christianity to use elements of Neoplatonism within its own discourse without submitting to external claims for ultimate allegiance. The schools can continue to teach Neoplatonic ideas, transformed by very different argumentative frames.

Zacharias also seeks to counter the potential for the school to remain a pagan stronghold by characterizing paganism as politically dangerous. Polytheistic politics is 'Corybantic frenzy' where the established order is overturned (312ff.). This seems to be a conventional deployment of the Bacchic rites to signal madness. Yet Proclus had characterized true interpreters of Plato as a divinely inspired Bacchic chorus, so Zacharias' attack may have a more pointed focus (cf. Proclus, *in Parm.* 618,5–8, where Syrianus is referred to as a fellow Bacchant with Plato). Zacharias again quotes Homer against the pagans:

> Further, they invent a chain of creators who are foreign and strange to the process of creation and production, such as [the chain] of evil and erring spirits, and have taken them up into the ranks of the gods, in no way paying attention to the Homeric wisdom which ordained that 'the rule of the

22. Cf. Pl., *Tim.* 31b; 40a; 58c against Arist., *Cael.* 1.2.

23. This passage is rich in allusions: Theodoret's *Cure for Greek Maladies* (*Graecarum affectionum curatio)* (pref. 1.5: τῷ γλαφυρῷ τῆς εὐεπείας; 1.52.2: τὴν ἀλήθειαν ἔχει ἐπανθοῦσαν τῷ χρόνῳ); Homer's *Od.* and Plato's *Ap.* (κεκαλλιεπημένοις ὀνόμασι). Such intertextuality is a good indication of the diverse cultures which helped to generate Zacharias' text.

> many is not good: let there be one ruler, one king' (Homer *Il.* 2.204–5). Instead, they affirm unbridled democracy, the most shameful of constitutions, perennially confused and revolting against divine principles, unable to perceive the beauty of monarchy, nor desiring its immaterial and blessed light. (316–24)

Here Zacharias echoes Aeneas' earlier claim that pagans 'make many principles and thousands of Gods, and bring in disordered democracy in place of orderly monarchy' [καὶ πολλὰς ἀρχὰς καὶ μυρίους θεοὺς ποιοῦντες, δημοκρατίαν ἄτακτον ἀντὶ τῆς τεταγμένης μοναρχίας εἰσοίσουσιν] (37.25–38.1). In quoting Homer, he uses a passage also favoured by Neoplatonists following Aristotle (*Metaph.* Λ 10, 1076a3–4), yet implicitly denies that they can validly appropriate it. Pagans are given the empty choice of accepting the incoherence of their tradition or accepting the charge that they undermine imperial power.

Aeneas adds to this political critique of pagan polytheism, making his Christian character claim that Neoplatonic arguments about creation are like bad laws and would lead to the collapse of the rule of law: 'The law of Solon does not permit a law to be given for a single man, but rather the same law is given for every Athenian. But you do not permit the law of the great lawgiver to be universal and you do not agree that the same law should be given to each and every man' (22.19–22). In each of these arguments, the Gazans seek to cast pagan polytheism as threatening to imperial ideology. In a political culture where the divinely mandated universal rule of the emperor had been emphasized since Constantine, Aeneas' and Zacharias' use of the doctrine of creation supports the imperial government by making monarchy a divine right, and marginalizes pagans as potential subversives. By using arguments about creation to emphasize the uniqueness of God in the face of pagan polytheism, Aeneas and Zacharias both recognize that the doctrine of creation could undermine the political influence of the pagans who might otherwise gain political power owing to their socially powerful education. 'God is One', the catch-cry that accompanied Christian aggression, including the destruction of the Marneion in Gaza in 402, was not simply a cry against polytheism.[24] In the hands of Aeneas and Zacharias it also became a way of marginalizing pagan political power within the schools.

24. See di Segni (1990a); Peterson (1920). Peterson had taken the inscription εἷς θεός as an exclusively Christian phrase, used against pagans, but di Segni has shown that the phrase could also be used against Christian Trinitarianism by Jews and Samaritans. For Neoplatonic authors who use Homer, *Il.* 2.204–5 in claiming their own monism, see Proclus, *in Tim.* 1.262.17; Ammonius *in Int.* 96,24; Asclepius *in Metaph.* 244,3; Olympiodorus, *Prolegomena* 9,22, *in Gorg.* 42.2.9. The Neoplatonists employ Homer in this way following Aristotle (see above).

Therefore Neoplatonic culture, with its claims for the authority and truth-value of Plato and Aristotle, its parading of a tradition with the authority of antiquity, and its polytheistic and political claims, poses fundamental problems which generate the claims to social power inscribed in the Gazans' works. The Gazans use their works to negate these claims. But the negation leaves room for engagement with Neoplatonic culture on Christian terms. Plato and Aristotle, as well as other thinkers within Neoplatonism, can be used within the Christian discourse, stripped of their totalizing religious claims. The attempt to cast polytheism as politically subversive may be read as a claim to power on the Christian side, in an age where imperial ideology was well-established, and firmly supported Christian religious claims.

3.3 Reconfiguring Neoplatonic Claims to Power through Narrative and Genre

If the dialogue form allows Aeneas and Zacharias to place different Christian and Neoplatonic cultures against each other and test their permeability, the direction of Aeneas' and Zacharias' narratives, their shape and implied goal, inscribes in the text a cultural reversal in the realm of religious identity which the authors wish to achieve in their own times. Aeneas' dialogue certainly begins in shared values, and for the first sixth of the dialogue, Theophrastus, while never allowed to win a point, as Egyptus' scornful interjections and his own explicit acquiescence to Euxitheus' arguments are meant to convey, at least has the lion's share of the conversation. But as the dialogue progresses, Theophrastus is reduced more and more to the status of simplistic interlocutor, and Euxitheus assumes the role of the teacher. Finally, Theophrastus is convinced of all Euxitheus' arguments, perceives (the Christian) God's grace, admits that God is wiser than Plato, and joins Euxitheus in prayer to the Holy Trinity. Zacharias' dialogue has a similar shape. The dialogue is set as a series of conversations retold to the questioning student inside a great church. In the mini-dialogues, the philosophers who are initially confident end up more 'speechless than stones or fish' and the student who was 'slipping towards paganism' faithfully joins a final prayer.

Thus their narratives achieve a series of striking reversals. The teacher becomes the student, the confident voice of pagan religion is silenced as Christian theology finds its voice, even Plato's unique, divine authority is relativized and subjected to Christian truth claims. In Zacharias' work, setting the discussions in a church colonizes philosophical thought. It includes, Christianizes, and limits Neoplatonic philosophy within the Christian literary context. Readers are implicated in this reversal and limitation, so the dialogue serves to bring people to Christianity while retaining an appropriately circumscribed role for

Neoplatonic ideas within Christianity. These literary reversals are further evidence that one cultural problem Aeneas and Zacharias try to solve in their dialogues is tension between the various Christian and pagan religious convictions of those educated in the schools.

In both dialogues, the Christian figures become progressively more dominant. The pagan figures are not allowed to win points, and by the end of each work they are written out entirely, except when they join in Christian prayer, itself a reversal that replaces Neoplatonic religiosity with Christianity. Therefore Aeneas and Zacharias both use the dialogue form to perform Christian victories over Neoplatonism, especially its religious claims. The literary reversal collapses the diversity of real-world conflict into a literary uniformity of belief. The writers both hope that their literary works will act on their readers to limit religious and philosophical diversity in the schools.

In both Aeneas and Zacharias, the literary reversal is also mirrored in a reversal of the types of arguments offered. Aeneas' dialogue begins with an extended doxography of the opinions of Neoplatonic philosophers. Such Neoplatonic argument runs through most of the work. But in the final section of the dialogue, which treats the possibility of resurrection, a different discourse is introduced. The final pages of the dialogue leave Neoplatonic argument behind, and instead offer mythological and Christian miracle stories. The Orestes myth becomes a somewhat macabre argument that it is possible to reconfigure the bodies of those long since dead. Theseus and Oedipus are invoked to demonstrate that even evil people 'are kept safe when they are under the earth' and so can be resurrected at the end of time (60.5ff.). Other characters from Greek myth prefigure the resurrection or suggest through their actions that it is possible (64.7ff.). Testimony from Plato, Zoroaster, and Theopompus completes the picture: 'Plato leads Harmonius back to the living from Hades in the body, and Zoroaster prophesied that there would be a time when there would be a resurrection of all the dead.[25] Theopompus knows what I say, and he himself teaches this to others'[26] (64.7–10). Yet these stories are all employed as part of a negative argument, as perhaps the close association of Plato and the shady figure of Theopompus may hint. In using the stories from Greek mythology, Aeneas does not grant the truth of the Greek stories. You believe these stories, he says, so why do you reject the possibility of Christian resurrection?

25. An erroneous allusion to Plato, *Rep.* 614b, where Er is the son of 'Armenius'. See Clement of Alexandria, *str* 5.14.103.3–4 for putative connections between Er and Zoroaster.

26. For Theopompus and 'resurrection', see FGrH 115 F 64.

The positive argument takes the form of Christian stories and the miracles of holy men:

> The scriptures of the Hebrews, which the oracles of Apollo praised, everywhere prophesy that not some part of man, but the whole man returns to life. Therefore certainly there are men, who, having learned self-control from childhood into old age, have raised their souls to the intelligibles, and have persuaded the body to serve the soul even in dreams. In this way, having arrived at the peak of philosophy by contemplation and practice, and having shown their kinship with God, calling on him purely, they have made corpses return to life, achieving by their actions sufficient demonstration of the doctrine. (64.15–23)

Aeneas claims to have seen a holy elder who had raised a child from the dead. The story is a trace of relationships between the monasteries around Gaza and the local Gazan population. This holy man had been visited, and kept in a good supply of grapes, by a father and son, who came frequently to learn from the holy man. Yet 'after a short time, the son became sick and died' [χρόνος βραχὺς καὶ ὁ παῖς νοσήσας τελευτᾷ τὸν βίον] (65.3f.). So the father brings his dead child, whom he covers in offerings of grapes and other produce in a basket, to the holy man. When the holy man came to eat the grapes after prayer, he was surprised that 'he finds not grapes but the corpse of the boy. The old man was amazed at the extent of the father's hope, and he turned his mind towards God, and fell upon the child and would not stand unless the child was raised' [ἐπὶ τὸν παῖδα καταπεσών, οὐ πρότερον ἔστη εἰ μὴ τὸ παιδάριον ἀνέστη] (65.11–13). This story avoids classical imitation, turning to the Bible for literary allusion instead, recalling Elijah in 1 Kings 17:21–24.[27] The biblical allusion underscores the change in the narrative. Acts of holy men shaped by the biblical narrative have taken over from the earlier classical allusions and philosophical arguments.

After the boy is duly raised, Aeneas argues 'that man could not achieve such a thing, if he had received a false doctrine. But having learned the word from God, he converted the doctrine into action with God's help. In this lies the best sort of proof, to achieve that which one promised was able to happen' (65.16–19). There is none of the irony in this passage which is apparent in the accounts of the Greek stories. The works of the holy man are the 'best sort of proof'. The holy man in question in this story has been identified as Zeno, disciple of Silvanus (Rufus, *Plerophories* 8).[28] The monastic community in Gaza provides Aeneas with

27. Such stories became a literary topos. In an amusing story from the Latin West, a man is proved to be a completely reprobate and irredeemable sinner when he does not get up after Bernard of Clairvaux lies down upon him no less than three times. See Walter Map, *De Nugibus Curialium* Dist. 1, chapter 24.

28. See Bitton-Ashkelony and Kofsky (2006), 19.

a standard for Christian truth and holiness. This story is immediately followed by the healing of a blind disciple of a Christian teacher and holy man. The blind man,

> who had been led around by hand up to this point, all of a sudden marvelled at the rays of the sun, and, having taken up the scriptures and reading them in public, amazed the audience and persuaded the hearer who loves strife both that the soul is immortal and that with noble nourishment and education, the soul comes back to revive that part of the body which has died. (66.2–6)

This restoration of sight had been promised by the holy man. The reference to 'the hearer who loves strife' also places the blind man, a disciple of a Christian teacher, within a more secular environment, that of agonistic enthusiasms. This is further evidence for some overlap between the monastic environment and the Hellenized culture of the rhetorical schools in Gaza. Crucially, in this narrative, Christian story rather than Neoplatonic argumentation has become, by the end of Aeneas' narrative, constitutive of truth.

A final story of the power of Christian faithfulness follows immediately. Here victims of Vandal persecutions under Huneric have had their tongues cut out for daring to profess their Christianity (66.15ff.). Just as Christ rose on the third day, three days after their tongues had been cut out, the victims began to talk, not with their old tongues, but because God had granted them a new nature 'so that they could converse without a tongue more clearly than before'. Aeneas proclaims:

> I saw the men and I heard [them] speaking, and, marvelling at the articulateness of their voices, sought out the instrument of the voice, and doubting my ears, I entrusted the judgement to my eyes. When I opened [their] mouths, I saw that their tongues had been completely dragged out from the roots, and, being astounded, I marvelled not that they could talk, but that they survived [οὐχ ὅπως τὸν λόγον συνήρμοσαν, ἀλλ' ὅπως ἐσώθησαν]. Let this dissolve the incredulity of the senseless man, if fallen bodies are made to stand again. (67.8–14)

A pious story about the 'African Confessors' is again made to carry the weight of the Christian argument—that the faithful will be resurrected, that this will be a bodily existence but that it will be a new form of existence, brought about by divine power.[29] The use of analogical arguments may also be a sign of the

29. This miracle tale is discussed in Edwin Abbott's *Philomythus* (1891), a response to Cardinal Newman, at 16–30, 196–97. In his *Essay on Ecclesiastical Miracles* (1901), section IX, 369–87, Newman had cited other ancient evidence for this miracle (Victor, Bishop of Vite *Hist Per Vand* 3, p. 613; Procopius of Caesarea *Bell. Vand.* 1.10; Justinian lib. 1 tit. 30; Gregory I, *Dial.* 3.32), although he cast doubt on it in later editions of the essay (391–93).

generative and regulatory role played by the Bible in the dialogue's transformed discourse.

In all these stories, the actions of holy men and the consequences of the faithfulness of believers are taken as definitive and unassailable proof of the truth of Christian doctrine. Coming at the end of Aeneas' dialogue, they have replaced Neoplatonic argument as the mode of narrative. Within a page of the final story, the dialogue ends in prayer. The work has moved from the classroom into the church, from philosophical dialogue into Christian discourse and finally to prayer. These changes in literary genre contribute to the reversal in power relations between the speakers which the dialogue performs.[30] Theophrastus submits to this transformation, and ultimately agrees to change his way of life: 'I am persuaded. For already I perceive the favour of God [τῆς εὐμενείας αἰσθάνομαι τοῦ Θεοῦ].[31] Farewell Academy: let us go to him. For Plato himself commands us to obey Plato up until there appears someone wiser than he is (*Rep.* 388e). And nothing is wiser than God' (68.5–8). While Zacharias' dialogue does not change its mode of discourse from Neoplatonic argument to Christian narrative in the same way that Aeneas' does, the final mini-dialogue of the work, after others which were set in the schoolrooms of Alexandria, returns to the church, and the student asks Zacharias not about contested philosophical questions, but about Christian problems concerning the resurrection of the body. The problematic has moved from philosophy to theology, just as the setting changes from the classroom to the church. Therefore both dialogues offer a new Christian discourse as a valid way of operating in the Christian incarnation of the classical rhetorical schools.

This transformation of classical discourse into Christian idiom may also be seen in how the Gazans employ their chosen genres. Dialogue links Aeneas and Zacharias to Neoplatonism by connecting their works to a prestigious philosophical genre. Their use of the genre asserts that Christians can write and think like Plato. It elevates Christianity above Platonic philosophy while claiming continuity with the classical past. But it also separates Aeneas and Zacharias from their philosophical contemporaries, since contemporary Neoplatonists seem to have moved away from writing their own dialogues, focusing on commentary instead. This complex use of dialogue, at a time when dialogue has atrophied in

30. My interpretation is opposed to that of Watts (2007), 155, who believes that the 'Christian significance' of these stories is 'downplayed'. Cf. also 162, where Watts claims that where Zacharias is explicitly Christian, Aeneas is 'understated' about his Christianity.

31. Augustine had earlier claimed that Porphyry explicitly acknowledged the grace (*gratia*) of God (*Civ. Dei* 10.29), though note that Aeneas' use of the term *eumeneia* rather than *kharis* suggests that God's general providence and goodness, rather than divine grace itself, may be all that is claimed here.

pagan circles, should make us question Goldhill's claim that Christianity killed the philosophical dialogue.[32] As we have seen, the use of the dialogue genre in this register embodies cultural conflict, but it may also be read as making a more fundamental claim for the superiority of Christian discourse. Aeneas and Zacharias seek to replace Platonic dialogue with a Christian version. They go back to the source of the Neoplatonic tradition, and seek to appropriate the classical genre for Christian purposes. The dialogues are partly designed to provide Christian students with suitable material for Christian philosophy, replacing and countering the standard curriculum of the philosophical schools. This is a further instance of the pattern of incorporating classical traditions into a new discourse, in the process performing a transformation, rather than a simple negation or rejection, of the original classical model. In going back to the Platonic source, Aeneas and Zacharias display a strong confidence to engage with Platonism and make the stronger claim that Christians can surpass Plato's achievement.

Something of the same dynamic may be seen in Procopius' use of the commentary genre, which dominated Neoplatonic philosophy and other intellectual disciplines in the fifth and sixth centuries. Using commentary thus ties Procopius firmly to contemporary intellectual endeavour, including standard Neoplatonic scholarship, although Origen's biblical commentaries had standard introductory questions and lemmata, and Procopius' commentary thus stands securely within a Christian tradition.[33] Like Origen and later commentators Christian and philosophical, he analyses his source text lemma-by-lemma after prolegomena which answer standard questions about, for example, authorship, classification of subject matter, and potential readers and their expected knowledge.[34] But instead of carefully recording the opinions of previous philosophers, Procopius buttresses Christian orthodoxy by transmitting the 'single spring' of truth (22A–23A). Procopius' decision to write a biblical commentary which collects the opinions of the Fathers suggests that his work is motivated partly by a Christian demand for authoritative collations of Christian truth. His commentaries, then, partly fulfil pedagogical purposes and are partly designed to provide Christian students with an established tradition of Christian scholarship which could counter the Neoplatonic 'golden chain'. Like Aeneas and Zacharias in the

32. Goldhill (2008).

33. If Procopius wrote a refutation of Proclus' commentaries, he could have had direct links to Neoplatonic commentary. My general point, that Neoplatonists would recognize his commentaries as being of the same general type as their own, stands whether or not his use of commentary is directly dependent on Neoplatonism.

34. For such prolegomena, see Westerink (1990).

case of dialogue, Procopius uses commentary to claim allegiance to Platonism and transform philosophical commentary into a new, Christian discourse. His use of genre, like that of Aeneas and Zacharias, figures changes in Gazan society. Like Aeneas and Zacharias, Procopius uses his chosen genres to achieve desired social changes. He too uses genre to legitimate Christian power and undermine Neoplatonic social influence as he replaces the Neoplatonic philosophical canon with a Christian biblical one. This new frame for the claims about creation devalues Neoplatonic claims for the authority of their heroes and constructs a new Christian chain of authority, creating a discourse in which Neoplatonists are silent.

Changes that the Gazans made to their chosen genres also reveal changes they would like to see in Gazan society. Some Platonic dialogues (particularly the early Socratic ones) end in aporia, with further questions to be answered. This sense of openness is one enduring attraction and defining feature of Plato's dialogues. While it is often clear who has the answers (despite Socrates' protestations), one key philosophical point of the Platonic dialogues is that truth may only be discovered in conversation (cf. Plato, *Epistle* 7) and that open discussion is preferable to discourses which foreclose argument. As we have seen, Aeneas' and Zacharias' works display a very different dynamic. No one could doubt what points they are trying to make. As their dialogues progress, they become less like open conversations and more like rigidly didactic catechetical instruction, with the teacher, who has all the answers, educating the student, who is supposed to accept the wisdom imparted to him by his teacher.

In the course of this transformation of the narrative, dialogue itself is transformed. The dialogue genre merges into a Christian variety of question and answer literature (*Erotapokriseis*) which is designed to place power in the hands of specifically Christian teachers and form a new tradition based around the authority of Christian teachers, thus sidelining Neoplatonic authority figures.[35] Procopius' *Commentary on Genesis* also tends in this direction. While his commentary shares a number of features with Neoplatonic commentary, it is also very close to the catena genre from which it heavily draws. In a catena, there is less of the connected argument found in a commentary. Its primary purpose, which overlaps with that of Christian question and answer literature, is to make the views of Christian authority figures available to students and exegetes. The transformation of the Gazans' chosen dialogues thus helps to establish Christian authority within the late-antique schools. It points to a cultural problem which

35. On this genre, see Volgers and Zamagni (2005). The 'Sayings of the Desert fathers' (*apothegmata*) is an associated genre.

the Gazans, each in different ways, want to solve, that of the continuing strength and authority of Neoplatonism in the schools.

In addition, the transformation of the dialogue into question and answer literature seems to be generated in part by the Gazan monastic local culture.[36] We have seen an example of such literature later in the sixth century, possibly drawing on Aeneas' example in a different register, as John and Barsanuphius established their spiritual authority by responding to questions from other monks, presbyters, and laity on a wide variety of social and spiritual or theological matters. By making their dialogues approximate the question and answer literature, the Gazans can claim spiritual authority for their arguments, and make their works understandable within the monastic communities.

Yet even this generic transformation, which is designed to undermine Neoplatonism, does not leave Neoplatonism behind. Many Neoplatonists themselves used question and answer to communicate their philosophy and establish their own authority.[37] The genre was accepted as valuable within the Neoplatonic intellectual community. Hence, similar conclusions to those presented above about dialogue may be drawn about Aeneas' and Zacharias' merging of dialogue and question and answer literature. They appropriate the genre from Neoplatonism and cast it in a distinctively Christian key partly to make a bridge between Christian and Neoplatonic local cultures, and partly to establish the dominance of the particularly Christian local culture in the schools.

The Gazans' work spans the different genres of commentary, question and answer, and dialogue. Each of these genres has both Christian and Neoplatonic precursors. Therefore the Gazans can use them to interact with people subscribing to different local cultures, including Neoplatonists and Christians in the schools, as well as monks in the monasteries, or those attracted to a monastic way of life. In different ways, Aeneas, Procopius, and Zacharias use their chosen genres to incorporate Neoplatonic discourse into Christianity, and simultaneously to marginalize Neoplatonists by silencing their claims to authority. This oscillation between contact and conflict, appropriation and rejection, characterizes late fifth-century Gaza. The choice of literary form by all three writers helps to consolidate Christian dominance in former pagan strongholds by implicating the audience in the fall of paganism and the rise of Christian philosophy and a distinctively Christian mode of discourse. Yet this rise and fall is not a story of the obliteration of one distinct local culture by another completely foreign one.

36. On this point, see the insightful remarks of Papadoyannakis (2006).

37. See, for example, Porphyry's *Questions and Responses* [*κατὰ πεῦσιν καὶ ἀπόκρισιν*] on Aristotle's *Categories* or various works by Alexander of Aphrodisias, including his *Ἀπορίαι καὶ λύσεις* [*Problems and Solutions*] and *Προβλήματα* [*Problems: Medical, Physical, Ethical*].

Rather, the new Christian discourse is built on its use of classical culture and continues to be shaped by it.

3.4 Conflict and Complexity

Gaza as constructed by Aeneas, Procopius, and Zacharias was characterized by complex interactions between individual agents, material factors, social institutions, and systems of meaning which constructed and deconstructed social power, and where different actors aimed for different truths. This picture is broadly consistent with my theorizing about culture in Chapter 1. The Gazans do try to define strongly demarcated acceptable religious belief in an exclusive manner, but their rejection of pagan religiosity leaves room for several aspects of the Neoplatonic culture they continue to value: conflict is joined by adaptation and appropriation in the process of the construction of distinctive local cultures. The creation-oriented works suggest that there were Christians in Gaza who were attempting to reject all elements of Neoplatonic culture, and inasmuch as Christian religious practices and discourses clash with Neoplatonism, Aeneas, Zacharias, and Procopius all try, in different ways, to marginalize Neoplatonists. Yet their works also seek to transform Neoplatonism to render it safe for Christian believers. Their works open a discursive space in which Christians and Neoplatonists could interact, so long as specifically religious identity was not paraded too boldly on the Neoplatonist side.

This chapter makes possible some provisional conclusions about how the Gazans' works were generated and simultaneously helped to configure the cultural horizons of late fifth-century Gaza. The dominant picture is one of complex interactions between different but permeable local cultures, despite the attempt on the Gazans' part to eliminate what they see as false religious claims or doctrinaire honouring of the Neoplatonists' traditional intellectual heroes. Conflict over one identity does not imply conflict across all allegiances that together create local cultures. Continuing tension over religious identity should not blind us to shared identities built on classical mythology, poetry, rhetoric, and philosophical reasoning.

Since people and their actions are not fully determined by the cultures they inhabit, there is a large measure of contingency in the decision to focus on creation instead of some other problem. Yet a plausible case can be made that Aeneas, Procopius, and Zacharias decided to analyse the doctrine of creation in part because of the perceived threat posed by polytheism and pagan power claims, both political and intellectual. Pagan polytheism directly threatened Christianity, and thus threatened the schools and many of the intellectual traditions to which Aeneas, Zacharias, and Procopius were committed, as well as much of the power they were able to wield in the wider community.[38] Justinian's closure of the Athenian philosophical school in 529 is evidence for the potential threat posed by some aspects of the schools' internal culture to their social authority. The Gazans' works inscribe negotiations and interactions between their relevant local cultures: classically educated and uneducated Christians, as well as monks, Neoplatonists, and pagans. These negotiations between different local cultures were partly designed to maintain classical education and its social power within a dominantly Christian culture. In Gaza, this necessitated both the use and the transformation of Neoplatonic culture, since this was a valued and lively component of the schools as experienced and constructed by Aeneas, Zacharias, and Procopius.

Since the Gazans valued the Neoplatonism by which they were simultaneously threatened, a central factor which generated their works was Neoplatonic argumentation within the schools. We now turn to investigate the arguments they faced from that quarter and the resources that were available to them within the Christian tradition on the question of the creation and eternity of the world.

38. Neoplatonists in fact offered a strong monistic view, so much so that Frede (1999) has spoken of pagan 'monotheism' (cf. the Neoplatonic use of Homer *Il.* 2.204–5). Yet in the schools, worship of a variety of deities persisted, if admittedly hostile accounts like Zacharias' *Life of Severus* are to be trusted (see also Marinus' partisan *Life of Proclus*). The multiplicity of levels in the Neoplatonic metaphysical hierarchy allowed many levels of divinities all derived from a single principle. This is what the Gazans' characterize as polytheism, obscuring the derivational monism which is at the heart of Neoplatonism for polemic purposes.

PART II

Explaining Creation

4

Christian and Neoplatonic Creations

To UNDERSTAND THE DISTINCTIVE FEATURES OF THE GAZANS' arguments about the creation and eternity of the world, we must first situate their ideas within earlier Christianity and Neoplatonism. While the Christian doctrine of creation from nothing had been formulated in the second century in the context of debates against Gnostics of various stripes, later Christian thinkers had revisited the doctrine in the following centuries. The Platonic tradition also continued to discuss related questions. As noted above, new impetus was given to such questions within Neoplatonism by Proclus' *Commentary on Plato's Timaeus* and *Eighteen Arguments on the Eternity of the World.* Given the Gazans' dependence on Alexandria for their philosophical knowledge, I also provide a brief overview of the contributions of Hierocles and Ammonius. Since other studies have analysed both the earlier Christian and Neoplatonic arguments in detail, I refer the reader to specialized treatments while identifying only the main contours of the sources and problems which were most useful for the Gazans and which will therefore provide the most relevant context for the arguments I analyse in the following two chapters.

4.1 Christian Creations

Many of the problems the Gazans explored had already been posed by earlier Judeo-Christian thinkers, and the Gazans regularly use solutions already offered within this tradition, adapting them to their own context. After a discussing early developments and their continuing application in the fourth century in Eusebius, I restrict attention to four areas of particular significance for Procopius, Aeneas, and Zacharias, two key debates and two influential individuals: the question of the pre-existence of matter, the definitive representative of the Hexameron tradition (Basil of Caesarea), an influential exemplar of Genesis exegesis in homiletics generally (John Chrysostom), and the question of relations between Trinitarian developments and accounts of creation.[1]

1. My treatment of each area is necessarily limited and should be read as exemplary of the debts to the wider Christian tradition demonstrated by Aeneas, Procopius, and Zacharias. I limit my discussion to the East; beside general similarity, occasionally noted below, there is no evidence for Western influence on the Gazans' arguments. In addition to the introductions to the SC editions of the ancient sources referred to in the text, the reader is referred to the following works for further illumination: May (1994); cf. O'Neill (2002); Osborn (1993), 109–29; Pagels (1985), 67–93; Pelikan (1997); Runia (1986, 1994, 2001, 2003); Wacht (1969), 85–98.

May has provided a detailed study of the development of the Christian doctrine of *creatio ex nihilo* from Hellenistic Judaism to Clement of Alexandria.[2] His argument, that it took some time for Jewish and Christian theologians to focus explicit attention on a philosophical analysis of the fundamental principles of creation, is persuasive. So too is his claim that the doctrine of creation from nothing was developed through a sustained process of biblical exegesis and disputation with Gnostics internal to (broadly defined) Christian communities. While scholars continue to use biblical texts to argue that the doctrine of creation from nothing had been established by the time of the New Testament (e.g. 2 Macc. 7:28; Rom. 4:5, 17ff.; Rev. 4:11 with emendation), on my reading the scriptural texts do not presuppose a doctrine of creation from nothing. It seems more likely that the question of whether 'creation' implies the absolute creation of matter or whether it should be understood as the formation of pre-existing matter was not controversial for Christian thinkers until Gnostic dualism and the associated threats to divine sovereignty brought it to the fore.[3] Alongside these debates within Christianity, Platonists were themselves rejecting matter as a co-principle of creation, and while these simultaneous developments may be purely coincidental, the coordinate changes in the Christian and Platonic schools may bear further investigation.[4]

Against Gnostics who argued that only a lesser God could be the creator of the world, the early apologists argued that the one good God created the cosmos. They claimed that this God is the unique principle of creation. *Creatio ex nihilo* was used to argue for one God who supremely governs his creation as the first principle of being and goodness.[5] The unification of the first principles of being and goodness continues, transposed into a new key, in the works of the three Gazans. This monadic answer raised a further problem, that of a derivational model of creation, where the cosmos derives from the Neoplatonic One, and which Christians believed elided the difference between creator and creature.

2. May (1994). See also Cox (2009) for exploration of relevant themes in Hellenistic Judaism, the New Testament, Middle Platonism, and Gnosticism.

3. Cf. O'Neill (2002). But May's argument that the conceptual framework for *creatio ex nihilo* is not present before the formula becomes explicit may be challenged. Osborn has provided a persuasive case that the concept of *creatio ex nihilo* can in fact be found earlier, and that May's claim that Basilides was the first to offer a doctrine of *creatio ex nihilo* should be revised. The question, however, requires further illumination. See Osborn (2001), 65–73. Wolfson (1968), 302–10, Reale (1979), 247–87, and (with caveats) Sorabji (1983), 203–9 have seen *creatio ex nihilo* in Philo of Alexandria (*Opif.* 29–32 and *Prov.* 1.6–8, cf. 2.50–51). Cf. May (1994), 9–21. To my mind, Runia's interpretation is more successful. Runia (1986), 453–55; (2003), 137–39; (2001), 152–55, 171–73 with further bibliography; Weiss (1966), 59–74.

4. See also the comments of Runia (2003), 146 along these lines.

5. Compare the arguments from Justin, Clement, Irenaeus, and Athenagoras collected and analysed in Osborn (1993), 116–24.

For Christian thinkers, it would be no good to reject matter as a co-principle of creation by eliding the distinction between creator and creature. The doctrine of creation from nothing was partly attractive because it avoided this difficulty. Within this doctrine, matter is neither a potential co-principle alongside god, nor is the world derived from God, and so potentially understood as divine.

By the time we reach Origen (c. 185–c. 254), the doctrine of creation from nothing is well established, although Origen provides detailed arguments in its support (*Princ.* 2.1.4).[6] For Origen, the creation of the cosmos is a divine act of volition which is therefore contingent.[7] 'Wisdom was in herself in no relation to anyone' [σοφία ὑπάρχουσα οὐδεμίαν σχέσιν πρὸς ἕτερόν τινα εἶχεν] (*frJohn* I).[8] That is to say, God in himself is ontologically prior to God the creator. But God wills to come into relation with the creatures which he brings into existence through his good will in an act of love (*frJohn* I). Father and Son give creation existence through their grace and generosity (*Comm Ep Rom* 10.38). God thus creates out of nothing freely and contingently in an act of volition that is just so an act of grace. Creation is 'from non-being', from 'non-existence' and all creatures are given being by God (*expProv* 16; *CommJn* 1, 17, 32; *Philocalia* 24.2; *selPs* 21, PG 12.1260).[9] Creation was not, for Origen, an eternally willed act. While the act of creation is consistent with God's eternal nature, the act to will the creation did not always exist: it is 'realized' in the creation which, for Origen, had a beginning.[10] Despite the later condemnations of 'Origenism' for positing an eternal world, there is no positive evidence that Origen himself believed that the world was eternal.[11]

A brief comparison with the Neoplatonist Plotinus' thinking on creation and divine will is instructive.[12] For Plotinus, the Intellect comes necessarily from the One 'without any act of will' [οὐδὲ βουληθέντος] as a sort of radiation from the Sun (*Enn.* 5.1.6.27–30). Creation follows from what the One is and the existence of the lower orders of the cosmos is necessary (e.g. *Enn.* 2.9.3).[13] The later Neoplatonists regularly speak of the Demiurge willing the lower orders of

6. For a more detailed account of Origen on creation in the context of Origenism in Gaza, see below, 6.6.

7. Tzamalikos (2006), 120–21.

8. *frJohn* = *Fragmenta 1-140 in Joannim*, CGS 4, pp. 485ff.; BGF 12, pp. 333ff.

9. *expProv* = *Exposita in Proverbia*, BGF 16, pp. 182–229; *selPs* = *Selecta in Psalmi* BGF 15, pp. 243–386, BGF 16, pp. 11–157.

10. Tzamalikos (2006), 122.

11. Tzamalikos (2006), chapter 4 provides copious evidence to the contrary. See also Edwards (2002), chapters 2–3.

12. See further below, 5.3, where Procopius introduces arguments against Neoplatonic creation which he thinks of as 'by the necessity of nature'.

13. See further Pépin (1964), 502–6.

reality into being, no doubt drawing on Plato's conception of the demiurge who wills the creation of the material world (*Tim.* 29E–30A, 41B), without challenging the basic idea that the cosmos is necessary given the nature of the One (see e.g. Iamblichus *de Myst.* 3.28; Proclus *in Tim.* 1.362, 1.371.4).

But it is also true that for Plotinus, the One can be said to exercise will, albeit only if one departs 'a little from correct thinking in our discourse' (*Enn.* 6.8.13.1–5). This is not the place to explicate this claim in detail, but it is worth following it a little further to delineate similarities and differences between Platonists and Christians on the question of divine will. For Plotinus, if the One can be considered to act, his acts must be considered to be acts of will and his activities must equally be understood as his substance, where 'will', 'act', and 'substance' are all used somewhat riskily of the Being who is beyond Being (6.8.13.5–59). The One is altogether unrelated to anything (6.8.8.13) and such ascriptions of attributes to the One should always be modified with the phrase 'as if' (6.8.13.49–50). His willing activity is his substance because even his own being or existence is in his power (6.8.13.11–12, 53–59). It is possible for him to will to be other than he is, since he instantiates himself. Yet the One does not will to change himself 'because there was nothing else at all that he might be drawn to' (6.8.13.39–41) and as the perfect entity he is satisfied with himself and absolutely self-sufficient (6.8.13.41–43). His thought and will are thus eternally turned towards himself, instantiating himself. It is this 'act' which defines him as perfect and good, and his perfection and goodness are seen in the generation of reality, originally in the production of Intellect. One and Intellect ultimately ground the necessity of the existence of the whole cosmos. This line of thinking will be seen below in Proclus' first argument for the eternity of the cosmos, where the 'generosity' of the One is the reason for the eternal generation of the universe.

There are many resonances between this account and later Christian thinking about creation and divinity. Plotinus' One instantiates himself independently of his 'creatures', and there is identity of will, activity, and substance in a similar way in the Christians' God.[14] It is too strong a distinction to claim that the Christian God wills creation whereas the Neoplatonic One produces involuntarily, although this is a claim that Procopius, for example, will make (see below, 5.3). Similarly, it is an overstatement to claim that Christian creation is an expression of divine goodness whereas the Neoplatonic creation merely follows what the One is necessarily, since for Plotinus and later Neoplatonists, the One is Good and 'wills' to be so.[15] Some Christian thinkers follow accounts like Plotinus' very closely (with or without direct dependence on it) to argue for

14. See 6.4 below and Lilla (1997) on 'Neoplatonic Hypostases and the Christian Trinity'.
15. Cf. Tzamalikos (2006), 130–32.

a willed act of creation characterized as an act of goodness, where God's will is the instantiation of his goodness.

Yet distinctions remain. For Plotinus, the One's willed self-thinking results in the production of difference in the cosmos, since it is the activity of his goodness. For early Christian thinkers like Origen, God's love for creatures other than himself is what causes him to create radical difference from nothing for the good of what did not yet exist. Creation does not, in this model, result from God's willed self-actualization but from a free act of love which is directed towards the other. This points to one further distinction, a distinction that may not be pushed too far, but which is worth holding in mind in the analysis of the Gazans' thought in later chapters. Since the production of lower metaphysical levels is the result of the One's self-actualization, in one sense for Plotinus creation is contingent, because the One could in principle have chosen to be what he is not. But in another sense, since his will and he himself are one, the act of production of the cosmos is an expression of the One's own being, and thus there is a sense in which the One produces simply by being what he is, and that what he produces is necessary, as Plotinus repeatedly claims throughout the *Enneads* (e.g. 6.8.9.10–13). For Origen, by contrast, we have seen that God can remain God without creating. His creative and loving will is certainly consistent with who God chooses to be, but God in himself stands beyond God's will to create.[16] In this scheme there is an ontological priority of the immanent over the economic Trinity as well as an absolute distinction between the infinite and atemporal immateriality of God and the temporal materiality of creation.

For if matter is taken to be coeternal with God, many impious consequences, Origen thinks, follow. Like the earlier Christians who developed the doctrine of creation from nothing, Origen carefully avoids the implication that matter is derived from God's being in any way. He explores the possibility that there is no such thing as matter, carefully setting out the view that bodily nature consists not of a material substrate to which qualities are added but may be defined purely by reference to the qualities themselves (*Princ.* 4.4.7). On this view, the qualities which define bodily things (e.g. hardness or softness) are all that there is. When they are taken away, literally nothing remains.[17] Yet he ultimately retains the idea of prime matter, conceptualizing it as the underlying substance or pure substrate which remains in thought once one imagines (albeit artificially) a body stripped of all its qualities. Such a body does not in fact exist in reality (*Princ.*

16. Ibid. 133–34.

17. Similar arguments are found in the author of *Philokalia* 24 (Armitage Robinson (1893), 212–26). See also Eusebius *Prep. Ev.* 7.22. See Armitage Robinson (1893) = Origen (1893), xl–xlix for questions of authorship of this extract.

4.4.7), but Origen thinks he has support for this view in Scripture (Ps. 39; Enoch 21:1) (*Princ.* 4.4.8). Throughout his writings, however, he insists that God creates prime matter from nothing (*Comm Gen* in Eusebius, *PE* 7.20.1–9; *Princ.* 2.1.4, 4.4.6–8).[18] Origen's arguments will recur in the works of the Gazans, placing them within a tradition of Alexandrian exegesis on this question.[19]

The Gazans all respond to the claim that matter is pre-existent, so it is useful to consider it in more detail. Eusebius' doxography of Christian opinions in the influential *Praeparatio Evangelia* may be taken as a starting point, given the popularity of this work in antiquity and the likelihood that it was known to Aeneas, Zacharias, and Procopius (*PE* 7.18–23).[20] Eusebius is convinced that the doctrine that God is the sole principle of creation is a Hebrew and Christian rather than a Greek philosophical idea (*PE* 7.18.12).[21] To make his case, he cites the opinions of Dionysius of Alexandria, Origen, Philo of Alexandria, and 'Maximus', who follows Origen's arguments about prime matter already noted.[22] According to Eusebius, Dionysius objects to matter as a principle for three reasons (*PE* 7.19). First, only God could be unoriginated. Second, matter, unlike God, is changeable, passible, moveable, and transformable. Finally, God does not work like an artisan.[23] These three points will recur in the works of the Gazans in expanded forms (see below, 5.2 and 6.1).

While Philo had argued that God, like artisans, knows how much matter he needs for creation (Prov. 1.6–8 in *PE* 7.21.1; cf. *Prov.* 2.50–51), Origen rejects the Platonic 'craftsman' analogy for the creation of the cosmos, using arguments we will see in Aeneas, Procopius, and Zacharias (see below, 5.2–4, 6.1).[24] God does

18. The loss of Origen's *Commentary on Genesis* leaves a large lacuna in our knowledge of the development of exegesis on Genesis. See Bammel (1989), 69.

19. See below, 6.6. Note, however, that there is no discernible tendency to favour either the Alexandrian or the Antiochian schools of exegesis in the body of Procopius' commentary. See further ter Haar Romeny (2007), 189.

20. For the use of Eusebius in Aeneas and Zacharias, see Minniti-Colonna (1958), 27, 238; (1973), 49, 55. Eusebius is a likely intermediary source for the Catena tradition on which Procopius' *Commentary* is dependent, although Procopius does have independent access to his sources.

21. But note again that later Platonists from Plotinus onwards had firmly rejected the idea that matter was a co-principle; their solution is a *derivational* monism. They saw no difficulty associated with the derivational model because the value of what was derived from the first principle was, reasonably enough, not taken to be identical with that principle. For Plotinus, see further O'Brien (1996), 171–95. For further discussion of creation in Eusebius, see e.g. *PE* 8.13.1; 11.14.1, 24.1; 13.18.12. Runia (1993), 223 cites these passages with Philonic parallels in his magisterial study of Philo in Christian literature.

22. Eusebius' Maximus may well be 'Methodius'. The section ascribed to Maximus in Eusebius is found in part or with some abbreviations in Joh. Meursius (*Var. Div. Liber,* Leyden, 1619) and Photius cod. 236 ascribed to Methodius' *Dialogue on Free Will.* See Armitage Robinson (1893), xl.

23. This fragment from Dionysius' *Against Sabellius* is preserved only in Eusebius.

24. Origen uses the image of an architect in referring to the role of the Logos in creation at *Comm. Joh.* 1.114.

not need bronze to make a statue, nor wood for woodwork, nor stones for building; rather, his creation is immediately contingent upon his will (*Comm Gen* in *PE* 7.20.1–2).[25] While Providence supplies the craftsman with the material for the artistic production, in God's case, the creation of material from nothing and the formation of it are part of the one, undivided, providential exercise of divine will (*Comm Gen* in *PE* 7.20.9).[26] There is no Providence separate from, or prior to, the good creator (ibid.). If matter is unoriginated, claims Origen, it would exist simply by a lucky chance: in his view only creation from nothing preserves God's providential concern for creation (*Comm Gen* in *PE* 7.20.3–8; cf. 5.5 and 6.3 below). In the section Eusebius attributes to Maximus, the purpose is again to separate God from the world so that the world cannot be considered to be derived from God (*PE* 7.22). Maximus also argues for the creation of matter from nothing on the basis that God can create forms out of nothing (*PE* 7.22.12ff.). We will see a similar argument recurring in Procopius' *Commentary on Genesis* 29B–29C; the argument has philosophical heritage in Aristotle (*Metaph.* VII 9 1034b16–19; see further below, 5.2). But its use in the Christian tradition gives Procopius a potential Christian source for his claims and is an example of the difficulties associated with distinguishing Christian and Platonic problems in the Gazans' thought. We will see that Procopius, like Zacharias and Aeneas, makes contact with Neoplatonism while solving Christian problems.

The question of the pre-existence of matter is a theme which continues to be discussed in fourth-century homiletics, although by now the main lines of the debate are clear. In commenting on Genesis 1:2 ('the earth was invisible and unformed' [ἀόρατος ἦν ἡ γῆ καὶ ἀκατασκεύαστος]), Basil of Caesarea begins his second sermon on the *Hexameron* by treating certain exegetical problems internal to Christianity (*Hex.* 2.1).[27] The Scripture has claimed that the heavens and the earth were created identically, but the earth (and not the heavens) now turns out to be invisible and unformed. Can this apparent discrepancy be explained? And what is the meaning of the terms 'invisible' and 'unformed'?

25. Like Irenaeus before him, Origen emphasizes what A. Torrance calls 'the immediacy (used in its literal, non-temporal sense!) of the totality of the created order's contingency upon God's creativity'. See Torrance (1997), 99, cited in Osborn (2001), 73. Basilides had earlier made a similar point. God does not create like a 'mortal man, who takes bronze, wood, or something [consisting] of parts of matter, when he is making' [θνητὸς ἄνθρωπος χαλκὸν, ἢ ξύλον ἤ τι τῶν τῆς ὕλης μερῶν ἐργαζόμενος λαμβάνει]. See Hippolytus, *Refutatio omnium haeresium* 22.2, and the discussion at May (1994), 73.

26. This is also the force of Irenaeus' use of the inseparable metaphors of wise architect and sovereign king. See Osborn (2001), 51–63.

27. For Basil's sources in the *Hexameron*, see Giet's *Sources Chrétiennes* introduction, Amand de Mendieta (1985), 349–67, and Runia (1993), 236–37. For the dating of the work, see Rousseau (1994), appendix 3.

Such close attention to the biblical text and the problems it generates is a characteristic of Basil's *Hexameron* sermons which distinguishes them from Aeneas' and Zacharias' dialogues and which is congruent with Procopius' understanding of the task of biblical commentary. That Aeneas and Zacharias do not engage in detailed biblical exegesis does not mean that they thought it was unimportant. It should rather be understood as evidence for their desire to debate within a different intellectual tradition.

Having dealt first with internal Christian problems, Basil turns to the 'corrupters of the truth' [οἱ παραχαράκται τῆς ἀληθείας] who think that the terms 'invisible' and 'unformed' are a coded reference to prime matter, which is without quality, form, and shape (*Hex.* 2.2.1–7). The independent existence of prime matter is taken to imply that God would be a craftsman, with no ultimate control over the matter he merely moulds (*Hex.* 2.2.7–9). Like Origen, Basil rejects the Platonic image of the craftsman, although his criticism would not greatly trouble a Neoplatonist, for whom prime matter is not independent despite being eternal.[28] In line with the earlier tradition, Basil is most worried about the putative eternity of prime matter. If matter is uncreated, he argues, it must be of equal rank with God, since both will share the quality of being uncreated (*Hex.* 2.2.9–11). This is a claim which Aeneas, Zacharias, and Procopius will make frequently. Basil has two further arguments, both also employed in some form by the Gazans. If matter can be moulded by God, it is capable of receiving all of God's wisdom, and thus the hypostasis of matter would be equal to the 'inaccessible power of God' [τῇ ἀνεξιχνιάστῳ τοῦ Θεοῦ δυνάμει], since it could 'measure the whole intelligence of God on its own account' [ὅλην τοῦ Θεοῦ τὴν σύνεσιν δι' ἑαυτῆς ἐκμετρεῖν] (*Hex.* 2.2.14–19). Matter could receive all the forms in the divine mind, and thus can be taken as having the same power as God. It is no good trying to avoid this difficulty by suggesting that there was less matter than divine ideas, for in that case matter would have limited what God set out to create (*Hex.* 2.2.19ff.). This argument will recur in Procopius. Basil's final argument against the pre-existence of matter is a statement of his monism. If matter pre-exists, he claims, there will be two principles of the cosmos: God, who gives it form, and Matter, which gives the cosmos its material essence (*Hex.* 2.2.31–37). This is an argument which would no doubt annoy, rather than trouble, a Neoplatonist, since as we will see Neoplatonists from Plotinus onwards had offered their own version of monism, rejecting the idea

28. Note also that Basil uses the term 'demiurge', as the Gazans do, to refer to God (*Hex.* 2.2.15). The key point is that he strips the demiurge of his need for pre-existing matter.

of multiple principles.[29] The argument may also rely on a conflation of different causes (material and formal) with different principles (Matter and God). Yet the argument again makes sense in the context of attempts to separate the creator from the creature as strongly as possible within Basil's Trinitarian theology. It is an argument which Aeneas, Zacharias, and Procopius all employ, again a reflection of the Christian problems which shape their thought at key points.

John Chrysostom also takes up the question of the pre-existence of matter in his *Homilies* and *Sermons* on Genesis.[30] For John, creation from nothing is the definitive answer to Manichaeans, Gnostics, and Greeks (*Hom. in Gen* 2.10; *Serm. in Gen* 1.154–275). As in Basil's case, the identified intellectual problems may appear more at home in the second century rather than the fourth. We will see ways in which allegiance to the earlier Christian tradition also makes Gazan arguments fail to connect with contemporary Neoplatonism. For John, matter is not ungenerated (ἀγένητος) as the Manichees claim (*Serm. in Gen* 1.154–60).[31] John also argues against Valentinians, Marcionites, and Manichees, that matter is not a principle of evil (*Serm. in Gen* 1.215–30). Finally, since matter is generated, it is not eternal, and cannot thus be taken as sharing a uniquely divine quality, which is taken to be the error of the Greeks. John does not engage with the Neoplatonic arguments which made the case for dependent eternal matter. John also assumes creation from nothing and thus rejects the craftsman analogy for creation (*Serm. in Gen* 1.231ff.). The creator is no artisan who needs materials for his creations; rather, he commands and the cosmos comes into being (*Hom. in Gen.* 3.5).

There are many other similarities of argument and imagery between Basil's *Hexameron* and John's *Homilies* and *Sermons* on Genesis and the works of the Gazans on the question of creation. Further particular correspondences will be noted as they appear below. But while I am exploring the relationship between the Gazans' works and the earlier Christian tradition, it is worth also anticipating ways in which the Gazans' works diverge from those of Basil and John.

29. Rist's comments that Basil seems to remain in a largely pre-Neoplatonic thought-world seem apt. Rist (1981), 190 et passim. There is some evidence that Basil knew *Enn.* 5.1 directly, and possibly 6.9 as well, but despite Platonic terminology, Basil often fails to provide 'any reason to believe that he is necessarily following any Neoplatonic source, or possibly any source at all' in apparently philosophically indebted passages (213) and remains largely uninfluenced by specifically Neoplatonic material (219).

30. The relationship between the *Sermons* and the *Homilies* is explored in the SC introduction, 17–22. English translations may be found in Hill (1986) (*Homilies*) and (2004) (*Sermons*). Markowicz (1963) and Baur (1927) help to disentangle the two series of works and provide commentary. Pagels (1985) notes differences between John's approach and that of Augustine, particularly in the realm of politics. For Chrysostom's life and times, see Mayer (1999); Baur (1959–60); Kelly (1995).

31. In keeping with the common Christian typology, John groups Valentinus and Marcion together. In reality, their systems were divergent.

Most importantly, Basil and John are both strictly governed by the demands of the genre of exegetical homily and by their pastoral concerns. Both writers follow the text of Genesis verse by verse. This is also Procopius' programme in his commentary, although the attack on the Greeks in his prologue suggests a particular concern with philosophical opponents and consequently a different audience. It again points to the distinctive interactions in Gaza between competing thought systems. Basil offers his reflections for the edification of the church (*Hex.* 2.1.15–17). His *Hexameron* homilies contain exhortations to good behaviour and to valuing the glories of the creation. John's *Homilies* are delivered in the season of Lent, he begins with (and returns repeatedly to) the virtues of fasting, and much of his rhetoric is directed towards the ethical improvement of his congregation (in *Homily* 6.2 he breaks off from his exegetical schedule to rebuke the congregation for returning to the horse races like dogs returning to their own vomit (cf. Prov. 26:11; cf. 2 Pet. 2:22). Aeneas, Zacharias, and Procopius do not have Basil's or John's pastoral responsibilities; Aeneas and Zacharias do not share their exegetical problems; and the three Gazans' audience of students and the classically educated elite demands a difference sort of engagement with the biblical text and with contemporary Platonism. Many of the arguments, images, and conclusions remain constant. But the dialogues of Aeneas and Zacharias give Platonism a much clearer, if still muffled, voice. Where John is convinced that Greek philosophers should simply be left to their own devices if they do not accept the Scriptures (*Hom. in Gen* 2.10), Aeneas and Zacharias (and Procopius in the prologue to his *Commentary*) only offer explicitly biblical arguments and evidence after attempts to offer non-biblical, philosophical arguments. While (as I hope to show) Christian problems and arguments remain at the forefront of the Gazans' minds, they engage with philosophy in a very different mode, and they leave pastoral exhortation and (with the exception of Procopius) biblical exegesis to the bishops.

This brief survey identifies much continuity in Christian thinking about creation from the apologists to the Cappadocians and beyond. One significantly consistent theme is the rejection of the model of creation as emanation or derivation. Neoplatonists favoured a kind of monism, where the whole cosmos derives from the One. The Christian doctrine of creation from nothing leads Christians to reject such a model. For Neoplatonists, creation as emanation may well make everything divine, with 'appropriate adverbial modification', as Siorvanes puts it, but the adverbial modification is sufficient, in their view, appropriately to distinguish the higher hypostases from the lower ones.[32] That

32. Siorvanes (1996), 154.

matter is eternal does not, as their Christian opponents will repeatedly claim, render it a co-principle of the cosmos for Neoplatonists. Depending ultimately and utterly on the One, matter, like all the subordinate levels of the metaphysical hierarchy, cannot compete with the sovereignty or divinity of the first principle. Yet the Christians see the idea of creation as emanation as implying that lower orders of being derive their existence from the Being of the One, and take this 'derivational monism' as an inappropriate divinization of the cosmos.

In part, I suggest that this misunderstanding is a consequence of the rhetoric of monotheism, which rules out the possibility of divinity outside of God and thus refuses to accept that there can be degrees of divinity. For a monotheist, so the argument might go, if matter is even vanishingly similar to God in substance, a plurality of gods has been admitted, and God's sovereignty and unique divinity are threatened. Yet this suggestion, unsatisfying as it would be to a Neoplatonist, cannot be the whole answer. Another part of the answer may lie, I suggest, in the use to which Christians in the fourth and fifth centuries put something like Platonic derivational monism in their discussions about the Trinity.

I compare ways in which the Gazans relate the questions of creation and Trinity in section 4 of Chapter 6. For present purposes, it is sufficient to note that in working out distinctions between the different persons of the Trinity, fourth- and fifth-century Christians employed something like the Platonic derivational monism. The Son is begotten of the Father: He derives from the Father's being and shares his substance completely. This is taken to be entirely different from the process by which God created the cosmos. Athanasius and Gregory of Nyssa may be taken as representatives of these ideas.[33] For Athanasius, God creates the cosmos from nothing by his word and because of his goodness (*de. Incarn.* 3.1–4); he is no mere demiurge (*de Incarn.* 2.3–4). But the Word of God is not, unlike the cosmos, created from nothing: that is the doctrine of the Arians (*Contra Arianos* 1.5.14–15). Rather, the Son is begotten of the Father, and eternally divine with him (*Contra Arianos* 1.4–5). This doctrine is similar to Platonic derivational monism, in that the Son derives eternally from the Father, and is of the same substance as the Father, as the Nicene Creed put it. Its key difference is that the Son and Spirit are understood to be identical to the Father with respect to divinity.

Gregory of Nyssa is, typically, more philosophically astute in his account, but similar ideas may be discerned. He sets out a 'scientific division' (διαίρεσις)

33. While Athanasius does not appear in Minniti-Colonna's *indices locorum* for Aeneas and Zacharias, Gregory of Nyssa was certainly known to them and to Procopius, and Athanasius' ideas may be taken as part of the *communis opinio* by the time the Gazans were writing.

of how things may be generated (*Ref.* [= *Refutatio confessionis Eunomii*] 88.5–90.10). Some things, such as houses, are caused by material and craftsmanship. Matter and nature cause other things, as in the generation of animals. Other things are caused by 'material emanation', as in the case of the sun and its ray, perfume and its fragrance, a lamp and its radiance. Finally, Gregory speaks of a final causal process. Such a cause is immaterial but the process of generation is sensible, needing a body as an instrumental cause. Gregory's example of this final category is the generation of the word by the mind. Scripture, says Gregory, speaks of each of these types of causes when describing divine activity, always remembering that the instruction excludes the spatial and temporal senses which attach to the ordinary, human sorts of generation (*Ref.* 91.5–92.10). Scripture uses the images of art and matter to speak of the creation of the cosmos, yet in reality it is affirming that God's will was sufficient for creation, excluding matter, place, time, affections, and dispositions, which are only appropriately predicated of created entities (*Ref.* 93.1–94.1).[34] Similarly, when speaking of the Son, who is consubstantial and from the Father (ἐξ αὐτοῦ), images referring to material emanation (Gregory's phrase is ἐκ τῆς ὑλικῆς ἀπορροίας) are used, always with the caveat about stripping human images of temporal-spatial associations (*Ref.* 96.7f.). The Son is the 'brightness of glory', the 'savour of ointment', and 'breath of God' (*Ref.* 94.10–11; cf. Heb. 1:3; Song of Songs 1:3; Wisd. 7:25).

This form of derivational monism within the Godhead is directly contrasted with the creation of the cosmos by God. When Eunomius denies that the Son is begotten through extension or emanation, but is rather created through the will of the Father, he makes the Son into a creature (*Eun.* [= *Contra Eunomium*] 3.2.28.1–29.1). God did not

> cast forth [προεβάλετο] the earth by being extended, nor bring its substance into existence by flowing or by severing himself [οὔτε ῥυεὶς ἢ τεμὼν ἑαυτὸν]...but [his] will [ἡ βούλησις] sufficed him for the origination of the substance of all things that were made [πρὸς ὑπόστασιν τῆς τῶν γεγονότων οὐσίας]. (*Eun.* 3.2.31.1–2,3,6–7)[35]

34. Gregory does not here offer his startling idea that body is the bundling together of intelligible qualities by the divine mind (*De An. et Res.* in PG 46, 124B–D; *in Hex.* PG 44, 69B–C; *de op. hom.* 24, PG 44, 212D–13B, where prime matter, not merely bodies, is referred to). These texts are collated and interpreted as ancient idealism in Sorabji (2004), vol. 2, 158–61. See also Sorabji (1983), 290–94; (1988), chapter 4.

35. For this sense of ὑπόστασις, see Lampe, loc. cit. IA.

Once one allows that the Father generates the Son like he does the cosmos, the Son, like the cosmos, will come to an end and will have a beginning in time (*Eun.* 3.2.35.1–4). Creation from nothing only applies to the creation of the cosmos; only the Son and Spirit are ungenerated and of the same substance as the Father, eternal, divine, and justly to be worshipped (*Eun.* 3.2.34.1–38.10; *Ref.* 97.1–98.15). To confuse the relation of Father and Son with that between God and the world thus has pernicious consequences, in Gregory's view. 'For either the elements of the cosmos must be revealed as worthy of veneration, according to the Greek fallacy, or the son must not be worshipped' [ἀνάγκη γὰρ ἢ καὶ τὰ τοῦ κόσμου στοιχεῖα κατὰ τὴν Ἑλληνικὴν ματαιότητα σεβάσμια φαίνεσθαι ἢ μηδὲ τὸν υἱὸν προσκυνεῖσθαι] (*Eun.* 3.2.35.10–36.1).

Hence, for Athanasius and Gregory, the internal relation between the persons of the Trinity displays some surface similarity to Neoplatonic derivational monism, but is fundamentally different from it, since all the persons of the Trinity are equally God. The claim is that the eternal generation or procession of the Son and Spirit makes them fully God. In this context, one might understand Christians seeing the eternal derivation of matter, in the Platonic scheme, as implying the real divinity of matter, divinity that would place matter on an equal footing with the One from whom it ultimately and eternally derives. This is not, of course, to claim that the Christian argument is a good Neoplatonic one, but it may go some way towards explaining the Christian rejection of the Neoplatonic version of derivational monism.[36]

This survey identifies the main Christian problems which helped to determine the grammar for Christian accounts of creation, including the governing ideas of creation from nothing and implications of Trinitarian doctrine. I will argue that the Gazans display their allegiance to the earlier Christian tradition in how they frame problems, what problems they take as important, and in what solutions they believe are acceptable (below, Chapters 5 and 6), although they do not use the resources of the Christian tradition slavishly. Yet their works do seek to engage with Neoplatonism even as they reframe its central concerns.

4.2 Gazans and Contemporary Neoplatonism

It is therefore natural to ask about the extent of the Gazans' knowledge of Neoplatonic ideas about creation and the eternity of the world. Minniti-Colonna

36. Further discussion of this question, and the Gazans' view of creation and Trinity, may be found below, 6.4.

has provided a useful summary of Aeneas' and Zacharias' sources.[37] Their familiarity with earlier Greek philosophy was sometimes direct and sometimes mediated through earlier Christian or Platonist sources.[38] Aeneas quotes from Plotinus, from whom he also cites the work of the pre-Socratic philosopher Anaxagoras (45.7ff.; 46.12ff.). He mentions a Boethus (12.6).[39] There are references to Middle Platonists, such as Atticus (e.g. 46.16ff.), and the Neo-Pythagorean Numenius is also mentioned (12.6). Other philosophers cited in the works include Plato, Aristotle, Zeno, Plutarch, and Porphyry.[40] Such a list demonstrates a basic familiarity with forms of Platonism, yet it may suggest that the Gazans' knowledge of their contemporary Neoplatonism was limited. After all, there is no unambiguous quotation of a Neoplatonist after Plotinus, whereas quotations from later Christian writers abound.[41] Perhaps the Gazans' knowledge of contemporary Neoplatonism was limited and indirect, mediated through other, better informed Christians.

Such a suggestion would, however, be overcautious. We have seen that Procopius plausibly wrote works directed against Proclus. Evidence from Aeneas and Zacharias is more certain. Zacharias' dialogue was set in Ammonius' classroom. Aeneas' investigation of different theories about transmigration of the soul accurately reports and attributes the philosophical positions of Porphyry, Iamblichus, Syrianus, and Proclus.[42] His dialogue refers obliquely to Proclus as the reason for Athenian predominance in philosophy (*Theophrastus* 4.6–12).

37. See Minniti-Colonna (1973), 45–55 and indices; Minniti-Colonna (1958). Further work is required to identify Aeneas' use of sources not noted by Minniti-Colonna and to check the level of influence which particular lexical similarities may imply. Minniti-Colonna's *index scriptorum* for Aeneas runs to one and a half well-spaced pages, whereas her index for Zacharias is five densely spaced pages. Particularly for Zacharias, Minniti-Colonna's indices are helpful; however, care is needed given that she sometimes cites passages where the similarity could be fortuitous, as in, for example, φθόνου πάθος οὐ διαφεύζεται (*Ammonius* 1180–81), which Minniti-Colonna relates to John Philoponus' (οὐ γὰρ τὸν φθόνον ἐκφεύξεται) (*Contra Proclum* 1.4, 14.18–19). Similar wording does not prove citation, especially when the subject matter is similar.

38. Again, further work is required to determine in each particular case whether the influence is direct or indirect. For example, while Minniti-Colonna thought that Zacharias' knowledge of Philo was indirect, the evidence may point in the other direction. Further work remains to be done on this question. For the case for direct influence, see Cumont (1891), xii.

39. The Peripatetic Boethus denied the immortality of the soul (see Porphyry in Eusebius, *PE* 11.28.1, 14.10.3, whereas Aeneas groups his Boethus with those who believe in the transmigration of souls within but not between species. This may point to Aeneas' Boethus being the Stoic of that name, although there are at least two other candidates, an Academic and a collator of Platonic sayings. See Goulet (1989), loc. cit. and Dobson (1914).

40. For Zacharias' citation of Porphyry at *Ammonius* 141ff., see Porphyry *in Tim.* fr. 39 Sodano, also quoted by Philoponus *Contra Proclum* 6.2, 126.10–24 Rabe.

41. See Minniti-Colonna (1973), 45–55.

42. *Theophrastus* 12.11–25 (Porphyry and Iamblichus); *Theophrastus* 14.7–9,12–17 (Syrianus and Proclus).

Scholars have noted similarities between the ideas explored in Aeneas' dialogue and works by Hierocles, both in his work *On Providence* and in his *Commentary on the Golden Verses* (see further below). The characters in his dialogue are supposed to have studied under Hierocles, again suggesting a link between Aeneas and Hierocles or his circle. While much of this evidence is drawn from the literary settings of the dialogues, which are intended to give the works an air of verisimilitude rather than to provide autobiographical detail, when placed against the knowledge of contemporary philosophy both Zacharias and Aeneas display, direct connections between Aeneas and Zacharias and Alexandrian philosophers are highly plausible. For Aeneas and Zacharias at least, there is evidence that the works and arguments of contemporary philosophers in Athens and Alexandria, had reached Gaza. Along these lines, Minitti-Colonna noted that many of the points raised by the pagan figures in Zacharias' dialogue accurately report arguments collected in Proclus' *Eighteen Arguments on the Eternity of the World.* When Aeneas turns to the problem of creation and eternity of the world, Proclus' treatise also seems crucial. A general familiarity with Proclus' ideas seems to be a plausible stimulus for their creation-oriented works.

Taking Zacharias as our main test case, the *Ammonius* displays close linguistic parallels with sections of Proclus' arguments Three, Five, Six, Nine, Thirteen, Sixteen, Seventeen, and Eighteen. These linguistic parallels are matched by wider conceptual similarity. Zacharias argues against the idea that God's goodness implies that the world is eternal (cf. Arguments One and Eighteen); against the claim that the demiurge's eternal actuality and unmoved or changeless existence and will mean he must always create (cf. Arguments Three, Four, and Sixteen); against the view that the simultaneity of time and the heavens implies the eternity of the world (cf. Argument Five); against the equation of corruptibility and evil with generation and dissolubility (cf. Arguments Six, Nine, and Seventeen); against the completeness of the cosmos (cf. Argument Eight); against the eternity of matter (cf. Arguments Eleven and Fourteen); and finally against a different heavenly material which causes eternal heavenly motion (cf. Argument Thirteen). Such broad conceptual similarities suggest that Proclus' detailed attack on the temporal finitude of the world, or at least the associated contemporary currents of philosophical debate in late-antique philosophical schools, was one stimulus for Zacharias' thought. Many of these themes are also taken up by Aeneas and Procopius; in some cases, Zacharias' arguments mirror Aeneas' earlier work.

Conceptual similarity, however, always depends on the level of generality of the analysis. The sceptic may argue that while Zacharias and the other Gazans argue against Proclus' conclusions, they do not always engage closely with the logic Proclus offered for these conclusions in his *Eighteen Arguments.* Others could object that while Zacharias and the others may have attempted to rebut many of Proclus' general conclusions, the *Eighteen Arguments* themselves cannot have been the crucial text, since the Gazans did not attempt to rebut all eighteen arguments, let alone the precise logical manoeuvres of each argument. Of Proclus' *Eighteen Arguments* it seems that the Gazans ignored five of them, namely Arguments Two, Seven, Ten, Twelve, and Fifteen. Within the arguments which the Gazans do seem to consider, elements of the logic are also ignored. Is there any pattern which might explain these omissions?

Proclus identifies six principles which, he thinks, cause the world whereas the Gazans collapse these causes into a single principle which is both the final and the efficient cause of Being, and try to make sense of this claim (see further below and Chapters 5 and 6). So Proclus' arguments for the eternity of the world from other possible causes, such as the Paradigm, Soul, Matter, or Form, miss the main line of their argument. I argue that this helps to explain why the Gazans do not respond to some of Proclus' arguments or enter into the detail of parts of his logic. I am not claiming that it would have been impossible for Christians to accommodate Proclus' six causes. They might have claimed, for example, that all subsidiary causes are created by God, bringing them close to the Neoplatonic position that the causes ultimately derive from and are dependent on the One. But their rejection of this possibility reframes the Neoplatonic arguments, rendering parts of them irrelevant to the Gazans. For example, Proclus' second argument proves the eternity of the world by arguing that the world is caused by the eternal Paradigm, on the basis that the Paradigm is the eternal pattern for the world and there is no copy without a pattern, just as there can be no son without a father. But since the Gazans allow no other cause than God, the final and creative cause of the cosmos, such an argument holds no force or relevance for them, and can simply be written off as the multiplication of Gods and creators which ends in anarchy. The other arguments which they ignore likewise do not concern either the demiurgic or the final cause.[43]

Similarly, those details of each argument which are not considered by the Gazans might be explained along these lines. For example, Zacharias has the Neoplatonist Gessius argue that if

> time is simultaneous with heaven [χρόνος δὲ ἅμα οὐρανῷ], and heaven with time, then time will also have come to be simultaneously with the heaven.

43. Argument Fifteen also champions eternity based on the characteristics of the Paradigm, this time its completeness, uniqueness, and eternity; Argument Seven argues for eternity given eternal motion instrumentally caused by the World Soul; Argument Ten is an argument from motion and the immanent ordering of the cosmos; Argument Twelve proves eternity based on the idea that matter could be a principle. Perhaps Argument Twelve is covered, to the Gazans' satisfaction at least, by their respective detailed rebuttals of the eternity of matter.

> For time is the measure of the revolution and rotation of the universe. But it is necessary that what is measured exists together with the measure, since they are related to each other and things that are related are simultaneous by nature [ἐπεὶ πρός τι, καὶ ἅμα τῇ φύσει τὰ πρός τι].[44] But if time came into being and everything came into being in time, then time came into being as well. There was time so that time could exist [καὶ ἦν χρόνος, ἵνα ὑπάρξῃ χρόνος]. It existed, therefore, even before the cosmos existed, which is impossible. But if this is absurd, then time is ungenerated [ἀγένητος], as also is this cosmos, since everything that comes to be, comes to be in time. (554–61)

The Christian character then denies that everything generated is generated in time and offers the solution that time could be generated in eternity rather than in time.[45]

This argument resonates with Plotinus *Ennead* 3.7 and offers particularly close parallels to Proclus' fifth and third arguments, especially Argument Five, which reads (in part):

> If time is simultaneous with the heaven [ἅμα οὐρανῷ χρόνος] and the heaven with time, then neither the heaven is, without time, nor is time, without the heaven.... For if the heaven was when time was not, it seems that when time was not, time was [ἔοικεν ὅτε οὐκ ἦν χρόνος ἦν χρόνος]... And the heaven is simultaneous with time and time with the heaven; for time is a measure of heaven's motion [μέτρον γάρ ἐστιν τῆς τοῦ οὐρανοῦ κινήσεως], as eternity is a measure of the living being itself. (103.2–4, 5–7, 18–20)

These marked similarities between Zacharias' text and Proclus' demonstrate a common thought-world and plausibly suggest direct influence from Proclus'

44. This logic and terminology is found in Proclus' third argument: 'in mutual relationships, however one stands towards the other, so also the other stands towards it' [διὰ δύο δειχθὲν ἀξιωμάτων, ἑνὸς μὲν ὡς ἂν ἔχῃ τῶν πρός τι θάτερον, οὕτω καὶ θάτερον ἔχειν] (43.18–20). The basis for the claim is found in Aristotle *Cat.* 7b15ff.

45. This is equivalent to Augustine's claim that time itself is created (Augustine, *Confessions* 11.13). The passage provides an example of Zacharias twisting Neoplatonic ideas against Neoplatonists. Proclus and other Neoplatonists could have agreed with Zacharias that time was generated in eternity, since they used this same formulation (not unnaturally) to argue that the world was eternal. In this argument, Zacharias simply uses it to avoid the infinite regress Gessius had seemingly trapped him into, understanding 'eternity' to mean 'God'. By saying that time is the moving image of eternity, Zacharias intends to argue simply that God, the eternal, created time, not that time and eternity stand in eternal, necessary relation to each other. The Neoplatonic phrase is used to mean something quite different from what the Neoplatonists meant by it. See further below, 6.2.

Eighteen Arguments.[46] But when Proclus goes on in Argument Five to talk of the living being—the Paradigm—Zacharias' text is silent. It might be objected that when Aeneas and Zacharias argue that God always had the ideas or forms of the cosmos in his mind, they have transformed Platonic forms into divine ideas, which approaches the role of the Paradigm in Proclus' argument. They should therefore, so the objection would run, have paid attention to Proclus' arguments for the paradigmatic cause of the cosmos had they been aware of it. Aeneas and Zacharias do in different ways use the concept of divine ideas in their accounts of creation (see below, 6.1).[47] But in maintaining a separation of God from the cosmos, they reject the idea that God's knowledge about an object necessarily implies the existence of the object, and use the concept of divine ideas to argue for a unique divine creative cause of the cosmos. The ideas are entirely dependent on God. Again, for the Gazans, a separate paradigmatic cause has no place in their scheme. Zacharias' emphasis on the final and demiurgic cause, I suggest, leads him to ignore logical moves and philosophical claims that were central for Proclus. Lack of engagement with the detail of Proclus' arguments is not evidence that Zacharias was unaware of it.

A further explanation for the prominence of Proclus' arguments for eternity based on the final and demiurgic cause of the universe has been suggested by scholars following Praechter. The Gazans learnt their philosophy from Alexandria, and in Alexandria, the argument goes, the complex hierarchy of being, so beloved of Athens, had been collapsed: the demiurge was the highest principle involved in the creation of the world. This would provide a further reason for the Gazans to focus on arguments about the demiurge in their own argument that the Christian God is both final and efficient cause of the existence of the cosmos. Yet such a view cannot be sustained following Hadot's reconstructions, which show that the Alexandrians did not differ significantly from Athenian philosophers in their account of the cosmic and hyper-cosmic orders. Certain works were indeed produced in Alexandria for pedagogical purposes, which played down the role of causes other than the demiurge in the creation of the world. Hierocles' work *On Providence* is one such case. Such works were designed for introductory purposes, to prepare the student of philosophy for more advanced material. Given that the Gazans were primarily rhetors rather than fully-fledged philosophers, it remains possible that they were most familiar with such introductory texts. This suggestion may be strengthened by

46. There is also a close parallel to Proclus *in Tim.* 3.50.2–4.

47. For the originally Middle Platonic concept of Platonic ideas as God's thoughts, see Alcinous *Did.* 9.1 and the texts collated in Dörrie-Baltes (1987–), vol. 4, 111–22. See also Dillon (1993), 93–100; Runia (2001), 151–52. See further, 6.1.

considering that Ammonius differed from Proclus at least in some works by uniting the Aristotelian final cause with the Platonic demiurge (see below, 4.3). These considerations may help to explain the Gazans' interest in those aspects of Proclus' arguments for the eternity of the world which focus on the demiurge to the exclusion of others. They would also make a plausible case that differences between Zacharias' and Aeneas' work and that of Proclus do not imply that the Gazans were ignorant of Proclus' work. Rather, different problems lead to arguments that look very different from their philosophical fellows.

4.3 Neoplatonic Creations

Having made a case for the Gazans' knowledge of contemporary Neoplatonism, I turn to the controversial features of the earlier Neoplatonic tradition. First, investigation of the physical nature of the cosmos was, for Proclus, a religious question. This aspect of contemporary Neoplatonism is one reason the Gazans took up the challenge to provide an alternative account. We have seen ways in which they sought to impose limits on pagan religious expression; their arguments also seek to counter pagan religious claims within circulating Neoplatonic arguments. Second, a key text within Neoplatonism on the question of the creation and eternity of the cosmos was *Timaeus* 28b. The ways in which different thinkers in the philosophical tradition interpreted this passage will be influential for the Gazans. Third, Neoplatonists linked questions of creation to questions of ethics. Hierocles is a representative of ways in which this was done within Neoplatonism, and I analyse his contribution as a foil for the Gazans' own treatment of creation and ethics in their respective works. Finally, Ammonius introduced the novel claim that Aristotle meant to unite the final and the efficient cause of the cosmos. The Gazans all seek to collapse Aristotle's causes into one divine cause, while not denying natural causal processes, so this move is particularly relevant to their own account of creation.

Proclus believed that the *Timaeus* 'has in all its parts as its purpose the explanation of nature' (Prologue). *Timaeus* 27d–28a provided the principles for natural science:

> 1) There is true being, which is comprehended by intuitive knowledge [νοήσις] together with a reasoned account [λογός]; 2) There is that which is generated [γενητόν], which is grasped by opinion together with unreasoning sense-perception [δόξη μετ' αἰσθήσεως ἀλόγου]; 3) All that is generated comes into being from a cause [ἀπ' αἰτίας γίγνεται]. What has not obtained existence from a cause is not generated; 4) That of which the model [τὸ παράδειγμα] is eternal being, is necessarily beautiful [καλόν

> ἐστιν ἐξ ἀνάγκης]. That of which the model is generated, is not beautiful; 5) Let the whole [of physical reality] be called heaven or cosmos [τὸ πᾶν οὐρανὸς καλείσθω ἢ κόσμος]. (1.236.21ff.)

An explanation of creation—of what is generated—is therefore provided by correctly identifying causes.[48] Following Aristotle (*Post An.* 1.2, 71b, 9–12 Bekker), Proclus argues that 'the task of scientific knowledge [ἐπιστήμης] is the recognition of causes [ἡ γὰρ τῶν αἰτίων γνῶσις], and only when we recognise [γνωρίσωμεν] the causes of things do we say that we know them [ἐπίστασθαι]' (*ET* 11). This task of explaining nature by explaining causes introduces an explicitly theological aim. If the whole purpose of the commentary is exploring *physiologia*, that can only be done, in Proclus' view, through an explicitly theological investigation. For Proclus as for other late-antique commentators, 'the activity of teaching Plato and writing works of Platonic philosophy was itself a spiritual exercise'.[49]

Proclus offers six causes of the cosmos' existence. These are all derived from the principles of natural science just described:

> The causes of the cosmos are thus the following: the final cause [τὸ τελικὸν], the paradigmatic cause [τὸ παραδειγματικὸν], the efficient cause [τὸ ποιητικὸν], the instrumental cause [τὸ ὀργανικὸν], the formal cause [τὸ εἰδητικὸν], the material cause [τὸ ὑλικόν]. . . . The result is that by means of these first principles [Plato] has tracked down for us the causes of the universe and taught them all in proper order. (1.263.19–21, 263.30–264.2)

This scheme is built around Aristotle's famous quartet of final, efficient, material, and formal causes: Aristotle's influence is marked. Yet Proclus is doing more than simply adding two causes to Aristotle's four. His scheme is also influenced by Plotinus. The One is the final cause, the paradigmatic and efficient, demiurgic causes operate at the level of Intellect, and the World Soul causes cosmic entities as a principle of movement or an instrumental cause.[50] Plotinian influence subtly transforms Aristotelian causes to provide a metaphysical explanation for the relation of the cosmos to beings higher up the metaphysical chain.[51]

48. For a general treatment of Neoplatonic thought on causation, see Hankinson (2001), chapter 12. General Proclus' bibliography may be consulted in Steel et. al. (2005, 2013).

49. Baltzly and Tarrant (2007), 7.

50. See further Tarrant (2007), 50ff. and Opsomer (2000, 2001, 2003) for the demiurge's ontological level.

51. The addition of causes to Aristotle's four is, of course, not an innovation. Seneca had already conflated Plato and Aristotle on causes (*Ep.* 65.4.14) and the sixfold scheme is found in Porphyry. See Karamanolis (2006), 274; Karamanolis (2004); Tarrant (2007), 50, 53–55; Tuominen (2009), 129. The

Ultimately, for Proclus, epistemology and ontology are intimately related. Physical inquiry is possible because of mathematics; physical entities gain existence from higher beings.[52] 'The science of nature is a kind of theology [ἡ φυσιολογία φαίνεται θεολογία τις οὖσα], because what is constituted by nature also has a divine existence in a way, to the extent that it is produced by the gods [ἐκ θεῶν ἀπογεννᾶται]' (1.217.25–27). Proclus' account of creation is of a universe suffused with divinity, congruent with his own spiritual experience, as a statement from one of his dreams suggests: 'There hovers the supercelestial and immortal radiance, leaping forth from the roaring fire that congregates at the source' (Marinus, *VProcl*, 28). Proclus thus connects physical, metaphysical, and epistemological concerns. Platonic physics, as Proclus understands it, is only able to make sound arguments because of the existence of higher realities (1.8.2–5). This equips readers 'also to comprehend the physical not only physically, but also theologically' [καὶ τὰ φυσικὰ οὐ φυσικῶς μόνον, ἀλλὰ καὶ θεολογικῶς νοεῖν ἡμᾶς παρασκευάζει] (1.8.3f.). A metaphysics of causes is developed which seeks to explain how diverse physical reality can emerge ultimately from the One.

The overlapping of physics and theology makes Proclus' account particularly relevant for Christian thinkers. The interpretation of the *Timaeus* is not a question of Stoic, or even simply Aristotelian, materialistic physics. Proclus, by beginning with Plato's discussion of principles in the *Timaeus*, gives physics theological or metaphysical foundations and implications. His interpretation of the *Timaeus* sets out a theology which has points of contact with the Gazan Christians, but which diverges from them at key points. Crucially, they refused to accept that created reality was in itself divine, along the lines sketched in the earlier Christian Trinitarian accounts.

Much of Proclus' discussion of causes could be helpful for Christians, and even what the Gazans reject of it could in principle have been accommodated, with careful interpretation. That the Gazans do not accommodate much of Proclus' account within their own works is evidence for their prioritizing of Christian ideas over those generated in the philosophical schools. Proclus' discussion of the demiurgic cause is most useful to the Gazans even as it demonstrates the wide gap between rival thought-worlds. To anticipate the argument below, the Gazans use Proclus' arguments for how the demiurge creates, but

systematic way in which Proclus employs the sixfold scheme is distinctive and demonstrates its importance for Proclus. For the following discussion, see Steel (2003), 183–87.

52. For further argument along these lines, see Martijn (2006a). This conclusion is at odds with Lernould's treatment, where geometrical reasoning is taken as inconsistent with dialectic, which he believes is the mode of discourse suitable for theology. See Lernould (2001), 35.

apply them to their highest being, instead of to a lower being. In specifying causes (physical explanations) of phenomena from entities beyond the genus which they cause, Proclus allows divine activity from the One down to influence terrestrial phenomena directly and indirectly, a point exploited by Christians. Physics as theology leaves room for divine action, although Proclus' scheme keeps the higher principles more distant from the material world than the Christian creation account does.[53] For the Christians, the only divine actor is the Trinity, and while there are superficial parallels between the instrumental agency of the demiurgic Intellect and, for example, the second person of the Trinity, in claiming that God's original and continuing creative activity is a tri-une act, the Christians make all creation depend directly on Father, Son and Spirit, collapsing the Neoplatonic hierarchy, and involving God more directly in the world of matter (see further 6.4 below).

In making the demiurge the principle of order and governor of multiple accessory causes, Proclus introduces a transcendent and providential agent as a valid explanatory category in physics. Finally, a providential teleology is perhaps the most important correspondence between Platonic and Christian thought.[54] This correspondence is strengthened by the unification of the final and efficient cause in the hypostasis of the demiurge. In rejecting spontaneity, the Gazans find common ground with Proclus, who conceives of a universe ordered by a divine principle. By making the distinction between a demiurgic and a hypostatic cause, Proclus' extensive divine hierarchy is brought into view. Christians, while happily claiming the creative cause of the universe as an efficient cause of existence, will seek to collapse this metaphysical hierarchy, and make their 'demiurge' more directly involved in giving and maintaining existence in terrestrial beings.

The fundamental difference centres on how causes work. Neoplatonists in general argue that causes differ from effects, sometimes quite drastically. For example, Proclus strikingly claims that only incorporeal causes can have physical effects (e.g. Proclus, *ET* 80).[55] Yet Proclus elsewhere argues that 'everything which by its existence bestows a character on others itself primitively possesses that character which it communicates to the recipients…if…the second [had] nothing in common with the existence of the first, [it] could not arise from its existence' (Proclus, *ET* 18). The difference is that the 'character as it pre-exists in the original giver has a higher reality than the character bestowed' (ibid.).

53. For the lesser gods and demiurges, see Opsomer (2003).
54. Rist (1996). For Platonism and teleology in ethics, see Murdoch (1991).
55. See other relevant texts collated at Sorabji (2005), vol. 2, 141–48, 151–53.

The Gazans want to claim that the cosmos has its existence from God, but that there is an absolute dissimilarity between God and the world. They propose a creator who makes something really new. In countering Proclus' account of the demiurge as father, the Christian thinkers reject part of what is distinctive about Platonic physics as Proclus understands it.

Interpretation of *Timaeus* 28b also provides grounds for creative tension between the Gazans and their Neoplatonic neighbours. For Proclus, 'whether [the cosmos] has come into being or is ungenerated' (*Tim.* 28b–c) is the fundamental problem of the *Timaeus* (1.235.32–238.5), because it provides the primary problem in Platonic physics and its ultimate theological orientation. Plato's answer to this crucial question is that '[the cosmos] came into existence; for it is visible and has body' [[κόσμος] γέγονεν· ὁρατὸς γάρ τέ ἐστιν καὶ σῶμα ἔχων]. Modern interpreters tend to take this passage literally: Plato, they say, thought the cosmos was created with a beginning in time.[56] Yet this apparently simple text caused major controversy in antiquity. The most obvious interpretation would make the world finite in time. This clashes with the Aristotelian view that the cosmos is eternal. Hence, in an attempt to harmonize Plato and Aristotle on this point, other ways to interpret the key terms were sought.

In the second century, interpretation was split between those who followed Plutarch and Atticus, and the majority position as found in Alcinous.[57] Plutarch and Atticus argued that Plato's γέγονεν implied that the world had a beginning in time (ἦν ποτε χρόνος ὅτε οὐκ ἦν [κόσμος]).[58] Yet this interpretation was widely rejected by Middle and then Neoplatonists. Alcinous' second-century *Handbook of Platonic Doctrines* (*Didaskalikos*) maintained that there was no time when the universe did not exist:[59] 'When he says that the cosmos is 'generated' [γενητὸν], he must not be understood [as saying] that there was ever a time when the cosmos did not exist; but rather that it is always in a state of becoming [ἀεὶ ἐν γενέσει], and reveals a more primal cause [ἀρχικώτερόν τι αἴτιον] of its own existence' (*Did.* 14.3). According to Alcinous (ibid.), god

56. For a more complete account, see Baltes (1999), chapter 14. For Proclus and his Platonic sources, see Tarrant (2007), 23–49.

57. Alcinous (1990); Alcinous (1993) represents the majority position on this question in Platonism traceable to Speusippus and Xenocrates. Neoplatonic interpretations of the *Timaeus* only followed the line back to Atticus and Alcinous. Alcinous has been wrongly identified with Albinus. See Whittaker (1987), 83–102.

58. The phrase is found in authors such as Philo of Alexandria (*dec.* 58.6), Sextus Empiricus (*Pyr.* 3.141.3), and Themistius (*in Arist. physica paraphrasis* 5.2, 211.25) and then finds its way into accounts of Christological arguments, for example, in Epiphanius (*Ancoratus* 71.5.2), Athanasius (*Orationes tres contra Arianos* 3.29), and Socrates (*Hist. eccl.* 2.18.31).

59. See also Osborn (1973), 47.

creates the eternal World Soul by ordering it eternally and through an act of non-temporal intellection (ἐγείρων καὶ ἐπιστρέφων πρὸς αὐτὸν τόν τε νοῦν).

The second-century head of the 'Athenian school', Calvenus Taurus, developed the Alcinous-type position, which was to become dominant in Neoplatonism. Taurus' contribution is preserved in Philoponus' *Contra Proclum* 6.8, 145,13ff.,[60] which reports that Taurus had argued that the question hung on the sense of the term γενητός. He therefore proposed four meanings. Something which is γενητός could be: (1) what is not actually created, but is of the same genus as what is actually created; (2) what is composite in theory but not in actuality; (3) what is always in the process of generation; or, (4) what is dependent on an outside source for its existence.[61]

Proclus, then, could draw upon a rich interpretive tradition. He begins by dismissing the Atticus-Plutarch interpretation. To say that Plato was speaking of generation in temporal terms (κατὰ χρονόν) introduces a number of problems. Proclus argues that Atticus' position means that disordered movement existed before the creation of the cosmos (1.283.19–285.7). With movement, time exists (Aristotle, *Phys.* 4, 11.219b2). But this suggests that disorder is superior to order, that order comes from disorder, that the good creator created disorder, and that the disordered is ungenerated (1.284.10–285.7). All such consequences are to be rejected as irrational and impious. Crantor and Plotinus have more appropriate views. The cosmos is said to be generated because it gains existence from a cause and because it is composite (1.276.30–277.32). In gaining existence from a cause, the cosmos is distinguished from beings which have existence on their own account:

> That which does not have its entire essence or its actuality [τὴν οὐσίαν ἢ τὴν ἐνέργειαν] together in a unified stable state is named 'generated' [γενητὸν], for an existent of this nature certainly subsists only through the process of becoming and the existence that belongs to it is always coming into being, but not [real] being. Of such a kind are (a) this sense-perceptible cosmos [ὁ αἰσθητὸς κόσμος], (b) the time which belongs to things which move and (c) the discursive intuitive knowledge [ἡ μεταβατικὴ νόησις] the souls possess. (1.277.27–32)

The cosmos is eternal in the sense that it is perpetual. It has been given 'acquired everlastingness' [τὴν ἀιδιότητα ἐπισκευαστὴν]:

> its perpetual [ἀεὶ] becoming is derived from another source. For if it had somehow taken hold of its own essential nature [τὴν οἰκείαν οὐσίαν]

60. See also Dillon (1977), 237ff.; Phillips (1997), 175–79.
61. Taurus seems to have preferred this final meaning. See Dillon (1977), 244.

> entirely, it would be self-sufficient [αὔταρκες] with respect to its being and would be separated from the maker who gave it its essential nature [κατὰ τὸ εἶναι καὶ τοῦ ποιοῦντος χωρισθὲν καὶ διδόντος αὐτῷ τὴν οὐσίαν]. (1.278.19–24)

Being a limited body, the cosmos cannot be properly eternal (1.279.5ff.). The statement that the cosmos is generated distinguishes it as a tangible composite body from self-sufficient beings. But it does not give the cosmos a temporal beginning (*pace* Plutarch-Atticus). To overcome this interpretation, Proclus reintroduces his distinction between temporal and atemporal eternity, found in compact form in the *Elements of Theology*. In that work, Proclus contrasts proper, atemporal, or simultaneous eternity (*ET* 50: πᾶν αἰώνιον ὅλον ἅμα ἐστίν) with perpetuity, or unending temporal duration (*ET* 55: τὸν ἀεὶ χρόνον).[62] Whereas the demiurge is eternal, the cosmos which it creates is perpetual (1.281.21–27).

Proclus thus combined Taurus' third and fourth meanings in his argument that the universe was eternal, while drawing on Plotinus.[63] The universe is always coming to be (meaning 3), since it is always being created and ordered by the perpetually creating demiurge on whom it depends for existence (meaning 4). It is entirely dependent on the demiurge as its cause since separation from its cause would imply it was incomplete. Unlike other entities which are generated, the universe is not completed by ending. Rather, since time is complete, and the universe spans time, the cosmos is complete without ending.

The other two thinkers whose influence may be felt in the Gazans' work, Hierocles and Ammonius, seem broadly consistent with Proclus on these questions. Hierocles attacks Platonists who 'do not maintain the right concept about god, the creator' (*Prov.* 251.1.460b).[64] Their problem, he says, is that they

> do not think that he is sufficiently capable, through his own power and wisdom, of bringing the cosmos into existence absolutely, acting from eternity, but that he can only create with the aid of uncreated matter and by using nature which does not derive its existence from him, whereby all things pre-exist potentially in the matter while he, as it were, paints things in and merely orders them and chooses from what matter presents. (*Prov.* 251.1 460b)

On the contrary, the universe is generated because it depends on the god who causes it eternally (e.g. *Prov.* 251.11.462b). In his metaphor of the cosmos

62. This terminology recurs in the *Timaeus Commentary*.

63. For this paragraph, see Phillips (1997), 175–79.

64. Attempts to compare Aeneas' dialogue and Hierocles' philosophy are especially fraught, since *Prov.* is extant only in Photius' epitome.

as a living being, complete in its continuous organic growth (*CPGV* I.12ff.), Hierocles' thought also approaches Taurus' third definition of the term γενητός, that the universe is generated because it is perpetually coming into being. When he argues that god does 'not begin to make from a point of time nor cease to make at a point in time, and that what comes to be does not lie outside the activity of that which produces it' (251.17.463b), this idea of eternal coming into being is further cemented, although the brevity of Photius' summary leaves us lacking detail. It seems, however, that Hierocles broadly followed Proclus in arguing that the world was created both in that it is causally dependent on the demiurge from eternity and in that it is perpetually coming to be.

If Photius' summary makes interpretation of Hierocles difficult, Ammonius' views on creation must be reconstructed from the reports of his students. Asclepius' *in Metaphysica* reports Ammonius' lectures on Aristotle's work (ἀπὸ φωνῆς Ἀμμωνιοῦ τοῦ Ἑρμειοῦ). Asclepius confirms Simplicius' account that Ammonius believed that the demiurge was both the efficient and final cause of everything in the cosmos (Asclepius, *in Metaph.* 108.23–25; 151.24–27; Simplicius, *in Phys.* 1363.2ff.).[65] The whole cosmos, both material and incorporeal, is continually being brought into existence by the generative potency of the creator, the spring of goodness and truth (ibid. 202.11,19; 21.19; 115.27). The relation between the cosmos and the demiurge is perpetual (Simplicius, *in Phys.* 1363.12–24). Zacharias claims that Ammonius draws on Porphyry to make the claim that the cosmos is temporally perpetual: 'for since the creative cause is eternal, the creation is eternal in time' [ἀϊδίου γὰρ ὄντος τοῦ δημιουργικοῦ αἰτίου, ἀΐδιον κατὰ χρόνον τὸ δημιούγημα] (142f.). Again, the similarity with Proclus' account is apparent. Ammonius seems to have argued that the cosmos came into being atemporally, is perpetually coming into existence, and depends absolutely for existence on an external cause. Therefore, he seems to subscribe, with Proclus, to Taurus' third and fourth meaning of the term γενητός.

Proclus' systematization of Neoplatonic ideas about creation was not original: his own doxographies show that he depends on earlier thinkers from Crantor to Iamblichus, through Taurus, Plotinus, and Porphyry, in his exegesis of the *Timaeus*. Yet he gave a new precision to Neoplatonic thought on this point and was influential within Neoplatonism among his contemporaries and immediate successors, including Alexandrian philosophers known to the Gazans. We will find *Timaeus* interpretation to be controversial in the dialogues of Aeneas and Zacharias and in the background to Procopius' arguments against the Greeks in his commentary. It is a case in which Christian knowledge of a dispute within

65. For discussion, see Verrycken (2001); Verrycken (1990), 205, 217.

Neoplatonism is used to make a case for the incoherence of the philosophical tradition.

Moving now from *Timaeus* interpretation to creation and ethics, Hierocles is the main relevant source, especially for Aeneas. Photius informs us that *Prov.* consisted of seven books. The first outlined Hierocles' theories about Providence, justice, and how rational creatures are judged according to their actions. Book Two explained Plato's views on the subject. Book Three offered possible objections. The following three books argued that Greek literature before and after Plato supported Plato's opinions. The argument covered at least the *Chaldean Oracles* (Book Four), Orphic and Homeric literature (Book Five), Aristotle to Ammonius Saccas (Book Six), and the Platonists after him—Plotinus, Origen, Porphyry, Iamblichus, and Plutarch of Athens (Book Seven). Aeneas' doxography of previous philosophical opinions on the transmigration of the soul might be drawn from this last book, although, as we have seen, he updates the list by including the opinions of Syrianus and Proclus. The detail of Photius' summary shows that Hierocles linked problems of creation to problems of providence and the eternity of the soul. These topics are also treated together in his *Commentary on the Pythagorean Golden Verses* (*CPGV*), strengthening the link between Hierocles and Aeneas, and, through Aeneas, the other Gazans.

While the Gazans all tie their arguments about creation to questions of ethics for Christian reasons—we will see them attempting to justify Christian salvation history through their creation accounts—the link between physics and ethics was dominant in Hierocles. It may have helped to sharpen the Gazans' thought about this relationship (see below, 5.5 and 6.3). Hierocles' account of creation has many points of similarity with that of Proclus.[66] Photius writes of the *de Providentia* that

> Following Plato, [Hierocles'] investigation posits the prior existence of god, the creator of both the whole visible and invisible world order, which, he says, the demiurge brought forth from no existing substrate [ἐκ μηδενός φησιν ὑποκειμένου προαγαγεῖν], since god's will suffices for the existence of things [εἰς ὑπόστασιν τῶν ὄντων τὸ βούλημα]. (*Prov.* 214.172a)

We have seen that Hierocles argued that creation is by a single principle, matter is eternally caused and that the act of creation is atemporal. Hence, his claim that the cosmos is ordered from no substrate is not a return to seeing prime matter as a principle of creation, and nor is it a statement of the Christian doctrine of creation from nothing. He merely argues that the matter from which the

66. My treatment depends on Schibli (2002), to whom the reader is referred for further detail.

cosmos is ordered is tenuous and insubstantial in comparison with the cosmos. He explicitly argued against those 'Platonists' who think that matter is either a principle or that its creation is temporal.[67]

Like Proclus, Hierocles' main argument for the eternal creation of the cosmos is the goodness of the demiurge. Divine goodness is all that is required for creation (*Prov.* 251.1.460b). The good demiurge, acting at the level of Intellect, creates the cosmos (*Prov.* 251.2.461a, 251.6.461b) as the 'father and maker' of everything (*Prov.* 251.6.461b). The destruction of the universe is an impossibility (*CPGV* I.12) because, as Proclus had argued, also drawing on *Timaeus* 29e, the demiurge is good: 'There is no other reasonable cause for his creation of all things except his substantial goodness [κατ' οὐσίαν ἀγαθότητος]' (*CPGV* I.13; 181 Schibli translation modified). This insistence that goodness is the reason for the creation of the universe leads directly to Hierocles' arguments about Providence.[68] The good demiurge is also pure Providence. Disorderly creation would imply no Providence (*CPGV* XI.27).[69] This claim, built upon Platonic foundations such as the Myth of Er, is the main point of Hierocles' *Commentary on the Pythagorean Golden Verses*:

> Law is the eternal and uniformly abiding activity of god that forever and invariably leads all things to their well-being [πρὸς τὸ εὖ εἶναι]....The main part of what has been said is that god, who is at once lawgiver and judge, ordains goods and removes evils; hence he is in every respect blameless of evils [διὸ καὶ πάντῃ κακῶν ἐστιν ἀναίτιος].[70] (*CPGV* II.1, XI.19)

The key point, that human choices, rather than god's action or inaction, are responsible for evil, was a traditional component of the Platonic tradition. Aeneas also uses this idea. God is blameless (Θεὸς ἀναίτιος) (*Theophrastus* 25.7f.) when good people suffer from the irrational (and therefore evil) choices of bad people (see below, 6.3).

While the demiurge is both Creator and Providence, he does not descend into the material realm to dispense providence. Instead, he remains in the level of Intellect, while a lower order of being is responsible for material providential

67. On this point, and similarities with Numenius, see Baltes (1976), 68f.

68. For fate and providence in Platonism, see Dörrie-Baltes (1993), 86–88, 320–27; Mansfeld (1999), 139–50 (on Alcinous); Schibli (2002), 129–63; Sorabji (2005b), vol. 2, 79–133.

69. 'If there were no providence of God, there would be no order in the cosmos' [εἰ γὰρ μὴ εἴη θεοῦ πρόνοια, οὐκ ἂν εἴη τάξις ἐν κόσμῳ] (*CPGV*, XI.27).

70. Cf. Pl., *Rep.* 614b–621d, especially 617e: ἀρετὴ δὲ ἀδέσποτον, ἣν τιμῶν καὶ ἀτιμάζων πλέον καὶ ἔλαττον αὐτῆς ἕκαστος ἕξει. αἰτία ἑλομένου· θεὸς ἀναίτιος [Virtue is free, and each person will have more or less of it as he honours or dishonours her. The blame is the chooser's: god is blameless]. The myth informs other sections of Hierocles' writing. See e.g. *CPGV* XXVII and *Prov.* 251.15ff. (463aff. Bekker).

intervention. The demiurgic intellect expands into contact with the world through the level of Soul.[71] The demiurge creates three levels of rational souls which derive their rationality from the demiurge (*Prov.* 251.5,7.461b,462a; *CPGV* I.14–15). The highest level is the heavenly divine beings, probably to be identified with the gods to whom the demiurge addresses his speech in the *Timaeus*, and who enjoy undivided contemplation of the demiurge, the divine Intellect.[72] Below these gods are the beings of the middle rank, who are perfectly rational good daemons, interpreters, and messengers of the demiurge who participate in Intellect through eternal but discursive contemplation. Finally, there are human souls, immortal men who only achieve partial, discursive, and temporal contemplation of the divine Intellect, and who are capable of falling into irrationality (and therefore vice) by their choices (251.12,14–17.462b,463a–463b). There can be no movement between these ranks, since everything was perfectly ordered eternally by the demiurge, rather than resulting from chance or human choices.[73] The second level of rational souls acts as material providence, governing human births and deaths, rewarding or punishing humans for their actions, and in every way, through their love for human souls, enacting the unmoved providential concern of the demiurge in the material realm (*Prov.* 251.8–9,20,28–29.462a–b, 464a, 465b–466a; *CPGV* I. 16ff.). This distinction is supported by a novel reading of the *Phaedrus* 249 and the *Theaetetus* 173–76: 'The one philosophises genuinely, that is, without need and heedless of human affairs, the other philosophises as a lover, which is the same as loving humanity and ordering the affairs of his fellow men' (*Prov.* 251.24.465a).[74] This maps well to the post-Plotinian order of the cosmos.[75] Plotinus himself had made a distinction between the intelligible realm, the heavens, and the perceptible cosmos (νοητόν; ἐν οὐρανῷ; αἰσθητὸς κόσμος) (Plotinus, *Enn.* 4.4.5.11f.) and wrote of Heracles the demigod being in heaven and, as a more truly transcendent divinity, in the intelligible realm (Plotinus, *Enn.* 4.2.32.23). Porphyry similarly makes this threefold distinction (e.g. *De regr An* fragments 4 and 6 Bidez). As in so much else in later Neoplatonism, the original division is in Hierocles and Proclus worked out in finer detail, and divisions within the basic scheme are multiplied.

71. See Schibli (2002), 72–80.

72. This may imply a deviation from Proclan hierarchy, where the demiurge was not the most pure Hypostasis of Intellect. The work's pedagogical purpose would explain the deviation.

73. The idea that movement between different ranks of existence was possible on the basis of human choice is championed by Origen. See below, 6.6.

74. See the discussion at Schibli (2002), 352–55, notes 368–79.

75. To the following, see Smith (1974), 56–58.

These different levels of being are essential to Neoplatonic eschatology, as different thinkers provided accounts of how the soul can ascend to higher levels of being. Much of Hierocles' account focuses on questions surrounding the third level of being, the human soul. Like Aeneas after him, he investigates transmigration of souls, arguing that only human-human transmigration is possible, because otherwise the orderliness of creation would be upset (*Prov.* 214.6.173b, 251.4.461b; *CPGV* XXIII.9–10).[76] Again, the created cosmic order should not be transgressed:

> The pinnacle of virtue [ἀρετὴ] is to remain within the bounds of creation, by which all things have been separated according to kind, and to follow the laws of providence [τοῖς τῆς προνοίας ἕπεσθαι νόμοις], through which all things in accordance with their own capacity are adapted to their proper good. (*CPGV* XXVII.9)

Human-human transmigration is accepted as part of the argument for providence (*Prov.* 214.6.172b). Divine justice is partly exercised through punishment of the evil soul by making it return in an inferior condition in its next incarnation. Similarly, good souls may be rewarded by a better station the next time around. The soul, which as a rational but partial creature is capable of choosing virtue or falling into vice, thus obtains justice in accordance with its choices (*Prov.* 251.15–16.463a–b). The emphasis in Hierocles falls on the possibility that a life of virtue can enable humans to come closer to the One; discussion of the role of theurgy in ascent is less marked (cf. Porphyry *De regr An* fr. 4 Bidez). This understanding of divine justice acting over many incarnations of the soul depends on the soul being immortal, as Proclus also recognized (*ET* 206). Therefore, the existence of providence is used to argue for the pre-existence of the soul. The soul and the body are different entities; the soul immortal and the body mortal. Hierocles argues that

> To be prepared to practise justice, to die nobly, and to be generously inclined with one's possessions requires most of all that the soul not die along with the body... [that] soul is superior to generation and destruction and is a different substance from the mortal body, since it is in itself eternal. For it is impossible for something that has come to be generated from some point in time to abide eternally, just as something that has its existence from eternity cannot ever submit to destruction. Therefore if the human soul, after the destruction of the body, survives and meets with

76. This is the view championed by the Neoplatonist character in Aeneas' dialogue. The debate can be traced at least to Porphyry.

> justice and judgement, if for the practices in life it receives recompense according to what it deserves, and if it is not possible for something generated in time to remain for eternity, it is clear that it has also existed previously for all time. Thus the human soul is disclosed to belong as well to the eternally generated things of the creator-god, whence it also participates in the divine likeness [τῆς θείας ὁμοιώσεως μέτεστιν]. (*CPGV* XI.39.1–4, 7—12—40.1–8)

For Hierocles, ethical action is impossible unless the soul is immortal, and the righteousness of the demiurge is justifiable only if the soul is immortal. In making the soul immortal, Hierocles is attempting to make his argument for divine providence credible.

Punishment and reward only make sense if the actions of the soul are really the soul's actions (*Prov.* 251.10.462b). That is, providence and lack of agency are incompatible, or, as Hierocles puts it more positively, free will and deliberate choice are the only options compatible with an intelligent providence (*Prov.* 251.11.462b). Rational creatures are not caused by chance; they are always looked after providentially (*Prov.* 251.14.463a), but this is not incompatible with free will: the soul always chooses 'what is up to us' and obtains justice according to these choices (*Prov.* 251.12,15.462b,463a–b). The soul is capable of virtue and vice and alteration from one to the other (*Prov.* 251.16.463b). It knows what it should do because of the existence of laws which are independent of individual choices, laid down by the demiurge to guide virtuous behaviour (*Prov.* 251.26–27.465b). Despite the universality of providential laws, the demiurge, through the second rank of intellectual beings, cares individually for each soul which he has made (*Prov.* 251.30.466a–b).

Hierocles' account thus has much complexity of detail but a clear outline. He insists on a close relationship between the first principle of physics and the first principle of ethics, making the demiurge both eternal creator of the world out of his goodness and the guarantor of providence in the cosmos. In order to allow the demiurge to be the ground of loving providence while remaining unmoved, material providence is allotted to the second rank of divine beings, who distribute providence by participating in the demiurge. The human soul is, like the creation, eternal. Because it is eternal, it is in the image of God. Providence is impossible if the soul is not pre-existent and eternal.

While Aeneas and through him Zacharias found much in an account like this to help them make a case for the unification of the first principle of physics and ethics, Hierocles' account also worries them. The multiplication of orders of being has analogues in Aeneas and, to a lesser degree, in Zacharias, with important modifications (see below, 6.1 and 6.3). Hierocles' arguments for the eternity of the world are rejected. Aeneas also attempts to rebut arguments for the pre-existence of the soul: Hierocles' interests partly explain the parallel Aeneas makes between this question and the question of the eternity of the world (see below, 6.5). Finally, Hierocles' emphasis on divine order is attractive for Aeneas and Zacharias, but in arguing that God will institute a radically new creation, they argue for the transformation and ultimate re-creation of divine order, although even in this move we will see important parallels between Christian and Neoplatonic thought.

Hierocles had strongly emphasized the harmony of Plato and Aristotle, praising Ammonius Saccas' 'proof' that 'the mind of Plato and Aristotle was in harmony regarding the most important and necessary doctrines' and attempting to show that Platonic and Aristotelian thought were intimately connected in the areas of providence, the immortality of the soul, and their views about creation (*Prov.* 214.2.172a).

The final thinker of importance to the Gazans, Ammonius, continued this line of thought.[77] Simplicius reports that

> my teacher Ammonius has written an entire book that provides many proofs of the fact that Aristotle considers god to be also the efficient cause of the entire world [ποιητικὸν αἴτιον ἡγεῖσθαι τὸν θεὸν τοῦ παντὸς κόσμου τὸν Ἀριστοτέλη] and I have here taken over some points sufficiently for my present purposes. (*in Phys.* 8.10, 1363.8–11, McKirahan translation)[78]

The problem is that Aristotle's unmoved mover appears to be best understood as solely a final cause.[79] But this clashes with Plato's account in the *Timaeus*, where the demiurge is understood as an efficient cause. It also clashes with Proclus' view, outlined above, that the demiurge is the efficient cause of being, acting at the level of Intellect or νοῦς. Simplicius recognizes the problem and endeavours to answer the probing question of 'why in the world Aristotle does not say that god is an efficient cause [ποιητικὸν αἴτιον τὸν θεὸν] as evidently as he said that he is a final cause [τελικόν]' (*in Phys.* 8.10 1363.12–14, McKirahan translation modified). Simplicius has two answers, which probably had some analogue in Ammonius' work. One answer is that since what is generated is, in ordinary

77. Proclus similarly found unlikely harmony: 'and it seems to me that the excellent Aristotle emulated Plato's teaching as far as possible so that he structured the whole method of investigation about nature [in accordance with him]' (*in Tim.* 1.6.21).

78. While the work Simplicius refers to is lost, given the final clause of Simplicius' statement, some of Ammonius' argument may be gleaned from Simplicius' work. See also Simplicius *in De cael.* 271.20 and the discussion at Sorabji (1990a).

79. For modern discussions, see Kahn (1985); Matthen (2001).

circumstances, mortal, and an efficient cause is normally the cause of this sort of generation (as in the case of terrestrial generation and corruption), Aristotle was careful to avoid using the terminology of efficient cause to refer to the creation of the eternal universe. This is not a real problem, though, because 'generation' can be understood as 'eternal generation', just as, Simplicius argues, Aristotle himself intended in the case of the eternal generation of eternal motion. The Neoplatonic exegesis used to elucidate *Timaeus* 28b is again operating. The second argument is more complete. Aristotle viewed the unmoved mover as the cause of the motion of the heavens, and through the heavens, of terrestrial motions such as generation and corruption. So far so Aristotelian, as the motion of the heavens is caused by desire for the unmoved mover, and the motion of the terrestrial world comes about by desiring the perfect motion of the heavens: the prime mover acts as a final cause of the motion of the heavens.[80] Simplicius then puts the unmoved mover at the level of mind, fitting the Aristotelian principle into the Neoplatonic hierarchy in a way that makes his thought cohere with Proclus'. But, argues Simplicius, 'what is moved by something else must also get its subsistence from something else, if in fact existence is superior to movement' [τὸ ἑτεροκίνητον καὶ ὑπόστασιν ἑτέρωθεν ἔχειν ἀνάγκη, εἴπερ κρείττων ἡ οὐσία τῆς κινήσεως] (McKirahan translation). This implies that 'just as [the terrestrial world] has its eternal motion from the unmoved cause [ἀπὸ τῆς ἀκινήτου αἰτίας], so also it receives its eternal corporeal existence from the incorporeal [cause]' (*in Phys.* VIII, 1363.5–7, McKirahan translation). As in Proclus, the Aristotelian efficient cause, which had been understood as a 'contact force', a push or a pull, is taken as a cause of existence, rather than a cause of motion. This allows Simplicius (apparently drawing on Ammonius) to unite the final and efficient causes at the level of Intellect.

Ammonius' account thus follows the general lines we have seen in Proclus and Hierocles. Like Proclus, he understands Plato's statement that the world is generated in a sense that allows him to hold to the eternity of the world. This logic also supports his unification of the final and efficient cause at the level of Intellect in the figure of the demiurge. In this move, Ammonius makes the efficient cause a cause of being, rather than simply of motion. This resonates with the *Timaeus*, where the demiurge is said to hold his creations in Being; again, the process of reading Plato and Aristotle as though they agreed on essentials leads to the creation of novel philosophical positions. While the Gazans could use the logic of the second move, they tried to undermine the claim that the

80. Simplicius provides Aristotelian texts for this claim at *in Phys.* 8, 1361.11–1363.24.

nature of the unified final and efficient cause implied the eternal generation and future eternity of the world.

4.4 Building on Different Traditions

In their different ways, all three Gazans were familiar with arguments presented by contemporary Neoplatonists, as well as arguments from the earlier history of Platonism and Christianity. The works of Proclus on creation and eternity, particularly his *Eighteen Arguments* and his *Timaeus Commentary*, are plausibly the main catalyst for the surge in interest in creation within late-antique Neoplatonism, which is seen both in the Gazans' response and in the works of other Neoplatonists such as Hierocles and Ammonius. Hierocles' and Ammonius' views on the topic seem to harmonize with those of Proclus, although they each have different emphases in the works that have come down to us, partly because of the introductory nature of their texts.

Members of the schools thinking about creation in Gaza at the turn of the sixth century were exposed to the explicit link between physics and theology made by Proclus and the later Neoplatonists, as well as to particular debating points in *Timaeus* interpretation. The emphasis on the relationship between physics and ethics represented by Hierocles and the unification of the first cause of being with the final cause of the perfection of the universe can also be seen as providing significant philosophical resources upon which the Gazans could draw.

Philosophers including Proclus, Hierocles, and Ammonius thus presented intellectual challenges, as well as potential solutions, to the Christian problems which interested Aeneas, Procopius, and Zacharias. Those Christian problems had a long pedigree, beginning in the decisive formulation of the doctrine of creation from nothing, and continuing through accounts influenced by developments in Trinitarian theology and exegetical and pastoral concerns. We will see that the doctrines of creation from nothing and the Trinity are the generative grammar for the Gazans' respective accounts of creation. They differ from many of the fourth- and fifth-century Christian deliberations by directing their works towards members of the rhetorical and philosophical schools of late antiquity, and to do that they appropriate and adapt ideas and literary forms from the philosophical tradition. How this different approach effects their particular creation-oriented works will emerge in the course of the following two chapters.

Procopius on Creation and Eternity

WHILE PROCOPIUS' TEXT POSTDATES THOSE OF AENEAS AND Zacharias, it provides a useful framework and introduction for analysis of their works in the following chapter. In the prologue to his *Commentary on Genesis*, Procopius outlines and rebuts various opinions ascribed to 'children of the Greeks' (29A). He investigates problems about creation including ideas about the eternity of matter, the temporal and causal origins of the cosmos, the relationship between matter and form, the origin and causes of evil, the workings and existence of providence, the existence and characteristics of non-terrestrial beings, and the eternity of the world. These arguments are the focus of this chapter.

Procopius' thought, like that of Proclus and other Neoplatonists, was foundationalist. Foundationalism has been attractive to many thinkers, at least from Aristotle's *Posterior Analytics*. It begins from a set of principles which are known directly, and so do not have to be proved. These principles then generate the acceptable statements in a given system, as in the case of axioms for linear algebra, from which valid algebraic expressions are derived. Changing the analogy, they provide the generative grammar for a language. These principles may be understood as generative of communal beliefs, actions, and interactions.

Procopius uses different strategies to undermine his Neoplatonic foundational opponents.[1] First, he seeks to show that the philosophers' axioms are mutually inconsistent. Like Philoponus, who, for example, later attempted to demonstrate that Aristotle's axiomatic claim that an infinity could not be traversed was inconsistent with his axiom that infinity is only potential rather than actual, Procopius turns philosophical arguments against the philosophers to rebut Neoplatonic claims about creation.[2] This use of philosophy against philosophy for Christian purposes is further evidence for the interpenetration of Christian and Neoplatonic cultures in Gaza.

Where Christian axioms are opposed to Neoplatonic ones, Procopius on occasions flatly denies the truth of Neoplatonic principles. He does this by introducing data which the original system did not take into account. This may be done along the lines of the first strategy, by adducing claims Neoplatonists

1. These criticisms of foundational systems are also criticisms of coherentism. I treat them as critiques of foundationalism, since Neoplatonists were epistemic foundationalists.

2. For Philoponus' infinity argument, see Sorabji (2004), vol. 2, 175–80.

should logically accept but which would contradict their other claims. But the new data may also be taken from outside Neoplatonism. In this case, the danger for rational argumentation is that Neoplatonists could not always rationally accept the data which Procopius adduces given the foundational claims of their system, so debate reaches a logical impasse. This happens when Procopius uses biblical, patristic, or liturgical claims as evidence to reject Neoplatonic ideas. Accepting this kind of new data requires an act of faith to embrace the new way of life and its new intellectual allegiances, and Procopius' use of this type of argument is designed to elicit such conversion. His privileging of Christian axioms over Neoplatonic ones is evidence from the field of intellectual history for the contests and transitions between different local cultures I sketched in Chapter 3.

In a related way, foundational systems may be rejected by placing the system in a new intellectual framework. In reframing the debate, some Neoplatonic ideas have no significance for Procopius. They are not so much untrue as irrelevant, as in my earlier explanation for the Gazans omission of argument about the Paradigm. In our modern context, for example, atheists have claimed that Christianity is untrue by placing it in a narrative of Darwinian science, quantum cosmology, individualism, and subjective truth, so that Christianity can only occupy a small part of the total picture, rather than taking the universal position it once claimed as the frame for all other cultures. Some Christian claims may be true, but they are given a new significance—they are made radically insignificant—by the new modern or postmodern frames. Procopius reframes Neoplatonic arguments about creation, making the creation of the cosmos part of an encompassing story about God's divine plan for human salvation. This new frame to the debates about creation helps to explain the aspects of Neoplatonism which Procopius ignores or combats. Yet in his arguments for the divine plan, we will see Procopius using philosophical arguments and images from the Platonic and Aristotelian tradition. In reframing the debate about creation and thereby sidelining Neoplatonic assumptions and world views, Procopius does not merely reject Neoplatonism. Rather, he uses it to bolster the rationality of his new scheme.

These three broad criticism strategies will recur at different stages of Procopius' argument. His major criticism of his Greek opponents is that the idea that the world is coeternal with God negates divine freedom, makes it impossible to argue that God is the first principle of being and ethics, inadequately separates God from the world, and makes Christian hope in the 'second coming' implausible, thus undermining good human actions. As a biblical commentator, Procopius has some unique concerns. But his account of creation has a clear overarching shape which will also be seen in Aeneas and Zacharias.

Creation solves ethical and soteriological problems which Procopius thinks are entailed by the Neoplatonic account. Like Aeneas and Zacharias, he analyses creation as an ethical problem, and frames his engagement with Neoplatonic ideas about creation (regarding matter, time, hierarchy of beings, and freedom and necessity) within an account of a divine plan of salvation.

5.1 Problems of a Commentator

Procopius begins with the established methods of late-antique commentary by dealing with questions of authorship and audience. He claims that Scripture comes from God and not humans (24A–B). The prophets act like a flute through whom God breathes (24A); Moses is the instrument through whom God wrote the Pentateuch. The divine origin of Scripture guarantees its truth: coming from an inspired agent of God, the Bible records nothing false or irrational (θεοῦ τὰ λόγια παρ' ᾧ ψεῦδος οὐδὲν ἢ ἄλογον) (24A). Procopius thus treats the Bible as trustworthy evidence, allowing him to deploy biblical claims against Neoplatonic ones, and to construct a new frame through which to view questions about creation.

But some passages of Scripture are obscure. Unclear statements make for bad evidence, so Procopius provides a justification for both the apparent obscurity of Scripture and for his particular interpretative method. His first approach to this problem is to make a claim for the primacy of prayer and pious thinking in scriptural interpretation. It is necessary, he says, to control oneself and be as pious as possible when thinking about Scripture (καὶ δεῖ ὅσα μὲν εὐσεβῶς δυνήσῃ νοῆσαι κρατεῖν) (24B). The student of Scripture has two other courses of action open to him. The student may 'learn from the fathers' or else he may 'attend directly to the God of knowledge, who teaches humanity knowledge' [ἢ Πατέρων μαθεῖν, ἢ τῷ Θεῷ παραπέμπειν τῶν γνώσεων, ὅς διδάσκει ἄνθρωπον γνῶσιν] (24B). These three ways of approaching scripture provide points of contact between Neoplatonists and Procopius' ideal Christian interpreter. Like contemporary pagan philosophers, Procopius' Christian interpreter is engaged in a spiritual discipline or practice when thinking about the canonical texts of earlier privileged thinkers. But the canon has changed, as has the hermeneutic community. As a Christian commentator, Procopius endeavours to construct a new authoritative interpretative community, based on Church Fathers rather than exalted philosophers, dependent ultimately and directly on God, rather than theurgic union with the One.

Yet these three methods of reading are insufficient for Procopius. The more fundamental problem of the simplicity of Scripture remains. The problem is sharper, because unlike all the other Jews, Moses spoke directly to God, so one might expect the Bible to be full of infinitely complex divine wisdom. Moses had direct knowledge about God's plan to send Jesus to redeem the world (24B–C). If the author was so wise about the divine plan, why, asks Procopius, is the text of *Genesis* apparently so simple? Why did Moses not use orthodox formulations and descriptions of God? Why are advanced subjects of Greek cosmology not included (24A–28A; 33C)?

Procopius' answer is that Moses' reticence is part of a divine plan. He was writing to the Hebrews and the Greeks, who are like children, incapable, through no fault of their own, of constructing difficult theories themselves or of understanding those proposed by others (28A). Therefore instead of confusing them, Moses 'stammered to the Jews, telling them only what they would be able to hear at that time. Just like a teacher of children, he introduced the first elements to them, knowing that once they had learned them, other teachers would come, who would teach and transmit the more perfect [knowledge]' (35A). Procopius believed that humans live their mortal lives in order to become 'accustomed' or 'habituated' to God and divine reality.[3] The process of habituation is evolutionary: it continues through the generations and history displays a definite progression. If people knew everything from the beginning, teaching them piety and good living would be superfluous (28A). Earlier peoples, in Procopius' view, are more primitive, less educated and less accustomed to divine glory than Christians who occupy the world after the events of the New Testament. This logic of a progressive divine plan supports Procopius' claim that the Old Testament is an introduction and preparation for the New Testament (28A). The Old Testament scriptures are a pinnacle of piety rather than the pinnacle of knowledge (28A). The place of the Genesis account within the divine plan explains its intellectual deficiencies. While Genesis does not cover advanced topics, its subject matter is essential for the Christian community and its content is true because of the wisdom of Moses and God's unchanging truthfulness.[4] This argument is similar

3. There is insufficient evidence to situate Procopius within debates about the difference between likeness (*homoiôsis*) and ideas of 'kinship' associated with the originally Stoic concept of (*oikeiôsis*) (see e.g. Pl. *Lysis* 222bff.). For the Stoic concept, see e.g. *SVF* ii.724; iii.178–79. See also Brink (1955–96), 139–41, 144; Long (1996), 253–63; Pembroke (1971), 114–49; Striker (1996), 281–97. For the Platonic ideal of 'likeness to God' (*homoiôsis theôi*), see Pl. *Theaet.* 176b. This ideal entered Alexandrian Christianity at least as early as Clement (*str.* 3.5.42). See also Osborn (2005), 108.

4. Procopius does not attack the Jewish community for their Jewishness. The inferiority of the historical Jewish community is not the fault of its members; rather, it is part of the divine plan. Jews who live in Christian times, however, have not grown up, in Procopius' view. This is a moral and intellectual failure on their part. So Jewish ideas of God are criticized, since they are not Trinitarian. Such a view sits all too easily with contemporary negative and discriminatory attitudes towards Jews; however, Procopius' text does not itself advocate persecution.

to John Chrysostom's claim that teaching has to be appropriate to the capacities of the audience (*Hom. in Gen* 2.8–9; *Serm. in Gen* 1.94–153) or Irenaeus' doctrine of *oikeosis* which we will see employed also in Aeneas and Zacharias. You do not give solids to babies, so Moses teaches the elements and leaves the more developed doctrine to John and Paul, whose audience, which has been granted knowledge of Christ, is ready for it (*Hom. in Gen* 2.9; *Serm. in Gen* 1.100–153).[5] For Procopius, this notion of God's progressive, evolutionary dealings with his creatures makes soteriology central to the doctrine of creation. For creation to be about salvation, it must be about history and ethics, and Procopius goes on to argue that Genesis is indeed a historical and ethical work. Genesis sets out the history of creation and the people of God, and explains and defines the laws which govern good ethical practices (23C).

Genesis is an authoritative account because of Moses' privileged relationship to God. When Moses saw God's back, he saw the demiurge or creator (δημιουργός) and grasped things that no mortal had ever seen (23C). This is equivalent to seeing the Son, since 'no-one has seen the father except the son and him to whom the son has revealed him' (23C; Matt. 11:27; John 1:18). Hence, the community which has access to the Bible as the source of truth about the Son thereby possesses new evidence that may be used to rebut Neoplatonic claims.

Procopius' use of such new evidence, however, eschews simple biblicism. When Procopius briefly treats the higher beings omitted from Moses' more simple account, instead of approaching the topic through Greek authorities, he uses the Bible to make claims about intelligible reality (33C–35B). This question had troubled earlier Christian commentators on Genesis, and Procopius' concerns are evidence that his argument stays within the bounds of the Christian interpretive community (see e.g. Basil, *Hex.* 1.5; John Chrysostom, *Hom. in Gen* 2.7; *Serm in Gen* 1.94–95). Unlike the Greek accounts, the Bible shows that the intelligible beings, like the changeable terrestrial ones, are created. There is no pre-existence of intelligible beings. On the contrary, heaven and earth were created in the same process. The texts used to establish these claims are taken from the Old and New Testaments (Ps. 148; Job 38:7; Prov. 16:5; Gen. 1:16; Col. 1:15).[6] In these arguments we may identify a rebuttal of Origenist ideas from the Gazan monasteries.[7]

5. A version of this claim was already known to Clement of Alexandria, who, like Procopius, emphasizes a divine plan of salvation. See e.g. *str.* 1. 6.5–6.

6. This treatment allies Procopius with Zacharias but differentiates him to a degree from Aeneas (see further Chapter 6).

7. Origen had proposed the idea of an intelligible creation before the material creation. Basil cited this as a possibility (*Hex.*), but thinks that one simultaneous creation of visible and invisible beings is more appropriate. Procopius draws on Basil's work at other points in his prologue.

Procopius' use of the Bible as evidence against Neoplatonist claims and epistemological presuppositions is extended into employing Patristic authorities. Basil's *Hexameron*, Gregory of Nyssa's *de opificio hominis*, and a wide range of sources collected in the earlier *Catena on Genesis* are allowed to determine the truth value of Neoplatonic propositions. A few examples from the main body of the *Commentary* may suffice to show how Procopius works out the prologue's programmatic statements about Christian truth standards. In a passage which uses Basil's *Hexameron* 3.3–4 as a springboard, Procopius investigates the shape of the cosmos (40–41, 65B–C, 67A–69B). Basil had simply dismissed such investigations as unbiblical. Procopius takes Basil's rejection of Hellenic investigations seriously and extends them. He begins by presenting a series of biblical texts which undermine the idea that the earth is spherical (65B–67C). These include statements about the number of heavens, again taken from Basil, but now applied to the problem of the shape of the universe. Procopius is indebted to Basil, but does not simply follow him slavishly. Biblical texts, not Greek natural science, support his arguments. But his argument moves beyond mere source-hunting. His use of the Bible is governed partly by his understanding of salvation history, or the divine plan of salvation. In Procopius' view, all history points to the coming of Christ, who redeems humanity. The purpose of the cosmos is its redemption by Christ. Procopius reads the Bible as a history of this purpose. So Procopius claims that the southern hemisphere does not exist, and therefore the earth is not spherical, because Christ never got there and it therefore has no purpose in the grand scheme of things (67C–69B).

Yet this use of Patristic authorities, and biblical texts supported by a reading of salvation history, does not mean that Procopius' *Commentary* is unable to enter into dialogue with philosophy; there is room for it within the picture. Procopius is aware that Christian theology cannot do without philosophy.[8] For example, in a section discussing the statement that humans are made in the image of God, which is based on a passage in Gregory of Nyssa (*de op. hom.* 145.36–47), Procopius explains the Pauline anthropology of σῶμα, ψυχή, and πνεῦμα (body, soul, spirit). Following Gregory, Procopius maps these distinctions onto the divisions of nutritive, animative, and intellective or rational parts of the soul (φυτικός, αἰσθητικός, νοερός) (117C–D).[9]

In another passage, Procopius rejects certain Christian interpretations of the statement in Genesis that 'darkness covered the face of the deep' (Gen.

8. The Gazans would subscribe to Aristotle's golden argument, that to argue against philosophy is to philosophize (*Prot*). See Aristotle, *Fragmenta*, Fragment 51, pp. 56–58 (Rose).

9. For the Aristotelian background to the nutritive soul, see (*An.* 2.2, 413b5–11; 3.12, 434a22–435a10; cf. *Tim.* 77c). Aristotle's preferred term for the part of the soul identified as *phutikon* here is *threptikos*.

1:2) (44B–C), drawing on the discussion at Basil, *Hex*. 2.4. Some had sought an allegorical explanation, that darkness referred to an ungenerated principle of cosmic evil, on the basis that Scripture uses ἦν without being explicit that the darkness was generated (Μακρὰ ληροῦσιν οἱ τοῦ κακοῦ φύσιν ἀγένητον ἐκ τούτων εισάγοντες διά τε τοῦ ἦν καὶ τοῦ μὴ γένεσιν σκότους εἰπεῖν τὴν Γραφήν) (44B). This is nonsense, in Procopius' view, again following Basil, because it would imply that sin and evil were coeternal with God. This is strong evidence for Procopius' main problem: how to counter the idea that the world is eternal, a problem that clearly was not on the radar screen for the allegorist. Procopius does use arguments with philosophical pedigree, claiming that darkness has no substance, being rather a privation of light (44B). A genus consists of things which are akin (συγγενές), so God and light are not the same sorts of things as evil and darkness (44B–C).[10] While a tantalizing sentence claims that much more could be said, were this his subject, possibly suggesting that Procopius had philosophical interests which went beyond his desire to use philosophy in an exegetical context (44C), the discussion quickly returns to exegesis of Genesis, and the venture into philosophy is general rather than particular.

Yet Procopius' text challenges attempts to define Christians as those who would have nothing to do with philosophy and suggests a group of Gazan Christians who wanted to hold open a place for philosophy within Christianity. Given this overlapping of categories, when I claim that Procopius is directing an argument against 'Neoplatonists', I mean both Neoplatonists who would not identify themselves as Christian, and people who would identify as Christians, but whose allegiance to Neoplatonism leads them, in Procopius' view, to hold beliefs which set them outside established Christian orthodoxy. This is another instance of the problem of fluid identities and cultural transitions which characterized Gazan life in the fifth and early sixth centuries.

5.2 God and Matter

The main intellectual opponents of the Mosaic account, according to Procopius, are Greek philosophers who believe that the 'creation is coeternal with God' [συναΐδιον τῷ Θεῷ] (29A):[11]

> Being unable, then, to discover how something will be generated from absolutely nothing, presuming to measure the power of God against their own understandings, they invented eternal matter for us.

10. This argument is partly based on Basil's *Hex*., 2.4, but goes beyond it in detail.
11. See below, 6.2 and 6.4, for the Trinitarian resonance of the term συναΐδιος.

[Μὴ δυνηθέντες γοῦν εὑρεῖν πῶς ἐκ μηδαμῆ μηδαμῶς ὄντος ὄν τι γενήσεται, μετρεῖσθαι τοῦ Θεοῦ τὴν δύναμιν ταῖς οἰκείαις ὑπολαμβάνοντες ἐννοίαις, ἀΐδιον ὕλην ἡμῖν ἀνεπλάσαντο] (29A)

The main problem that Procopius identifies with the Greek viewpoint is that the eternity of matter limits divine power. Procopius fears that this would make matter equal to God and confuse the proper distinction between the creator and his creations (29B). Later in his argument he returns to the question of how the eternity of matter would constrain God. His first problem is to combat the idea that matter is eternal. The Greeks claim that matter is eternal, Procopius reports, on the basis that since God is always a creator, his creations exist eternally alongside him (29A). This claim, says Procopius, rejects the true account (creation from nothing) and measures the power of God against human notions, perhaps an oblique reference to the Platonic 'craftsman' analogy for creation, where the creator needs material with which to create (29A).

In his statement of the Platonic case, Procopius claims that the Greeks say that matter is 'coeternal' (συναΐδιος) with God. Zacharias will later use the term in describing Ammonius' arguments (*Ammonius*, 1078). The term is somewhat perplexing, because I cannot find Proclus or any other extant pagan Neoplatonist using it (although it occurs in Philoponus' refutation of Proclus). Procopius and Zacharias, and later Philoponus, may have imported the term into Platonism from Christianity, where it is used most commonly to describe the relations between the ungenerated members of the Trinity. As I argued above, this background is one reason why the Gazans reject the Platonic idea that both matter and God are eternal. Their understanding of the concept of coeternity is coloured by their understanding of the Trinity; only the Son and Spirit can be coeternal with the Father, hence the cosmos cannot be coeternal with God (see also 6.4 below).

Yet Procopius does not object on these Christian grounds. His rebuttal, signalled by the adversative particle καίτοι, begins with a proof by contradiction (29B). If matter is eternal, it will also be changeless (29B), for it could only be changed in respect of its eternity, since that is the only quality ascribed to it by Platonists. They claim that prime matter, while eternal, is without quality, size, or form (29B). But change with respect to eternity is impossible.

Without the καίτοι, this might look like a perfectly good Neoplatonic argument for the eternity of the world.[12] Aristotle, we may remember, had argued

12. The most detailed study of related issues is F. Haas (1997). For an influential debate later in the sixth century, see Philoponus and Simplicius (1991). Simplicius claimed that Aristotle thought of prime matter as indefinite extension (*in Phys* 229,5–7), but was equivocal about whether such prime

that prime matter has neither quality, place, nor form. It is to be thought of as what remains when such attributes are removed. As such, prime matter is eternal and cannot undergo change (e.g. *Metaph.* VII 3 1028b36–1029a20; *Phys.* IV 2, 209b6–11).[13] A Platonic strand of the philosophical tradition aligned Plato's 'receptacle' from the *Timaeus* with Aristotelian prime matter (e.g. Proclus, Argument 11; cf. *Tim.* 49a, 51a). As we have seen, the demiurgic act of creation was conceived of as an eternal ordering of the disorder of the receptacle (e.g. *in Tim.* 1.381.22–382.12). The receptacle or material substrate of the universe is eternal, since it has no qualities which could undergo change. So in both cases, prime matter exists eternally, is not changed when it is ordered, and the eternity of matter implies that the world is eternal. But Procopius is claiming that if matter is eternal, it is equal to God. Matter is not equal to God, therefore it is not eternal. Although this is not made explicit, I understand Procopius as also suggesting that if matter is changeless, it would be equal to God, which is impossible. This implies that matter is capable of change, which is then supposed to defeat the claim that matter is eternal.

On what grounds could Procopius argue that if an entity is eternal and changeless it is equal to God? Procopius offers no explicit defence of this claim. As we have seen, it is not one that Neoplatonists, with their derivational monism, would accept. For Neoplatonists, if one were unfortunate enough always to stand in the light, a shadow would be 'coeternal' with one's body without being in any meaningful sense equal to it (for more shadow arguments, see below, 6.1).

This is an area where Platonic and Christian thought are irreconcilable. Procopius, unlike Neoplatonists, axiomatically takes eternity as the distinguishing mark of God: 'God alone does not have a beginning... which belongs to the eternal alone' [Θεὸς δὲ μόνος τὸ ἄναρχον... ἃ δὴ μόνῳ τῷ ἀιδίῳ συμβέβηκεν] (32C–D). It is what distinguishes the uncreated from the created (32C). This argument relies partly on an equation of eternity with necessity: God alone is eternal because God alone is necessary. Everything created is contingent on God's will. Any form of derivational monism is only possible with respect to the persons of the Trinity. For Platonists, however, eternity is not proper to only one entity, and Procopius never explores the detailed logic of Neoplatonism on this point. Instead, he seeks to offer an attractive alternative picture.

matter actually existed: prime matter 'flows from all sides away from Being into non-Being' (*in Phys.* 230,25f.). Philoponus believed prime matter extended in three dimensions. See the discussion at F. Haas (1997), 121f.

13. The precise nature of prime matter in Aristotle is controversial. See F. Haas (1997), xii, n. 2.

Procopius' further arguments against the eternity of matter are intended to offer such an alternative account. He argues that the Platonist belief in uncreated matter makes it an accidental event in the creative process: God is not in control. If matter is uncreated, 'God's invention of matter is just accidental [εὐτύχημα]' (29B). Coeternity, for Procopius, confuses the relationship between cause and effect: 'for in what respect could eternal differ from eternal? And how will one be the maker and the other the made?' ['Αίδιον γὰρ ἀιδίου τίνι διοίσειε; πῶς ἔσται τὸ μὲν ποιοῦν, τὸ δὲ γινόμενον] (29B). It strips God of proper divine authority and precedence, and impiously attributes confusion rather than intentionality to God.

As we have seen, in Procopius' view the solution which preserves God's authority and establishes a proper order of cause and effect is *creatio ex nihilo*. Yet like Philoponus after him, Procopius thinks that Neoplatonists have no reason to reject this doctrine (29B–C).[14] 'How', he asks,

> was [God] unable to make matter, which is inferior, although making the forms, which indeed are also better, from nothing?
>
> [πῶς δὲ τὰ εἴδη ἐκ μὴ ὄντων ποιῶν, ἃ δὴ καὶ κρείττονα, τὴν ὕλην οὖσαν χείρω, ποιεῖν οὐκ ἠδύνατο] (29B–C)

Procopius then extends the claim to all intelligible beings and the human soul (29C).[15] In this claim, which anticipates the more detailed argument offered by Philoponus later, we have an argument that engages Neoplatonists on Neoplatonic terms, although it, like Procopius' other arguments, has a precursor in earlier Christian thinking (see *PE* 7.22, discussed above, 4.1; cf. Philoponus, *Contra Proclum* 9.9, 340, 9.11, 347, 365,3). Aristotle had argued against the creation of matter from nothing on the basis of arguments against a vacuum and infinite regress (*de Cael.* 3.2, 301b30–302a9; *Phys* 1.9, 192a27–32). But his views about how qualities come to be left the field more open in the case of form. For Aristotle, when an entity gains a new quality, that quality need only have previously existed potentially and does not go through a process of coming to be. Rather, proximate matter takes on form instantaneously: whiteness does not undergo the processes of generation and corruption (*Metaph.* 7.15, 1039b23–27; 8.3, 1043b14–16; 8.5, 1044b21–22). For example, an object may become white or cease being white, and the form of whiteness need only exist potentially before it qualifies a particular body (*Metaph.* 7.9, 1034b16–19, 1039b26; 8.5, 1043b14,

14. For Philoponus on this question, and the Aristotelian background, see F. Haas (1997), 4f, 281–83. Sorabji (1983), 247–49 cites a long history of Christian and Islamic thinkers who read Aristotle as accepting the creation of form from nothing.

15. This argument seems similar to Augustine's *City of God* XII.16, but direct influence is unlikely.

1044b21–24).[16] These considerations render plausible Procopius' claim that Greek philosophers accept the creation of form from nothing.[17]

Procopius uses this background to turn the Neoplatonic-Aristotelian argument about the instantaneous creation of form against the Neoplatonists. If form were created from nothing, then form comes from God. Form is better than matter, so if God has control of form, he should also be able to create matter from nothing. Otherwise one must assume that God could do something harder (creating form) but not something easier (creating matter). This, in Procopius' view, is absurd. Procopius probes difficulties in the Neoplatonic treatment of form and matter, as Philoponus would do with greater logical rigour later in the sixth century. Procopius' attempt to use Neoplatonic arguments and axioms against the Neoplatonists points to the heterogeneous boundaries between local cultures in Gaza.

In a final argument for *creatio ex nihilo*, Procopius utilizes the Neoplatonic idea of matter being suitable for form. Plato had argued that the receptacle can receive each and every form, whereas proximate matter on earth is only suitable for particular forms (e.g. *Tim.* 50c).[18] If forms are created from nothing, then matter must also be created from nothing in order to be suitable for the forms it receives. If the Platonists maintain that matter is not created in this way and hence is not identically from God, there can be no affinity between form and matter:

> How did [matter] come into being as suitable for the forms which are from God, if it is alien to God and did not come into being through him?
>
> [πῶς δὲ ξένη οὖσα Θεοῦ καὶ μὴ παρ' αὐτοῦ γενομένη, τῶν εἰδῶν τῶν ἐξ αὐτοῦ γέγονε δεκτική] (29B)

This argument combines the idea of the suitability of matter with the idea of the instantaneous creation of immanent forms. Again, it seeks to show that Neoplatonic arguments are mutually inconsistent. Certainly, Neoplatonists would have been surprised to see themselves depicted as believing that matter is

16. See further Sorabji (1983), 11 n. 5 for entities which come into being without a process.

17. Philoponus also argued that Aristotle accepted that form was created from nothing, using this claim within an argument that motion was not eternal. Aside from the *Contra Proclum* texts already cited, see *Contra Aristotelem* in Simplicius *in Phys.* 1142,1–28. In another argument, Philoponus argues by analogy that God can destroy matter into not-being, just as he does with form (*Contra Aristotelem* in Simplicius *in Phys.* 1177,10–26).

18. See F. Haas (1997), 4ff. for discussion and further texts from the history of Platonism to support the widespread acceptance of this distinction. Aubry (2008) has recently discussed the concept of *epitêdeiotês* in the context of the question of whether matter has an active ability to receive form or whether it should be conceptualized as purely passive.

an independent principle. Procopius' argument makes sense within his strong distinction between the eternal creator and the contingent, limited creations but fails to do justice to Neoplatonism.

5.3 Matter, Freedom, and Determinism

Immediately following this discussion, Procopius begins to approach a new set of problems associated with the idea that the cosmos is coeternal with God (Πῶς δὲ καὶ ὁ κόσμος τῷ Θεῷ συναΐδιος). If the creation is coeternal with God, Procopius believes that it will be given its existence 'by the necessity of nature, not by the [divine] will' [ἔσται γὰρ ἀνάγκῃ φύσεως, οὐ βουλήσει, τὸ εἶναι λαχών] (29D). Here is an explicit statement of the equation between 'eternal' and 'necessary' which we have been observing, and relates to the earlier discussion of Plotinus and Origen on the divine will.[19] Later in his *Commentary*, Procopius makes the same point: the Son and Spirit create along with the Father voluntarily and with power (βουλήσει, ἐξουσίᾳ) (77C). In the Prologue's response to the Greeks, Procopius argues that if matter is coeternal with God, then God is not free. We have seen that Neoplatonists such as Proclus do not think that the eternity of matter constrains any creative principle in any way, so we need to ask how Procopius tried to make sense of his (for Neoplatonists) novel claim.

What does Procopius want the phrase ἀνάγκη φύσεως to communicate? The first thing to note is that the phrase is predominantly a Christian usage.[20] Christian authors begin to use the phrase in extant literature from the fourth century. Authors represented include Synesius, Gregory of Nyssa, John Chrysostom, Athanasius, Cyril of Alexandria, John of Caesarea, and Epiphanius. A number of the Christian writers employ the term in discussion of heresies, particularly Manichaeism, to attack the idea that nature is deterministic and evil. Non-Christian sources also use variants, using phrases derived from cognates of ἀνάγκη and φύσις. It is therefore worth investigating some of these non-Christian uses to begin to define the semantic possibilities of the phrase within the community against which Procopius argued.

Plutarch represents a wide variety of phrases derived from ἀνάγκη/φύσις cognates. In one passage, Plato is praised for subjecting the compulsions of the

19. See above, 4.1.

20. There is one possible usage in Satyrus, 'possible', because it relies on editorial emendation. See Satyrus, *Vita Euripidis* (*P. Oxy.* 9.1176, fr. 37.3 Arrighetti): 'Ζεὺς/ [εἴ]τ' ἀνάγκ[η]/ [φύσεω]ς εἴτ[ε]'. The conjecture is plausible. Cf. Euripides, *Troiades*, 886. Philo of Alexandria also uses the term, suggesting that the Christian usage is part of a wider Judeo-Christian discourse. See *Hypothetica sive Apologia pro Judaeis* (Cohn-Reiter, vol. 6, 200).

physical world to divine principles (Plutarch, *Life of Nicias* 23.5.4). The 'necessity of nature' stands for the non-rational elements of the physical world, the constraints of desires and bodily or material existence, which for Plato are not characteristics of intelligible reality.[21] In another passage, Plutarch distinguishes the demands of nature from customs, actions which are preferable rather than necessary (Plutarch, *Life of Romulus* 11.2.3). There is no denigration of the physical world, but there is again an acknowledgement that physical existence provides a set of boundary conditions for human existence. In a third possibility, necessity (circumstances) can make people act against their nature (Plutarch, *Life of Lucullus* 6.2.3). Necessity is uncoupled from nature and can be set aside for the purposes of this discussion. In a fourth usage, perhaps most relevant to the present discussion, the concept is removed from the physical world and applied to a higher metaphysical level. 'Natural Necessity' becomes a divine power which distributes good and evil fortunes to humans (Plutarch, *Life of Marius* 23.1.4: πραγμάτων ἀναγκαία φύσις). In this fourth usage of ἀνάγκη/φύσις cognates, it would be ridiculous to suggest that the divine power was constrained by nature as Procopius seems to think possible. Rather, necessity is the divine power which can act to infringe human freedom.

If we move to more explicitly philosophical texts, Plotinus employs the concept of the necessity of nature far more frequently than the later Neoplatonists (Plotinus, *Enn.* 3.3.1.10; 4.8.7.20; 5.5.12.8; 6.8.2.14: τῇ τῆς φύσεως ἀνάγκῃ). In his treatise *On Free Will and the Will of the One* (*Enn.* 6.8), the phrase is akin to Plutarch's first and second usages. One possible way in which things might be up to us, Plotinus argues, is that free action happens when there is both correct rational identification of right action and correct motivation for that action (τῷ ὀρθῷ λογισμῷ καὶ τῇ ὀρθῇ ὀρέξει) (*Enn.* 6.8.2.10).[22] But if this is the case, which comes first? If correct desire is first, and if that desire includes physical elements, then the soul, which is responsible for rational evaluation (τῷ ὀρθῷ λογισμῷ), is attendant on the desires of the body and is in that sense constrained 'by the necessity of nature' (τῇ τῆς φύσεως ἀνάγκῃ) (*Enn.* 6.8.10–15). Higher hypostases cannot be constrained by lower ones, but they can be led astray, as it were, by directing their attention improperly towards lower levels of the hierarchy.[23] When this happens, they fall down the chain by necessity. Hierocles looked at the same problem from the opposite angle. If we align our desires to reason, we

21. Cf. Plato, *Tim.* 47eff., where the cosmos is a compromise between reason and necessity.

22. This idea is given modern form in Iris Murdoch's essay 'The Idea of Perfection', in her example of the conscientious mother-in-law. See Murdoch (2001), 16ff.

23. Damascius makes a similar point in an approximately contemporary work (*in Phaed I*, 274).

can overcome the necessity of nature (*CPGV* XIII, 14.7f.: κοσμήσαιμεν τῇ ὀρθῇ προαιρέσει τὴν ἀνάγκην τῆς φύσεως).

These ideas take us back to the idea of 'persuaded necessity' (Plato, *Tim.* 48a): for Plato the cosmos is a product of necessity and intellect, and intellect rules necessity by persuading it to some good end. This is congruent with Plato's account of 'necessary desires' in the *Republic* (*Rep.* 558d–e). Desires which serve a good purpose, say health or survival, are naturally necessary and reasonable, since they have been teleologically ordered (cf. *Tim.* 69c–d).[24]

In the other three passages where Plotinus employs the phrase, he utilizes this idea of the teleological ordering of the cosmos. The 'necessity of nature' is supposed to refer to the ineluctability of the operation of eternal procession and return which provides the metaphysical order of the cosmos. So Plotinus writes: 'Everything desires [the One] and aims towards it by the necessity of nature, as if everything had been given the prophecy that without it they could not exist' [Πάντα γὰρ ὀρέγεται ἐκείνου καὶ ἐφίεται αὐτοῦ φύσεως ἀνάγκῃ, ὥσπερ ἀπομεμαντευμένα, ὡς ἄνευ αὐτοῦ οὐ δύναται εἶναι] (*Enn.* 5.5.12.7–9).[25] Similarly at *Ennead* 3.3.1.9–10, the return to unity is a 'necessity of nature': Ἐκ γὰρ ἑνός τινος ὁρμηθέντα πάντα εἰς ἓν συνέρχεται φύσεως ἀνάγκῃ. Proclus has a similar thought: *in Parm.* 1116,14–15: φύσεως γὰρ ἀνάγκῃ πάντα τὰ μετὰ τὸ πρῶτον ἐφίεται τοῦ πρώτου.

'Necessity of nature' can describe the teleologically ordered procession of a lower hypostasis from a higher one, as in the case of Soul from Intellect:

> So the way out of the Intellect is a descent into its worse extreme—for it does not ascend [in the movement of procession] into the transcendence of the One, but it necessarily operates out from itself and does not have the power to remain within itself, and it comes rather by the necessity and law of nature to Soul [ἀνάγκῃ καὶ νόμῳ μέχρι ψυχῆς], since that is its goal. (*Enn.* 4.8.7.17–21)[26]

Creation by procession from the One, the act of elaboration of the simplicity of the One into the multiplicity of the Many, is characterized as a necessity of nature and recalls the logic supporting the procession of Proclus' metaphysical hierarchy analysed above. 'Nature' (φύσις) does not signify the physical world. Rather, it seems to

24. My thanks to Peter Adamson for this point in his paper 'Making a Virtue of Necessity: *Anangkê* in Plato and Plotinus'. Adamson notes that Plotinus is more negative about these goods, rejecting the idea that they contribute to the purpose of humanity and accepting only that they contribute to our existence (*Enn.* 1.4.6–7).

25. Quotations from Plotinus are from Armstrong's translation.

26. Cf. Damascius *Princ.* 42.

describe both the essential ontological characteristics of an entity and the essential metaphysical structure of the cosmos. It is a physical necessity for Soul to process from Intellect or for the human soul to return to Soul simply both because of what Intellect, Soul, and the human soul are, and because of the sort of universe they inhabit. Similarly, the production of matter is necessary because it results naturally from the metaphysical constraints of the operation of the higher principles (*Enn.* 3.2.3.3–5; cf. 3.3.1.9–10). The entities of the physical world are necessary not by their own nature, but because their intelligible causes are necessary. All the processions from the One are a 'necessity of nature' because procession and return are part of the nature of the One. In this sense 'necessity' signals that there are metaphysical (rather than logical) reasons why something must or cannot happen.[27]

This may appear to imply that the One is bound by the necessity of nature, since the One does not stand outside the metaphysical structure of reality. In this reading, the category of 'nature' would be understood as even more primal than the One.[28] We have already seen, however, that Plotinus firmly rejects this view, as would later Neoplatonists.[29] Necessity does apply to the lower orders of the metaphysical hierarchy, but does not apply to the One, who can be said, albeit with the necessary caveats, to will his own nature. Furthermore, the One is understood as constitutive of the whole of reality, so there can be nothing external to the One which could act as an external constraint or compulsion on him.

This brief survey shows that within the Greek philosophical community, phrases such as τῇ τῆς φύσεως ἀνάγκῃ were capable of communicating a small but flexible range of meanings.[30] In the context of ethics and discussions of human free will, such phrases contrasted with the freedom which Platonists believed consisted in rational action. In discussions of the generation and reunification of different hypostatic levels, the phrase identified basic truths about the metaphysical structure of the universe. In both contexts, it communicates key aspects of a Neoplatonic account of freedom.

27. See Adamson (n. 24 above).

28. For a detailed argument along these lines, see Foster (1934, 1935, 1936).

29. See above, 4.1.

30. A wider survey of the concept of necessity in Platonic thought is needed. For pertinent comments on necessity in Plato and Plotinus, see Adamson (n. 24 above). The Platonic cosmos is a 'union of necessity and intellect' (*Tim.* 48a Zeyl trans.). Necessity may be persuaded by intellect and thus teleologically ordered or unpersuaded. If unpersuaded, it cannot be otherwise and is to be regretted. If persuaded, it may be otherwise, but may still be regrettable. In this case, necessity determines what exists when regrettable alternative possibilities compete. For detailed discussion of this schema, see Adamson (n. 24 above). He argues that Aristotle *Metaph.* V.5, 1015a20–b9 sets out senses of *anangkê* which are consistent with this schema.

Procopius has both these sets of meanings in his sights, and he also adds a distinctively Christian twist to his argument. To make matter coeternal with God, he argues, is to make God dependent on, and therefore constrained by, something which should be on a much lower ontological level. Procopius should be understood as claiming that the Neoplatonic view of the eternity of matter makes it possible for God to be constrained by material reality in the same way that humans are.[31] This argument builds on his earlier claim, repeated at this point of his argument, that making matter a co-principle of creation necessarily eliminates divine sovereignty. God is necessarily constrained by matter in the sense that he cannot exist as an independent principle of creation. If matter did not exist, God would not exist, which again, in Procopius' view, makes God improperly dependent on matter. This claim recalls Origen's insistence that God in himself is beyond the action of willing creation. God can be God without the creative act of volition.

More fundamentally, Procopius' attack on the coeternity of matter is an attack on Neoplatonic claims about the universe's metaphysically necessary structure. Plotinus had argued that the lower orders of creation from the Intellect down were produced necessarily, and we have seen that such statements can be reconciled with the claim that the One acts 'as if' voluntarily, given the freely willed 'activities' of the One which just are his 'nature' (*Enn.* 6.8.13). Procopius' claim that divine choice defines the metaphysical framework thus does not yet get to the point at issue with the Neoplatonists. It is not that Procopius' God does not freely enact his own nature; as in the case of the One, he does. But 'freely enact' for Procopius means choosing real difference rather than the eternal self-thinking and self-actualization which characterizes the 'activity' of the One and results in the production of the necessary lower orders of reality. Thus, Procopius' God's independent, sovereign choice in creation is properly characterized as an act of grace and love, rather than the necessary consequence of the One's goodness. Procopius' creation is thus radically contingent, in harmony with ideas we saw in Origen.

This criticism draws on a large body of Christian literature in which 'necessity of nature' stands in opposition to free, gracious choice. In Christian texts, the phrase ἀνάγκη φύσεως is often contrasted with verbs of willing (βούλομαι, θέλω) and nouns expressing freedom of choice and individual freedom from constraint (ἐξουσία, ἐλευθερία, βούλησις). For example, Athanasius claims that mortality is a necessity of nature, not something which humans intend, or

31. Of course, the whole point of the Neoplatonic scheme of procession and return was to avoid such a criticism. Procopius is not, I think, ignorant about this point. Rather, he simply thinks it is rationally unsustainable.

which they have the power to avoid (*Or. tres contra Arianos* 3.57.5 (Metzler and Savvidis): οὐ κατ' ἰδίαν ἐξουσίαν, ἀλλ' ἀνάγκῃ φύσεως καὶ μὴ θέλων ἀποθνήσει). John Chrysostom contrasts the necessity of nature with the freedom and enacted capability of choice (*in Ep. ad Romanos* PG 60 p. 517, line 1f, ἀνάγκῃ φύσεως versus ἐλευθερία προαιρέσεως; *in Ep. ad Titum* PG 62 p. 667 line 28f, ἀνάγκῃ φύσεως versus ἐξουσίᾳ προαιρέσεως). Procopius' argument fits neatly into the assumptions of these texts: creation may either come into existence by an act of will (βούλησει) or by the necessity of nature (ἀνάγκῃ φύσεως) (see also 77C).

Of course, Neoplatonists might have ready answers to Procopius' argument, or simply be mystified by it. They might claim that god is coeternal with matter, but that matter is not a principle alongside god. In every moment, they might claim in harmony with Plato, it depends on God's will for its eternal existence. Again, Procopius' unstated and axiomatic premise is that eternity equals necessity, whereas something that is willed implies contingency. What is contingent cannot be eternal. The eternal existence of matter, for Christians, means that matter necessarily exists. It is thus non-contingent; its necessary existence impedes God's ability to will it.

Thus, Procopius tries to show that the necessary procession of matter is an incoherent idea, and that it leads to impious or absurd consequences about God's continual engagement in his creation. He also argues that the eternity of matter limits divine freedom and sovereignty. For Procopius, procession is untenable first because it would mean that God did not control the creative process. The 'procession' account of creation means that 'God does not have the power to control his creative impulses' [μὴ δυναμένου τοῦ θεοῦ τὰς ποιητικὰς ἐπέχειν ὁρμάς] (29D). The first stage of this claim is an *ad hominem* smeer: Procopius draws on the connotations of ἡ ὁρμή, which refers to irrational desires rather than rational judgement, for example, in Platonic psychology to mischaracterize Neoplatonic procession as impulsive and irrational.[32]

Of course, a Neoplatonist is able to reply that it is precisely the One's perfection, not any impulse, which rationally results in creation. Procopius is on firmer ground when he argues that there seems to be no reason that the perfection of the One should result in a limited creative act. The One's perfection and goodness should imply an unlimited creation produced by the one's perfect and hence unlimited goodness, so the perfectly good One has no power to 'hold back' his creative acts. Therefore, Procopius argues, there is no mechanism in the Neoplatonic system to stop the One creating many worlds

32. He shows knowledge of this psychology, at least as mediated by Gregory of Nyssa, at 117C–D, which is modelled on *de op. hom.* 145.36ff.

(29D): 'How did he stop making, and not create a series of cosmoses?' [πῶς ποιῶν ἐπαύσατο, καὶ μὴ καθεκάστην κόσμους δημιουργεῖ?]. Procopius does not need to spell out explicitly the absurd implications of the theory of many worlds to his Neoplatonic audience, since Platonists from Plato onwards had ruled out this possibility (although believing in multiple worlds is a minority position found in Epicurus, Anaximander, and Democritus: Lucretius *De rerum Natura* 1.73; Diogenes Laertius 2.1,2; 9.44; cf. *Tim.* 11a–e). This argument again turns Neoplatonic premises against Neoplatonists.

Procopius also claims that procession inadequately distinguishes between the being of God and the being of the cosmos. God will come to depend on his creatures, who will fill out the divine being (29D). We will see a similar argument in Aeneas and Zacharias. Procopius' objection to creatures being able to fill out the divine being may be related to Trinitarian distinctions between the being or substance of God and that of the world (see above, 4.1 and below, 6.4), although there is no mention of Trinitarian problems in the prologue to Procopius' *Commentary*. 'How', asks Procopius, 'will the creations not be forming an essential part of the divine being, if indeed when these things are not, he will not be a creator by nature' [Πῶς δὲ οὐκ ἔσται συμπληρωτικὰ τὰ ποιήματα τῆς θείας οὐσίας, εἴ γε τούτων οὐκ ὄντων, οὐκ ἔσται φύσει δημιουργός] (29D). This again raises the subtle difference between Procopius' account of creation and schemes such as that we have seen, for example, in Plotinus. Since in Plotinus, the cosmos arises from the 'willed' nature of the One, if there were no creations, the nature of the One would not be that of a creator. In Procopius' scheme, however, God may be understood as a creator even were there no material creations, since his freely willed act of creation is externally directed.

Furthermore, if what is created does derive ultimately from God's substance, then God is, for Procopius, dependent on his creations in a way that strips God of his proper freedoms. When one of his creations ceases to exist, God will also cease to exist (29D). This argument is meant to apply not to individual cases of creations dying, but rather to the original state of the cosmos and hence is a criticism of eternal matter, although Procopius is not explicit on this point, framing it only as a rhetorical question emphatically expecting the answer 'no': Πῶς... εἴ γε τούτων οὐκ ὄντων, οὐκ ἔσται φύσει δημιουργός; (29D). In these arguments, Procopius insists on a radical separation of God from the world in order to guarantee divine freedom. Divine freedom consists both in radical independence and in freedom of choice. God cannot depend on any other necessary existent, and if the creation is eternal, it is also necessary.

This argument is radically different from Neoplatonic monism. It is designed to justify his Christian version of creation by making it appear more plausible than the philosophical one. The central claim is that creation by emanation from the One cannot provide an appropriate account of divine freedom in that it inadequately separates God from the world. But Christians and Neoplatonists are poles apart on the question of what is taken to be 'appropriate' and 'adequate' on this question. Certainly, some arguments (such as the claims about the creation of form from nothing and the inability of Neoplatonists to give reasons why emanation from the One does not result in multiple worlds) may give committed Neoplatonists pause for thought. Yet the argument surely works most forcefully against Christians in the schools tempted to give up on Christian distinctions between creator and creature, and the subsequent identification of eternity and necessity, than against an audience already committed to the detail of Neoplatonism. Such an audience would require a coherent set of claims to offer in response to Neoplatonism, but may not have felt the need to employ the principle of charity towards Neoplatonic opponents.

Because the eternity of matter is taken to limit divine freedom, Procopius then offers arguments against the idea that the cosmos is eternal. His central argument probes the idea of the eternity of matter in relation to the divine creation of forms. A series of *modus tollens* arguments tries to show that divine creation of form is inconsistent with eternal matter. Suppose, says Procopius, that there is eternally pre-existing matter. Even the Neoplatonists agree that God had to give form to the disordered substrate. This leaves a number of possibilities. Perhaps there was, by a stroke of luck, just enough matter for the forms God wanted to create. But in this case, God was dependent on an accidental contingency, and since (says Procopius, drawing on Neoplatonic assumptions) accidental contingencies are not eternal, matter is not eternal (e.g. *ET* 97).[33] Also, since God was dependent on an accidental circumstance, and only what is necessary could be eternal, God is not eternal, which is absurd. Two alternatives remain. God could have devised more forms than he strictly wanted or fewer than he was able to. If more, then the 'mass of matter conquered' the divine will (32A), by making God do more than he really wanted to. The other option in this prong of the dilemma is that God devised only as many forms as he could, but left some matter unformed because he lacked power. This is impious (32A–B).

If, however, God created fewer forms than he was able to, Procopius thinks that the picture is somewhat brighter, though still to be rejected. In this case, we could argue that God 'unwillingly held back the abundance of his power' [τὸ πλεονάζον τῆς ἑαυτοῦ δυνάμεως ἄκων ἐπέσχε] and devised no form for any further creation (32B). This is a further argument against the eternity of matter, on the grounds that eternal matter would constrain God's will. God would have

33. This argument can be found in the Alexandrian tradition of Genesis exegesis. See e.g. Origen, *Comm Gen* in Eusebius, *PE* 7.20.

had to do less than he could have, because there was insufficient matter for his ideas. Yet if God created fewer forms than he was able to and 'held back part of his power, then he was also able to hold back the universe, and not establish the cosmos as coeternal' [Εἰ δὲ μέρος ἐπέσχε τῆς δυνάμεως, καὶ τὸ πᾶν ἐπέχειν ἠδύνατο καὶ μὴ συναΐδιον ὑποστῆσαι τὸν κόσμον] (32B). This argument should be linked to his earlier argument against Neoplatonic derivational monism, namely that Neoplatonists fail to explain how procession from the One can be limited. While God was unwilling to create less, and hence was limited by the quantity of matter at hand, he would not create less involuntarily. In this prong of the dilemma, we see God able to will to hold back his power.

This is the possibility which Procopius wants to hold open for the Christian God. Holding back his power would not be a mark against God, because he remains a priori capable of further creations, despite deciding to stop creating when he did.[34] Rejecting the logic of creation by derivation, and preferring instead a biblically based doctrine of *creatio ex nihilo*, Procopius finds grounds to argue against the idea of the eternity of matter and proposes a view of creation and divine freedom—independence and freedom of choice—which differs from the standard Neoplatonic views outlined above.[35]

Procopius offers one further argument against the eternity of matter. We might term it the 'Goldilocks argument' (cf. Basil, *Hex.* 2.2). If matter is eternal, either God was faced with too much matter, too little matter, or it was just right. If there was too little, it is difficult to see where he could have got the rest from, unless you accept *creatio ex nihilo*, which the Neoplatonists do not (33C). If there was too much, another uncreated universe remains ready to be given form. At the very least, there is a lump of disordered matter still in existence. Both of these things are absurd (32C). The 'just right' option has already been explored, when Procopius argued that it would make God dependent on a fluke (32A). In this argument, Procopius shifts ground and argues for the other possibility, that the quantity of matter in the universe was both just right and rationally planned. But if it was rationally planned, then there must be a power that did the planning:

> some fortune before God prepared its measure, both in proportion to the requirement of the cosmos and in proportion to its own power.
>
> [τύχησις πρὸ Θεοῦ τὸ μέτρον αὐτῷ καὶ πρὸς χρείαν τοῦ κόσμου καὶ πρὸς τὴν ἰδίαν παρεσκεύασε δύναμιν] (32C)

34. Procopius has given two reasons for this decision: that if God was incapable of stopping his creative impulse, he is dependent on irrationality, and that multiple worlds would exist.

35. Since Procopius rests his argument when he has shown that God could refrain from creating the cosmos, all he has proved is that matter could be non-eternal. This seems to me to be a valid criticism of Procopius' argument as it stands. His polemic against the coeternity of matter with God shows that he wanted to argue for a stronger case than he has at this point.

This leads either to the untenable position of God being dependent on another deity, or perhaps to an infinite regress, and is therefore taken to be further grounds to reject the eternity of matter.

5.4 Time and Cause

Procopius then turns his attention to how the universe was caused.[36] His guiding assumption, which he now attempts to make plausible, is that 'what is atemporal is uncreated and what is uncreated does not have a beginning' [τὸ γὰρ ἄχρονον ἄκτιστον, τὸ δὲ ἄκτιστον ἄναρχον] (32C). He argues that 'And God alone does not have a beginning [Θεὸς δὲ μόνος τὸ ἄναρχον], in whatever way you would have understood the sense of 'the beginning' [τὴν ἀρχὴν], whether with respect to cause [καθ' αἰτίαν] or with respect to time [κατὰ χρόνον] which belongs to the eternal alone' (32C–D). We should read Procopius as alluding to and rejecting the distinctions between temporal and causal origins which Taurus had made, and which inspired contemporary Neoplatonists to argue that the cosmos was created (has a causal origin) but eternal (does not have a temporal origin) (32C–D).[37] Procopius claims that God is uniquely eternal, and so uniquely necessary.

Thus far, Procopius has tried to show that matter is temporally finite, but he now turns his attention to how the universe is caused. Procopius again seeks to preserve divine freedom, freedom which he thinks could be threatened by particular causal accounts of the universe. He begins by focusing on two alternative modes of the causation of the cosmos. The first is causation which is analogous to the sun causing a ray; the second is of a colonizer constructing a city (32D) (cf. Basil, *Hex.* 1.7). For Procopius, the second analogy is closer to the truth, since he wants to prove that God may be an eternal creator without his creations also being eternal. God is like the founder of a city who must build a community where before there was none. In this section Procopius returns to the first 'Greek' objection to the Christian account, which was that the creations must be eternal if the creator is eternally creating. The new aspect of his argument, however, is elucidation of problems about causation instead of temporality.

The 'sun and its ray' analogy is rejected because it does not distinguish between the eternity of God and the finitude of the creation: 'It is not possible

36. He has already rejected procession, but the main focus of his earlier argument was on procession and matter. He now tries to find further arguments to reject procession as a causal mechanism.

37. For Taurus' synthesis, see above, 4.3. Aeneas and Zacharias similarly display knowledge of this debate within Neoplatonism and come down on the opposing side with Plutarch and Atticus. See below, 6.1.

for what is created to exist eternally and to be coextensive with the eternity of the maker' [ἀλλ' οὐκ ἠδύνατό τι γεννητὸν ἀεὶ εἶναι καὶ συμπαρεκτείνεσθαι τῇ τοῦ ποιοῦντος ἀϊδιότητι] (32D). This should be seen as a further rejection of the Neoplatonic idea of creation by procession and return, this time on the grounds that such a view of *causation* is inconsistent with divine uniqueness and freedom. It is inconsistent with uniqueness, because the ray is of the same substance as the sun. It is inconsistent with divine freedom because the sun cannot choose to produce the ray. It just has to produce the ray because of what it is. This view of causation is inconsistent with the view that God's act of creation was an act of will; we have already seen that divine will is central to Procopius' view of divine freedom.

Christological debates may influence Procopius' rejection of the sun/ray analogy on the basis of divine uniqueness.[38] If God begets the cosmos like the sun does a ray, God and the cosmos would be both coeternal and consubstantial (συναΐδιος, ὁμοούσιος) and the uniqueness of God would be undermined. The account of causation suggested by the sun/ray analogy is rejected because it elides the difference between how the Son is generated by the Father (coeternally and consubstantially) and how the world is generated by God (as a truly other entity).

While the sun/ray analogy is rejected because it implies that the ray is eternal, its attractiveness for Christians consists in the fact that it implies that the creator is eternally and unchangeably creating. Procopius wants to preserve this aspect of the Neoplatonic position. Like the Neoplatonists, Procopius believes that God is unchangeable. Yet his account of a God who creates a finite world makes this claim particularly problematic. If the world is not eternal, then it looks like there was a time when God was not creating, and God either changed when he finally decided to create, or else was at one time ignorant of how to create, or unreasonably decided not to display his goodness by creating, at least for a while, or was inactive for a time before he created. All of these arguments had been used by Proclus in the *Eighteen Arguments* to demonstrate the eternity of the world; the problem is formulated in just these terms by Zacharias (*Ammonius* 115ff.). Procopius thus uses the builder analogy for cosmic causation in order to begin to make a case for the mutual consistency of believing in a finite creation and an eternally creative creator who could avoid these Neoplatonic criticisms. He argues that 'the building does not come into being with the builder, nor the boat with the ship-maker. For the creative activity is

38. Christological and Trinitarian considerations are brought into the argument explicitly by Aeneas and Zacharias. See below, 6.4.

in the creator [Η μὲν γὰρ δημιουργία ἐν τῷ δημιουργῷ]; the creation is after [μετὰ] the creator' (32D–33A). When the builder is not building, he is still a builder. What the builder builds is different from what the builder is, and is subsequent to his act of construction. The analogy has its roots in the Platonic tradition, drawing on the connotations of *demiourgos*, the 'craftsman' of Plato's *Timaeus*. The builder analogy was used by Atticus (Eusebius, *PE* XV,6) and by Philo, and is also used by Aeneas and Zacharias.[39]

This account of causation preserves God from the charge that he is subject to change by suggesting that God's being is not affected by his creative actions and it protects him from the charge that he was ever idle. God simply is the creator, regardless of whether he is creating.[40] Note that it also goes some way to avoiding the charge of capriciousness, which is a main concern of Aeneas and Zacharias (see below, 6.3). If God is sometimes creating and sometimes not, might run the objection, then humans have no grounds for trusting in the steadfastness of God. We would instead be dealing with a God who might do one thing today, and another thing tomorrow. The builder analogy cuts this objection off by pointing to God's unchanging essence and thus secures trust in God's promise that he will transform the present world into immortality.

The builder analogy is somewhat dangerous because it may put God into the realm of time, making him subject to the constraints of temporal existence. Procopius does not deal with this problem or acknowledge its existence. He never uses uniquely temporal vocabulary. Words like συνυπάρχει, συνεισάξει, συμπαρεκτείνεσθαι, μετά, and ἅμα do not necessarily have temporal connotations, and suggest that Procopius does not conceive of God as creating temporally. Procopius elsewhere defines the act of creation as the beginning of time, in commenting on Genesis 1:1 to avoid infinite regress to an unreachable beginning which would result from conceding that the initial act of creation was capable of being divided (36C–37B).[41] The aorist (ἐποίησεν), he argues, is intended to convey this point: divine will and creation are indivisible (Δηλοῖ οὖν ὡς ἅμα δὲ Θεὸς ἠβουλήθη καὶ γέγονε τὰ γενόμενα) (37B).

Up to this point, Procopius' argument has dealt with problems current among contemporary Neoplatonists. However, in a short section which concludes his comments on causation, Procopius turns his attention towards Stoic views

39. Baltes (1976), 45–63. It is plausible that Procopius, Aeneas, and Zacharias all had access to some of the works of Atticus and Philo directly, perhaps through the library at Caesarea. Aeneas is one source for Atticus' thought, apparently independently of Eusebius (*PE* XV, 4–6).

40. Procopius does not meet the objection that the builder is merely a potential, rather than an actual builder. For this move, see Philoponus' adept use of Aristotle to argue that this is not the sort of change that a god need worry about (*Contra Proclum* 3,44.1–55,22).

41. This passage paraphrases Basil, *Hex.*, 1.6.

about creation. This may be best understood by considering Procopius' sources. A key source was Basil's *Hexameron*, from which Procopius quotes directly at times, and which was partly directed against contemporary (third- and fourth-century) Stoic determinism, and determinism associated with astrology (especially *Hex.* II). Like contemporary Neoplatonists, Procopius rejects Stoic theories. This is further evidence for the particular character of his main Greek opponents, as well as showing that Procopius has a grasp of topics in the history of Greek philosophy. Procopius' main argument is directed against the idea that the cosmos comes into being necessarily and repeatedly in an infinite series of cosmic cycles.[42] For Procopius, this idea is again inconsistent with the free creativity of God.

A number of factors combined to produce the Stoics' strongly deterministic outlook.[43] The Stoics claim that material causes necessarily entail material effects. The effect of any cause is also unique. There is a one-to-one mapping of material cause to effect and effects always have material causes. This claim also draws strength from the idea of eternal recurrence. Eternal recurrence claims that the universe comes into being and is destroyed before coming into being again. But world $n + 1$ is otherwise exactly the same as world n. The uniqueness of the possible world, in any of its incarnations, means that causes are both unique and always produce the same effect. Within this scheme of unique and deterministic material causes, it is difficult to see where a Platonic demiurge or a Christian God could fit.

Therefore Procopius is antagonistic. He has no complex argument about Stoic determinism, presumably because his main audience (Neoplatonists, including Christians who had been exposed to Neoplatonism) and his main intellectual opponents (pagan Neoplatonists and Christians too close to Neoplatonism) had long rejected it. But he does offer two arguments against the Stoic conclusions. First, he argues that Stoic determinism limits God's creativity. If everything is preordained, 'there is nothing new in the cosmos' (33B). The Stoic system makes God subject to fate (33B). Procopius' argument returns to a critique of a putative pre-existing natural structure of the cosmos which he thinks sets limits on how God can act. Part of his argument for divine freedom is that God chooses (and so constructs) what is natural. God chooses the form that the basic structure of the universe has, rather than being bound by a logically prior natural system. Procopius then argues that the Stoic doctrine of eternal recurrence removes

42. The notion of cosmic cycles, of course, had pre-Socratic antecedents, which Procopius could have known about had he read Aristotle's *Physics*.

43. For two recent treatments, see Bobzien (2001); Salles (2005). See also the section on Stoic logic in Baltzly (2008). On Stoic causation, see Hankinson (2001), chapter 7, especially 238–47.

the need for a creator. If there is an eternal restoration of the world in a series of cycles, there is no reason to believe that God created any iteration of the cosmos (33B).

In this argument against the Stoics, a further fundamental Christian objection to the eternity of the world appears. If the world is eternal, there is no grounds for believing in the 'second coming', the re-creation and transformation of the cosmos into a really new heavenly creation, when everything is perfected by Christ. The Stoic cyclic creation of identical realities removes the possibility of change for the better. This is a particular problem for the Christian belief in a final transformation of reality into paradise. But it also more generally renders the Christian view of salvation history implausible. We have already seen that Procopius believed that human history moves towards a goal and that the coming of Christ brings in a new sort of reality to which earlier peoples only had veiled access. But the Stoic idea that each world is just like the last provides no grounds for such a view of history, which is partly founded on accepting the possibility of radically new events within history. These are objections that we will see Aeneas and Zacharias make much of—more than Procopius himself does in the prologue to the *Commentary*—but I suggest that they also sit behind Procopius' rejection of the eternal creation of the world.

5.5 Theodicy

Much of Procopius' discussion of creation is closely tied to ethics. Within the arguments about causation, Procopius includes a discussion of whether evil is a first principle of the universe. The problem, as Procopius sees it, is that since the putative coeternity of the cosmos would upset the proper order of causation, there is no reason to suppose that good precedes evil (note again the collapsing of the distinction between beginning in cause and beginning in time):

> If the cosmos is simultaneous with [God] and is nothing new, evil is simultaneous with the cosmos. But if this is the case, then evil is simultaneous with God. And either [evil] is entirely without beginning, or from Him. Both alternatives are absurd.
>
> [Εἰ ἅμα κόσμος ⟨ὁ Θεὸς⟩ καὶ οὐδὲν καινὸν, ἅμα τῷ κόσμῳ κακία· εἰ δὲ τοῦτο, ἅμα Θεὸς ἡ κακία· καὶ ἢ ἄναρχος αὕτη παντελῶς, ἢ ἐξ αὐτοῦ. Ἄμφω δὲ ἄτοπα] (33A)

The problem is only magnified when one considers that God and evil demons would also be coeternal, if the cosmos is coeternal with God (εἰ ἅμα Θεὸς ἅμα κόσμος, ἅμα Θεὸς καὶ δαίμονες πονηροί; cf. Basil, *Hex.* 2.4) (33A). Like thinkers such as Plotinus and Augustine before him, Procopius rejects the idea of substantial evil (33A). But if evil and God are coeternal, then evil does have substance, and either there are two first principles, or God gave substance to evil. In this section, Procopius is addressing Neoplatonic debates about the nature of evil. His argument is brief, but it is sufficient to show that (along with contemporary Neoplatonists) he rejects the idea that evil is a principle of being, again allying him with post-Proclan Neoplatonism.

Closer inspection of Procopius' argument through a more detailed comparison with Proclus' yields a more subtle difference. Proclus argued that since there is only one first principle, pure or absolute evil does not exist, whereas absolute good does (Proclus, *On the Existence of Evils*, chapter 9). However, evil mixed with good does exist in Proclus' scheme (ibid.), by virtue of the limited and provisional nature of particular entities.[44] These two premises yield two further conclusions: first, that there is no evil contrary to the Good; and secondly and more generally, that anything evil must be contrary to a particular, rather than an absolute, good.

The first conclusion is what we have already seen Procopius accept, and then use against the Neoplatonic claim that the world is coeternal with God. The subsequent commentary makes this position crystal clear: 'It is quite impossible for contrary things to belong together' [Συνυπάρξαι δὲ ἐναντία, λίαν ἀδύνατον] (44C). The second conclusion may alert us to more subtle differences between the two thinkers on the question of creation. Procopius believes that the idea that evil is coeternal with God implies that the demons (particular evils) are coeternal with God. This misrepresents Neoplatonic arguments such as those of Proclus. Procopius can see this, and accordingly uses a counterfactual argument. Since particular evils do not have substantial being, according to the Neoplatonic logic of participation they must have acquired evil by participating in something evil. But this returns us to the problem of an absolute evil existing alongside God, in which particular evils can participate (33A). Since such participation is (in Neoplatonic terms) eternal, Procopius derives a further conclusion, namely that God is coeternal with particular evils as well as an absolute evil.

Yet I think that Procopius' move to claim that the coexistence of evil with God implies the coexistence of evil demons with God also relies, at least implicitly, on the Christian biblical idea, stressed in the earlier tradition, that God is directly involved in the creation of all his creations: 'Adam never left the hands of God' (Irenaeus, *haer.* 5.1.3).[45] Procopius collapses the extended metaphysical

44. Plato *Theaet.* is the canonical text.

45. For discussion of this image within Irenaeus' treatment of the economy of salvation, see Osborn (2001), 91ff. Basil's *Hexameron* and John Chrysostom's *Sermons* and *Homilies* on Genesis repeatedly emphasize the direct, unmediated role God plays in creation.

hierarchy that was characteristic of Proclus' scheme and claims that only God is responsible for all creations in the universe. If particular or absolute substantial evil exists, God must have created it, which is an impious conclusion. This alternative view about creation is therefore responsible for shifting the locus of evil in the created order. For Neoplatonists such as Proclus, evil necessarily exists in the world because of the nature of particularity. For Procopius, it is human choice, rather than the nature of created existence, which causes evil.[46]

Procopius has a special interest in denying the existence of an absolute evil. We have already seen that he treats the Christian creation account in Genesis as primarily an ethical account. He claims that one cannot know the law if one does not know the lawgiver. So his account of creation is primarily designed to make the claim that the first principle of being is the first principle of goodness (23C–25D). The lawgiver is the father and maker of the cosmos (23D). This reading of Genesis grants the text a similar function to that which Neoplatonists gave to the *Republic* and the *Timaeus*. The dramatic setting of the *Timaeus* as an extension of the discussion in the *Republic* offered an interpretive key for Neoplatonists (e.g. Proclus, *in Tim.* I 4.11ff.). They interpreted this setting to imply a similar relationship between political organization or ethics and physical causation and characteristics. For Procopius, the proper order of cause and effect in the universe is preserved by God, the creator and first principle of Goodness, and this order allows the possibility of ethical action, because one's actions can be assumed to have regular, ordered effects.

A passage in the main body of the commentary combines many of these themes (108C–109B). The creation of Adam was not an evil act, despite the fact that God foreknew that Adam would fall into evil. Rather it is the act of the highest Good (108C–D). The act of creation proves that God is Good. Procopius argues that Being is better than non-Being, positive qualities are better than privation, and what exists is better than what does not (τὸ εἶναι τοῦ μὴ εἶναι κρεῖττον· τὸ μὲν γὰρ ἕξις, τὸ δὲ στέρησις... τὸ ὂν τοῦ μὴ ὄντος) (108D).[47] Therefore, the God who creates Being displays greater goodness than one who does not (108D). The goodness of God is shown, argues Procopius, in his preferring order over disorder, sight over blindness, and virtue over vice (108D). The God who created humans is true Being, the Good who creates beings out of nothing (ὁ Θεὸς, ὡς ἀγαθὸς, τὰ ὄντα ἐκ μὴ ὄντως δημιουργῶν) (109A).

46. For Aeneas and Zacharias on this point, see below, 6.3.

47. While such arguments resonate with Aristotle, Rist's remark (1981, 213) that Basil's use of philosophical language need not imply 'that he is necessarily following any Neoplatonic source, or possibly any particular source at all' might aptly be transferred to Procopius in this instance.

The absolute supremacy of God, the first principle of Being and Goodness, is emphasized still further and tied to human dependence on God:

> Everything created from nothing is lesser than eternal Being, and every creation is lesser than the creator in every respect [πᾶν δὲ ἐκ μὴ ὄντος τοῦ ἀεὶ ὄντος, καὶ ποίημα τοῦ ποιήσαντος ἐν ἅπασιν ἔλαττον]. Otherwise there would be no difference [διαφορά] [between these entities]. If God is changeless [ἄτρεπτός] and immutable [ἀναλλοίωτος] and good by nature [φύσει... ἀγαθὸς], it necessarily follows that what is made, by the fact that it exists from nothing and must be lesser than the creator, is changeable and does not hold the good in its judgement by nature, but rather by participation by choice [κατὰ δὲ μέθεξιν τὴν ἀπὸ τῆς αἱρέσεως]. (109A)

The logic of this passage moves from God as the first principle of Being and Goodness (God is naturally Good and pure Being) to the dependence of the creatures on this God for their own existence and ability to act ethically. The story of creation is the story of ethics, which becomes explicit as the passage progresses:

> For [humans] were established by God as a mean [μέσος], able to incline in whatever direction they choose. The divine is Good by nature, and possesses this not taking hold of it by participation. Every rational nature has established it as an object of participation according to its goodness [μεθεκτὸν δὲ κατὰ τὴν ἀγαθότητα πᾶσα λογικὴ καθέστηκε φύσις]. But in the process of participation, there is better and worse, intensity and slackening, guarding of possessions and a discarding of sluggishness from that which is up to us... For substantial Good [οὐσιῶδες... ἀγαθὸν] belongs to the Divinity alone, who also alone is eternal. And if [the divine] is unmoved [ἀκίνητον], our good must be created in motion, with the result that the one participates and the other is participated in. The one that participates wants a share of what is participated in.... If there was a choice of inclination to the worse, there also arose [an inclination] to the better, for an inclination is a turn from something. Therefore it is [a motion] from something which is not of such a kind, towards something which is of such a kind. (109A–B)

This extended passage employs Platonic concepts of participation and essential goodness, as well as Aristotelian ideas of created beings who are in motion towards a final goal, ideas which were thoroughly integrated into Procopius' contemporary Neoplatonism. It also demonstrates how close a connection Procopius wants to make between creation and ethics. Humans are utterly dependent on God for their existence, and any human goodness is possible only by participation in true goodness, the life of God.

God's goodness is seen in his dealings with his creatures. Procopius' account of salvation history is meant to provide a defence against charges that God's freedom makes him capricious. If God is not bound by a given metaphysical structure, the possibility that God might choose to act evilly arises. For Procopius, God looked after the Abrahamic race with diverse economies of salvation (28B). The ultimate act which shows God's providential concern for his creation is the incarnation (28B). Christ came to save those who had transgressed the law, to extend the gospel universally, so that no one in the economy might remain in a state of corruption, and so that all races, at the appropriate time, might be brought to salvation (28B–C). Everything in this divine economy is directed towards one end, which is to 'lead everything into the presence of Christ' (28C). Moses was able to show this, says Procopius, because he was filled with the Holy Spirit, who comprehends past, present, and future (29A).

Therefore, Procopius' account of creation, as we will also see in the case of Aeneas and Zacharias below, is ultimately directed towards soteriology. Procopius thinks that an eternal world, and the sort of creator which he believes that cosmology implies, undermines Christian claims about salvation history. By apparently calling into question the sovereignty of the creator, the Neoplatonic view, as Procopius reads it, weakens God's claim to be the first principle of goodness. Most crucially, a putatively eternal world undermines Christian hope in God's ability to perfect the cosmos in the future. Both these problems weaken the grounds for human ethical actions, by removing the first principle of ethics and weakening the motivation for good action. These claims are worked out in more detail by Aeneas and Zacharias.

5.6 Problems and Solutions

Procopius was aware of contemporary questions within Neoplatonism about the eternity of the world, how to think about matter and its relation to form, how to talk about creation with respect to time and cause, and how to relate beliefs about the existence of evil to accounts of creation. His attack on Stoic views displays a wider knowledge of Greek philosophy, possibly mediated through his Christian sources. In most arguments, Procopius' engagement with Neoplatonic philosophy seems to be general rather than detailed. Most importantly, he does not provide a charitable reading of Neoplatonic derivational monism, which provides reasons to think that coeternity of matter with God does not undermine the sovereignty or uniqueness of the One. His arguments often rely on an equation of eternity with necessity. This equation is motivated by a desire to separate creator and creature as strongly as possible, in the context of the two doctrines which provide the grammar for his account: the Trinity and creation from nothing.

His two strongest arguments in Neoplatonic terms are his claims that Neoplatonists accept the creation of form from nothing and that the Neoplatonic process of creation by emanation cannot guard against multiple worlds. In other areas, the connection between his arguments and Neoplatonism is more tenuous, although he does show knowledge of contemporary philosophical arguments, images, and assumptions in other areas of his thought in passages where he seeks to offer an alternative Christian account instead of countering Neoplatonism on its own terms (e.g. concepts of participation, being and privation, impossibility of substantial evil, debates about beginnings in time and cause, standard Platonic analogies for creation, including the builder, craftsman, and the sun and its ray). Many of these more general resonances with Platonism are to be found in earlier Christian texts. Yet together with Procopius' identification of Greek philosophy as an intellectual opponent, and the more particular attacks on Neoplatonists, we can see that conflict and collaboration between Christianity and Neoplatonism was an intellectually stimulating tension in the Gazan schools.

Procopius' reading of Genesis led him to radical departures from Neoplatonism, and his interaction with Neoplatonism is always subordinated to his account of the Christian story of creation. His strong emphasis on divine sovereignty is one result of his tradition-oriented reading of Genesis. The doctrine of creation from nothing guides his argument. These two factors led Procopius to reject Neoplatonic ideas about the causation of the cosmos and to argue strongly against procession and return. They also led him to a view of divine freedom as choice which constitutes the structure of the universe.

Most fundamentally, an account of the economy of salvation is the pattern that governs his work. In his understanding of the economy, all creation is radically dependent on the independent first principle of being and goodness. History works towards the incarnation, which is a radically new event within the cosmos, with cosmic significance. Humans live out their lives being educated into Christian life and becoming appropriated to divine reality through *oikeôsis*. All creation will be perfected by Christ and made new again in the final resurrection. This story of salvation history has parallels in earlier Christian literature from Irenaeus onwards.[48] It fundamentally grounds Procopius' account

48. The question of precise influence in this instance is beyond the scope of this book. I would simply state, however, that this quasi-Irenaean economy of salvation is also found in writers as diverse as Aeneas, Zacharias, Romanos the Melodist, and Cosmas Indicopleustes. Was there an 'Irenaean revival' in the early sixth century? A possible vector of Irenaean ideas is Theodoret. Further work needs to be done on such questions.

of creation. He must separate God and the world more radically than he thinks the Neoplatonists do in order to make clear who depends on whom and hence preserve God's unique place as the first principle of ethics and being, the lawgiver and father of the cosmos. If the account of creation leads to any confusion about the lordship of the lawgiver, it must be modified, because the lawgiver is the necessary foundation of human ethical action which is itself an integral part of the process of *oikeôsis* through participation. The eternally proceeding world of the Neoplatonists, or the unchanging material cycles of the Stoics, rules out the possibility of real change, and thereby renders implausible Christian belief both in the incarnation and in the ultimate eschatological transformation of reality. This story of salvation governs how Procopius addresses problems about creation which are generated within Neoplatonism. Where Neoplatonic assumptions can fit within this story, he leaves them intact and uses them to make his case. When, as in the case of procession or the eternity of matter, they come into conflict, the Christian story trumps Neoplatonic claims.

Aeneas and Zacharias on Creation and Eternity

LIKE PROCOPIUS, AENEAS AND ZACHARIAS INCORPORATE THEIR creation accounts into narratives about God's saving interventions in human history. They both argue for a created and temporally finite cosmos and attack Neoplatonic arguments for the eternal beginning of the cosmos. They emphasize that the cosmos is perishable in order to guarantee the final act in the divine plan of salvation: God's transformation of the present cosmos into a new and perfect creation. The creation of this new and perfected reality is the event to which all human history and ethical action is directed. Their accounts thus move from physics to eschatology, as they seek to ground arguments for Christian hope in the case for a created, finite, and therefore redeemable, cosmos.

I map their individual arguments against particular problems in Neoplatonism before arguing that some of these problems are also related to Christian Trinitarian debates and to Evagrian Origenist ideas from the local monasteries. Communication between the schools and the monasteries helped to generate some of the terms of the debate. Overlap between Christian and Neoplatonic problems again points to the intertwined, heterogeneous, and shifting cultures of late-antique Gaza.

6.1 Matter, Cause, and Time

As noted above, the basic problem concerning creation and matter was formulated by Plato in *Timaeus* 28b: Is the cosmos created or not? Theophrastus asks this question in the early stages of Aeneas' dialogue and returns to it later (e.g. 45.12–15):

> In the case of matter, in one place Plato shows that it has been created [γεγενῆσθαι], while in another place he shows that it is uncreated [ἀγένητον]. But later [interpreters], both because they were ignorant of the depth and diversity of Plato's knowledge, and because they each desired to be the first to formulate something new, were thrown into disorder among themselves, and having been scattered, follow neither Plato nor one another. (8.22–26)

As Basil had put it, 'if matter is uncreated, in the first place it is equal in honour to God, being deemed worthy of the same honours' [εἰ μὲν οὖν ἀγέννητος αὕτη, πρῶτον μὲν ὁμότιμος τῷ Θεῷ, τῶν αὐτῶν πρεσβείων ἀξιουμένη] (*Hex.* 2.2.9–11). In all his claims about creation and matter, Aeneas tries, like Basil before him, to preserve divine sovereignty and autonomy. Matter, he argues, is not a principle; rather, it is a secondary entity which is necessarily a composite (28.5–6). This argument unites him with earlier Christian claims about creation.[1]

The Christian character Euxitheus, whose views most often represent Aeneas', employs Neoplatonic philosophers to make his point that matter is not a principle:

> For God creates different things at different times according to his power, and he always creates and supplies the matter for the universe; he arouses, harmonises, orders and adorns it. For matter is not unbegotten, nor without a beginning [ἀγέννητος, ἄναρχος]. The Chaldeans also teach you this. Further, Porphyry gives to the book which he publishes the overall title, *On the Chaldean Oracles*, in which he insists strongly that matter came into being and, explaining Plotinus' book 'Whence Evil', while saying that matter is certainly not ungenerated, says somewhere that placing [matter] among the first principles [ἐν ἀρχαῖς] should be refused as an atheistic dogma. Therefore if matter is generated and not a first principle, but rather is the last [ἔσχατος], how can the perceptible cosmos be ungenerated, without a beginning, or exist before time [ὁ αἰσθητὸς κόσμος ἀγέννητος, ἢ ἄναρχος, ἢ πρὸ τοῦ χρόνου]? In fact, what is made from matter does not exist before matter. (45.2–12)

Aeneas presses the case that matter is created, both from nothing and continually, by the only first principle, who is earlier in the argument identified as the Christian Trinity (43.1ff.). Since matter is created from nothing, and the universe is material, the creation of the universe is *ex nihilo*. The cosmos—matter included—enjoys 'life from an external cause, not on its own account' [ὡς ἔξωθεν, οὐ παρ' ἑαυτῆς, τῆς ζωῆς ἀπέλαυσεν] (32.22). This means that it is naturally mortal. Aeneas grants the material cosmos the possibility of immortality; but its potential eternity is not achieved by virtue of its own nature, since it was dependent from the beginning on God's creative act.

To relegate matter to the 'last things' and establish God as the sole first principle is to declare that everything in the created order shares its createdness and its dependence on God. Philoponus has been credited with unifying terrestrial and celestial physics for the first time, in his claim that celestial bodies are subject to the same laws as terrestrial ones (*contra Aristotelem ap.* Simplicius, *in*

1. See e.g. Basil, *Hex.* 2.2; John Chrysostom, *Hom. in Gen* 2.10–12, 6.12–13, 9.4. See also 4.1 above.

Cael. 88,28ff.; 133,28f.). Aeneas does not offer Philoponus' detailed arguments about the physical composition of the universe, but he does make a strong claim for uniform terrestrial and celestial physics, on the basis that God equally created both realms:

> He caused the moon, alone of the stars, to wane and its light to depart, then to wax and become new, so that we might not at all suffer, supposing irrationally that any of the bodies above are ungenerated. . . . Therefore, just as we learn from the lowest of the stars, which is even now visible and vanishing, that the upper bodies are also generated so from the lowest rational substance, the human soul which has recently been produced, reason grasps well that the rational powers prior to it take their origin [τὴν ἀρχὴν] from the Creator [ἐκ τοῦ Δημιουργοῦ]. (38.10–17)

This set of arguments may be seen as a rejection of Aristotelian physics. In standard Aristotelian cosmology, the moon and everything below it were subject to change and part of the terrestrial world of decay. By contrast, the upper heavens were perfect and unchanging, subject to different physical laws, and made of a kind of substance not found in the terrestrial regions. Since Neoplatonists (and other educated late-antique thinkers) knew that the phases of the moon are caused by the sun's light falling on the moon, Aeneas can only be read by Neoplatonists as making the moon symbolic of heavenly change. The key point is that Aeneas uses the biblical creation story from Genesis, where the heavens include the sun and the moon, to undermine the Aristotelian-Neoplatonic separation of physical reality into terrestrial and heavenly realms. The biblical account authorizes Aeneas' departure from Greek cosmology, just as the biblical stories governed Procopius' account. It allows him to argue that everything in the material universe is created and subordinate to God, the unique first principle of Being. The relevant ontological difference is between God and creation, not between different parts of God's cosmos. The world is utterly contingent on God's will.

But the physical argument is only a minor concern for Aeneas. It is more profitably read as an attack on Neoplatonic eschatology and ethics. We have seen the threefold division of the universe into perceptible cosmos, heavenly realm, and intelligible realm, with its late-Neoplatonic variations. A key question was how or whether the soul could ascend through the regions after death, and such eschatological considerations were connected to arguments for the immortality of the soul. By collapsing the distinctions between different orders of the created cosmos, Aeneas makes the immortality of the soul independent of ethical and metaphysical ascent.

Continuing this theme, Euxitheus declares that everything created is entirely different from God and similar only to other created things. This rules out the encosmic gods of Neoplatonism (39.14–40.7); there is no place for anything equivalent to Plato's 'lesser gods':

> Now God foresaw that men, marvelling at the rational powers [τὰς λογικὰς δυνάμεις], and believing that they were without beginning and were ungenerated [ἀνάρχους τε καὶ ἀγενήτους], thereby making many principles and thousands of gods, would introduce disordered democracy in place of orderly monarchy. Such men, having praised the perceptible cosmos and placed God in it, said that the cosmos is uncreated and that it does not have a beginning, and those people, full to bursting with philosophy, came to grief in irrational fantasy. (37.25–38.3)

Matter is the lowest element in Aeneas' cosmology. It is not conceptualized as a basic substrate, since it is created *ex nihilo* by God, rather than simply being formed by him. In these assessments of matter, Aeneas' aim is to remove any competing necessary existent from the field. God alone is the first principle of Being. As such he is the only necessary existent and is the only entity who can be described as essentially eternal.

While everything in the cosmos is created, the cosmos includes material and immaterial substances. Within the cosmos, God created 'rational substance'. This is higher than matter, though it is not self-sufficient, because it too is created. The highest rational substances are the 'first beings' who circle the (material) heavens, reflecting the glory of their maker and helping the lower terrestrial beings to recognize that glory. As we have seen, our rational souls are also created, and occupy the rank of the lowest rational substance (38.15–18).

Nor is the perceptible universe all that there is in Aeneas' scheme. Our rational souls are produced

> as a paradigm of [God's] power [παράδειγμα τῆς αὐτοῦ δυνάμεως] and as an instruction about the pre-existent beings [προϋφεστώτων], that everything is from one creator and that from a single principle every rational and intellectual power and substance proceeded and still proceeds [ἐξ ἑνὸς Δημιουργοῦ πάντα καὶ ἐκ μιᾶς ἀρχῆς πᾶσα λογικὴ καὶ νοερὰ δύναμις καὶ οὐσία προῆλθε καὶ ἔτι πρόεισι]. (38.5–7)

Aeneas gives scant detail about these 'pre-existent beings'. However, they function within his cosmology to safeguard God from the charge that he changed when he started to create or was ever too envious to share his blessed state with mortals. If the creations are not eternal, there was a time (argues Theophrastus) when God was not creating (43.22ff.). Aeneas uses the standard Christian argument that we have already seen about an architect—that just as an architect is not changed by the building he makes, so too God is not changed by his creation of the world (36.11ff.). But he also offers another argument, when he claims that there is an eternal universe—an intellectual one, rather than a perceptible one—which God was always creating:[2]

> a single substance also made and put in order the intellectual substances before time [τὰς νοερὰς οὐσίας πρὸ τοῦ χρόνου]. For he wanted to have <beings> to whom he could act well,[3] and for that reason he produced the upper powers [τὰς ἄνω δυνάμεις προβάλλεται] to be capable of enjoying the Good and the first benefaction, for in the Good there is no envy about anything [ἀγαθῷ γὰρ οὐδεὶς περὶ οὐδενὸς φθόνος] (*Tim.* 29e). In this way he did not remain inactive before [creating] the perceptible cosmos. (44.21–25)

The creation of an intelligible cosmos to inoculate God against charges of idleness had a long history (Seneca *Ep.* 65.7; Philo *Prov.* 1.7, 21; Origen *Princ.* 1.4.3–5). Aeneas takes up Origen's important contribution that the creation of an intelligible cosmos before time rebuts charges that God was ever inactive. Later in the dialogue, Euxitheus calls on a Hellenic divinity to support this theory of double creation:

> Apollo also once uttered the oracles, proclaiming that the *daimones* in Hades were also created and that they were created before humans, and before the building of the cosmos, and that they served the creator for humanity's benefit. This was the oracle: 'They were created before you, and of divine generation of the cosmos, incorruptible spirits for your benefit' [Εκτίσθη πρὸ ὑμῶν, θείας τοῦ κόσμου γονῆς, ἄφθαρτα πνεύματα εἰς ὑμῶν χρείας].[4] (47.5–9)

Aeneas refers to Plato's statement that the Good has no envy about anything (*Tim.* 29e) on two occasions (44.24f.; 49.6). Each time, he uses the idea of the creation of a pre-existing, intelligible, and immaterial cosmos to preserve God from the charge of being envious or inactive. The 'first creation' is therefore directed against the charge that the creator is not also the Good.[5]

2. Cf. Zacharias, *Ammonius* 383ff. This is similar to Gregory of Nyssa and Eruigena later on. See Sorabji (1983), 203–9, 240–42, for the Judeo-Christian tradition from Philo to the Cappadocians and Augustine on this question, including the Platonist objection that a non-eternal creation means that God was idle before creating the cosmos.

3. See the emendation suggested by Donald Russell, p. 64, n. 156, in Sebastian Gertz's translation in the Ancient Commentators on Aristotle series (2012).

4. Aeneas is, as far as I can tell, the only source for this oracle.

5. This schema laid Aeneas open to charges of Origenism, for which, see below, 6.6.

Aeneas comfortably inhabits a shared world, where the boundaries between Christian and pagan writings, even sacred writings, can be freely employed in common debate. His theory of double creation—eternal intelligible realm and finite perceptible world—is a case in point, built from complex interactions between Christian and Platonic schemas. One of the names of God is Nous, and the second person of the Trinity is defined as the 'Intellect that gathers together all things in thinking' (44.13). Such claims bring Aeneas close to the Middle Platonic doctrine that the Forms are thoughts in the mind of God (e.g. Seneca *Ep.* 65.7). Aeneas does not buy into Plotinian arguments about whether each form should be understood as an Intellect, although they may help to make sense of Aeneas statement that the *logoi* are created to contemplate God eternally. Yet Basil's *Hexameron* also speaks of an intellectual, eternal world, to which a perceptible world was added as a training ground for mortals, drawing on earlier thinkers in the Alexandrian tradition.[6] Basil's argument has both Platonic and biblical warrant, as is clear from the biblical quotation which is used to support his supposition.[7] The biblical and patristic model, rather than a Platonic one, may be the best candidate for Aeneas' reference to the intellectual world inhabited by the 'upper beings'. This example demonstrates some difficulties involved in identifying and separating Christian and Neoplatonic problems and influences in Aeneas' thought.

When arguing about what matter is, we have seen that Aeneas wanted to make a strong claim that God is the unique first principle. This claim recurs when he turns to creation and causes. The Trinity, which is different from the cosmos in substance, and is prior to the cosmos in cause and time, causes the cosmos. Only God can establish order, create and supply matter, and create time (44.1ff.). There are no causes within the universe which could compete with God as the first principle of Being (38.6f.). God is the direct cause of the cosmos, and the causal process leaves God independent of his creatures:

> God, remaining what he is, makes the things that come into being. For he is not diminished when he makes other things, and when he produces [προβαλλόμενος] many things he is not spent but remains still more a whole, even more in so much as he produces multiplicity. For it is not because of the things that come into being individually, but on his own account, that the creator is the creator [δημιουργὸς], just as among men an architect is not divided into his creations. (36.12–16)

6. Philo *Prov.* 1.6–7; Origen, *Princ.* 1.2–4; *Contra Celsum* 5.39; Basil, *Hex.* 1.5.
7. Col. 1:16.

The example of the architect is used to make points with which Neoplatonists could agree, although again, detailed discussion of actuality and potentiality would have to wait for Philoponus' later contribution. Aeneas is content to leave the argument with the claim that architects, like God, do not lose part of their soul or knowledge, when they build churches, houses, or dockyards. When God produces multiplicity, he remains the same.

Aeneas draws on Plato's argument in the *Timaeus* that everything visible and tangible is created to argue that the cosmos is both caused and has an origin in time (*Tim.* 28b) (45.14ff.). After drawing aid from Porphyry and Plotinus, Euxitheus claims:

> How is the perceptible cosmos ungenerated, without a beginning, or before time [αἰσθητὸς κόσμος ἀγέννητος, ἢ ἄναρχος, ἢ πρὸ τοῦ χρόνου]?... Plato himself, you remember, appears to us as not taking a particular position in the *Timaeus*, earlier asking whether the cosmos came into being or did not come into being [πότερον γεγόνεν ὁ κόσμος ἢ οὐ γέγονεν]; then the reason [it did] was added: [the cosmos] is visible and tangible [ὁρατός, ἁπτός]. (45.10–15)

Aeneas takes the Plutarch-Atticus position on the interpretation of *Timaeus* 28b. Recall that they had argued that the generation of the cosmos means that there was a time when it was not (see above, 4.3). On this view, generation is linked to temporality and only an ungenerated cosmos would be eternally without a beginning. This was not the standard Neoplatonic reading, which we saw appropriated by Proclus from Taurus. But given that Proclus felt the need to rebut the Plutarch-Atticus position, it was a live interpretive possibility in late-antique Gaza. By taking the minority Neoplatonic line, the Gazans point to a point of internal disagreement within Neoplatonism and seek to exploit it for their Christian case.

Aeneas extends his argument, again drawing on resources within the Platonic tradition to make his case for a Christian interpretation of *Timaeus* 28b:

> Great Atticus, the lover of Plato, when he examined the opinions of his beloved, declared somewhere that he was investigating the nature and order of the cosmos and that given what it was like, it was neither unbegotten nor eternal [οὐκ ἀγέννητον οὐδ' ἀΐδιον], but that it came into being through the agency of one who is greater and more perfect in power, the pre-eminent and intelligible God. Since it is visible, tangible and has bodily form in every respect, it is impossible for it to be ungenerated. The substance of such things needs support from another for their being. How can we not agree that these things have come into being [γεγονέναι] and are preserved by the maker? (46.15–23)

Thus for Aeneas, the cosmos is corruptible from beginning to end. God is needed to override its corruptibility at all moments of its existence: 'the substance of such things needs support from another for their being', hence such things require a maker for their beginning as well as for their continued preservation.[8] Having argued that the cosmos would dissolve without God sustaining it in being, Aeneas again draws on Plato's argument at *Timaeus* 41b that the demiurge can dissolve everything he bound, to ridicule Aristotle's claim that the cosmos is eternal:[9] '[Atticus] also calls Aristotle laughable, since Aristotle agrees that the universe is visible, tangible and corporeal, yet, being a great controversialist, he says that it is ungenerated and uncorrupted [ἀγένητον δὲ καὶ ἄφθαρτον]. How is this man not ridiculous...?' (46.24–47.2). Through all these foregoing arguments, the reader has been left to assume that Plato's '*gegonen*' must refer to a beginning in time. We have seen that this position is rejected by the greater part of the Platonic tradition from Calvenus Taurus onwards. The Gazans' contemporary Neoplatonists all rejected a temporal interpretation of *Timaeus* 28b, preferring to understand it as referring to causal dependence. Aeneas shows that he is aware of this debate within Neoplatonism: 'The interpreters of Plato say that "*gegonen*" means not "has come to be" but "came into being through a cause" [τὸ γέγονεν οὐ γέγονεν λέγουσιν, ἀλλὰ κατ' αἰτίαν ἐγένετο], just as my body is a cause of my shadow, but did not make it, rather it follows along with it incidentally' (45.21–23). In this passage, Aeneas is making fun of Platonic interpreters who 'say that "gegonen" is not "gegonen"' but try to force discussion of causes into the term's semantic range. As in the case of Neoplatonic monism, Aeneas seems to know the position of his opponents. Yet Aeneas' polemic fails to give airspace to the careful discussions in Neoplatonism about just how the cosmos is causally dependent (ultimately) on the One. Philoponus will be more successful philosophically in the later generation, outlining the terms of the Platonic exegesis before engaging with it in detail.

Instead of such detailed engagement with the Platonists, Aeneas latches onto the analogy of cosmos as a shadow, found in Neoplatonism from Plotinus onwards (*Enn.* 6.3.8). The shadow analogy for creation is also to be found in Porphyry, and Baltes has argued that the ἀλλά clauses, especially the final

8. Philoponus' argument about the natural corruptibility of the cosmos is different but perhaps related. He argues that God cannot override the natural dependence of the cosmos on beginning (*Contra Proclum* 6.28,225,14–226,9). The Gazans merely make the claim that substances other than God depend on God's being, which is uncontroversial for Neoplatonists, who are, of course, working with a different and more sophisticated (causal) definition of 'came into being' (*gegonen*). For Philoponus' argument, see Judson (1987).

9. On this passage, see Baltes (1976), 60.

one, misrepresent Porphyry's original analogy within the Christian polemic.[10] Porphyry simply wanted to emphasize the dependence of the creation on God and the eternity of the cosmos and its cause. Within the Neoplatonic scheme, the shadow analogy functions precisely as an example of something which may be eternal but only tenuously connected to being, clearly secondary to the higher entity from which it derives. Baltes argues that Aeneas and Zacharias polemically draw another inference from the analogy by treating the cause as involuntary in order to attack the Neoplatonic arguments about creation.

While Baltes is right that Porphyry did not intend to use the body/shadow analogy to imply that the cosmos is involuntarily caused, Iamblichus' exegesis of Plato's simile of the divided line (*Rep.* 509dff.) shows that the resources for the Christian reconfiguration of the body/shadow analogy were available within Neoplatonism:

> All the intelligibles are divided into two kinds, both into those that are called and known as properly intelligible objects and into the mathematical objects. The first group are the *noeta*, the second inferior group are the *dianoeta*. Furthermore, from these is another *ousia*, the *ousia* of the perceptible objects. Of these, on the one hand there are the objects which are properly perceptible, which are matters of opinion, and, on the other hand, there are images. The proper *aistheta* are objects of opinion because they share in bodies, like stones, wood and the four elements, and these are the superior objects among perceptible things. Weak and dissimilar objects come after these things, and accompany the primary perceptible objects. These are shadows. For shadows accompany bodies, and unless they had some other underlying body, they would not be visible. Therefore shadows are images and they are also the images in water, in reflections and in other things, and they do not have their own being, nor do they appear separately from other bodies, but rather, because they have fallen into other bodies, when the bodies have been taken away, they do not appear. Therefore the perceptible objects are in one genus, in that they fall into [the category of] perception, but the images are objects of belief rather than substantially existent, defined according to belief which is not susceptible to positive demonstration. (Iamblichus, *de communi mathematica scientia* 8.6–25)

Iamblichus here elucidates Plato's claim that shadows are metaphysically and epistemologically inferior to other objects. This explains the force of the body/

10. Ibid. for relevant texts and discussion.

shadow analogy as Porphyry intended it. Throughout, Neoplatonists argue that the dependence of an effect on its cause renders it secondary to the cause. However, this passage also shows that the analogy of body and shadow could be used within Neoplatonism to explain the idea of an involuntary cause, an effect that needs only matter, not will, for its production. Aeneas (and Zacharias) drew on this possible element of the analogy, exposing what they saw as an internal inconsistency.

Aeneas initially criticizes the body/shadow analogy by noting that shadows are produced when bodies stand in the way of the sun, but the creator is 'non-corporeal, invisible, subsisting as light itself' [ὁ δὲ Δημιουργὸς ἀσώματος, ἀόριστος, αὐτὸ τὸ φῶς ὑπάρχων] (46.5f.). This builds on Iamblichus' definition of a shadow as something which requires body for its production. Second, he goes to the heart of the problem, and argues that the sort of cause implied by the analogy is impious. 'The creator is not the creator, if he creates what he made involuntarily': the universe will be an accident if God did not create it in the proper sense [οὐκ ἄρα δημιουργὸς ὁ Δημιουργός, εἰ μὴ βουλόμενος ὃ πεποίκεν δημιουργεῖ· ἀλλ' αὐτόματον τόδε τὸ πᾶν, εἰ μὴ γέγονεν] (46.1f.). Aeneas insists that the production of a shadow does not fit the bill: 'Who could will to order or destroy his own shadow?' [τίς δ' ἂν τὴν ἑαυτοῦ σκιὰν κοσμεῖν ἢ καθαίρειν βούλοιτο] (46.8f.).

Through such strategies, Aeneas argues that God creates independently and freely, without conceding a symmetric relation of dependence between God and the cosmos. Yet the insistence on the voluntary nature of the initial cause of the cosmos also allows Aeneas to explore a second problem, namely the question of how the first principle of Being is also the first principle of Goodness. If the initial act of creation was necessary rather than voluntary, Aeneas thinks that there is no reason to believe that God is able to act voluntarily for the good of creation at any time. Any argument which suggests that God did not voluntarily create the cosmos therefore undermines claims that God can act providentially for his creation. Euxitheus concludes: 'Therefore this reasoning of senseless men would also destroy Providence [Πρόνοιαν], since care for a shadow would be impossible' (46.9–11). A Neoplatonist may object that providence only applies to ensouled beings rather than to prime matter,[11] although this objection is not available if the cosmos as a whole is taken to be a shadow, since the cosmos is ensouled for Neoplatonists. But Aeneas' argument on this point had a strong pedigree in Christian thought, and it is to there that we should look to explain his link between creation and providence. Eusebius cites Atticus' attacks on

11. See Sorabji (2005), vol. 2, 79–89 for relevant texts and discussion.

Aristotle for (a) undermining the centrality of virtue (*PE* XV.4); (b) rejecting divine providence by isolating the prime mover from the terrestrial world (*PE* XV.5); and (c) rejecting the idea that the world was created (*PE* XV.6). The latter two arguments are related because there can be no providential concern for creation if there is no creator. The first two are related because if there is no divine providence, there is no foundation for the virtuous life. The same logic supports Aeneas' argument.[12]

Aeneas, like Procopius later, also rejects the body/shadow analogy because it makes the cause coeternal with the product:

> Further, a shadow appears alongside the body simultaneously [ἅμα] with it. But it is impossible to imagine matter as simultaneous with the Creator. Moreover, Plotinus, after he had investigated matter thoroughly, very clearly declared this and ridicules Anaxagoras because he does not also declare it (Plotinus, *Enn.* 2.4.7.2–10), but rather proposed that the creator and matter exist simultaneously. But simultaneous existence [ἀδύνατον δὲ ἅμα] is impossible, since the maker is superior [πρεσβύτερον] to what is made. (46.11–16)

This rejection of a temporal equivalence between creator and creature contributes to Aeneas' case for one sovereign first principle of Being. Yet it is based on a mischievous reading of Plotinus, for whom matter is causally rather than chronologically secondary. Aeneas also (mis)uses the ambiguity of the Greek term ἅμα, which can mean 'temporally simultaneous' or 'together', in the sense that two entities are on the same ontological level. God is not ἅμα with anything in the second sense, therefore, Aeneas seems to be arguing, he cannot be ἅμα (temporally simultaneous) with anything either. Again, however, we may see the same Trinitarian distinction between creator and creature sitting behind this argument, and see in it the intuition that eternity implies necessity.

Aeneas' discussion of causes and time highlights three points. First, God is directly involved in creation as the sole cause of everything in the cosmos. Secondly, Aeneas explicitly distinguishes the sort of cause involved in creation from the Neoplatonic idea of procession. The creation of multiplicity is not the overflowing of divine being. Rather, it is the creation of something different and new. Thirdly, creation is contingent on an act of divine will; arguments for divine freedom are based on an idea of freedom as choice between alternative possibilities (see further below, 6.7). Aeneas' argument on creation, causes, and time thus separates God from the world. It is based on a particular view of

12. Zacharias has similar concerns. See below, 6.3 and 6.7.

divine freedom and is designed to establish the first principle of being as the first principle of goodness.

Aeneas attempts clearly to separate God from the world, making him the supreme first principle of Being. By eliminating a hierarchy of creative causes, he radically simplifies the sort of scheme offered by contemporary Neoplatonists. Only God is the efficient cause of the universe. Proclus' scheme of six causes does not map onto Aeneas'. Aeneas rejects the idea that the creation of the cosmos involves a 'pre-existing', ungenerated material cause. Nor is there a pre-existing formal cause of the universe's generation, although both formal and material causes, which mediate divine actions, are allowed in the terrestrial realm after the initial act of creation. Compounds of δημιουργεῖν can be used to describe God's creative activity, but Aeneas does not distinguish between demiurgic and hypostatic causes: God is personally involved in causing the existence of the cosmos. Nature does not have its own soul; only God, not nature, can be a truly creative principle. Nor is the idea of the original creation of an intelligible realm analogous to Proclus' paradigmatic cause, because the intelligibles thus created have no necessary part in the creation of the perceptible world. The perceptible world is dependent on God's will alone, not on the intelligible creation. The last cause in Proclus' scheme is the final cause. Like Neoplatonists, Aeneas makes God the final cause of creation. He identifies the Holy Spirit as the final cause, the person who 'always turns [creation] to the Father and draws up everything which it touches' [ἐπιστρέφει γὰρ ἀεὶ πρὸς τὸν Πατέρα τὸ Πνεῦμα καὶ πᾶν ἀνέλκει, οὗ ἂν ἐφάψηται] (44.18f.). Likeness to God is the ultimate purpose for creatures, but the Holy Spirit is involved in achieving this perfecting of creation. God the final cause is identified not only with God the first cause of Being, but also with God the first cause of Goodness. Therefore defining God as the final cause identifies him as the perpetual creator and as a providential first principle of goodness within the physical world.

Zacharias' treatment of matter, cause, and time is similar to Aeneas. Matter is not a co-principle, everything in the visible cosmos is bodily, created, and corruptible and there are no encosmic gods (e.g. 653–715). Zacharias has three emphases which distinguish his work from Aeneas'. First, he uses more explicitly orthodox language. The arguments used by both Aeneas and Zacharias draw on *creatio ex nihilo*.[13] But it is Zacharias who uses the formula more explicitly. God, he argues, 'creates substance itself out of absolutely nothing [ἐκ μηδαμοῦ μηδαμῶς ὄντος παραγαγὼν].... We say that God is the maker of substances, not indeed of shapes alone' (493–96). Secondly, he brings the argument back more

13. Cf. Aujoulat (1987), 76.

consistently to Plato, rather than to contemporary figures. In an extended section of *Timaeus* exegesis (667ff.), Platonic texts are used to demonstrate that the cosmos is made from sense-perceptible matter which is therefore corruptible. The idea that matter is a receptacle or nurse (*Tim.* 52d) is quoted and refuted, since accepting such an idea would imply that matter is a co-principle alongside God:

> If, Plato says when he wrote the *Timaeus*, a treasure trove for you [πίθος δὲ ὑμεῖς], that the creator took matter, which you love to call 'receptacle' and 'nurse',[14] without form or shape, and furthermore mixed and moved chaotically in disorder, and [took] it with [its] disorder and put it into order, introduced tranquillity instead of confusion and made it and shaped it and removed it from its earlier shapelessness, then there was a time when there was disorder in the universe—according to Plato—and also a time when the cosmos and the present harmony did not exist.[15] But if this is admitted, matter will be coeternal with God [συναΐδιος τῷ θεῷ]—at least according to Plato—but the cosmos itself will not yet be. If this is so, then you [philosophers] also agree that the things which exist have been created with time and you say that God was not at all a benefactor from eternity, which is what you babble and carry-on about in order to scare the simpler people. That is, the disorder of matter and the lowest formlessness will be, with God, equally without beginning, coeternal, and equal to him in honour [τῷ θεῷ συνάναρχος ἔσται καὶ συναΐδιος καὶ ὁμότιμος]. Indeed this will follow: it will be deemed worthy of the same rank and the same privilege as the wise and absolutely beautiful God, since it is ungenerated [ἀγένητος]. (843–58)

This passage proposes a significant conceptual move which helps to specify the gulf between Zacharias and his Neoplatonic contemporaries. Zacharias does not draw upon the Neoplatonic distinctions between eternity (ἀίων) and perpetuity (ἀιδιότης κατὰ χρόνον) (*ET* 52–5). This allows him to argue that coeternity means that 'there is a respect in which God is not better than the cosmos' (833–35). What is perhaps more surprising is that Ammonius (as presented by Zacharias) does not make this distinction either. Zacharias has Ammonius say that both God and the cosmos are eternal; both exist perpetually. They are eternal in exactly the same way (ὁ δὲ θέος, ἀΐδιος ὢν ἀεὶ ὢν ἐστιν; ὁ κόσμος δὲ, ἀΐδιος ὢν… ἀεὶ ὢν ἐστιν) (982, 984). For Ammonius, God and the cosmos are coeternal (συναΐδιος) (1078).[16] As we have seen above, the term συναΐδιος is not

14. The reference is to *Timaeus* 49a.

15. Reading ὅτε for ὅδε. If the printed text stands, the translation is 'and this cosmos and the present harmony was not'. The parallelism and the νῦν suggest the emendation.

16. This is the only place where Ammonius uses this term. Zacharias puts it in his own mouth repeatedly (e.g. 1073, 1069, 1062).

used by Proclus or any other pagan author. Neoplatonists would not attempt to predicate eternity identically of God and the cosmos. It seems that Zacharias may be landing Ammonius with a concept foreign to him. Yet Philoponus uses the term, which leaves open the possibility that both Zacharias and Philoponus learnt to employ the terminology in this cosmological context from Ammonius, their common teacher.

What does Zacharias mean by 'συναΐδιος'? The term first appears in the work of Pseudo-Justin (third century A.D.). Across varied works, he uses it to describe pagan ideas. He rejects matter as a second principle alongside God (*Confut. dog. quor. Arist.* 120D–E). The terrestrial and the celestial worlds can also be described using this term (ibid. 159A). The relation between God and time and God and the cosmos is described (wrongly, thinks Ps.-Justin) as συναΐδιος (ibid. 138B,D; *Quaest. Christ. ad gent.* 186D). What is generated is not coeternal with what is ungenerated. Thus, the cosmos cannot be coeternal with God. Ps.-Justin goes beyond Zacharias, when he describes the model for the creation as generated, and so not coeternal with God (ibid. 191Aff.). Ps.-Justin also employs the terminology to describe the relations between the ungenerated members of the Trinity (*Expositio rectae fidei* 111B, 380B,D).[17]

This final usage is the one which is most widely used in Christian authors. This meaning of the term συναΐδιος is a key reason why Zacharias rejects the coeternity of the world with God. His understanding of the concept of coeternity is coloured by his understanding of the Trinity; his understanding of the coeternity of the Son and Spirit with the Father will not allow him to make the world 'coeternal' with God since coeternity is only applicable to the relations between the persons of the Trinity.

Zacharias is working with a number of assumptions about 'coeternity'. Something 'coeternal' is as timeless as that with which it is eternal. Coeternity is achieved by begetting or procession. But for Zacharias, such coeternal procession implies equality and identity of substance between the thing which emits from eternity and that which is emitted, something Neoplatonists deny. Trinitarian debates provide influence. For Zacharias, something 'created' coeternally is 'ὁμοούσιος' and 'ἀΐδιος' with what 'creates'. These associations of 'συναΐδιος' suggest why understanding the world as 'coeternal' is anathema to Zacharias. If the world is 'συναΐδιος', it is eternal like God is, and is of the same substance as God. The cosmos becomes a god and all is plunged into the irrational, chaotically democratic Hellenic system of divinities (1120).

17. This work may be better attributed to Theodoret of Cyrus (early 5th century). See Sellers (1945).

The third and final difference between Aeneas and Zacharias on the question of matter concerns the relation between the intellectual and the material worlds. We have seen that Aeneas proposes the creation of an immaterial world to safeguard God from the charge that he changed when he decided to create the perceptible cosmos, and to link God the Creator to God the Good.

Zacharias has a similar argument, extending it to 'creative principles' or 'creative thoughts' (δημιουργικοὺς λόγους) which God has eternally within himself (370). Aeneas also speaks of these 'creative principles' in a different context at 58.12, where he claims that the creative principles are not destroyed in terrestrial processes of generation and corruption, an idea which resonates with Origen (see below, 6.6), who had developed the idea within Christianity that the creative principles are eternally in the Creator's mind and set within matter to order it. Zacharias, however, draws on this concept explicitly in his creation account. He argues that God does not always bring the creative principles 'into the open' (382–85). He creates willingly and freely on the basis of the creative principles he has within him, so he is not constrained by an external power or dependent on the existence of a creation in order to be a creator. This argument is consistent with the analogy of the architect, who has the plans of the building in his head, but does not always actualize the plans.[18]

When Zacharias turns to arguments about creation and time, his concern again is to make a radical distinction between God and the world. Only God is eternal (605–13), whereas the cosmos is temporal (573). Nothing created can share in divine eternity (609).[19] There is no possibility in Zacharias' cosmology of a universe which is coeternal with God: the cosmos and time itself were generated (571ff.).

Similarly with causes. God is the 'first principle of being, the most fertile nature...the fount of life' [ἡ γὰρ ἀρχὴ τῶν ὄντων, ἡ γονιμωτάτη φύσις...ἡ πηγὴ τῆς ζωῆς] (1099f.). This insistence on God as the unique cause of the universe, as with Aeneas, is directed at removing the possibility that the cosmos could be thought of as a necessary existent alongside God. So Zacharias argues:

> If he is not able to be separate [χωρὶς] from this universe, the universe gives him, through its existence, the greatest part of himself, or perhaps the whole, that is, his very being. According to this argument at least, the

18. Thus, it does not meet the potential Neoplatonic charge that God has changed by going from being a potential to an actual builder. For such an argument, we should look to Philoponus, who uses similar arguments about creative principles in his *Contra Proclum*, but extends them with detailed analysis of Aristotle's concepts of actuality and potentiality. See Aristotle, *De An.* 2.5 and Philoponus *Contra Proclum* 47.18–48.7.

19. For the relation between this claim and contemporary Trinitarian concerns, see 6.4 below.

universe is the cause of him and he himself is not the cause of the universe. Certainly, the sort of thing which needs something for its composition would be the thing caused by it and not the cause [αἴτιον]. (742–46)

Such an argument rejects any idea of cause by procession, or any other causal process which could imply that God depends in any way on the cosmos. As in Aeneas, it is designed to protect God's absolute freedom. It also removes the possibility that any element of the cosmos could be equally responsible for causing the existence of things within the cosmos. So, again like Aeneas, Zacharias rejects the idea that the sun is the cause of anything in the terrestrial realm (217, 247–88, 335ff.). Zacharias thus rejects the 'common ground for all Platonists, that between God and man there must be a host of intermediaries, that God may not be contaminated or disturbed by too close an involvement with matter.'[20] On the contrary, Zacharias claims that God constructs all human life directly. Biological fathers are only instruments of the divine power and will (219). Through his transformative power (διὰ τῆς ἀλλοιωτικῆς δυνάμεως), God binds the soul into the body which he formed and creates each human as 'a rational, living mortal, capable of intelligence and understanding' [ζῷον λογικὸν θνητὸν…νοῦ καὶ ἐπιστήμης δεκτικόν] (226f.).

God causes the cosmos voluntarily. 'How would the creator be the creator, unless he made his creations purposefully?' [πῶς γὰρ ἂν εἴη δημιουργὸς ὁ δημιουργός, εἰ μὴ βουλόμενος ὃ πεποίηκεν εἴη δημιουργός?] (758–59; cf. 393). God creates order through his good will (652–55). As in Aeneas and Procopius, the idea that God is an involuntary cause of the universe is rejected, in an extended attack on the body/shadow analogy (521–34) which falls into the tradition of Christian rebuttals of claims such as Plotinus', that the Intellect proceeds from the One in an involuntary act, as radiation from the sun (*Enn.* 5.1.6.27–30). Zacharias shares with Aeneas the argument that accepting the analogy would make God dependent on the cosmos and would undermine belief in the possibility of providence.[21] If the cosmos were merely incidental, as the shadow is with respect to the body, God would be a 'purposeless and involuntary cause in the composing of what exists' [ἀπροαίρετον αἰτίαν καὶ ἀβούητον τῇ συστάσει τῶν ὄντων] (528f.). Zacharias draws on the Proclan idea that 'the uncaused is also spontaneous' [τὸ γὰρ ἀναιτίως καὶ αὐτόματον] (*ET* 97). Proclus had argued that spontaneity, 'could never happen where there is order, continuity and perpetual changelessness' [τὸ δὲ αὐτόματον

20. Dillon's claim in his introduction to Alcinous (1993), xxxiv f., and compare Alcinous, *Did.* 16.

21. As with Aeneas, this seems to be a deliberate misreading of the Neoplatonic argument, which is, of course, precisely designed to show that God is superior to the cosmos despite being simultaneous with it.

ἐν οἷς τάξις ἐστὶ καὶ ἀλληλουχια καὶ τὸ ἀεὶ ὡσαύτως οὐκ ἄν ποπε γένοιτο] (*ET* 97). Since God is order, argues Zacharias, creation is not spontaneous; rather, it is voluntary (τὸ γὰρ ἄτακτον οὐ θεοῦ, ἀλλὰ τοῦ αὐτομάτου) (653). Hence the idea that the universe springs spontaneously from God, without his will directly causing it, is rejected by Zacharias using Proclus' logic, in order to guarantee God's freedom in relation to his creation.

Of course, even for Plotinus, who speaks regularly of the necessity of the lower orders of creation, something like will is attributable to the One, and in the later Platonists the demiurgic intellect is represented as willing the terrestrial cosmos into order.[22] So one might justly claim that Zacharias simply misses the mark in this criticism. He has one further argument that perhaps signals a deeper criticism, although the suspicion remains that he is arguing at cross purposes. Zacharias argues that creation is no 'by-product' or mere attendant circumstance (παρακολούθημα; cf. Plotinus, *Enn.* 3.7.10). This again recalls the Plotinian idea that creation arises from the One's self-reflection rather than being an outwardly directed act of grace and we have seen that shadows are by-products of bodies in Iamblichus (*Comm. Math.* 8). In this argument Zacharias leaves room for the claim that will is involved in Neoplatonic creation, but signals that the kind of volition attributed to the One is insufficient to explain creation as an act of love and grace that purposefully creates a cosmos radically different from God.

6.2 Creation and Eschatology

Much of Aeneas' dialogue is devoted to arguing that the cosmos will come to an end. This eschatological focus transforms the usual Neoplatonic terms of the debate, which characteristically focused on protology.[23] Aeneas focuses on arguments for the future infinity of the cosmos more than contemporary Neoplatonists, who framed their arguments about the temporal infinity of the cosmos in terms of an eternal origin of the world. His argument is motivated by his claim that the good God will bring this creation to an end and create a new, perfect paradise. Christian problems, rather than Neoplatonic ones, govern the argument.

'Do you think', asks Theophrastus, 'that this cosmos will be destroyed at some point in time?' 'Yes', answers Euxitheus, 'given that it came into existence and given that this fine scene did not come into being by chance' (42.21–43.2f.). This

22. See above, 4.1.
23. See Rousseau (1994), 334 for similar comments about Basil.

argument has two prongs. The universe must come to an end because it came into existence, and because it has a purpose.[24] This 'purpose' is explicitly ethical, and so I analyse it in the following section. In this section, I focus on the first set of arguments.

In his first argument, Aeneas draws on tenets of Aristotelian physics which were commonly accepted in Neoplatonism. What is generated is also corruptible; no generated entity is eternal (Aristotle, *Phys.* II). This basically Aristotelian physics is supplemented by an interpretation of *Timaeus* 41a–b which Aeneas shares with Zacharias, but which leads him away from standard Neoplatonism. In this passage, Plato's demiurge addresses the lesser gods. Aeneas quotes the relevant passage as: 'Gods of gods, of whom I am father and demiurge, you are not wholly immortal, given that you have come into being. You will not be dissolved at all, because you have been allotted as your portion my will, which is stronger than death'[25] (40.3–5).

Instead of understanding this statement to imply that the lesser gods are immortal (as Simplicius would later), Euxitheus exploits the statement that the gods are 'not completely immortal', given that they depend on the creator's will. He takes this to mean that the cosmos is not naturally immortal, but that it is capable of being changed into immortality: 'Plato thought that this whole cosmos came into being, is mortal, and is continually preserved as immortal. For what is capable of being burnt is not burnt without qualification'[26] (40.14–17). But this argument throws up a number of objections. The first is that destroying the universe leaves God open to the charge that he is evil: Why would God will to destroy what he made harmoniously in the first place (*Tim.* 41b)? Aeneas' answer, presented by Euxitheus, is that the final dissolution does not add destruction to the universe. The universe is properly mortal and is therefore already corruptible. Aeneas is arguing that the corruptibility is not problematic for God, since the corruption is natural and what is natural is good. One does not blame a rock, Aeneas writes, because it cannot think (23.16ff.). Far from introducing corruption into an incorruptible universe, making the universe

24. See Judson (1987) for the logic (or irrationality) of this claim.

25. Θεοὶ θεῶν, ὧν ἐγὼ πατήρ τε καὶ δημιουργός, ἀθάνατοι μὲν πάμπαν οὐκ ἐστέ, ἐπείπερ ἐγένεσθε· οὔ τί γε μὴν λυθήσεσθε, τῆς ἐμῆς βουλήσεως κρείττονος θανάτου λαχόντες. Cf. *Tim.* 41a–b: Θεοὶ θεῶν, ὧν ἐγὼ δημιουργὸς πατήρ τε ἔργων, δι᾽ ἐμοῦ γενόμενα ἄλυτα ἐμοῦ γε μὴ ἐθέλοντος. τὸ μὲν οὖν δὴ δεθὲν πᾶν λυτόν, τό γε μὴν καλῶς ἁρμοσθὲν καὶ ἔχον εὖ λύειν ἐθέλειν κακοῦ· δι᾽ ἃ καὶ ἐπείπερ γεγένησθε, ἀθάνατοι μὲν οὐκ ἐστὲ οὐδ᾽ ἄλυτοι τὸ πάμπαν, οὔτι μὲν δὴ λυθήσεσθέ γε οὐδὲ τεύξεσθε θανάτου μοίρας, τῆς ἐμῆς βουλήσεως μείζονος.

26. This argument draws on earlier discussion of modality, for example among the Stoics, which continued into Neoplatonism. See Philo the Logician reported in Alexander, *in. An. Pr.* 183,34–184,18; Boethius, *in Int.* 234,10–26; Simplicius, *in Cat.* 7.195f. Cf. Chrysippys in Diogenes Laertius, 7.75. See Bobzien (1993), 76–84; Frede (1974), 107–17; Papazian (2007), especially 200–202.

finally eternal in fact removes corruption from the mortal world of change and decay (48.13–17).

However, even if this rebuttal is sustained, another objection arises: If God were going to make the universe perfect, why not make it perfect from the beginning, instead of putting mortals through all kinds of suffering before bringing them to perfection? Theophrastus puts this objection, and argues that there could only be two logical reasons for God not creating a perfect universe from the beginning: either he was impotent or else he was unwilling to share his perfection with others through envy (48.20ff.). We have already seen the argument against the first prong of the dilemma, when Aeneas introduces the concept of the initial creation of an eternal, imperceptible world. In the earlier argument, this act preserved God from the charge of inactivity in creation. Here, the argument is extended to demonstrate the associated point that God never lacked the power to create. It is also a first defence against the charge of envy. Quoting Plato, again without attribution, Aeneas agrees with the Neoplatonic position that 'in the Good there is no envy about anything'. The eternal creation of rational and intelligible beings is taken as evidence that this premise applies to the Christian God. The goodness of God also leads to diversity in creation:

> Second, [God] established the perceptible creations, which are fine and great, but lesser than the first [creations]. Adding the second creations was not a mark of envy, but was to not neglect any of the fine creations which he was able to make. Furthermore, creating an invisible and visible good order is the essence[27] of power, not weakness. It is a quality of the perfect Logos and Creator not only to make difference, but even things that are contrary to each other, such as white and black, hot and cold, immortal and mortal, which, by his surpassing power, he will transform into immortality. (49.9–16)

Far from being evidence for divine impotence, Aeneas argues, the creation of mortal beings is evidence for infinite divine power, since God will transform these mortal beings into immortality. This is one key reason why Aeneas rejects the eternity of the world. His scheme justifies God's actions from the future. God's goodness implies that he will transform the cosmos at the end of time. If Aeneas were to accept the Platonic eternal world, he could not provide good reasons to believe that his God is good. So the first set of arguments for the universe being brought to completion turn out to be directed at ethics. The universe must come to an end since the creator is the principle of Goodness.

27. Reading αἰτία for αἴτια with *Bt*.

This idea binds the continual and ultimate transformation of the cosmos towards ethical perfection to a claim that God is good. God would not create a mortal world without ultimately transforming it, nor would he create it without using its mortality for the process of perfecting humans (see further 6.3 below). The creation is good because it is one where human progress towards perfection is made possible and ultimately guaranteed by God's final act of re-creation.[28]

Like Procopius, Aeneas attacks the Stoic idea of eternal return, because it denies the possibility of real change. If the heavens and the earth are repeatedly destroyed, he argues, then 'to change is superfluous' (51.18ff.). The change from mortality to immortality is, *pace* the Stoics, a real change. Aeneas concludes:

> Therefore a change once and for all [ἅπαξ μεταβολή] is better, after which there will be no more change, and man will live again, not to die again. For nothing will be mortal [θνητόν], but everything will be new and immortal, both this whole cosmos and mankind [πάντα καινὰ καὶ ἀθάνατα καὶ ὁ πᾶς οὗτος κόσμος καὶ ὁ ἄνθρωπος]. (51.21–23)

The Stoic cycle is futile: if all the future holds is cyclical destruction, there is no point, Aeneas argues, in continual renewals (51.18–20). Aeneas' arguments about creation are thus motivated by his expectation of the radical alteration, rather than the destruction, of the created cosmos at the promised eschaton. As such, the argument for the cosmos becoming new requires the argument Aeneas has offered for the finitude of the world *ex parte post*.[29]

The question of whether the eschatological transformation of the universe is credible given contemporary philosophical cosmology recurs in Zacharias' dialogue. The pagan interlocutor Gessius asks whether 'the good [God shall] be changed' and whether 'he would will to destroy what was beautifully made and well fitted together' (cf. *Tim.* 41b) (579–81). The ensuing argument partly rehearses the arguments we have already seen in Aeneas about whether the world is naturally eternal, based on the demiurge's speech in the *Timaeus*, so I will not analyse them in detail. Yet in the philosophical discussions staged in the classrooms of Alexandria, the focus remains on origins. Zacharias emphasizes the Platonic axiom that anything that came into being is also perishable (e.g. 693–96). If Zacharias can prove that the universe came into being, he can simultaneously prove that the universe will come to an end. Therefore he focuses his discussion with the philosophers on origins; the terms of the

28. This claim again shows strong similarities with Irenaeus.

29. Philoponus' views on future infinity are somewhat unclear, since the relevant sections of the *Contra Aristotelem* are not extant. Yet there is evidence to suggest he took a similar line to that proposed here. See further Wildberg (1988).

argument largely stay within a philosophical framework, although the discussion does focus more on the implications for the future infinity of the cosmos than earlier philosophical discussions.

However, when the dialogue setting moves away from the philosophical classroom and into the church, the first question the student asks concerns creation and eschatology:

> If God intends to render this cosmos immortal and to transform it and form it anew for the better, what is the reason for not making it such from the beginning.[30] ... either he did not make such [a cosmos] because he was ignorant of what is fine, in that he would make it sometime as if from changing his mind, or because he could not do it; or, which is not lawful to say, he will not escape the passion of envy. But ignorance, weakness, envy and changing one's mind are far from the blessed nature. What do you have to say about this? (1176–78, 1179–82)

The student soon reiterates his concern about why God 'did not make everything immortal at the same time as its generation' [τί δὲ μὴ ἅμα τῇ γενέσει ἀθάνατα πάντα ἐποίει] (1223). This demarcation of arguments—origins with the philosophers and eschatological interests in the church—is a clear example of the way in which Christian and Neoplatonic problems jointly generate Zacharias' discourse. Certainly, the student's questions about the new creation raise standard Neoplatonic objections to the idea (that God would change, be envious, or be incompetent). Yet the Christian emphasis on the possibility of the transformation of the universe at the second coming suggests that his discussion of the future infinity of the world is generated by Christian claims about creation and re-creation.

6.3 Creation and Ethics

For Aeneas, the whole purpose of creation is to bring something other than God to divine perfection. God 'not only makes difference, but even things that are contrary to each other ... which, by his surpassing power, he will change to immortality' [μὴ μόνον διάφορα ποιεῖν, ἀλλὰ καὶ ἀλλήλοις ἐναντία ... ἃ δι' ὑπερβολὴν δυνάμεως ἀθάνατα μεταποιήσει] (49.14–16). God's creations are not perfect, but they are able to be perfected, 'ascending almost to the Good and the wisdom of the Good' [μέχρι τοῦ ἀγαθοῦ καὶ τῆς τοῦ ἀγαθοῦ σοφίας ἀναβαίνων] (24.1f.).

30. Cf. Aeneas, *Theophrastus* 48.19.

This ethical scope of Aeneas' creation account has implications for the kind of cosmos that Aeneas thinks God created:

> The generation of bodies, which is indeed a kind of motion, does not want to remain still; for what sort of motion wants to remain still? Rather, it desires perfection and the One from which it proceeded [προῆλθεν], and always hastens and presses on towards it. The motion is not in vain, so it will never stand still, until it finds what it desired. It will find [what is desired] whenever the creator himself wills, and the creator shall so will it when it is appropriate. Indeed, after the trial of souls and the visible testing of evil, he will change the perceptible universe into immortality [τὸ αἰσθητὸν ὅλον ἐπὶ τὸ ἀθάνατον μεταλλάξει], so that it would be in accord with [συνᾴδειν] the immortality of humans and could again become a suitable [οἰκεῖον] place for the happiness of its inhabitants [τῶν ἐνοικούντων εὐδαιμονίᾳ]. This is because a mortal creature must live in a mortal cosmos, but an immortal [creature must live in] an immortal [cosmos]. For there is a unique harmony of everything, and no disorder or discord, but each thing is well-disposed and suitable for each, and has made the will of the creator its nature. But I think that it is a quality of wisdom and power to have recast the same mortal creatures as immortal ones. Is it not the work of great wisdom and power that we are not ignorant about our mortality, yet do not remain in it? (43.6–21)

Because they sinned, humans are not immortal, so they need a training ground in ethical perfection to lead them back up to heaven (49.6–51.23).[31] Hence, the cosmos must be suitable for mortals, and therefore mortal and finite. But the cosmos has an ethical and ontological goal: participation as much as possible in the perfect life of God. Therefore, God is both the efficient and the final cause of the cosmos, and the cosmos as a whole, like humanity, is both mortal and capable of receiving immortality. The destruction of the present cosmos is a change for the better which demonstrates the creator's 'power, righteousness, gentleness and love for mankind' [εἰς ἐπίδειξιν δὲ τῆς τοῦ Δημιουργοῦ δυνάμεως καὶ δικαιοσύνης καὶ πραότητος καὶ φιλανθρωπίας] (51.11f.).

God knew that the first rational beings would look away from him in an improper use of their divinely ordained freedom. Yet he does not want to be a god of automatons, so the freedom (τὸ αὐτεξούσιον) of his creatures is not removed and God uses the cosmos to heal the creatures who have become sick

31. The earth as a training ground is a common image in earlier Christian literature. See, for example, Basil, *Hex.* 1.5.

(50.20ff.). This scheme allows Aeneas to propose a theodicy where evil in the world is part of God's providential concern for humanity. The worst apparent evils, such as infant mortality, disability, or deformity, are really part of the divine purpose of education, punishment, and reward, which is all designed to bring humans to perfection (27.20ff.): suffering brings benefit (25.16–19).

Direct ethical consequences follow from the creation of this sort of cosmos within this particular account of divine providence. Aeneas devotes large sections of his dialogue to a description of individual virtues and vices. The list of virtues and vices is largely shared with his Neoplatonic contemporaries, although humility is repeatedly emphasized as a cardinal virtue, pointing to the Christian foundations of his ethic. Correct ethical action means living a life aligned to God's purpose for humanity, and this is a far remove from the attainment of social honours: 'God made [virtue] free from riches, sovereignty and pleasure, so that the good athletes do not grasp virtue for the sake of external reward, but for its own sake, and so that they might not confound virtue with passion [πάθει τὴν ἀρετήν]' (25.19–22). Throughout his account of creation and ethics, Aeneas is silent about Christology, although the quotation above about the possibility of reaching the 'wisdom' of the Good might be a Christological reference. He remains largely within Neoplatonic ideas about human freedom, the origin of evil, and the propriety of striving towards the Good; however, this congruence is general rather than particular. He does assume the workings of a personal providence. God is directly involved in creation, but this is understated. It is 'Providence' rather than 'God' who is involved in perfecting human beings, and while his Christian readers could readily understand this to refer to persons of the Trinity, Neoplatonists might equally well substitute an impersonal Providence as the divine mechanism for regulating good actions in the cosmos.

As I indicated above, Zacharias' discussion of creation and eschatology leads him immediately into an extended discussion of the divine plan of salvation. Thus his ethics are explicitly eschatological. The universe was not made immortal and indestructible from the beginning because it had to have a certain affinity (ἐμφέρεια) with mortals, so that mortals could live within it to be trained for perfection (1195ff.). This account has strong parallels with Aeneas' view that the cosmos is created as a training ground for ethical perfection. But the Christian student is not put off by Zacharias' initial exposition of this element of the divine plan. It still begs the question, in the student's view, about why God did not choose to create a perfect universe together with perfect creatures in the first place. The student's insistence on the point separates Aeneas' interests from Zacharias', in that Aeneas' interlocutors had been satisfied by the initial answer. Zacharias' Christian teacher has more work to do.

In response to the student's persistent questioning, Zacharias lays out the divine plan in more detail (1221–1284). The divine ruler originally created the heavens and the earth fit for kings, and set humans within the royal creation, binding the soul to the human body and thus scattering the seeds of immortality in bodies (1235f.). The human is therefore created as the 'governor of his fate, free from necessity [ἀνάγκης ἐλεύθερον], independent and autonomous [αὐτόνομον]—since that above all is the mark and sign of a rational nature, and the image and imitation [εἰκὼν καὶ μίμησις] of the kingdom above' (1239–41). Then God gave humans the law, so that they would know how to distinguish good from bad action.[32] Zacharias does not have Aeneas' interest in the particular details of the virtues, but he shares with Aeneas and Procopius the identification of the creator of the cosmos with the creator of social rules. The disintegration of the cosmos, or the introduction of mortality, came about because humans disregarded the law. Evil is again brought into the world by human choice (1413ff.; Pl. *Rep.* 617e). But God did not abandon his creatures. In his pity towards his creations, God leads them back to perfection from their chosen evil state. Ultimately, God leads humans back to perfection through the incarnation; ethics in Zacharias is explicitly Christological:

> For this reason, through the creator himself, who remained God and became human, in whom evil found no trace or movement of itself—since he is the fount of virtues and holiness, and is changelessness and sinlessness—the foundation of immortality and the tokens of incorruptibility will be conferred upon the human race. (1278–83)

This scheme of creation, fall, education, incarnation, and ultimate perfection is Zacharias' 'explanation of why [God] did not render us immortal in the beginning at the same time as [our] generation' [τὴν αἰτίαν τοῦ μὴ τὴν ἀρχὴν ἡμᾶς ἀθανάτους ἅμα τῇ γενέσει κατασκευασθῆναι] (1283f.). But most importantly, this divine plan is also the ground for human ethical action. Humans are created as free creatures by a God who proves his goodness through creation, who continues to act throughout history for human benefit, and who underwrites all human ethical striving with the promise that such virtuous actions will be rewarded with the new creation.

For the divine plan to be comprehensible, for evil to be explained, and for human action to be worthy of the name 'virtue', humans must be free agents. Yet Zacharias claims that while humans are created to be kings on earth, they are really subjects of God, the divine king (1243f.).[33] Being a slave to God, for

32. Cf. John Chrysostom, *Serm. in Gen* 8.37–58.

33. This passage in Zacharias is ultimately (and, perhaps directly) dependent on Philo, *Opif.* 78. Gregory of Nyssa also uses the image in *Opif. Hom.* 2, 131D.

Zacharias, has its ethical advantages: 'The recognition of servitude is certainly a fine thing. It banishes arrogance, wilfulness, vanity and pretension, the first and last evil. In general, it controls one's thoughts and recalls to mind what was written at Delphi: "know yourself"' (1244–48). But now there are two obvious objections to Zacharias' account. If humans really have free will, does Zacharias' claim that the new creation will liberate humans mean anything? Furthermore, the servitude of free agents looks incoherent. Again, the divine plan is Zacharias' solution to this apparent incoherence. The suitability of the cosmos means in part that it has a rational, harmonious order, which is fitting for the rational creatures who inhabit it (1198–1280) and is evidence for the rationality of God which establishes human rationality. In creating humans as free agents, God bestows on them the divine mark of rationality (1239ff. above). This rationality is the divine image, in which humans are called to participate. In giving them freedom and rationality, God creates humans to serve him willingly and lovingly: he has no desire to dominate. Rather, he desires 'this alone for us, that we are saved' [τοῦτο μόνον ἀπολαύων ἡμῶν ὃ σῳζόμεθα] (1399f.; cf. Clement of Alexandria, *prot.* 1.6.2; *str.* 7.3.14.6). This explains the paradox of free servitude for Zacharias (see further below, 6.7).

But there is still the problem of the liberation of free beings. For Zacharias, humans bring improper servitude upon themselves. In disregarding the law (ὀλιγωρήσας δὲ τοῦ νόμου), humans separate themselves from the immortality they would otherwise have shared (1375ff.). Bondage to sin is self-inflicted, and God provides humans with the means to escape this bondage. While humans cannot escape their sin through their own efforts, God provides a training ground for their purification, and recapitulates human history in the person of his son, reforging human nature by becoming human while remaining God, and correcting and perfecting the life of the first sinful man (1276ff.). By assuming human flesh, Christ makes all human flesh again worthy of immortality (1274ff.). Humans who became slaves by irrationally disregarding the law through misdirected acts of free will are liberated by God who returns sinful humanity to its original free state through the divine plan of salvation. The divine plan re-creates the possibility that humans will employ their freedom properly so that free will leads to real freedom rather than servitude to evil.[34]

6.4 Creation and Triunity

Developments in Trinitarian theology provide a set of boundary conditions for what Zacharias means by the term συναΐδιος, and what Aeneas and Procopius

34. Irenaean and Augustinian themes are again marked.

are getting at when they insist that the cosmos does not always exist together with the creator. The problematic is dominated by Christian theology, rather than Neoplatonic philosophy, although the Gazans appropriate philosophical concepts when it suits them. One reason that Christian thinkers in the fourth to sixth centuries returned to the doctrine of creation—which had been decisively formulated by the end of the second century—was that aspects of the fourth- and fifth-century Trinitarian controversies brought to the fore new problems in the doctrine of creation.

The more precise formulation of the doctrine of the Trinity also made a Neoplatonic system of derivational metaphysics, perhaps, even newly attractive. If the language of derivation could usefully be applied to the inner workings of the Trinity, why not extend it by analogy to explain the necessarily mysterious mechanism of creation? Proclus' rigorous systematization of how reality flows from the One made such an analogy intellectually respectable. Proclan sympathies later became a mark of heterodoxy, as in the case of John Italus (c. 1023–1085).[35] But in the early sixth century, the question could still go either way. Ps-Dionysius, of course, used large swathes of Proclus directly in his system of Christian mysticism. Attacks on Proclus' views, like the general rebuttals of Aeneas, Procopius, and Zacharias, and later the more developed attacks of Philoponus, helped to shape the later orthodoxy.

Aeneas' account of creation and the Trinity arises in answer to a two-pronged question from Theophrastus. 'Is the cosmos,' Theophrastus asks, 'not ungenerated and without a beginning? How is the creator a creator, if there was a time when he was not constructing his own creations?' [οὐκ ἀγένητος ὁ κόσμος καὶ ἄναρχος;"Η πῶς δημιουργὸς ὁ Δημιουργός, εἰ χρόνος ἦν ὅτε μὴ τὰ ἑαυτοῦ εἰργάζετο;]. The two prongs of the question are linked, since one way the cosmos could not be eternal *ab initio* is if there were any point on the timeline before which it was not being created. We have seen that all three Gazans recognized this as a problem for their account of God in the context of arguments with Neoplatonists, since such a scenario could imply that the changeless might be changed and leave open the objection that their God was idle before he created the cosmos. In the arguments about creation and Trinity, Aeneas gives these arguments stronger metaphysical foundation:

> The ruler of the universe, from whom [ἐξ οὗ] all things are, the origin and source [ἡ ἀρχὴ καὶ πηγή] of the things that exist—for he is not an unproductive source—the Good itself [τὸ ἀγαθόν], the Father of Wisdom

35. For the controversy surrounding John Italus, see Browning (1975); Clucas (1981); Siniossoglou (2011), 82–85.

> and the Creator [ὁ Δημιουργός] of the universe, did not in time originate the power and activity of his Son, since he is eternally [ἀεί] Father of the Word and of Wisdom. He did not suffer when he begat [γεννήσας], since he did not beget by necessity. Nor did he introduce an accessory cause [συναίτιον] through the act of begetting, for nothing else existed. Again, he did not empty himself of power, since he always holds what he begat in himself, being all in all, filling and being filled. He wished to be the single Father of the single [Son]. Further, what was begotten was not superfluous, for he would not have possessed him in himself, and he is of the same substance, since God is not a composite. Through this act, the Father begat the Word substantially, so that the Word might express in full the person [ὑπόστασιν] and power of the Father. The Word is very reason, very intellect, and gathers all things together by thinking [τῷ νοεῖν]. Through him [δι' αὐτοῦ], the Father creates everything. Wisdom required that this universe be brought to perfection and together with the Son he led forth from the same substance the Holy Spirit, not by the constraint of nature, but by the authority of power, and this is why he willingly begat, and led forth with power. Further, inspiring the intelligible and perceptible creations with this Spirit, he fills them with power and holds them together and draws them up to himself. For the Spirit always turns [them] to the Father and draws up everything which it touches. In this way the great wisdom and power of the Father, the Monad [ἡ Μονάς], the Divine Trinity, is timeless, not admitting degrees of more and less. (44.1–21)

Aeneas employs Neoplatonic terms for God. God is 'the Good', and the 'Monad', 'self-sufficient', the fount of being, atemporal and holding everything in himself. Use of Platonic 'prepositional metaphysics', prominent since Aristotle and developed in Middle Platonism, is also a point of contact with Neoplatonism, with the prepositions ἐξ, διά, and εἰς used to identify the particular ways that each member of the Trinity causes their communion of eternal being. The Father is the source or origin (ἐξ) of the Trinity itself; all the acts of the Trinity are mediated by the Son (διά); and all such acts are liberated, empowered by, and find their goal in the Spirit (εἰς). Use of prepositional metaphysics has been defined as derivational, and so it is, within Platonism.[36] But for Aeneas, the main force of the prepositional statements is to underline the unity of God in his extra-Trinitarian creating. In this way, Aeneas argues for a single first principle which is triune. Father, Son, and Spirit have identical substance and all create

36. Runia (2003).

together; there is a single cause, rather than one main cause and two accessory causes (συναίτιον).[37]

In speaking of the return of all things to the origin, there are hints of the Neoplatonic concept of procession and return. But Aeneas attempts to separate the cosmos from God more strongly than he thinks the Neoplatonists do. He distinguishes the act of inner-Trinitarian creation from the creation of the world. The Word is not other than the Father, unlike the cosmos, which is not created as consubstantial. To underline his point, and to bring his thinking into line with credal formulations, Aeneas talks consistently of the 'begetting' (γέννησις) rather than the genesis or creation (γένεσις) of the Son. Plato's statement at *Timaeus* 29e, which is axiomatic for all subsequent Platonists, and was so dear to Proclus, that the demiurge is Good and so desires everything to be *like* himself, is inconsistent with Aeneas' thought (*Timaeus* 29e: ἀγαθὸς ἦν... τούτου δ' ἐκτὸς ὢν πάντα ὅ τι μάλιστα γενέσθαι ἐβουλήθη παραπλήσια ἑαυτῷ). God's goodness, for Aeneas, requires the creation of something radically different and new, even as what is created is capable of achieving likeness to God. Again, *creatio ex nihilo* is the subtext and creation by derivation is implicitly rejected.

Aeneas also explicitly rejects the idea that the Father begets the Son *by nature*. For Aeneas, this possibility makes God subject to some sort of compulsion. If the Trinitarian persons originate by necessity, God would be passible: 'He did not suffer when he produced, since he did not produce by necessity'. Instead, Aeneas maintains that the Father begets by an act of will: 'He willed to be the single Father of the single [Son]' (cf. Plotinus, *Enn.* 6.8.18). Instead of distinguishing between 'natural' inner-Trinitarian creation and 'voluntary' extra-Trinitarian creation Aeneas pushes acts of will back within the Trinity itself. God chooses what he naturally is.[38] This is consistent with Cappadocian and Neoplatonic arguments that God's properties are his nature and hence there is no external constraint on his action (e.g. Gregory of Nyssa, *de Vita Mos* I (40.10–11); Plotinus, *Enn.* 5.5.13).[39]

Zacharias also sees intimate connections between Trinitarian theology and the doctrine of creation. God, says Zacharias

> is a Triad in a Monad and a Monad in a Triad, by being three hypostases [ὑποστάσεις],[40] but a single substance [οὐσίαν μόνην]. For the first

37. See *Tim.* 46d for the idea of an accessory cause.

38. The same contrast of will and necessity as we saw in Procopius' thought seems to inform Aeneas' earlier account. This move has clear parallels with Plotinus, *Enn.* 6.8. For modern treatments, see Gunton (1997).

39. See Lilla (1997), 162 for further discussion of this point.

40. See Lampe, loc. cit., for this term in Christian usage, which came to be the standard terminology to refer to the persons of the Trinity by the council of Chalcedon, although it is used in this sense earlier.

> principle of being, the most fertile nature [φύσις], unstinting goodness, the fount of life, the intellectual light, both the good itself and one, the first cause, the one who is and who really has being and is always self-identical, as indeed being Intellect [Νοῦς] and Father. He begat the Logos from eternity, [the Logos which is] not uttered, nor again in thought,[41] but real and substantial and of the same substance [οὐσίας] with himself from eternity and co-eternal, since he is of the same divinity with him, and the same substance [ταὐτὸν ὄντα] with him, not in hypostasis but in substance. He also emitted [προβαλόμενος] another hypostasis from eternity, of the same substance with him and with the Logos, which the divine scriptures call the Holy Spirit, together with the begetting of the Logos, that is, with the Son and Wisdom. [This did] not involve any flowing or cutting or emptying (as these are properties of bodies). (1097–1109)

In thinking of God the Father as Mind and Being, Zacharias reconfigures the Neoplatonic identification of Nous with the second hypostasis and stands in the Cappadocian tradition (e.g. Gregory Nazianzus *Or.* 20.10). Zacharias' divine Father is certainly described in terms familiar to Neoplatonists: νοῦς, ἄρχη, τὸ ὄν, τὸ ἀγαθόν, τὸ νοέρον, πρώτη αἰτία, ἀεὶ ὡσαύτως ἔχον. But while such terms have distinguished philosophical pedigrees, Zacharias is also evoking the meanings they have taken on within Christian credal discourse by the end of the fifth century. Zacharias uses credal language and language authorized by Church Fathers more prominently than Aeneas in his account.

Like Aeneas, Zacharias rejects the Neoplatonic idea of emanation to explain the internal relations of the Trinity, dismissing metaphors of 'flowing', although arguments against division in the overflowing of the One may be found in Plotinus (e.g. *Enn* 5.1.2; cf. Gregory Nazianzus *Or.* 31.1). He draws on Gregory's caveats against thinking about God in material terms, warnings Neoplatonists would all observe:

> The Spirit is able to be conceived beyond eternity, time and every extension [διάστημα] imaginable.[42] [The Father] is one together with the Logos, that is, Creator and Wisdom, and with the Holy Spirit, since these are being referred back to the cause itself,[43] the Logos through begetting,

The philosophical meaning of 'substantial entity' is part of the attraction of the term for Christians, but, as Philoponus would discover to his disadvantage when he was accused of tritheism under Justinian, the technical philosophical usage of the term is not simply transferable.

41. προφορικόν versus ἐνδιάθετον.
42. Inserting punctuation after δυνάμενον.
43. Cf. Alcinous, *Did.* 14.3 on the World Soul and Nous.

> the Spirit through emanation or procession [τοῦ μὲν γεννητικῶς, τοῦ δὲ προοδικῶς, εἴτ' οὖν ἐκπορευτικῶς], given that Wisdom, that is, the Logos, superintends the composition, creation and substantification of what exists, while the divine Spirit is the one who inspires all rational and intellective substances and the perfection of their existence. 'For we say that the Father of the Logos (that is, Wisdom), [the Father] who produced [προβολέα] the Holy Spirit, is the first cause and principle of divinity, the timeless principle of what is observed in the Son and the Spirit', as our theologian Gregory says.[44] (1109–1119)

The Son is begotten and the Spirit proceeds. Like Aeneas, in reference to the Spirit, Neoplatonic language about procession enters the account. Yet Zacharias is faithfully representing credal statements, which use different terminology for how the Son and the Spirit come from the Father. The Nicene Creed uses ἐκπορεύω to describe the Father's originating of the spirit; this term has been translated into προβαλόμενος as a more readily understandable term for a Neoplatonic audience, as well as to pick up the term *probalea* used by Gregory. The apologetic context, where points of contact with the opponent need to be emphasized for rhetorical purposes, again allows use of the language of the Neoplatonic theory of emanation.

The prologue to Procopius' *Commentary on Genesis* is largely silent about the relationship between the doctrine of creation and the doctrine of the Trinity. He makes the same distinction as Aeneas and Zacharias do in their Trinitarian discussions between the coeternity of Father and Son and the temporal and causal priority of God (Father, Son, Spirit) over the world, suggesting that his thought is in line with Trinitarian discussions from the earlier patristic sources and in Aeneas and Zacharias.

As I have noted, a fragmentary text attributed to Procopius exists, which is directly relevant to the question of how Trinitarian thought relates to the problem of creation. Since the attribution is uncertain, I label this text Procopius(?) and offer the following discussion somewhat tentatively as providing aspects of a possible sixth-century Gazan view about creation.[45]

The fragment in question reads (in part) as follows:

> The divine procession [πρόοδος] is without beginning and without end; only one might speak about the begetting from [ἀπό] the one and only Father of the one and only Son and the emanation [πρόβλησις] of the

44. Gregory Nazianzus, *Or.* 23.7 is the major patristic source for this section.

45. All but the first phrase of this fragment Θεία πρόοδος ἄναρχος καὶ ἀτελεύτητος, μόνη ἄν, which is at PG 87.2 2792e, may be consulted at PG 87.2, 2792h.

> one and only Spirit, according to which both the paternal and originating power, or rather the pre-eminent unoriginated monad, having moved itself into the dyad which 'being beheld in the Son and Spirit is established as far as the Trinity', as says our theologian Gregory. And this is the unique divine procession according to nature, if indeed one should say 'according to nature' about matters beyond nature and divine. The Father is the unoriginated origin of this [procession], for it is from him [ἐξ αὐτοῦ]. The co-original Son is the mediator [μεσότης], for it is through him [δι'αὐτοῦ]. The surpassingly perfect and unending Spirit is the goal [τέλος], for it is towards him [εἰς αὐτό]. This procession has been set apart from the other processions. For what are from it are not at all outside the origin.

Procopius(?) buys into Neoplatonic language about emanation, procession, monads and dyads, and this language suggests that he thinks that Neoplatonic procession provides a good model for explicating the relations between the persons of the Trinity. He also uses the same prepositional metaphysics which we saw employed by Aeneas. Care is taken with the limits of language about God, especially when describing internal Trinitarian relations. His attention to this nuance is an attempt to ensure that God is not reduced to natural categories. Platonic ideas about the One, who for the later Platonists is beyond nature and being, at least helped to bring this concern into the open and keep it relevant. To say that the members of the Trinity process by nature is also implicitly to contrast this procession with how Procopius(?) argued that God creates the universe, which is by will, a free, unconstrained choice.

What is particularly striking in this passage, however, is the adoption of Neoplatonic categories to make sense of the inner relations of the members of the Trinity, coupled with a rejection of the view that the same process can be called upon to explain the existence of the world. For Procopius(?), the inner-Trinitarian procession is unique. Speaking about procession is only proper when speaking about the inner-Trinitarian relations, and the procession of the members of the Trinity transcends all other putative processions. There may be some analogy between how the members of the Trinity eternally come to be and how the world comes into being, and Procopius(?) goes on to talk about how created things come to be using terms like 'procession', 'production', and 'creation' more or less interchangeably. But for Procopius(?), the analogy is weak, since what is caused when the Trinity eternally comes to be has 'one nature' and 'identity of being', whereas, in all other things produced by the Trinity, there is a different substance between the maker and the made. Procopius(?) continues: 'Further, none of the [processions of created beings] lacks a principle [ἄναρχος], since none of what exists is without origin, but everything was created [γέγονε] by the Father through the Son and has been made perfect in the Spirit.' While we may see parallels between the instrumentality of the Son and the instrumentality of Nous in Plotinus, the focus is on the claim that creatures are caused, temporal, and finite. In this context, Procopius(?) draws an explicit comparison with the Trinity. We recall similar stressing of this difference between creator and creature from the prologue to the *Commentary on Genesis*. *Creatio ex nihilo* is assumed in this text: when God creates, he creates something completely new, different from himself. He does not depend on what he makes in any way.

He then concludes with a reference to the Genesis creation account. His problem is how to accommodate *creatio continua*—the continual creative acts of God in the world—with the biblical statement that God rested on the seventh day. He writes:

> But on the seventh day God rested from all his works (Gen 2:2). And there was no procession of another cosmos and what had been made was completely accomplished in its totality, according to the reality of the present age. But in its parts, there is still operation, as is said by the saviour: 'My father is still working, and I am also working' (Jn 5:17).... And there will be another procession [πρόοδος] at that time in which God will be all in all. And everything will return to him [ἐπιστρέψουσιν], the elements of the whole, and there will be an alteration from corruption into incorruption [ἐκ φθορᾶς εἰς ἀφθαρσίαν μεταποίησις].

This account might seem to call into question the careful work that has been done to separate God's being from that of his creatures, in that all reality will return to God (the Neoplatonic term *epistophê* is used explicitly). Yet the key phrase is the last one: 'corruption will change into incorruption'. In this final act of creation, God will again make something decisively new, and mortals will put on immortality.

This final passage displays marked similarities with Procopius' treatment of the seventh day of creation in his *Commentary on Genesis*, giving further weight to treating the ideas in the *Refutatio* as reflecting prevailing views in sixth-century Gaza. In his *Commentary*, Procopius first deals with the use of the construction τὸ συνετελέσθη for τὸ ἐπληρώθη (140D). As in the *Refutatio*, the former verb is used to highlight, says Procopius, the ultimate perfecting of the creatures which God had produced (παρήγαγε) (140D) and to signal the restoration of what has been corrupted (ὁτὲ μὲν τὴν φθορὰν σημαίνει, ὁτὲ δὲ τὴν συμπλήρωσιν) (140D). Armed with this parallel, we should not interpret the *Refutatio* passage as referring to a Neoplatonic concept, although the Neoplatonic language may have sweetened these ideas for Neoplatonists. The discussion in the *Commentary* then moves to divine providence (141A) and *creatio continua*. Divine providence (in this context best understood as a name for God) demands that creation will continue down to the consummation of the age. Procopius quotes the same passage from John's gospel (5:17) to demonstrate God's continual concern for creation and his continual creative acts (141A), again to deal with a supposed problem for *creatio continua* raised by the statement that God completed or stopped his work on the seventh day (ὅτι Θεὸς οὔποτε παύσεται τοῦ ἐργάζεσθαι, μαρτυρεῖ Χριστὸς ἐν τῷ κατὰ Ἰωάννην Εὐαγγελίῳ) (141A). Finally, the idea that the passage from Genesis 2 removes the possibility of more than one cosmos is found in the *Genesis Commentary* in a discussion about the importance of the plural in the phrase 'works that he had made'. This refers, in Procopius' view, to the totality of nature, not to many universes.

Ideas such as these are congruent with trends in the Gazan contributions to the creation debates. Taking biblical ideas as regulative for the Christian account of creation makes God directly involved in creation, throughout the history of the world, a marked departure from Neoplatonic thought. The reference to Gregory, the same quotation found in Aeneas and Zacharias, as well as biblical quotations which are congruent with the exegetical work of Procopius, shows the author of the *Refutatio* drawing on resources from within Christianity alongside his Neoplatonic arguments, and looking outside standards of rationality established in the Greek philosophical tradition. In the case of Procopius(?), there is no easy way to separate problems which arise and are played out within Christianity from those that are generated and worked on within Neoplatonic philosophy. The *Refutatio*, like better authenticated works of Procopius, and those of Aeneas and Zacharias, seeks to play in both worlds.

It is therefore worth asking, finally, about just how the three Gazans' respective concepts of the Trinity relate to earlier Christian ideas and contemporary Neoplatonic thinking about divine hypostases.[46] Gregory of Nazianzus is clearly a key figure, and his knowledge of Plotinus is one way in which the Gazans' accounts may seem indebted to Platonic thinking. In Gregory, we find repeated statements about God as divine monad and triad. God is one in substance, divinity, and will, but three in hypostases. This formulation is not, of course, distinctively Christian. It may be found in the *Chaldean Oracles* and in Porphyry, who conceives of the highest principle as a threefold unity of existence [ὕπαρξις], power/life [δύναμις, ζωή], and intelligence [νοῦς, νόησις].[47] Proclus rejected this account of the highest principle, reinstating Plotinus' pure

46. See also 4.1 above.

47. *Chaldean Oracles* fr 26 (μουνάδα…τριοῦχον) and 27 des Places (παντὶ…ἐν κόσμῳ λάμπει τριάς, ἧς μονὰς ἄρχει); Porphyry *in Parm.* XIV.10–12, 15–16.

unity, but Porphyry's post-Plotinian scheme provided intellectual resources to Christian thinkers as they constructed their doctrine of the Trinity. The Gazans have, for example, the Father as the originating source of being (existence), the second person of the Trinity is named by Aeneas and Zacharias as Wisdom while Aeneas has 'mind itself' holding all things in himself by thinking, and the Holy Spirit can be thought of as the animating principle of what exists in both Aeneas and Zacharias (life). Yet for the Gazans, existence, mind, and life do not map to the different hypostases neatly. Zacharias speaks of the Father as Being itself (existence), as a productive source, perhaps approximating Porphyry's life/power, and as Intellect [νοῦς]. Similarly, Aeneas and Zacharias have the Son and Spirit as equal in substance to the Father. Father, Son, and Spirit are held to animate and sustain created beings, and where Zacharias has the Father named as Nous, we have seen that Aeneas is closer to making the Son a Platonic Intellect (αὐτονοῦς καὶ τῷ νοεῖν ἅπαντα συναθροίσας) (44.12–13) (cf. Plotinus, *Enn.* 5.1.4, 5.3.8). The Gazans' hypostases cannot be clearly separated by activity, although they do have characteristic ways of acting, as the prepositional metaphysics of Aeneas and Procopius(?) is intended to communicate.

The most important Neoplatonic concept for the doctrine is the perfect 'unity-in-distinction' of the intelligibles where the intelligibles are understood as an organic unity of difference.[48] Lilla quotes Gregory of Nyssa (transmitted in Basil *Ep* 38):

> neither can the distinction between the hypostases break the contiguity of nature nor can the community of essence blur the peculiar features by means of which the hypostases can be recognized. Do not be surprised if we say that the same reality is at the same time united and divided and if we enigmatically think of a new and extraordinary kind of united distinction and divided union. (*diff ess* 4, 87.85–91)[49]

Given the long history within Platonism of similar ideas about the intelligibles, Gregory's claim that this conceptualization of the Trinity heralds an entirely new line of thinking is overstated. The Gazans stand within this shared Christian-Platonic tradition. God is beyond time and space (Gregory Nazianzus, *Or.* 41.9; cf. Plotinus, *Enn.* 6.8.20). Gregory Nazianzus, whom they all cite in their Trinitarian discussions and who also emphasized the unity-in-difference concept (e.g. *Or.* 31.3, 14; 40.41, 42.15), is one possible source for their thinking on this point.

48. See Lilla (1997), 158–60 and Dodds (1963), 291–92; cf. Beierwaltes (1994), 16.
49. See the discussion at Lilla (1997), 158.

The perfect sharing of divine substance partly explains the distribution of characteristics of Neoplatonic hypostases in ways Neoplatonists could not accept. For all three Gazans, following in the footsteps of thinkers like Gregory Nazianzus (e.g. *Or.* 23.7, 29.2,5), the Father is the source of being.[50] The act of generating the Son is identical with the Father's will, as is the procession of the Spirit, in a similar way to the One's productive willing of Nous (βουλόμενος, οὐ βίᾳ φύσεως ἀλλ' ἐξουσίᾳ δυνάμεως) (cf. Gregory Nazianzus *Or.* 29.6; Plotinus, *Enn.* 5.3.12, 6.8.18). This is the closest they get to the absolute priority of the One in Neoplatonism, and may finally make the insistence that all members of the Trinity are equal in divinity difficult to sustain. But they differ from contemporary Platonists in equating God with Being, Intellect, and Goodness, instead of putting the highest principle beyond them.[51] We might have expected the Holy Spirit to parallel the World Soul, but where Plotinus has the World Soul holding created things in being (*Enn.* 2.3.13), in Zacharias and Aeneas, as in Origen (*De Or.* 23.1), this function is more clearly given to the Logos, although Aeneas emphasizes the unity of the God and comes close to Platonism in claiming that the Father sustains creation and draws it to him 'by the Spirit' (44.17–18). Similarly, where Zacharias calls the Son the demiurge and allocates to the Spirit the demiurgic function of perfecting and inspiring the rational and intellectual substances, in Aeneas the title *demiurgos* is reserved for the Father, who 'creates everything through the Son' [πάντα δι' αὐτοῦ ὁ Πατὴρ δημιουργεῖ]. Zacharias' distribution of demiurgic functions to Son and Spirit has parallels in Cappadocian theology (e.g. Gregory Nazianzus *Or.* 41.14) and resonates with Plotinus, whose Nous is the demiurge and whose World Soul inspires prime matter with rational substances (e.g. *Enn.* 3.9.1, 5.1.8. 5.9.3).

Throughout this discussion of the Gazans' Trinity, it is clear that Cappadocian influence is marked and is one source for concepts which overlap with Neoplatonism. While similarities with Neoplatonic concepts and language will have helped to build a bridge between the Gazans and their Neoplatonic interlocutors in the schools, in this case Christian problems and earlier solutions mainly motivate and shape the Gazan accounts.

50. On Gregory Nazianzus' Trinitarian theology, see the careful exposition of Beeley (2008), 187–233.

51. Platonists had argued about whether God should be equated with Mind and Being or whether he should be thought of as beyond these categories. See Lilla (1997), 141–43 and Whittaker (1969), 92–93. The Cappadocians had come down on the side of God as Being to counter their Arian opponents, and the Gazans follow this line without showing detailed knowledge of the problem which continued to exercise contemporary Platonists, although see Procopius(?). Gregory of Nazianzus leaves open the claim that God may be beyond *ousia* in *Or.* 6.12.

6.5 Creation and the Soul

I treat Aeneas' discussion of the pre-existence of the soul as a case study for the problem of the creation and eternity of the world.[52] As in his discussion on the eternity of the world, Aeneas argues against the pre-existence of the soul to preserve God as the unique first principle of being and goodness. The creation of the soul is, just like that of the cosmos, an act of divine will: 'The creator embraces all things that have come into being, are coming into being and will come into being, and he creates each thing as he wills and when it is appropriate and as would be best, always with wisdom and skill' (37.11–14). All rational powers, including the soul, receive their origin from the creator (37.16ff.). Like the cosmos, the soul proceeds in time (38.13–18). All this marks God out as the supreme first principle of Being.

Aeneas expounds many different theories about the pre-existence of the soul early on in his dialogue (9.16–14.17).[53] But Aeneas also explores particularly Platonist problems. Diverse positions on the transmigration of the soul, referred to in several Platonic dialogues, had been taken up by Platonists and are referred to in Aeneas' dialogue.[54] According to Plato, a human soul could either migrate from humans into humans only,[55] or potentially into beasts. If the latter, this cross-species transmigration of souls could occur by the human soul transforming into a bestial soul or by accompanying an animal soul.[56] The latter option avoids problems associated with a rational soul becoming united with an irrational beast.[57] Porphyry, by contrast, had used his belief in the transmigration of souls from humans to animals as an argument for vegetarianism (*On Abstinence* 1.6.3, 1.19.1–3).[58] If the human soul could only migrate into humans, punishment might be achieved by making the resulting soul weaker than the originally evil soul, perhaps by making the soul of a man return into a woman or into an inferior type of human. On this account, a person who had been stupid in a previous life might return as an asinine man.[59] This position is found,

52. For discussion not limited to questions about creation, see Aujoulat (1987).

53. Problems arising from the Origenist controversy may partly influence Aeneas' work (below, 6.6).

54. For key Platonic texts, see *Phaed.* 81d ff., *Phaedr.* 249c and *Rep.* 620a ff. On transmigration in the Platonic tradition, see Dörrie (1957) and Smith (1984).

55. The view of Hierocles.

56. Aeneas attributes the view that the soul can achieve cross-species transmigration to the Egyptians, Plato and Plotinus, Harpocrates, Boethus and Numenius. The idea that the human soul returns attached to a bestial soul is attributed correctly by Aeneas to Syrianus and Proclus.

57. Syrianus and Proclus deny this possibility, drawing on the thinking of Theodorus of Asine. See Proclus, *In Remp.* 2.309.28ff.

58. For further discussion of related arguments, see Sorabji (1993), chapter 13.

59. The view attributed by Aeneas to Porphyry. See Plutarch *De Sera Numinis Vindicta* 563B–568A for an early version of this view. On this model, Nero's soul goes through fiery torments, is changed into

for example, in Plotinus *Enn.* 3.4.2.16–30, who also argues that the choices one makes are partly dependent on one's previous lives (*Enn.* 4.3.8.6–10).[60]

Aeneas rebuts positions such as these with humour. If a drunk returns as a person suited to being a drunk, so much the better for him. If the evil person returns with his soul attached to an animal's soul, perhaps Odysseus would return hanging onto the leg of an ant, just as he clung to the underbelly of a sheep in the cave of the Cyclops.

But his serious objection is that life on earth is an education for a good life. In this he is largely in line with the Platonic tradition, except that he is even more optimistic about the efficacy of moral education. If the soul continually returns, the education is in vain and ethical progress never reaches its goal. Aeneas argues against the eternal pre-existence of the soul, as he does against the eternity *ab initio* of the cosmos, because it would undermine the ethical purpose of creation, and therefore undermine the idea that God is the Good. As we have seen, Aeneas' God is a just judge, the providential power who guides his creation into harmonious order. From his perfect knowledge of present and future, God allots fitting outcomes for all his creatures while maintaining room for creaturely freedom (29.1–3; 30.10–13; cf. Plotinus *Enn.* 3.2–3).[61] Drawing on a Plotinian argument (*Enn.* 3.2.5.21–3), he claims that God makes even evil, which is caused by humans, subject to his harmonious ordering of the cosmos: God can bring good out of evil and bring to perfection the things human evil has left deformed (26.16–23). His arguments about the pre-existence of the soul are partly designed to leave room for this providential power.

His final argument against the pre-existence of the soul emphasizes this ethical point. Euxitheus states the argument for the pre-existence of the soul based on the Platonic theory of recollection (Plato, *Meno* 82aff.). Euxitheus interprets this argument as providing evidence that the soul pre-exists because humans can remember good and true things. But this also threatens the goodness of the providential creator: 'readily and justly one despises the judge if, despite knowing no crime in one's self, one undergoes punishment' (17.13–14). Why remember what is good but not the evils by which the soul was educated in its previous life? Humour is used against Theophrastus' objection that some

a Pindaric viper, and finally, out of divine compassion due to him for showing favour to the Greeks, ends up as a frog. See further Smith (1984) on Porphyry's view and its relation to Iamblichus', whose opinion is recorded in Nemesius, *de natura hominis* 2.35.7–17 Morani.

60. Plotinus countenances the idea that souls of errant humans migrate to animals at e.g. *Enn* 1.1.11.8–15.

61. Aeneas' discussion of providence is deeply influenced by Plotinus, with very close parallels to 3.2.5.6–7, 21–3, 3.2.9.1–4, 3.2.11.9–12, and 3.2.13.7.

historical figures recalled not just the Forms but also details of their previous terrestrial existence. For example, Pythagoras remembered that he was a warrior at Troy (17.19; cf. Diogenes Laertius *Lives of the Philosophers* 7.4.7ff.):

> If he says this, he misleads, in an attempt to persuade [us] about his teaching that the soul is pre-existent. With the same intention he hid in a hole under the ground for ten years, and then, doubtless, rose up from Hades, and claimed to have heard from Pluto that the soul was immortal, and he was believed!... Certainly, as soon as the sun rises, the phantasm is also destroyed. Thus the babbling is an old wives' tale and in no way persuasive. (17.21–24, 19.8–9)[62]

Irony and sarcasm aside, the arguments against the pre-existence of the soul all seek to demonstrate the absolute dependence of the created soul on the first principle of Being who is also the providential first principle of Goodness. The argument is therefore directly analogous to the more general argument about the creation of the cosmos.

Similarly, the potential eternity of the soul paralleled the manner in which the cosmos could be said to be eternal. In the debates about the eternity of the cosmos *ex parte post*, Aeneas argues that the cosmos is mortal and so is not eternal in the future direction on its own account. Rather, it will be made immortal by a free act of the creator, who will, at some point in the future, make everything immortal. Plato's *Timaeus* (41b) was used to make this point. The same argument, and the same passage from Plato, is used with respect to the soul. God created the soul and did not make it from his own substance (40.2ff.). But it is rational, and so resembles something that is immortal, in that it is independent (within its own sphere of influence), has its own animating principle, and distributes life to the organic body.

These statements seem to give the soul a higher place in the hierarchy than the material cosmos, and Aeneas is not clear about the sort of *transformation* which would be involved in the Being of the soul by making it immortal. 'Transformation into immortality', in his account, seems to apply mainly to the material world, whereas the immortality of the soul seems to follow from its rational nature, which remains the same (and hence is immortal), rather than being transformed into immortality. In arguments such as this one, Aeneas' account seems to move by analogy from bodies to souls, an analogy which Neoplatonists could not accept.

Yet the new creation is also a change for God's rational creatures. A clue about this new sort of soul is given in the discussion about the resurrection of

62. Cf. Hdt., *Hist.* 4.95–96.

the body in the last third of the dialogue. The resurrection body will be the same individual, but the formal principle of matter will predominate, rather than the changeable stuff of the body (58.20–59.15). Perhaps the resurrected soul, since it would be bound to an immortal body, would be able to express its rationality perfectly, and so more fully participate in the immortal quality given to it by the creator. But the soul's immortality remains dependent on the creator, who grants it a taste of immortality as a gift. There is no sense that the soul is independently immortal, just as the cosmos gains its immortality by virtue of the divine will, and so cannot, even in eschatological perfection, be thought of as equal to God. The soul is not immortal in the same sense that God is. This argument is intended to make the case that God and his creation do not share relevant properties, so God's uniqueness or sovereignty remain intact.

Arguments about the causal processes involved in the soul's coming into being are also equivalent to those responsible for the generation or creation of the world (e.g. 39.14ff.; 41.1ff.). The soul is not generated by procession or emanation. As Neoplatonists would agree and Aeneas emphasizes, there is no diminution of the divine substance when God creates the multiplicity of souls. Aeneas then argues that the soul is neither coeternal nor consubstantial with God. The first principle, rather than a lower hypostasis, produces the soul, just as God created the rational, heavenly powers (39.14–15). God the first principle is directly involved in the creation of each individual human soul. Aeneas considers Plato's argument (*Tim.* 30b–c) that the soul is a 'blessed god', willingly created out of the demiurge's goodness, as a means of making the world possess intellect (7.5–11). But the Christian character in the dialogue rejects such a divinization of the soul (8.3–6). This all parallels the causal processes outlined in the discussion directly concerning the cause of the cosmos, and is designed to preserve God in his unique role as ground of Being.

The direct creation by God of the soul and God's continuing providential care for the soul were examples of a wider argument about divine providence in creation and the possibility of *creatio continua*. God directly created souls having already commanded the land to nurture herbs, drugs, and medicines for the welfare of his creations (37.22ff.). God has foreknowledge of the afflictions that will beset human souls and establishes an ordered cosmos in which they are capable of recognizing the signs of his divinity. God's divine will continually holds the souls he created in existence.

6.6 Monastic Problems: Aeneas and Origenism

The problems Aeneas explores, and the arguments with which he seeks to make his case, are congruent with wider discussions and controversies in

Neoplatonism, although in the discussion of creation and Trinity, Christian problems seem crucial, and the wider logic of Aeneas' argument is securely founded on claims about the nature of the Christian God and his saving plan for his creatures. But did other Christian problems, specifically those generated in the local monastic communities, also help to generate aspects of Aeneas' argument? The Gazan monasteries, as I argued in Chapter 2, were a possible source for the rise of Origenist ideas in the early sixth century. So one way of determining intellectual influence from the monastic communities is to explore the question of whether Aeneas' dialogue displays any evidence for Origenist ideas about creation.

According to Origen, God is entirely immaterial; in this he is unlike creation, which is thoroughly material (*Princ.* I.1.1–6).[63] Yet the act of creation includes the creation of the reasons for creation. In creating these incorporeal *logoi*, God providentially creates the principles—relations, laws, possibilities, causes, and purposes—which govern creation (e.g. *CommJn* 13.42).[64] The material creation evolves in accordance with this providential creation of principles: 'It is because of this creation that the entire world has been able to have come into existence' (*CommJn* 1.34). These created principles are understood to be in the Word of God, the second person of the Trinity, who contains, but is not defined by 'the *logoi* of everything which has been created' (*Contra Celsum* 5.39). These *logoi* decorate the divine Logos, but they are not, for Origen, co-substantial or coeternal with him. As Tzamalikos points out, it thus makes sense for Origen to say that the 'rational creations' in paradise were perfect, since the created *logoi* of the providential creation were perfect, incorporeal principles awaiting individuation. Yet this is not yet the embodied life of creatures, for it is a world without time, time which only comes into being with the creation of matter.[65]

The real temporal world is a material creation, and some explanation is needed for the way in which bodily creatures act against the providential operation of creation. For Origen, reason implies freedom, which he defined as a choice between good and evil (*Princ.* I.7.5). The creation of the material realm occurs when the first beings sin and fall away from the body of the Logos by inappropriately applying their god-given freedom. Such a fall modifies a reading of Origen which makes the created principles merely lifeless ideas in the mind of God, a formulation already found in Philo of Alexandria (*Prov.* 1.7).

63. The following account is indebted to Williams (2004). Standard accounts of Origen's cosmology have been questioned by Tzamalikos (2006) and Edwards (2002), 87–122, on whom I also draw in the section. See also 4.1 above.

64. In this analysis I follow Tzamalikos (2006), 39–48.

65. Ibid. 49.

Origen's principles have some degree of agency, although at this distance from Origen's writing it is impossible to specify exactly what the mechanism for this agency is.[66] As they fall they assume bodies, which God gives them in the new material creation in order that they might rise again through a process of education and purification (*Princ.* IV.3; II.8.2; I.4–5). At this point it makes sense to speak of the creation of material individuals (*Princ.* I.5.3) and the beginning of temporality.[67] Humans as embodied personalities live a life of their own, but it is a life now radically apart from God (*Princ* IV.4.1; *CommJn* 20.28), although all share in the rationality that links them to God the Logos (*CommMt* 17.34).[68]

Education that allows humans to ascend from their fallen state is the purpose of the material cosmos. Fallen souls can rise to different levels of creation and there is a variegated hierarchy of creaturely existence (e.g. *Princ* II.1.1, II.4.3; *CommJn* 1.31).[69] For example, the heaven is more pure than the earth. But this is different from reincarnation, since each new level of spiritual maturity is matched by a different material environment (*Princ.* II.11.6; *HomNum* 27).[70]

The Logos is the ground of plurality which is seen first in the intelligible creation. The Logos is the perfect expression of God's rationality: God the Father is alone *autotheos* (*CommJn* II.2). All created minds participate in the Logos' eternal contemplation of the Father. The Logos does not derive from the οὐσία of the Father, since this implies the possibility that God is divided or diminished (*CommJn* XX.18). Rather, the Logos is generated (γενητός), since there cannot be two first principles.

These ideas led to continued controversy. The account of fallen rational principles and their re-training to original purity may, later thinkers thought, separate the essential soul, understood as a principle, from the contingent body, which was only created at the fall. This in turn may cast doubt on the biblical idea of the resurrection of the body.[71] The account of the Trinity is suspicious to

66. Ibid. 73–79. But Tzamalikos' suggestion at p. 74 that the incorporeal principles could be understood as living, yet not living a life of their own by the Pauline analogy of 'I live; yet not I but Christ lives in me' (Gal. 2:20) is not to the point, since Christ living in the *logoi* confuses the created logoi with the uncreated Logos, and cannot explain evil choices without unwanted doctrinal consequences. The claim at *Princ.* II.2.2 that there is no purely incorporeal being other than God may provide a mechanism for a form of incorporeality that distinguishes the *logoi* from divine Wisdom sufficiently to ground the independence necessary to explain the fall.

67. Tzamalikos (2006), 82–83.

68. Ibid. 96.

69. See further ibid. 108.

70. Williams (2004), 136.

71. Sorabji has argued that Origen believed the resurrection body was made from impassible air and fire. For precursors, texts and discussion, see Sorabji, (2006), 58ff., 72. Williams notes that Origen is ambiguous here, since there is no absolutely incorporeal reality except God (*Princ.* II.2.2), which might imply that there are bodies of some sort even in the immaterial realm.

the doctrinal sniffer-dog, trained only to hunt out concepts that smell different from fourth- and fifth-century credal definitions, to which Origen's ideas contributed, but about which he could have known nothing. Finally, the creation of the intelligible beings, since it may be interpreted as the timeless creation of something like God, could be claimed by unsympathetic interpreters to add a further divine principle.

During the late fifth and early sixth centuries, the form of Origenism which was influential in the monasteries was that adopted by Evagrius. Hence, Evagrian ideas are part of the shared discourse between the schools and monasteries, and it is reasonable to ask about the relationship between Evagrian Origenism and Aeneas' dialogue.

Evagrius' writings about the spiritual life provided an important theory of monastic living and made him popular in the eastern monastic tradition. His version of Origenism has many of the features just outlined. He shares Origen's tendency towards allegorical interpretation.[72] More importantly, Evagrius' account builds on Origen's regarding the nature, purpose and origin of the world, souls and corporeal existence, and the role of the Logos in salvation, but takes Origen's ideas in directions that are more difficult to harmonize with orthodoxy as it was constructed in the fourth and fifth centuries.[73] On questions of creation, Evagrius argues that the soul pre-exists and that there is a double creation (*Keph. Gnost.* I, 50).[74] Origen's *logoi* are understood as pure, invisible, and rational creatures which were created and existed in a perfect unity with God.[75] However, all of these creatures, except the Logos, sought to become independent, and introduced a movement in attempting to separate themselves from this perfect unity (*Keph. Gnost.* III, 22). This separation or fall from stable unity was the cause of evil in the cosmos (*Keph. Gnost.* I, 51). Christ the Logos, the only rational being who remained united to God as pure *nous*, is the creator of the material creation.[76] Before the separation of the rational beings from the divine unity, there was a cosmic unity of intelligible beings, gazing in perfect unity at the Divine Monad: 'Before the movement, God was good, wise, knowing, creator of the incorporeals, father of the intelligible beings and

72. For example, in his treatment of Exodus, Evagrius follows Origen, arguing, 'Egypt signifies evil; the desert the *praktikê*; the land of Juda symbolises the contemplation of the body; Jerusalem the incorporeal and Sion is the Symbol of the Trinity' (*Keph. Gnost.* VI, 49). As Guillaumont notes, such a method of interpretation is not unique to Origen, but does help to place Evagrius in a general 'Weltanschauung' consistent with Origen. See Guillaumont (1962), 102–3.

73. Ibid. 103. See also Konstantinovsky (2009), especially 20ff., 180–82.

74. See Guillaumont (1962), 103–13.

75. Konstantinovsky (2009), 31.

76. Guillaumont (1962), 39.

all-knowing; after the falling away, he became the creator of the body, judge and governor' (*Keph. Gnost.* VI, 20; cf. II, 64).[77] Like Origen before him, Evagrius claims that the rational beings can fall to different levels of this new material world, depending on the extent of their rebellion.[78] The material cosmos therefore has distinct realms with different materialities.[79] While Evagrius' opponents attacked this scheme for an improper negative evaluation of the material world, Evagrius himself may not have despised the material creation. While the material cosmos results from the evil separation of rationality from divine unity, Evagrius sees it as a good consequence of the fall, part of God's providential plan for the rehabilitation of the rational beings (*Keph. Gnost.* VI, 75). The creation of bodies is intended to make the ascent of the rational creatures back to their original perfection possible (*Keph. Gnost.* II, 64; III, 38, 59, 66; VI, 20, 75). The body is evaluated positively, perhaps to guard against charges of Manichaeism (which were levelled anyway) (*Keph. Gnost.* IV, 60).[80] The body is not the prison of the soul, but the cause of its purity, because in the body the soul can contemplate Being (*Keph. Gnost.* IV, 70). I conclude, with Guillaumont, that while it is possible to assimilate the idea of two creations to a Neoplatonic belief in the distinct intelligible and perceptible worlds combined with a Manichean rejection of the visible world, Evagrius seeks to guard against such interpretations. For him, matter is not despised, and the visible world has its own providential part to play in the good God's providential plan for his creations.[81]

Given that the material creation is the result of the fall of rational beings, Evagrius' account depends on the idea of pre-existent souls. He also believes that souls are immortal and return within the material cosmos.[82] However, as in Origen's case, this idea should not be confused with standard ideas of reincarnation. There are indeed multiple resurrections to better planes of material existence. Souls which have taken the advantage of education within the material world are resurrected into a more excellent material existence (*Keph. Gnost.* III, 25, 47; V, 19). While the resurrected body is not the fleshly body, it is always formed of the four elements and is therefore material, best understood as a purer

77. My translations and general sketch are taken from Guillaumont's French translation in ibid.

78. Konstantinovsky (2009), 29.

79. For relevant texts, see Guillaumont (1962), 108.

80. The body is a necessary good, so suicide is forbidden (*Keph. Gnost.* IV, 76; cf. IV, 70). See ibid. 112: 'Le corps est, en effet, indispensable pour l'accomplissement de la praktikê.' See also *Practicos* 156, PG 140, 1248.

81. See ibid. 113.

82. For a more complete discussion of Evagrius' eschatology, see ibid. 114ff. See also Konstantinovsky (2009), 11–15.

mix of material elements (*Keph. Gnost.* III, 48, 50).[83] These resurrections are not unique, but part of a vast cycle of multiple changes in a long hierarchy, which includes archangels, angels, psychic beings, demons and humans (*Keph. Gnost.* V, 11). So while Evagrius may be able to claim that he professes the doctrine of the resurrection of the body, he does not consider this resurrection as a unique event, and there is some tension in his account, because the goal is to return to pure immateriality: 'Just as the first trumpet signified the creation of bodies, so too the last trumpet will signify the destruction of the body' (*Keph. Gnost.* III, 66; cf. I, 26, 29; II, 62; III, 68).

Christ is essential to the eschatological perfection of fallen rational souls.[84] The goal of the education of the rational souls in the material creation is a return to the unity they moved away from initially. But *pace* systems such as those advocated by Plotinus and later Neoplatonists, this return is not able to be achieved naturally. Soteriology is founded in Christology. That the Logos did not fall from God makes it possible for other rational beings to return to God. Evagrius has a distinction between Christ, the rational Logos who always stayed with the Father, and the Son, or Word of God, who works in the world to be a model for the perfection of the rational creatures (*Keph. Gnost.* I, 77; VI, 14).[85] While Guillaumont regards this as perfectly orthodox, it is not difficult to see how it was taken by Evagrius' opponents as too strong a subordination of the Son to the Father.[86]

These ideas probably continued to circulate during the fifth century, despite the relative silence of our sources.[87] Cyril of Scythopolis praises his hero Euthymius for rejecting the Origenists, whom he describes as those who accept the 'myth of the pre-existence of souls', and rejects the idea that the resurrection of souls is not bodily, which leads to other 'godless and impious doctrines to which these tenets give birth' (Cyril of Scythopolis, *Life of Euthymius* 26).

83. This has intriguing parallels with Platonic debates about the composition of the heavens. Cf. Philoponus *contra Aristotelem ap.* Simplicius, *in Cael.* 84,15–22; 88,28–34; Proclus *in Tim.* 2.43,20–44,24; Simplicius *in Cael.* 85,7–15. See also Wilberding (2006), 10ff.

84. For Evagrius' Christology, see Guillaumont (1962), 117–19.

85. See further ibid. 151–53.

86. Guillaumont declares that Evagrius was a faithful disciple of the Cappadocians in his Christology (118). Epiphanius, Jerome, and Theophilus all see in such Origenist ideas similarities with Arianism. See Epiphanius, *Panarion* 4.3 Holl p 410,9–11; Jerome, *Contra Joannem* 7, *PL* 23, 360ff.; Theophilus, *Lettre synodale de 400*, also preserved (in Latin) by Jerome, *Ep.* 92 (Hilberg CSEL 55, 147–55). See ibid., 85, 90, 97. Despite Guillaumont's doubts, Clark has shown that Theophilus did know Evagrius' work, but masked explicit references to him. See Clark (1992), 7, 39. Guillaumont's conclusions about Evagrius' orthodox Christology are questioned by Konstantinovsky (2009), e.g. 6–9.

87. Guillaumont (1962), 124.

He describes the Origenist ideas as particularly strong in Palestine.[88] They next appear in the years immediately preceding Justinian's condemnation of Origenism in the sixth century. Eight letters in the correspondence of John and Barsanuphius allow us to pinpoint Gaza as one place where Evagrius' ideas had some traction. In these letters (*Q&A* 600–607) the main concerns are the pre-existence of the soul, and whether the post-resurrection person continues to have a bodily nature.[89] Barsanuphius and John are at first unwilling to provide a detailed analysis of the proper response to these views, urging their correspondent to take more care of his soul through practising humility, instead of wondering about matters of abstract theology. But they finally come down against Evagrius' position, while noting that Evagrius may still be relied upon in other matters. This advice points to the high value placed on Evagrius' *Practicus* by the monastic communities.[90]

The condemnations of Origenism in 553 were probably directed against Evagrius' brand of Origenism. The *Edictum contra Origenem* Anathemas 6 and 8 (*ACO* iii) condemns the idea that there was an eternal creation and that Christ was a demiurge of the material creation (cf. *Keph. Gnost.* III, 24, 26). On the question of sin, the Council insisted that original sin is caused by Adam, rather than by a fall of eternal, rational souls. The resurrection of the body is explicitly affirmed, partly in order to separate the sort of body that resurrected creatures have from the divine substance. The edicts reject the idea of multiple resurrections, advocating instead one bodily resurrection of the saved and the eternal suffering of the damned.

How does this brand of Origenism relate to Aeneas' work? We have seen that Aeneas, somewhat like Origen, elevates the soul over the body. In contrast to Evagrius, Aeneas defends bodily resurrection at great length. Human bodies are capable of contact with rational souls and can therefore receive immortality (61.8–12). He identifies standard arguments against bodily resurrection, rebuts them, and offers stories of bodies coming back to life to support the idea that corruption is not the only possibility for the body. On the question of the pre-existence of the soul, Aeneas is fundamentally opposed to Evagrius, although, as I argued above, his immediate arguing partners appear to be Neoplatonists, not Origenists. Furthermore, on the question of whether

88. While this passage could be read as evidence for Origenism in the years leading up to Chalcedon, the ideas Euthymius combats are all ideas which were condemned in Cyril's own lifetime. The denial of Origenism is closely modelled on Justinian's *Edict against Origen*. It may therefore be better to read this as evidence for sixth-, rather than fifth-century Origenism.

89. For this correspondence, see Guillaumont (1962), 124–28.

90. See further Kofsky and Bitton-Ashkelony (2004).

the resurrection is unique, he argues that one life is sufficient for the perfection of bodies; the arguments I have identified as opposing the Stoic idea of eternal return could equally well be directed against this element of Evagrian Origenism. While this argument is framed in the Neoplatonic terms of metempsychosis, it may also be read as rebutting the Evagrian Origenist idea that multiple lives, deaths, and resurrections are possible for created beings as part of a series of lives aimed towards perfection. Aeneas does not offer the possibility that there are gradations of being to which a soul might be resurrected. With the exception of the 'first beings', where we have noted similarity with Origen himself, the whole created cosmos is material and corruptible. Stars, the moon, and terrestrial rocks share these basic qualities. In place of the Evagrian notion of resurrection to different metaphysical levels, Aeneas offers a stark choice between souls who have been good, and are crowned as victors and enter paradise, and the souls who have acted evilly, who suffer eternal punishment.

Likewise, the charge that Aeneas' account of the Trinity is excessively subordinationist is a misreading.[91] Even if Aeneas' Christology were counted as subordinationist, it would not subordinate Christ in the way that Evagrius did. Christ is not separate from the Logos for Aeneas. Again, similarity to Origen is closer than parallels with Evagrius.

The similarity between Aeneas' account of the intelligible cosmos and that of Origen is close. A similar sort of thinking appears to operate, in that God's rationality is sufficient reason for the eternal creation of an intelligible realm. Concern with the first intelligible creation seems to arise in the relation between this intelligible realm and the material realm. The 'orthodox' suspect that this is the relation between something superior and something inferior, however highly Evagrius might have prized the material universe as a creation of God within the divine plan of salvation. The souls of mortals remain fallen pure souls. Aeneas' treatment is fundamentally different. There is a distinction between human souls and the first beings. God creates both, but he created the first beings eternally to be an example of divine governance and power, whereas he creates each human soul individually up to the present (37.16ff.). The first beings are not governors, but they serve God and thereby represent divine rule to mortals in the perceptible realm (50.13–22).

Aeneas accepts that the first beings might exercise their freedom evilly. Their particular evil is that they imagine that they are independently powerful and

91. Cf. Gallicet (1978).

'desire tyranny and govern illegally' (50.22–25). Such beings do not become mortal, for

> they were created as immortals in the first place by [God], but they will perceive mortals as though in darkness, and, as though they have fallen into a river, they are carried here and there, being ruled rather than ruling (cf. *Tim.* 43a).... When [Becoming] is dissolved, tyranny is also destroyed along with it. And after the destruction of the tyrants, he will make immortal again that part which because of them he caused to be mortal at first. (50.26–51.2, 51.7–9)

Mercifully causing the first Beings to experience the mortal world to allow them to regain their place as immortal beings should not be confused with the idea that the mortal world is created because of the fall of immaterial beings. Aeneas does come close to this idea, and does not, unlike Zacharias, emphasize the Adamic fall. Yet even if the fall in Aeneas is a fall of the original intellectual beings, Aeneas' account of the fall is different from Evagrius', where, as we have seen, the fall is a separation from the divine unity. For Aeneas, the rational beings are clearly designated as different from the divine substance and nature from the beginning. Only the Trinity is timeless; time comes into being with the creation of the intelligible heavens (44.80).

I therefore conclude that Aeneas' thought should not be interpreted as conforming to fifth-century Origenism. Evagrius had made the idea of the pre-existence of the soul attractive for a substantial group of Christians in Palestine. Aeneas' dialogue rebuts this idea, taking Neoplatonists as his explicit opponents. But given the relevance of these questions to internal Christian disputes, it may be appropriate to read Aeneas' rejection of the pagan idea of the pre-existence of the soul as a way of rebutting the Christian (Evagrian or Origenist) idea of pre-existence. If this reading is accepted, Aeneas' dialogue implicitly attacks those who would support Evagrius by identifying them with pagans. A similar rhetorical move could be seen in Aeneas' arguments about the repeated return of souls to the material realm.

An alternative direction of influence may be posited, given the general lack of evidence for fifth-century Origenism. The increased number and urgency of debates about creation at the turn of the sixth century, for which the works of Aeneas, Zacharias, and Procopius are evidence, may provide one stimulus for renewed controversies over Origen's account of creation. Aeneas' dialogue and the associated works by Zacharias and Procopius may therefore be one stimulus for the sixth-century Origenist controversy. Further work remains to be done on this question.

6.7 Problems and Solutions

Attention at Gaza to the doctrine of creation is related to Proclus' formalization of Neoplatonic arguments for cosmic eternity. What led Aeneas and Zacharias to reject this idea so forcefully? I suggest that two central problems govern their thought. The first is how to make sense of divine freedom. The second is how to defend God's goodness, and the possibility of eschatological re-creation, given their account of divine freedom. In elucidating these two problems—divine freedom and eschatologically justified divine goodness—Aeneas and Zacharias expound the doctrine of creation from nothing and grapple with other related problems which emerge both from within Neoplatonism and within Christianity.

The primary reason that Aeneas and Zacharias reject the Neoplatonic doctrine of the eternity of the world is that they think it limits divine freedom. They understand freedom as choosing between multiple, real alternatives. While this idea may be found in Peripatetics such as Alexander of Aphrodisias, a Neoplatonist like Plotinus (e.g. *Enn.* VI.8) rejects the idea that freedom is identical with the possibility of deliberation. Alternative choices only arise if something has first gone wrong, for example, if the soul is subjected to the external influence of the body, which is, of course, impossible in the case of the One. So where Aeneas and Zacharias often think of divine freedom as choice between alternative possibilities, Neoplatonists prefer to think of this as absence of external constraints. Armed with this different view of divine freedom, they set out a view of creation which makes the world radically contingent on the divine will. God's choices create the conditions or structure of the universe. In Neoplatonic accounts, by contrast, while God may be said to will the creation, the act of will is not deliberative.[92]

Yet this different view of divine freedom leads to several sub-problems for Aeneas and Zacharias. All these problems are thus generated within Christianity, and their subsequent use of Neoplatonism becomes less important as they explore problems in Christian ethics, eschatology, soteriology, resurrection, and Trinitarian formulations. First and most importantly, they have to meet the charge that the absolute contingency of creation implies that God can be capricious. They seek to meet this objection by setting out a view of history that proves that God is always faithful to his promises. Furthermore, God created the cosmos and human history with it precisely in order to train humans up for divine perfection. This account of human and divine history links the problems of divine freedom and divine goodness. But since they seek to preserve divine freedom by insisting on a finite cosmos, they then attempt to counter Neoplatonic objections to a finite cosmos. For example, they seek to rebut

92. See Proclus, *in Tim.*, 1.321.10ff.; 362.2f. and Hadot (1978), 91.

the inference that creating a finite universe means that God must have changed from a state of inactivity to a state of activity. The major challenge from within Neoplatonism to the idea of a finite universe is that it is incompatible with the idea that God is good. This argument is put cogently in Proclus' first argument for the eternity of the world. The Neoplatonists had identified goodness with sameness and unity. 'In the Good there is no envy at all', so God makes the cosmos 'like himself'; anything else is to undermine God's goodness.[93] By making the world fundamentally different from God, Aeneas' and Zacharias' account of creation runs up against this Neoplatonic idea of goodness.

These factors go a long way towards explaining the mass of material about ethics in arguments about creation. The construction of a physics which is congruent with Christian ethics and soteriology is a dominant concern for Aeneas and Zacharias. The historical account of creation, which is tied to an interventionist God who enters history repeatedly, from creation, to incarnation, to the eschaton, widens the view of what can be relevant to discussions about creation. This view of how God acts in history makes the Gazans emphasize the finiteness of creation into the future, and means that their views of creation are intimately tied up with ethics, soteriology, and eschatology.

Crucially, Christian ideas of salvation history both cause Aeneas and Zacharias to reject the Neoplatonic idea of the eternity of the world and provide the resources for their account of divine goodness. The account of the divine plan proves God's continual providential concern for his creatures. Such an account depends on God being able to enter history and inaugurate a new creation. This possibility is denied by Neoplatonic accounts of the eternity of the world, and their denial is a principal reason why Aeneas and Zacharias reject Neoplatonic cosmology and direct their arguments at the impossibility of the infinite world in the future direction, instead of merely focusing their attention, as contemporary Neoplatonists did, on the eternal origins of the cosmos.

The space which Zacharias and Aeneas each give to the question of the resurrection of bodies is a further Christian concern related to their two main problems. God retains his freedom with respect to his creatures even after they die. The resurrection of the body is a particular case of creation and re-creation, proclaiming that the body that God freely created will come to an end and be changed into a new bodily creation. At the level of individual souls, as in cosmic changes, we again see the Christian emphasis on the end, rather than simply the beginning, of

93. While contemporary Neoplatonists tempered Plato's text somewhat here, arguing, in effect, that everything is *as like to God as possible* (e.g. Nous is unlike the One because it is multiple), the emphasis is still emphatically on unity.

time. Making sense of the resurrection of the body forms a part of the justification of the Christian God's goodness. The new creation of perfect bodies in the general resurrection is the pinnacle of the divine plan which justifies divine goodness.

For Aeneas, the resurrection of the body is tied to an argument about the pre-existence of souls, which is similarly related to the problems of creation of a finite world by a good creator. Aeneas argues that souls are not pre-existent: they are created from nothing and are radically dependent on God, just as the cosmos is. The pre-existence of the soul is a case study for the wider rejection of the Neoplatonic idea of the eternity of the world. Rejecting the pre-existence of the soul causes Aeneas a range of ethical problems relating to theodicy. How are the misfortunes that befall humans just if they cannot be explained by evils committed in past lives, and how is the success of evildoers just, unless evildoers can be punished in a future life? To the first part of the question, Aeneas responds by arguing that the world is a place for the education of the soul. This forms part of Aeneas' defence of divine goodness and freedom, because the God who created the soul from nothing is the same God who provides the conditions which allow the soul to learn goodness. Reward for human goodness is found in the transformation to immortality; conversely, eternal punishment awaits those who acted evilly.

Zacharias is more concerned than Aeneas with the problem of human freedom. He recognizes that his account of divine freedom, with God the sovereign ruler over his creations, may cause problems for an account of human freedom. For Zacharias, humans are slaves of the absolutely free God. So there is a problem about how he can coherently call humans free at all. Aeneas would agree that humans should serve God, but he does not find this problematic. Rather, he assumes that serving goodness is what people would always happily do simply because it is the rational thing to do. This draws on Platonic psychology, where to be free is to do what is in accordance with the promptings of the rational part of the soul.

For both thinkers, however, a Platonic logic of the twofold Good operates. The Good is both the source and the goal of goodness. There is the Good and the blessedness of participating in the Good. Zacharias draws on this idea in his somewhat different account of human freedom. For Zacharias, God is the origin and goal of human freedom, and human freedom is achieved by participating in divine freedom. This participation is achieved through good actions—following the divine law—as well as through the action of God in the believer, drawing the believer towards likeness to God. Humans are free when they are enacting their intended purpose, which is to serve God within the divine plan.[94] As I argued on

94. For exercise concepts and freedom, see Taylor (1979). Making human freedom an exercise concept means that God's freedom (choice between alternative possibilities) is only partially analogous to human freedom for Zacharias. Humans do have alternative possibilities, but only one set of choices

slightly different grounds above, this explains the apparent paradox of freedom as servitude.

In Aeneas, the story is somewhat simpler. The fact that humans have rational souls implies that they have freedom, a choice between good and evil. Participation in divine freedom is achieved by utilizing one's divinely given reason, which is equivalent to acting well. If Zacharias' problem concerns how humans could be free given that they are servants of God, Aeneas' is the more traditional problem of evil: What is the origin of evil given that God is Good? His answer is that evil lies in the exercise of human freedom. In arguments recognizable from Neoplatonism and which draw on the discussion in Plato's *Laws*, he claims that God cannot be blamed for what is up to us. The different approaches to human freedom in Aeneas and Zacharias suggest a stronger governing Christian problematic for Zacharias. On this question, Aeneas remains more clearly within the established Neoplatonic argument frame, whereas Zacharias deals with a problem generated primarily within Christianity.

Thus despite their shared problems and Zacharias' direct dependence on Aeneas, there are also differences between the two dialogues. Aeneas, with his interest in theories about the soul, covers a wider range of philosophical topics than Zacharias. The material about the soul in the *Theophrastus* is intimately related to questions of cosmology, but it also emphasizes the direct relevance of questions of cosmology to anthropology and the direct dependence of humans on God's creative acts. Zacharias' work, while clearly cognizant of contemporary Neoplatonism, does not mention as many Platonists, and the language of Christian orthodoxy is more frequently employed. These differences reveal different rhetorical strategies and point to the different ways in which Gazan Christians could interact with the overlapping and dynamic Christian and Neoplatonic communities in the late fifth century. This interaction between different local cultures was expanded into the monasteries, particularly in Aeneas' dialogue, through sections of argument which display a creative relationship with strands of Evagrian Origenism. Zacharias, like Procopius after him, is more careful to limit the possibility that his work may be counted as Origenist, perhaps pointing to a rise in the Origenist controversy in the years soon after Aeneas wrote his dialogue.

will lead to the true freedom of serving God. Zacharias' account of human freedom may thus appear to approach compatibilism. Further work is required to explore the relation of human and divine freedom in late-antique Christian thought.

7

Conclusion

Creation Creating Cultures

7.1 Creatio Continua

The debate about the creation and eternity of the world continued well into the sixth century. In the same year that Justinian closed the Neoplatonic school in Athens, the Christian Neoplatonist John Philoponus wrote a work entitled *Against Proclus on the Eternity of the World*.[1] The Neoplatonist philosopher Simplicius took up the standard for Athens, and Jerusalem found its champion in Cosmas Indicopleustes, an Alexandrian traveller, merchant, and monk, who was incensed to find a fellow Christian accepting so much Neoplatonic philosophy.[2] The Gazans' contribution may be read as keeping the philosophical conversation alive between Proclus and Philoponus and as one stage in the development of Christian rebuttals of the Neoplatonic idea of the eternity of the world.

The debates between Philoponus and Simplicius have been extensively studied; more perhaps remains to be written on Cosmas' contribution.[3] In this brief section I gesture towards these debates and suggest possible intersections between the Gazans and the later Alexandrian controversies, identifying initial similarities and differences for further exploration.[4]

While Philoponus' Christian beliefs led him to criticize Neoplatonic arguments for the eternity of the world, his *Contra Proclum* stays within a Neoplatonic frame to the extent that it may be read as aiming to remove inconsistencies within Neoplatonism. This work, together with the *Contra Aristotelem*, shows Philoponus sharply and perceptively using Neoplatonic arguments and turning

1. For Philoponus, see Bohm (1970); MacCoull (1995); Philoponus (1984, 1997, 2004, 2005, 2006); Rashed (2004); Scholten (1996); Sorabji (1987); Wildberg (1988). On the closure of the Neoplatonist school, see Blumenthal (1978); Cameron (1969); Sorabji (2005); Watts (2004).

2. For Simplicius, see Baltussen (2008); Foulkes (1992); Hadot (1978, 1990); Hoffmann (1987); Simplicius (vol. 9: 1882, 1894, vol. 10: 1895, 1989, 2001); Watts (2005). For Cosmas, see Anastos (1953); Cosmas (1897, 1968); Mouriki-Charalambous (1970); Wolska (1962).

3. On Philoponus and Simplicius, see essays in Sorabji (2010); Wildberg (1988); and the relevant volumes of the Ancient Commentators on Aristotle Series. On Simplicius, see Balthussen (2008). For Cosmas Indicopleustes, see Wolska (1962).

4. Watts (2006), 237ff. reconstructs potential social connections between Zacharias and Philoponus. See also Sorabji (2012) and my chapter in Fowler (2014), *Plato in the Third Sophistic* for further comparisons.

them against Neoplatonists. He knows the detail: we know Proclus' arguments for the eternity of the world because Philoponus quoted them in order to provide a point-by-point, systematic, and penetrating rebuttal. If we take Procopius' most successful argument against the Neoplatonists, that they should accept the creation of matter from nothing since they believe in the creation of form from nothing, we find Philoponus arguing with much greater philosophical rigor and precision, and with much clearer knowledge of the detail of the Aristotelian basis for the Neoplatonic position. He makes the claim within an argument that motion was not eternal (*Contra Aristotelem* in Simplicius *in Phys.* 1142,1–28) and strengthens it with the claim that God can destroy matter into not-being, just as he does with form (*Contra Aristotelem* in Simplicius *in Phys.* 1177,10–26).

This brings out one important difference between the Gazans and Philoponus. While the Gazans were interested in Neoplatonic philosophy, they did not attempt to advance a Neoplatonic 'research programme'. They might have applauded Philoponus' lemma-by-lemma refutation of Proclus, but they would simultaneously have been bemused by it. Philoponus' engagement with Neoplatonism reaches a very different level of philosophical sophistication and points to a stronger and more vibrant contemporary Neoplatonic scholarly community in Alexandria well into the sixth century.

Nevertheless, I have identified some areas where the Gazans' thought overlaps with Philoponus'. Some, including treatment of the Atticus-Plutarch interpretation of *Timaeus* 28b can be put down to shared general knowledge of key points in Neoplatonic interpretations of the origins of the cosmos. In this category, they share arguments about the standard images of God as a craftsman or an architect, or standard models for creation, including the image of the shadow and the emanation of light from the sun. Many similarities can be explained by shared stimulus from Proclus' fifth-century works. For example, both the Gazans and Philoponus deal with questions Proclus asks in his *Eighteen Arguments*. If god is good, how could he allow the cosmos to be dissolved? If there was a time when the universe did not exist, how can we speak of God as a creator? Given that time and the heaven coexist, and time has neither beginning nor end, how can the heaven come to an end? Other shared problems seem to arise from standard school criticisms of Christian ideas about creation. For example, the Gazans and Philoponus both respond to the criticism that God should have created the world to be eternal originally, instead of making it mortal first, and then promising to transform it into immortality. Further, Zacharias and Philoponus both attribute the concept of coeternity to the Neoplatonists (Zacharias to Ammonius and Philoponus to Proclus), and attempt to show the weakness of this concept in similar ways, perhaps pointing to ways in which a Trinitarian frame shapes the arguments in both episodes.

Other passages suggest a connection between the Gazans' works and Philoponus'. This is not the place to enumerate all of them. A brief look at one example may suffice to demonstrate both the ways in which the Gazan episode can be seen to be contributing to the long-running Christian-Neoplatonic debate about creation as well as the ways in which the Gazan arguments differ from Philoponus' more explicitly and carefully philosophical contribution. I take the case of Proclus' fourth argument, which is about the impiety which follows if one believes that the cosmos is not everlasting, given that if the cosmos is not everlasting, there is alteration in the creator, who is sometimes not creating and sometimes creating.

Zacharias' arguments against these points have in part been analysed above. His key argument was that since God does not create in time, the initial act of creation is not an alteration in time. Near the end of his dialogue, he uses the example of the creation of individuals. Socrates, Plato, and any individual are created by God, as Ammonius agrees. So how is it, asks Zacharias, that they are not everlasting? And why does the generation and corruption of individuals not worry the Neoplatonists? Zacharias does not drive home the point that the alteration of creatures does not imply the alteration of God, but the background of Proclus' fourth argument suggests that that is the direction in which he is heading. By contrast, Philoponus has an extended passage on different kinds of alterations which sits within the Iamblichan tradition of Neoplatonic thought about whether God can have knowledge of individuals or the future without thereby being bound up in particulars or time (*Contra Proclum* 4.9; 16.1–4). Returning to Zacharias, Ammonius is made to agree that even though individuals undergo corruption, God is still Good. He is also made to agree that the generation and corruption of such individuals does not make them less good, or imply envy in God. This goes to Proclus' first argument, that if God creates a creation which is not everlasting, he would be creating ungenerously. That is, the creation of a finite universe would be the act of a jealous God, and in the Good there is no envy at all, as Plato put it, so God would not be the Good. Ammonius goes on to argue that the sun is the cause of corruption and generation on earth, making a Neoplatonic distinction between the different sorts of causes at the different levels of the cosmos and Zacharias responds with the arguments outlined above against the divinity of the sun and the heavens, suggesting that a major concern for Zacharias was pagan religious practices in the schools, such as those of Antonius, whom we recall the Neoplatonist Damascius praised for making Gaza more reverent than it had been.

In his response to Proclus' fourth argument, Philoponus also uses the example of the generation and corruption of individuals (*Contra Proclum* 4.9, 79,16ff.). Like Zacharias, he uses the example of the creation and destruction of Socrates and Plato. Like Zacharias, he points out that God's goodness is not called into question by the generation and corruption of individual creations. But unlike Zacharias, he makes the argument about change and alteration much more clearly, and he explicitly makes an argument about the types of changes which should and should not concern a Neoplatonist to support his claim for the continued goodness of God along Neoplatonic lines. Philoponus also goes on immediately to propose an argument about the operation of the sun, but he does not offer the distracting argument about the sun's divinity. Rather, he uses the analogy of how individuals are differently affected by the sun's rays to point out that the sun is not itself altered by the individuals it changes. He completes his argument with the claim Zacharias had earlier made, namely that God has no need of time to produce, but brings all creatures into existence at the instant that he wills them.

It is clear that the structure and content of Philoponus' argument is much more firmly tied to Proclus' Neoplatonism. Philoponus sticks tenaciously and perceptively to the logic of Proclus' arguments, and shows a stronger interest in the detail of arguments within the Neoplatonic tradition. Zacharias, by contrast, does not follow Proclus' logic, and while his arguments resonate against the backdrop of Proclus' treatise, he has other concerns, partly generated from within Christian doctrinal debates, and partly a function of immediate social problems in the schools, which help to generate arguments that are very different from Philoponus', for all their shared material. Christians among Philoponus' audience needed to be much more deeply knowledgeable about Neoplatonism, and care more about its internal consistency, than the implied audience of either of the dialogues of Aeneas or Zacharias.

Despite the arguments they share, in general, while the Gazans occasionally provide arguments which might bother Neoplatonists on Neoplatonic grounds, and show knowledge of contemporary Neoplatonism even as they misrepresent it in their arguments, their general strategy is to present a coherent picture of their own instead of entering into detailed Neoplatonic argument. In this task, they were aided by discussion about creation in the Judeo-Christian tradition from the New Testament and Hellenistic Judaism to the Cappadocians and beyond. Their deployment of Neoplatonism is mostly general and superficial rather than particular and penetrating; they do not want to be Neoplatonic philosophers. Philoponus, by contrast, was thoroughly at home in Neoplatonism.

Yet despite his undoubted Neoplatonic interests and expertise, Philoponus' *de opificio mundi* left such extended and rigorous Neoplatonic argument behind. It rebuts the scientifically and philosophically questionable but biblically based cosmology of Cosmas Indicopleustes. Scholten has shown that there is a complex relationship between Philoponus' text and the catena tradition on which

Procopius also drew for his commentary on Genesis.[5] They inhabit a similar thought-world, where biblical and philosophical discourses concerning creation and the eternity of the world are intertwined. One thinker may mix freely in philosophical and exegetical communities, although Cosmas attempted to construct a new intellectual framework to avoid the philosophers altogether.

Cosmas was appalled that Philoponus would even talk to philosophers. Such Christians are two-faced and lack proper foundations, like empty houses standing high in the air without supports (*Christian Topography* 1.4). He rejects an infinite universe on the grounds that God would have no power to redeem matter or resurrect bodies (*Christian Topography* 3.87). He rejects the idea of revolving heavenly spheres by taking Plato's side in the dispute about whether there are four or five elements. He argues that none of the four elements can move in a circle and that Aristotle's aether could not account for some physical properties of stars and planets even if it existed (*Christian Topography* 1.5–8). The epicycles proposed by astronomers make a mockery of the spherical model of the heavens (*Christian Topography* 1.9–13).

Yet while references to epicycles and Platonic and Aristotelian theories of the elements suggest some knowledge of contemporary science, the reader soon learns that the argument thus far is driven by a purely negative logic. Cosmas does not think that anything like the Greek theory of the elements is true, whether in Platonic or Aristotelian garb. He argues instead for passive matter moved by the divine will alone. Rain falls not because it is water seeking its proper place but because angels carry it according to providential commands (*Christian Topography* 2.84f.). The argument seeks to ensure that God has complete control over matter, thus making belief in the resurrection plausible (cf. 3.61). Cosmos also believed that the earth is flat (e.g. *Christian Topography* 1.5–7; 4.24). The heavens are not spherical because the tabernacle is a type for the universe (e.g. *Christian Topography* 2.3).[6]

With such arguments we have moved into a new epistemology and a new set of truth claims that would utterly transform Christian thought, privilege the Bible as a unique standard of truth, and render Neoplatonic argument unnecessary. Cosmas' arguments on the creation and eternity of the world share only their conclusion with Philoponus and the Gazans. They are evidence for the eclipse of Neoplatonic argumentation in sections of late-antique society, despite

5. Scholten (1996), 89ff.

6. For Cosmas' literal typology and the centrality of prophecy for Cosmas' epistemology, see MacCormack (1982), 291.

the Gazans' best efforts in the earlier generation to demonstrate the utility of Greek philosophy for Christian thinking.

But Philoponus was also attacked from within Neoplatonism by the pagan Neoplatonist Simplicius. According to Simplicius, Aristotle's best achievement was that he 'proved that the entire structure of nature depends on a cause which is above nature, and that the study of nature depends on metaphysics' [τὴν ὅλην φυσικὴν σύστασιν τῆς ὑπερφυοῦς αἰτίας καὶ τὴν φυσικὴν θεωρίαν τῆς πρώτης φιλοσοφίας ἐξηρτημένην ἔδειξεν] (*in Phys.* VIII, 1366.19–20). Such statements point back to Proclus and his insistence that physics depends on theology. This goes some way towards explaining Simplicius' strong anti-Christian polemic (e.g. *in Phys.* VIII, 1326.37–1327.4).[7] Philoponus is a drunkard who inverts the natural order of things, bringing the sun down to earth and a human into heaven (*in Phys.* VIII, 1330.27ff.). The strength of the polemic, and the explicit rejection of Christianity, is a far cry from Proclus' stony silence about Christianity.[8] Simplicius' explicit rejection of Christianity points to stronger Christian attacks on Neoplatonism by Simplicius' day, consistent with Cosmas' more universally negative attitude towards Neoplatonism. Gaza's late fifth-century engagement with Neoplatonism was possible in part because of a greater cultural acceptance of Neoplatonism in the schools.

7.2 Creation of Ideas and Local Cultures

As Pelikan has it, if counterpoint between Platonism and Christianity is a defining feature of the western intellectual tradition, the *Timaeus* provides the *cantus firmus*.[9] The creation debates in late-antique Gaza, partly stimulated by Proclus' commentary on the *Timaeus*, are one restatement of the theme. They illumine Gazan society by revealing creative, productive, and violent tensions between diverse, overlapping and heterogeneous local cultures, with each performing different allegiances and intellectual stances.

The works of Aeneas, Zacharias, and Procopius reveal late-antique Gaza as a diversity of heterogeneous, changing, and mutually interacting local cultures. Groups that helped to form and define the late-antique schools included the students and teachers, philosophically minded Christians and pagans, Neoplatonists, Christians who were uncomfortable with philosophy, the local bishop, and the Gazan monasteries. Further afield, other educational centres, most importantly Alexandria, Caesarea, and Athens, influenced how the

7. For Simplicius' polemic, see Hoffmann (1987).
8. Cf. Saffrey (1975).
9. Pelikan (1997).

Gazan schools operated. Negotiating lives between these local cultures, Aeneas, Zacharias, and Procopius sought to solve cultural problems about the authority of Christian teachers and holy men, the power of Neoplatonists in the schools and wider society and the fluid religious affiliations of students and teachers.

The defining characteristics of these individual local cultures were contested and only ever loosely coherent; the explanatory categories for this section of Gazan society are interaction, transformation, fluidity, and contest, and no local culture was static or entirely insulated from the others. Terms like 'Christian' and 'pagan' are too blunt for this cultural reality. Monks interacted with teachers and left their mark on the thought of Aeneas and Zacharias; Procopius' biblical commentary draws on Neoplatonism. Since local cultures consisted of members with shared though heterogeneous beliefs, values, and practices, identity in this period was itself heterogeneous, context dependent, contested, and shaped through mutual interaction and adaptation of valued characteristics as well as through the construction of oppositions.

The broad interests of the teachers in Gaza are congruent with these heterogeneous and dynamic local cultures. The Gazan schools are well known for their achievements in rhetoric. Sophists wielded power in society in Kaster's terms as 'guardians of language', and Aeneas' letters cast light on the extent to which social power still inhered in the classical education of late fifth-century Gaza. Yet Aeneas, Procopius, and Zacharias all display much wider interests, generated by the diversity of the local cultures which interacted with the schools in Gaza. Gaza at the turn of the sixth-century took elements from other intellectual centres, especially Alexandria, Caesarea, and Athens to forge its own distinctive identity, open to differing intellectual systems, engaged in philosophy, science, literary criticism, rhetoric, and theology. The standard picture of Aeneas, Zacharias, and Procopius as sophists rather than philosophers requires re-evaluation. The overlap of philosophy and rhetoric in their cases suggests that the frequent conflation of the categories of rhetor and philosopher in earlier periods continues into the sixth century, although given their allegiance to Christian problems and arguments, and the extent of their rigorous engagement with Neoplatonism, this may be better understood as the merging of the categories of theologian and rhetor in their case.

Their philosophical interests suggest that while classical *paideia* still commanded respect and social power, there was a new need to demonstrate the continuing utility of central elements of classicism, such as Neoplatonism, which were beginning to threaten some Christians. In employing Neoplatonic philosophy within their Christian account of creation, the Gazans reinforced their social power as guardians of classical knowledge and made the case that philosophy remained helpful to explicate and construct Christian theology.

Simultaneously, in rebutting Neoplatonic arguments and Neoplatonic philosophers, they neutralized the perceived threat of Neoplatonism to Christian doctrine and belief, reinforced the position of Christian teachers and students in the schools, and sought to defeat Neoplatonic religious claims.

Their theological claims may indicate the rise of the monasteries as potential alternative providers of education. Christian education was beginning to compete with traditional classical education in Gaza, and the Gazans' theological interests may be read as attempts to provide Christian resources within a classical idiom to remain attractive in this new environment. The monasteries may also have provided specific intellectual stimulus, in the case of the Origenist problems explored in Aeneas' dialogue.

Wider Christianization helps to explain other cultural transformations which figure in the Gazans' works. The literary reversals enacted in the dialogues and the way the three authors employed and altered their chosen genres both performed desired cultural transformations and configurations, and provided glimpses of other possible cultural alliances and identities. Aeneas rewrote the philosophical tradition by using the dialogue genre, displaying Christian confidence to engage with and appropriate the classical philosophy while simultaneously displaying the continuing utility and strength of Neoplatonism. Yet in changing the dialogue genre in the direction of question and answer literature, he attempted to develop widespread Christian education and revealed the influence of monasteries on Gazan schools. Zacharias recounted his dialogues in a churchyard, symbolizing the Christian colonization of philosophical thought even as his mini-dialogues set in the Alexandrian classrooms perform real tensions within the schools. Procopius employed the commentary tradition in order to be comprehensible within the classical tradition while constructing a new Christian chain of authority figures.

Late-antique education in Gaza was thus vibrant and culturally diverse. It was at the heart of a number of transformations which constituted and continued to reshape late-antique Gazan society. While there were strong conflicts between competing local cultures in the schools, conflict is much too blunt a category with which to characterize late-antique Gazan society. Gaza's dependence on Alexandria, Athens, and Caesarea, together with its mix of schools and monasteries, suggests an openness in the schools which encouraged overlapping cultures and continual adaptations of elements taken from local cultures different from one's own.

In their different ways, the Gazan authors contributed to the process of framing a new intellectual discourse and thus transforming the wider society. Problems arising in the monasteries and contemporary Trinitarian disputes were explored alongside traditional questions of school philosophy. All three thinkers wrote about creation partly because of tension between foundational Neoplatonic statements and Christian claims. Neoplatonism retained rational weight, yet was reframed and thus ultimately marginalized by (various versions of) the divine plan of salvation. Aeneas, Zacharias, and Procopius sought to marry Greek logic and aspects of Neoplatonic argument and imagery to the proclamations of holy writ and patristic authorities, as well as to liturgical practices and the actions of holy men and other Christian stories.

Hence, among the literary elites to which Aeneas, Procopius, and Zacharias belonged, there was a shared discourse which allowed figures to move between traditionally Hellenic or Christian stories and read them in new ways. Plato was read afresh to support the idea that the creation had an origin and that God will transform mortals into immortality; mythological figures can prefigure events in Christian history and biblical texts can be interpreted using Platonic ideas. The contributions of Aeneas, Procopius, and Zacharias to the debate about creation were made possible by this discourse and simultaneously helped to strengthen and create it. In this way, the creation debates provide a rich case study of the creation of a Christian discourse during a time of intellectual and social transition.

Given the formation and characteristics of this shared discourse, problems apparently internal to Neoplatonism as well as those apparently internal to Christianity were generative of the Gazan works. The *Timaeus* antinomy at 28b and its interpretation among contemporary Neoplatonists were central, but so too were debates about the Trinity and how properly to separate the Christian God from the world. Platonic thinking about the problem of evil, perhaps especially by Hierocles, also influenced Aeneas and Zacharias. The Neoplatonic account of goodness as unity and sameness and its non-deliberative account of the divine also posed problems for the three thinkers, while Origenist ideas from the monasteries entered the debate. These diverse problems help explain why the three Gazans explored the doctrine of creation three centuries after *creatio ex nihilo* had been established in Christian doctrine.

Each writer moved his argument against the eternity of the world from physics to ethics, and ended in soteriology. All three writers claimed that God the creator is also God the lawgiver. Thus creation became part of the story of the history of God's salvific acts. The Neoplatonic belief in the eternity of the world threatened the happy ending of this story, demanding a Christian response. The Gazans argued that God is the efficient and final cause of creation: this would be a crucial continuing claim in the history of ideas, seen again in Simplicius and Philoponus and central to Thomas Aquinas' account of creation. It allowed them to join the first principle of Being with the first principle of Goodness and grounded Aeneas' and Zacharias' interest in ethics.

Especially in Aeneas and Zacharias, but also in Procopius, the problems surrounding creation raised questions about divine and human freedom. The Christians differ from their Neoplatonic contemporaries in insisting that creation is a gracious, outwardly directed act of choice by the divine will. God is not free if he did not choose to create, and since what is eternal is necessary, an eternal creation means that God is not free. In this scheme, God's will to create is not dependent on the actual existence of the cosmos. God's act of creation is thus free and entirely gratuitous.

The unification of the first principle of Being with the first principle of Goodness in this gracious act of creation forms a crucial component of the divine plan of salvation, which was central to each of the Gazans. Each writer played with the categories of creation, fall, education through mortal sufferings, incarnation, and final recreation. The precise configurations of these elements are slightly different in each author. For example, Aeneas did not emphasize the incarnation as strongly as Zacharias did, but spent considerable time discussing the creation and resurrection of souls; his views on the soul would repay more detailed study. Yet for each writer, these basic plot elements provide a framework for their arguments. This frame means that Neoplatonic conclusions must be re-evaluated and often jettisoned. The divine plan of salvation had been crucial to the original Christian apologetic of the second century, especially in Irenaeus and Clement of Alexandria, and its centrality in the works of the three Gazans points at least to a revival of this theme, and possibly to a deeper continuity in Christian thought, a sort of 'Irenaean revival' between the second and the sixth centuries.

The divine plan also provides a view of history which helps to explain the facility and confidence with which the Gazans interacted and employed ideas from Neoplatonism. If God is continually providentially present in human history, and if all human experience has been summed up and perfected in the incarnation, then Christians can approach Neoplatonism confident that Christian truth sums up and perfects the earlier truths that God communicated to the weaker, childlike intellects of the Jews and the (pre-Christian) Greeks. Christian truth has different yardsticks: the Bible, liturgy, fathers and church councils are authoritative sources of truth. But God also communicated truths to earlier generations in other dispensations of the divine plan. This was a key argument at the start of Procopius' commentary; Aeneas claimed that earlier doctrines should be adhered to where they are truthful. The key point is that truths may be found outside the church, and this facilitates cultural and intellectual interaction between Christians and others.

Of course, the divine plan could be recast to emphasize the perfection of Christians at the present moment of divine–human history. That was how

Cosmas Indicopleustes took it, enabling him to argue for a nearly complete rejection of non-Christian claims; the Gazans' own polemic rejection of Neoplatonic ideas often trivialized the thought of their opponents and may be based in part on such an evolutionary triumphalism. Yet the Gazans join the idea that God is perfecting human history to the idea that God has always assisted humans throughout history. Because they recognized that God has not yet completely perfected the cosmos, they could appropriate the 'imperfect' thought systems of the Neoplatonists to construct better but still provisional Christian truth.

This is an example of how the method that runs through this book may unite cultural and intellectual history. The analysis and reconstruction of argument through the elucidation of problems, which brought out the centrality of the divine plan, sheds light on the motivations, mechanics and extent of cultural interactions. Beliefs, symbols, and intellectual commitments, along with power differentials and material constraints, shape cultural action. Similarly, my analysis of the Gazans' cultural problems, especially their anxieties about the social power of pagan Neoplatonists, helps to explain parts of their argument which may otherwise sound somewhat shrill. It reveals groups which were posing social challenges to the members of the schools, thus helping to situate the thinkers' ideas and to identify relevant sources of opposing arguments. Through the different cultural and intellectual reconstructions I have offered in this book, I have presented a case that cultural history should be more expansive than power discourse theory, while intellectual history should be embedded in wider cultural analysis. What this method reveals in late-antique Gaza is a set of cultures in transition, mutually constituting and transforming each other through a fugal pattern of exchange, adaptation, conflict, and collaboration.

Bibliography

1. ANCIENT TEXTS AND TRANSLATIONS

Acta conciliorum oecumenicorum. Sub auspiciis Academiae Scientiarum Bavaricae edita, ed. Bayerische Akademie der Wissenschaften (Berlin, 1984).

Aeneas, *Teofrasto*, ed. Maria Minniti-Colonna (Naples, 1958).

———, *Epistole*, ed. Lydia Massa Positano, 2nd ed. (Naples, 1962).

Aeneas of Gaza, *Theophrastus with Zacharias of Mytilene Ammonius*, trans. Sebastian Gertz, John Dillon, and Donald Russell, Ancient Commentators on Aristotle (London, 2012).

Alcinous, *Alcinoos: Enseignement des doctrines de Platon*, ed. J. Whittaker, Collection des universités de France (Paris, 1990).

———, *The Handbook of Platonism*, ed. John M. Dillon, Clarendon Later Ancient Philosophers (Oxford, 1993).

Ammonius Hermiae, *Ammonius in Aristotelis de interpretatione commentarius*, ed. A. Busse, CAG 4.5 (Berlin, 1897).

———, *On Aristotle's on Interpretation 1–8*, trans. David L. Blank, Ancient Commentators on Aristotle (New York, 1996).

Ammonius Hermiae, and Boethius, *On Aristotle's on Interpretation 9*, trans. David L. Blank and Norman Kretzmann, Ancient Commentators on Aristotle (Ithaca, N.Y., 1998).

Apophthegmata Patrum. Latine reddidit Victor Arras, ed. Victor Arras, CSCO 459. Scriptores Aethiopici Tomus 78 (Leuven, 1984).

Aristotle, *Aristotelis qui ferebantus librorum fragmenta*, ed. Valentine Rose (Leipzig, 1886).

———, *The Works of Aristotle*, trans. W. D. Ross and J. A. Smith, 12 vols. (Oxford, 1910).

———, *Aristotle: In Twenty-Three Volumes*, Loeb Classical Library (Cambridge, Mass., 1932).

Asclepius, *Asclepii in Aristotelis metaphysicorum libros A–Z commentaria*, ed. M. Haydruck, CAG 6.2 (1888).

Athanasius, *Contra gentes and De incarnatione*, trans. Robert W. Thomson, Oxford Early Christian Texts (Oxford, 1971).

Augustine, *Confessions*, trans. Henry Chadwick (Oxford, 1991).

Barsanuphius, and John the Old Man of Gaza, *Correspondance. Barsanuphe et Jean de Gaza. Introduction, texte critique et notes par François Neyt, Paula de Angelis-Noah. Traduction par L. Regnault*, ed. François Neyt and Paula de Angelis-Noah, 5 vols., SC 426, 427, 450, 451, 468 (Paris, 1997–2002).

Basil, *Basile de Césarée. Homélies sur l'hexaéméron*, ed. S. Giet, 2nd ed., SC 26 (Paris, 1968).

Choricius of Gaza, *Choricii Gazaei Opera*, ed. Richard Foerster and Eberhard Richtsteig, Bibliotheca Scriptorum Graecorum et Romanorum Teubneriana (Leipzig, 1929).

——, 'Choricius of Gaza: An Approach to His Work. Introduction, Translation and Commentary by Fotios K. Litsas'. Ph.D. Dissertation, Department of History, The University of Chicago (1980).

Chrysostom, John, *Against the Games and the Theatres (Contra ludos et theatra)*, ed. J. P. Migne, PG 56.263–70 (Paris, 1857–1866a).

——, *Homilies on Genesis*, ed. J. P. Migne, PG 53, 54 (Paris, 1857–1866).

——, *On the Letter to the Romans*, ed. J. P. Migne, PG 60 (Paris, 1857–1866b).

——, *On the Letter to Titus*, ed. J. P. Migne, PG 62 (Paris, 1857–1866c).

——, *On Vainglory and on the Education of Children*, ed. A.-M Malingrey, SC 188 (Paris, 1972).

——, *Homilies on Genesis*, trans. R. Hill (Washington, DC, 1990).

——, *Sermons sur la Genèse. Introduction, texte critique, traduction et notes pa L. Brottier*, SC 433 (Paris, 1998).

——, *Sermons on Genesis*, trans. R. Hill (Washington, 2004).

Clement, *Clemens Alexandrinus*, ed. Otto Stählin, Ursula Treu, and Ludwig Früchtel, 4 vols. (Berlin, 1905–1936 (Stählin); revised by Treu and Früchtel, 1970–1985).

——, *Stromateis*, trans. John Ferguson (Washington, D.C., 1991).

Cosmas, *Christian Topography of Cosmas, an Egyptian Monk*, trans. J. W. McCrindle (London, 1897).

——, *Topographie chrétienne*, ed. and trans. W. Wolska-Conus, 3 vols., SC 141, 159, 197 (Paris, 1968).

Cyril of Scythopolis, *Lives of the Monks of Palestine*, trans. R. M. Price and John Binns, Cistercian Studies 114 (Kalamazoo, Mich., 1991).

Damascius, *De principiis*, ed. C.É. Ruelle, *Damascii successoris dubitationes et solutiones*, Vols. 1 and 2 (Paris, Vol. 1: 1889; Vol. 2: 1899 (repr. 1964)).

——, *Damascii Vitae Isidori Reliquiae*, ed. Clemens Zintzen, Bibliotheca Graeca et Latina Suppletoria 1 (Hildesheim, 1967).

——, *In Phaedonem*, ed. L.G. Westerink, The Greek Commentaries on Plato's *Phaedo*, Vol. 2 (Amsterdam, 1977).

——, *The Philosophical History: Text with Translation and Notes*, ed. Polymnia Athanassiadi (Athens, 1999).

Des Places, Edouard, ed., *Oracles chaldaïques: Avec un choix de commentaires anciens*, Collection des universités de France (Paris, 1971).

Dionysius, *Pseudo-Dionysius: The Complete Works*, trans. Colm Luibeid (New York, 1987).

Dorotheos of Gaza, *Dorothée de Gaza. Oeuvres spirituelles. Introduction, texte grec, traduction et notes par Dom L. Regnault et Dom J. de Préville*, ed. J. de Préville and Lucien Regnault, Sources chrétiennes 92 (Paris, 1963).

——, *Dorotheos of Gaza. Discourses and Sayings*, trans. Eric P. Wheeler, Cistercian Studies Series 33 (Kalamazoo, Mich., 1977).

Edwards, M. J., *Neoplatonic Saints: The Lives of Plotinus and Proclus by Their Students* (Liverpool, 2000).

Eunapius, *Eunapii vitae sophistarum*, ed. J. Giangrande (Rome, 1956).

Eusebius, *Eusebius Werke,* Band 8: *Die Praeparatio evangelica*, ed. K. Mras, Die griechischen christlichen Schriftsteller 43.1 and 43.2 (Berlin, 43.1: 1954; 43.2: 1954).

——, *Eusèbe de Césarée. Histoire ecclésiastique*, ed. G Bardy, 3 vols., SC 31, 41, 55 (Paris, 1: 1952; 2: 1955; 3: 1958 (repr. 3: 1967)).

Evagrius, *The Ecclesiastical History of Evagrius with the Scholia*, ed. Joseph Bidez and L. Parmentier (London, 1898 (repr. 1979)).

Friedländer, Paul, *Johannes von Gaza, Paulus Silentiarius und Prokopios von Gaza: Kunstbeschreibungen justinianischer Zeit* (Hildesheim, 1969).

Garitte, Gerard, 'Textes hagiographiques orientaux relatifs à saint Léonce de Tripoli. ii. L'Homélie copte de Sévère d'Antioche', *Le Muséon* 79 (1966), 335–86.

Gregory Nazianzus, *Orations*, ed. J. P. Migne, PG 35 (Paris, 1857–1866).

Gregory of Nyssa, *De opificio hominis*, ed. J. P. Migne, PG 44: 124–256 (Paris, 1857–1866).

——, *Gregorii Nysseni Opera. Contra Eunomium libri*, ed. W. Jaeger, 2 vols. (Berlin, 1921).

Guillaumont, Antoine, *Les 'Képhalaia gnostica' d'Évagre le Pontique et l'histoire de l'origénisme chez les Grecs et chez les Syriens*, Patristica Sorbonensia 5 (Paris, 1962).

Herodotus, *Herodoti Historiae*, ed. Haiim B. Rosén, 2 vols. (Leipzig, 1987–1997).

Hierocles, *Hieroclis in aureum Pythagoreorum carmen commentarius*, ed. F. G. Köhler (Stuttgart, 1974).

Hippolytus, *Refutatio omnium haeresium*, ed. Miroslav Marcovich, Patristische Texte und Studien Bd. 25 (Berlin, 1986).

Homer, *Homeri Opera*, ed. D. B. Monro and Thomas W. Allen, Scriptorum Classicorum Bibliotheca Oxoniensis (Oxonii, 1912).

Iamblichus, *Iamblichi de communi mathematica scientia liber*, ed. U. Klein (Leipzig, 1891 (repr. 1975)).

——, *Protreptique*, trans. Edouard Des Places, Collection des universits de France (Paris, 1989).

——, *On the Pythagorean Way of Life*, trans. John M. Dillon and Jackson P. Hershbell (Atlanta, Ga., 1991).

——, *Les Mystères d'Egypte; traduit du grec par Edouard des Places; preface de François Vieri*, ed. Édouard des Places (Paris, 1993).

——, *Iamblichi Protrepticus*, trans. Ermenegildo Pistelli, Editio stereotypa editionis 1. (1888); ed. Bibliotheca Scriptorum Graecorum et Romanorum Teubneriana (Stutgardiae, 1996).

——, *De Anima*. Text, translation, and commentary by John F. Finamore and John M. Dillon (Leiden, 2002).

Irenaeus, *Contre les hérésies V*, ed. A. Rousseau, B. Hemmerdinger, L. Doutreleau, and C. Mercier, SC 152, 153 (Paris, 1969).

——, *St. Irenaeus of Lyons against the Heresies*, Books 1 and 2 trans. Dominic J. Unger and John J. Dillon, Book 3 trans. Matthew C. Steenberg, Dominic J. Unger, Ancient Christian Writers, No. 55, 65, 66 (New York, 1992).

Jacob, Bishop of Batnan in Serug, *Jacob of Serugh's Homilies on the Spectacles of the Theatre. Extracts from the Syriac Text, with an English Translation by C. Moss*, ed. Cyril Moss (Louvain, 1935).

Jerome, *Letters and Lives*, ed. J. P. Migne, PL 22, 23 (Paris, 1845).

——, *Vivre au désert: Paul, Malchus, Hilarion*, ed. Jean Miniac (Grenoble, 1992).

——, *Trois vies de moines: Paul, Malchus, Hilarion*, ed. Pierre Leclerc, Edgardo Martín Morales, and Adalbert de Vogüé, Sources chrétiennes 508 (Paris, 2007).

John of Gaza, Ignatios, Leo, Elias, and George, *Cinque poeti bizantini: Anacreontee dal Barberiniano greco 310*, ed. Federica Ciccolella, Biblioteca Apostolica Vaticana (Alessandria, 2000).

John of Gaza, Paul Silentiarius, and Procopius, *Johannes von Gaza, Paulus Silentiarius und Prokopios von Gaza: Kunstbeschreibungen justinianischer Zeit*, ed. Paul Friedländer (Hildesheim, 1969).

John Rufus, *Plérophories, c'est-à-dire témoignages et révélations (contre le concile de Chalcédoine). Version syriaque et traduction française*, ed. F. Nau (Paris, 1911).

Julian, *The Works of the Emperor Julian*, trans. Wilmer Cave Wright, 3 vols., Loeb Classical Library (London, 1913).

Julianus, *Oracles chaldaïques: Avec un choix de commentaires anciens*, ed. Édouard des Places, Collection des universités de France (Paris, 1971).

——, *The Chaldean Oracles: Text, Translation, and Commentary*, ed. Ruth Dorothy Majercik, Studies in Greek and Roman Religion, Vol. 5 (Leiden, 1989).

Justinian, *The Digest of Justinian*, ed. Theodor Mommsen, Paul Krueger, and trans. Alan Watson, 4 vols. (Philadelphia, Pa., 1985).

Leontius, *Leontii Presbyteri Constantinopolitani Homiliae*, ed. C. Datema and P. Allen, Corpus Christianorum, Series Graeca 17 (Leuven, 1987).

——, *Leontius, Presbyter of Constantinople: Fourteen Homilies*, trans. P. Allen and C. Datema, Byzantina Australiensia 9 (Brisbane, 1991).

Libanius, *Lucianus ex recensione Caroli Jacobitz. Accedunt scholia auctoria et emendatiora, index et rerum et verborum*, ed. Karl Gottfried Jacobitz, 4 vols., Vols. I, IV (Leipzig, 1836, 1841).

——, *Libanius' Autobiography (Oration I)*. The Greek text, edited, with introduction, translation, and notes by A. F. Norman (London, 1965).

Lucretius, Carus Titus, *De Rerum Natura: Libri Sex*, ed. Cyril Bailey (Oxford, 1947).

Map, Walter, *De Nugis Curialium*, ed. M. R. James, Christopher Brooke, and R. A. B. Mynors, Oxford Medieval Texts (Oxford, 1983).

Marinus of Neapolis, *Vita Procli sive de felicitate*, ed. R. Masullo (Naples, 1985).

Mark the Deacon, *The Life of Porphyry, Bishop of Gaza*. Translated with introduction and notes by G. F. Hill (Oxford, 1913).

——, *Vie de Porphyre, évèque de Gaza. Texte établi, traduit et commenté par Henri Grégoire et M.-A. Kugener*, ed. Henri Grégoire and Marc Antoine Kugener (Paris, 1930).

Massa Positano, Lydia, ed., *Enea di Gaza. Epistole*, 2nd ed., Collana di studi greci 19 (Naples, 1962).

Mayer, Wendy, and Pauline Allen, *John Chrysostom*, The Early Church fathers. Selections from John Chrysostom (London, 2000).

Moss, Cyril, 'Jacob of Serugh's Homilies on the Spectacles of the Theatre', *Le Muséon* 48 (1935), 87–112.

Nemesius of Emesa, *Nemesii Emeseni de natura hominis*, ed. Moreno Morani (Leipzig, 1987).

Nikolaos of Methone, *Νικολάου Μεθώνης. Ἀνάπτυξις Τῆς Θεολογικῆς Στοιχειώσεως Πρόκλου Πλατωνικοῦ Φιλοσόφου. Nicholas of Methone. Refutation of Proclus' Elements of Theology.* A critical edition with an introduction on Nicholas' life and works, ed. Athanasios D. Angelou (Leiden, 1984).

Origen, *The Philocalia of Origen*. The text revised with a critical introduction and indices by J. A. Armitage Robinson (Cambridge, 1893).

——, *Origines Werke*, Bd. 4, ed. E. Preuschen; Bd. 5, ed. P. Koetschau (Berlin, 1903, 1913).

——, *Origenes vier Bücher von den Prinzipien [De principiis]*, ed. H. Görgemanns and H. Karpp (Darmstadt, 1976).

Orphicorum Fragmenta, ed. O. Kern (Berlin, 1922).

Petit, Françoise, *La Chaîne sur la Genèse. Édition intégrale*, 4 vols., Vol. 1, Traditio Exegetica Graeca 1–4 (Leuven, 1991).

Philo, *Quaestiones in Genesim et in Exodum. Fragmenta Graeca*, ed. Françoise Petit, Les oeuvres de Philon d'Alexandrie 33 (Paris, 1978).

——, *On the Creation of the Cosmos According to Moses*, trans. and commentary by David T. Runia (Leiden, 2001).

Philoponus, John, *De opificio mundi Libri VII*, ed. Walther Reichardt, Bibliotheca Scriptorum Graecorum et Romanorum Teubneriana (Leipzig, 1897a).

——, *In Aristotelis libros de generatione et corruptione commentaria*, ed. H. Vitelli, CAG 14.2 (Berlin, 1897b).

———, *De Aeternitate Mundi Contra Proclum*, ed. Hugo Rabe, Bibliotheca Scriptorum Graecorum et Romanorum Teubneriana (Leipzig, 1899).
———, *De aeternitate mundi: Contra Proclum*, ed. H. Rabe, 2. Nachdruckaufl. ed. (Hildesheim, 1984).
———, *Against Aristotle, On the Eternity of the World*, trans. Christian Wildberg, The Ancient Commentators on Aristotle (London, 1987).
———, *De opificio mundi*, ed. Clemens Scholten, Fontes Christiani, 23/1, 23/2, 23/3 (Freiburg, 1997).
———, *Against Proclus On the Eternity of the World, 1–5*, trans. Michael J. Share, Ancient Commentators on Aristotle (London, 2004).
———, *Against Proclus On the Eternity of the World 6–8*, trans. Michael J. Share, Ancient Commentators on Aristotle (London, 2005).
———, *Against Proclus On the Eternity of the World 12–18*, trans. James Wilberding, Ancient Commentators on Aristotle (London, 2006).
Philoponus, John, and Simplicius, *Place, Void, and Eternity*, trans. D. J. Furley and Christian Wildberg, Ancient Commentators on Aristotle (Ithaca, N.Y., 1991).
Photius, *Bibliothèque. Texte établi et traduit par René Henry. Index par Jacques Schamp*, ed. René Henry, 9 vols., Collection byzantine (Paris, 1959–).
Plato, *Plato: With an English Translation*, trans. Harold North Fowler, Robert Gregg Bury, and W. R. M. Lamb, The Loeb Classical Library (London, 1914).
———, *Platonis Opera*, ed. E. A. Duke, Scriptorum Classicorum Bibliotheca Oxoniensis (Oxford, 1995).
———, *Complete Works*, ed. John M. Cooper and D. S. Hutchinson (Indianapolis, Ind., 1997).
Plotinus, *Plotinus*, trans. A. H. Armstrong, 7 vols., Loeb Classical Library (London, 1966).
———, *Plotini Opera*, ed. Paul Henry and Hans-Rudolf Schwyzer, 3 vols. (Leiden, Vol. 1: 1951; Vol. 2: 1959; Vol. 3: 1973).
Plutarch, *Plutarch's Lives*, trans. Bernadotte Perrin, Loeb Classical Library (Cambridge, Mass., 1914).
Porphyry, *Porphyrii Philosophi Platonici: Opuscula selecta*, ed. August Nauck (Lipsiae, 1886).
———, *Porphyrii isagoge et in Aristotelis categorias commentarium*, ed. A. Busse, CAG 4.1 (Berlin, 1887).
———, *Porphyrii Philosophi Fragmenta*, trans. Andrew Smith and Devid Wasserstein, Bibliotheca Scriptorum Graecorum et Romanorum Teubneriana (Stuttgart, 1993).
Priscian, and Procopius, *Procope de Gaza, Priscien de Césarée, Panégyriques de l'empereur Anastase Ier; textes traduits et commentés par Alain Chauvot*, Antiquitas Reihe 1, Abhandlungen zur alten Geschichte Bd. 35 (Bonn, 1986).
Proclus, *In Platonis Timaeum commentaria*, ed. E. Diehl, 3 vols. (1903–1906).
———, *De malorum subsistentia. Procli Diadochi tria opuscula*, ed. H. Boese (Berlin, 1960).
———, *The Elements of Theology*, ed. E. R. Dodds, 2nd ed. (Oxford, 1963).
———, *Commentaire sur le Timée*, ed. A. J. Festugière, Bibliothèque des textes philosophiques (Paris, 1966–1968).
———, *Theologie Platonicienne*, ed. H. D. Saffrey and Leendert G. Westerink, 6 vols., Collection des universités de France (Paris, 1968–1997).
———, *Commentaire sur la République*, ed. A. J. Festugière (Paris, 1970).
———, *Commentaire sur le Parménide de Platon: Traduction de Guillaume de Moerbeke*, ed. Carlos G. Steel, Ancient and Medieval Philosophy (Leiden, 1982).
———, *On the Eternity of the World: De Aeternitate Mundi*, ed. Helen S. Lang, A. D. Macro, and Jon McGinnis, The Joan Palevsky Imprint in Classical Literature (Berkeley, Calif., 2001).

——, *Commentaire sur le Parménide de Platon*, ed. Concetta Luna and Alain-Philippe Segonds (Paris, 2007a).

——, *Commentary on Plato's Timaeus Volume I. Book I: Proclus on the Socratic State and Atlantis*, trans. with an introduction and notes by Harold Tarrant, with a general introduction by Dirk Baltzly and Harold Tarrant (Cambridge, 2007b).

——, *Commentary on Plato's Timaeus Volume III. Book 3, Part I: Proclus on the World's Body*, trans. with an introduction and notes by Dirk Baltzly (Cambridge, 2007c).

——, *Proclus on Plato's Cratylus*, ed. Harold Tarrant, trans. Brian Duvick. Ancient Commentators on Aristotle (London, 2007d).

Commentary on Plato's Timaeus Volume II. Book 2: Proclus on the Causes of the Cosmos and its Creation, trans. with notes by David T. Runia and Michael Share, with an Introduction by David T. Runia (Cambridge, 2008).

Procopius, *Commentary on Genesis*, ed. J. P. Migne, PG 87.1 (Paris, 1857–1866).

——, *Refutatio Procli*, ed. J. P. Migne, PG 87.2 2792e–h (Paris, 1857–1866).

——, *Procopii Gazaei Epistolae et Declamationes*, ed. Antonio Garzya and Raymond Joseph Loenertz, Studia Patristica et Byzantina 9 (Ettal, 1963).

——, *Procopii Gazaei Catena in Ecclesiasten: Un nuovo testimone della Catena sull'Ecclesiaste di Procopio di Gaza, il Cod. Vindob. Theol. Gr. 147*, Corpus Christianorum, Series Graeca 4 Supplementum (Turnhout, 1983).

——, *Panegirico per l'imperatore Anastasio*, ed. Giuseppina Matino (Naples, 2005).

Procopius, and John Ps-Chrysostom, *Procopii Gazaei Catena in Ecclesiasten necnon Pseudochrysostomi Commentarius in eundem Ecclesiasten*, ed. Sandro Leanza, Corpus Christianorum Series Graeca 4 (Turnhout, 1978).

Psellus, Michael, *Épître sur la Chrysopée. Opusclues et extraits sur l'alchimie, la météologie et la démonologie, publiés par Joseph Bidez. En appendice-Proclus: Sur l'art hiératique; Psellus: Choix de dissertations inédites*, ed. Joseph Bidez, Catalogue des manuscrits alchimiques grecs, Vol. 6 (Brussels, 1928).

Pseudo-Dionysius, *De divinis nominibus (DN)*, ed. B. R. Suchla, Corpus Dionysiacum I, Patristische Texte und Studien 33 (Berlin, 1990).

——, *De mystica theologia (Myst)*, ed. G. Heil and A. M. Ritter, Corpus Dionysiacum II, Patristische Texte und Studien 36 (Berlin, 1991).

Romanos, *Cantica*, ed. Paul Maas and C. A. Trypanis (Oxford, 1963).

——, *Romanos le Mélode Hymnes. Introduction, texte critique, traduction et notes par José Grosdidier de Matons*, Vol. 5, SC 283 (Paris, 1981).

Severus, *A Collection of Letters of Severus of Antioch, from Numerous Syriac Manuscripts*, edited and trans. E. W. Brooks, Patrologia Orientalis. Tom. 12. Fasc. 2; Tom. 14. Fasc. 1 (1916).

Schibli, Hermann Sadun, *Hierocles of Alexandria* (Oxford, 2002).

Simplicius, *In Aristotelis quattuor libros de caelo commentaria*, ed. J. L. Heiberg, CAG 7 (Berlin, 1894).

——, *Simplicii in Aristotelis physicorum libros octo commentaria*, ed. H. Diels, CAG 9, 10 (Berlin, Vol. 9: 1882; Vol. 10: 1895).

——, *On Aristotle's Physics 6*, trans. David Konstan, Ancient Commentators on Aristotle (London, 1989).

——, *On Aristotle's 'Physics 8.6–10'*, trans. R. D. McKirahan, The Ancient Commentators on Aristotle (Ithaca, N.Y., 2001).

Socrates, *Historia ecclesiastica*, ed. Pierre Maraval and P. Périchon, Cerf (Paris, 2004–2007).

Sozomen, *Sozomenus. Kirchengeschichte*, ed. Joseph Bidez and G. C. Hansen, Die griechischen christlichen Schriftsteller 50 (Berlin, 1960).

Tertullian, *Quinti Septimi Florentis Tertulliani Opera*, Corpus Christianorum, Series Latina, I, II (Turnholt, 1954).
Themistius, *Themistii Orationes Quae Supersunt*, ed. Henricus Schenkl, Glanville Downey, and A. F. Norman, 3 vols., Bibliotheca Scriptorum Graecorum et Romanorum Teubneriana (Leipzig, 1965).
Theodoret, *Théodoret de Cyr. Thérapeutique des maladies helléniques*, ed. P. Canivet, 2 vols., SC 57 (Paris, 1958).
Theodosius II, *The Theodosian Code and Novels and the Sirmondian Constitutions*, a translation with commentary, glossary, and bibliography by Clyde Pharr in collaboration with Theresa Sherrer Davidson and Mary Brown Pharr. With an introduction by C. Dickerman Williams. Corpus of Roman Law, Vol. 1 (Princeton, N.J., 1952).
Timothy of Gaza, 'Excerpta ex Timothei Gazaei libris de animalibus,' ed. M. Haupt, *Hermes* 3, 5–30 (1869).
von Arnim, H., *Stoicorum veterum fragmenta*, 3 vols. (Leipzig, 1903–1905).
Zacharias, *Sévère, Patriarche d'Antioche, 512–518*, ed. M. A. Kugener, 2 vols., Patrologia Orientalis T. 2, Fasc. 1, No. 6 (Turnhout, 1907).
———, *Vitae virorum apud Monophysitas celeberrimorum*, ed. E. W. Brooks, CSCO Scriptores Syri series 3, t. 25 (Paris, 1907).
———, *Ammonio. Introduzione, testo critico, traduzione, commentario*, ed. Maria Minniti-Colonna (Naples, 1973).
———, *Historia ecclesiastica Zachariae Rhetori vulgo adscripta*, trans. E. W. Brooks and F. J. Hamilton (New York, 1977).
Zosimus, *New History*, ed. and trans. Ronald T. Ridley (Sydney, 1982).

2. MODERN SCHOLARSHIP

Abbott, Edwin, *Philomythus. An Antidote against Credulity. A Discussion of Cardinal Newman's Essay on Ecclesiastical Miracles*, 2nd ed. (London, 1891).
Abu-Lughod, Lila, 'Writing against Culture', in *Recapturing Anthropology: Working in the Present*, R. G. Fox ed. (Santa Fe, N.M., 1991), 137–62.
Alexander, P. J., 'La Topographie chrétienne de Cosmas Indicopleustès. Théologie et science au VIe siècle', *Isis* 55.1 (1964), 115–17.
Allen, Pauline, 'Zacharias Scholasticus and the *Historia Ecclesiastica* of Evagrius Scholasticus', *JThS* 31.2 (1980), 471–88.
Altman, Janet Gurkin, *Epistolarity: Approaches to a Form* (Columbus, Ohio, 1982).
Aly, Wolf, 'Prokopios 20', in *Paulys Realencyclopädie der classischen Altertumswissenschaft*, Pauly and Georg Wissowa eds. (Stuttgart, 1957), 259–73.
Amand de Mendieta, E., 'La Preparation et la composition des neuf Homélies sur l'Hexameron de Basile de Césarée: Le Problème des sources littéraires immédiates', *StudPat* 16 (Berlin, 1985), 349–67.
Amato, Eugenio, *Rose di Gaza: Gli scritti retorico-sofistici e le Epistole di Procopio di Gaza* (Alessandria, 2010a).
———, 'Sul discusso plagio della *Refutatio Procli* di Procopio di Gaza ad opera di Nicola di Metone: Nuovi apporti della tradizione manoscritta', *MEG* 10 (2010b), 5–12.
Amato, Eugenio, and Jacques Schamp, eds., *Ethopoiia: La Représentation de caractères entre fiction scolaire et réalité vivante à l'époque impériale et tardive* (Salerno, 2005).
Anastos, M. V., 'Aristotle and Cosmas Indicopleustes on the Void: A Note on Theology and Science in the Sixth Century', *Hellenika* 4 (1953), 35–50.

Armitage Robinson, J. A., ed., *The Philocalia of Origen.* The text revised with a critical introduction and indices by J. A. Armitage Robinson (Cambridge, 1893).

Armstrong, A. H., 'The Background of the Doctrine "that the intelligibles are not outside the intellect"', in *Les Sources de Plotin*, Fondation Hardt, Entretiens 5 (Vandoeuvres-Geneva, 1957), 393–425.

——, ed., *The Cambridge History of Later Greek and Early Medieval Philosophy* (London, 1970).

Ashkenazi, Yakov, 'Sophists and Priests in Late Antique Gaza According to Choricius the Rhetor', in *Christian Gaza in Late Antiquity. Jerusalem Studies in Religion and Culture*, Vol. 3, Arieh Kofsky and Bruria Bitton-Ashkelony eds. (Leiden, 2004), 195–208.

Athanassiadi, Polymnia, 'Persecution and Response in Late Paganism: The Evidence of Damascius', *JHS* 113 (1993), 1–29.

——, ed., *The Philosophical History: Text with Translation and Notes* (Athens, 1999).

Athanassiadi, Polymnia, and Michael Frede, *Pagan Monotheism in Late Antiquity* (Oxford, 1999).

Aubry, G., 'Capacité et convenance: La Notion d'epitêdeiotês dans la théorie porphyrienne de l'embryon', in *L'embryon: Formation et animation. Antiquité grecque et latine, traditions hèbraïque, chrétienne et islamique.* Histoire des doctrines de l'Antiquité classique 38, Luc Brisson, Marie-Hélène Congourdeau, and Jean-Luc Solère eds. (Paris, 2008), 139–55.

Aujoulat, N., 'Le Théophraste de Énée de Gaza: Problèmes de chronologie', *Koinonia* 10 (1986), 67–80.

——, 'Le De providentia d'Hiéroclès d'Alexandrie et le Théophraste d'Énée de Gaza', *VChr* 41.1 (1987), 55–85.

Austin, J. L., *How to Do Things with Words*, 2nd ed. (Oxford, 1980).

Avi-Yonah, M., 'The Economics of Byzantine Palestine', *IEJ* 8 (1958), 35–51.

Bach, Kent, 'Speech Acts and Pragmatics', in *The Blackwell Guide to the Philosophy of Language*, Michael Devitt and Richard Hanley eds. (Oxford, 2006), 147–67.

Bagnall, Roger, 'Introduction', in *Alexandria: Auditoria of Kom el-Dikka and Late Antique Education. Journal of Juristic Papyrology Supplement 8*, Tomasz Derda, Tomasz Markiewicz, and Ewa Wipszycka eds. (Warsaw, 2007), 3–7.

Ballet, Pascal, 'Introduction à l'étude des échanges: La Céramique', in *Gaza dans l'antiquité tardive: Archéologie, rhétorique et histoire: Actes du colloque international de Poitiers, 6–7 Mai 2004*, Catherine Saliou ed. (Salerno, 2005), 41–50.

Baltes, Matthias, *Die Weltentstehung des platonischen Timaios nach den antiken Interpreten. T. 1*, Philosophia Antiqua 30 (Leiden, 1976).

——, *Dianoêmata: Kleine Schriften zu Platon und zum Platonismus*, ed. Annette Hüffmeier, Marie-Luise Lakmann, and Matthias Vorwerk (Stuttgart, 1999).

Baltussen, H., *Philosophy and Exegesis in Simplicius: The Methodology of a Commentator* (London, 2008).

Baltzly, Dirk, Review of *Proclus: On the Eternity of the World (de Aeternitate Mundi).* Helen S. Lang and A. D. Macro. *Bryn Mawr Classical Review* 2002.10.19 (bmcr.brynmawr.edu/2002/2002-10-19.html, 2002).

——, 'Stoicism', in *The Stanford Encyclopedia of Philosophy (Fall 2008 Edition)*, Edward N. Zalta ed. (http://plato.stanford.edu/archives/fall2008/entries/Stoicism/, 2008).

Baltzly, Dirk, and Harold Tarrant, 'General Introduction to the *Commentary*', in *Proclus. Commentary on Plato's Timaeus Volume I. Book I: Proclus on the Socratic State and Atlantis.* Translated with an introduction and notes by Harold Tarrant, with a general introduction by Dirk Baltzly and Harold Tarrant (Cambridge, 2007), 1–20.

Bammel, C. P., 'Adam in Origen', in *The Making of Orthodoxy: Essays in Honour of Henry Chadwick*, R. Williams ed. (Cambridge, 1989), 62–93.
Bardy, G., 'Zacharie le Rhéteur', in *Dictionnaire de théologie catholique* (Paris, 1950).
Barnes, T. D., 'The Baptism of Theodosius II', in *Studia Patristica XIX. Papers Presented to the Tenth International Conference on Patristic Studies, Held in Oxford, 1987*, Elizabeth A. Livingstone ed. (Leuven, 1989), 8–12.
Bassett, Sarah, *The Urban Image of Late-Antique Constantinople* (Cambridge, 2004).
Baur, C., 'Chrysostomus in Genesim', *ThQ* 108 (1927), 221–32.
———, *John Chrysostom and his Time*, 2 vols. (Westminster, Md., 1959–1960).
Beck, Hans-Georg, *Kirche und theologische Literatur im byzantinischen Reich*, Byzantinisches Handbuch; II T., 1. Bd. (Munich, 1959).
Beeley, Christopher A., *Gregory of Nazianzus on the Trinity and the Knowledge of God: In Your Light We Shall See Light* (Oxford, 2008).
Beierwaltes, W., 'Unity and Trinity in Dionysius and Eriugena', *Hermathena* 157 (1994), 1–20.
Bennett, Tony, Lawrence Grossberg, Meaghan Morris, and Raymond Williams, *New Keywords: A Revised Vocabulary of Culture and Society* (Malden, Mass., 2005).
Berg, R. M. van den, *Proclus' Hymns: Essays, Translations, Commentary*, Philosophia Antiqua 90 (Leiden, 2001).
———, *Proclus' Commentary on the Cratylus in Context. Ancient Theories of Language and Naming*, Philosophia Antiqua 112 (Leiden, 2008).
Berlin, Isaiah, and Henry Hardy, *Liberty: Incorporating Four Essays on Liberty* (Oxford, 2002).
Binns, John, *Ascetics and Ambassadors of Christ: The Monasteries of Palestine, 314–631* (Oxford, 1994).
Bitton-Ashkelony, Brouria, and Arieh Kofsky, 'Gazan Monasticism in the Fourth–Sixth Centuries: From Anchoritic to Cenobitic', *PrOC* 50 (2000), 14–62.
———, *The Monastic School of Gaza* (Leiden, 2006).
Blank, David, 'Ammonius', in *The Stanford Encyclopedia of Philosophy (Fall 2008 Edition)*, Edward N. Zalta ed. (http://plato.stanford.edu/archives/fall2008/entries/ammonius/, 2008).
Blumenthal, H., '529 and its Sequel: What Happened to the Academy?' *Byzantion* 48 (1978), 367–85.
———, 'John Philoponus: Alexandrian Platonist?' *Hermes* 114 (1986), 314–35.
———, 'Alexandria as a Centre of Greek Philosophy in Later Classical Antiquity', *ICS* 18 (1993), 307–25.
Bobzien, Susan, 'Chrysippus' Modal Logic and Its Relation to Philo and Diodorus', in *Dialektiker und Stoiker*, K. Döring and Th. Ebert eds. (Stuttgart, 1993), 63–84.
———, *Determinism and Freedom in Stoic Philosophy* (Oxford, 2001).
Bohm, J., 'Philoponus', in *The Cambridge History of Later Greek and Early Medieval Philosophy*, A. H. Armstrong ed. (London, 1970), 478–79.
Bourdieu, Pierre, *Outline of a Theory of Practice*, Cambridge Studies in Social Anthropology 16 (Cambridge, 1977).
Bowersock, Glen W., *Greek Sophists in the Roman Empire* (Oxford, 1969).
———, 'The Greek Moses: Confusion of Ethnic and Cultural Components in Later Roman and Early Byzantine Palestine', in *Religious and Ethnic Communities in Later Roman Palestine*, Hayim Lapin ed. (Potomac, Md., 1998), 31–48.
Brakke, David, Michael L. Satlow, and Steven Weitzman, eds., *Religion and the Self in Antiquity* (Indianapolis, Ind., 2005).

Brightman, Robert, 'Forget Culture: Replacement, Transcendence, Relexification', *Cultural Anthropology* 10.4 (1995), 509–46.

Brink, C. O., 'Οἰκείωσις and Οἰκειότης: Theophrastus and Zeno on Nature in Moral Theory', *Phronesis* 1.2 (1955–1956), 123–45.

Brinkmann, A., 'Die Homer-Metaphrasen des Prokopios von Gaza', *RhM* NS 63 (1908), 618–23.

Brock, Sebastian, 'Greek and Syriac in Late Antique Syria', in *Literacy and Power in the Ancient World*, A. K. Bowman and G. Woolf eds. (Cambridge, 1994), 149–160.

——, *From Ephrem to Romanos: Interactions between Syriac and Greek in Late Antiquity*, Variorum Collected Studies (Aldershot, UK, 1999).

Brown, Peter, 'The Rise and Function of the Holy Man in Late Antiquity', *JRS* 61 (1971), 80–101.

——, *Power and Persuasion in Late Antiquity: Towards a Christian Empire*, The Curti Lectures 1988 (Madison, Wis., 1992).

——, 'Holy Men', in *Cambridge Ancient History*, Vol. 14, Averil Cameron, Bryan Ward-Perkins, and Michael Whitby eds. (Cambridge, 2000), 781–810.

——, *The Body and Society: Men, Women, and Sexual Renunciation in Early Christianity*, Twentieth anniversary ed. with a new introduction (New York, 2008).

Browning, R., 'Review: The Letters of Aeneas', *CR* 13.2 (1963), 164–65.

——, 'Enlightenment and Repression in Byzantium in the Eleventh and Twelfth Centuries', *P&P* 69 (1975), 3–23.

——, Education in the Roman Empire', in *Cambridge Ancient History*, Vol. 14, Averil Cameron, Bryan Ward-Perkins, and Michael Whitby eds. (Cambridge, 2000), 855–83.

Cabrera, Miguel A., 'On Language, Culture and Social Action', *H&T* 40.4 (2001), 82–100.

Cameron, Alan, 'The Last Days of the Academy at Athens', *PCPhS* 195 (1969), 7–29.

——,'Earthquake 400', *Chiron* 17 (1987), 332–50.

——, 'On the Date of John of Gaza', *CQ* 43.1 (1993), 348–51.

Cameron, Averil, *Procopius and the Sixth Century*, Classical Life and Letters (London, 1985).

——, *Christianity and the Rhetoric of Empire: The Development of Christian Discourse*, Sather Classical Lectures, Vol. 55 (Berkeley, Calif., 1991).

——, *The Mediterranean World in Late Antiquity, AD 395–600*, Routledge History of the Ancient World (London; New York, 1993).

Cameron, Averil, B. Ward-Perkins, and M. Whitby, eds., *Late Antiquity: Empire and Successors, AD 425–600*, New ed., Cambridge Ancient History, Vol. 14 (Cambridge, 2000).

Cameron, Euan, *Interpreting Christian History: The Challenge of the Churches' Past* (Oxford, 2005).

Cancik, Hubert, August Friedrich von Pauly, and Helmuth Schneider, eds., *Der neue Pauly: Enzyklopädie der Antike*, New ed., 16 vols. (Stuttgart, 1996–2003).

Caseau, Béatrice, 'Polemein Lithois: La Désacralisation des espaces et des objets religieux païens durant l'Antiquité tardive', in *Le Sacré et son inscription dans l'espace à Byzance et en Occident*, M. Kaplan ed. (Paris, 2001), 61–123.

Cavallo, Guiglielmo, 'Places of Public Reading in Late Antiquity', in *Alexandria: Auditoria of Kom El-Dikka and Late Antique Education. Journal of Juristic Papyrology Supplement 8*, Tomasz Derda, Tomasz Markiewicz, and Ewa Wipszycka eds. (Warsaw, 2007), 151–56.

Cavinet, Pierre, and Alice Leroy-Molinghen, eds., *Théodoret de Cyr, Histoire des moines de Syrie* (Paris, 1977).

Childers, Jeff W., 'The *Life of Porphyry*: Clarifying the Relationship of the Greek and Georgian Versions through the Study of New Testament Citations', in *Transmission and*

Reception: New Testament Text-Critical and Exegetical Studies, Jeff W. Childers and D. C. Parker eds. (Piscataway, N.J., 2006), 154–78.

Chitty, Derwas J., *The Desert a City: An Introduction to the Study of Egyptian and Palestinian Monasticism under the Christian Empire* (London, 1977).

Chuvin, Pierre, 'Christianisation et résistance des cultes traditionnels', in *Hellénisme et christianisme. Collection 'Mythes, imaginaires, religions'*, Michel Narcy and Eric Rebillard eds. (Villeneuve d'Ascq, 2004), 15–34.

Ciccolella, Federica, 'Text, Interpretation and Fate of Some Anonymous *Ethopoiiai* of the Sixth Century', in *Ethopoiia: La Représentation de caractères entre fiction scolaire et réalité vivante à l'époque impériale et tardive*, Eugenio Amato and Jacques Schamp eds. (Salerno, 2005), 163–75.

Clark, Elizabeth A., *The Origenist Controversy: The Cultural Construction of an Early Christian Debate* (Princeton, N.J., 1992).

Clifford, James, *The Predicament of Culture: Twentieth-Century Ethnography, Literature, and Art* (Cambridge, Mass., 1988).

Clifford, James, and George E. Marcus, *Writing Culture: The Poetics and Politics of Ethnography* (Berkeley, Calif., 1986).

Clucas, L., *The Trial of John Italos and the Crisis of Intellectual Values in Byzantium in the Eleventh Century* (Munich, 1981).

Cohen, S. M., and D. Keyt, 'Analysing Plato's Arguments: Plato and Platonism', *OSAPh Suppl* 11 (1992), 172–200.

Collinet, P., *Histoire de l'école de droit de Beyrouth* (Paris, 1925).

Collingwood, R. G., *The Idea of History* (Oxford, 1961).

Cormack, Robin, 'Byzantine Aphrodisias: Changing the Symbolic Map of a City', *PCPhS* 216 (1990a), 26–41.

——, 'The Temple as the Cathedral', in *Aphrodisias Papers: Recent Work on Architecture and Sculpture. Journal of Roman Archaeology Supplement 1*, Charlotte Roueché and Kenan T. Erim eds. (Ann Arbor, Mich., 1990b), 75–88.

Cox, Ronald, *By the Same Word. Creation and Salvation in Hellenistic Judaism and Early Christianity*, Beihefte zur Zeitschrift für die neutestamentliche Wissenschaft Bd. 145 (Berlin, 2009).

Cramer, J. A., ed., *Anecdota graeca e codd, manuscriptis bibliothecarum Oxoniensium*, Vol. 4 (Oxford, 1835–1837).

Cribiore, Raffaella, *Gymnastics of the Mind: Greek Education in Hellenistic and Roman Egypt* (Princeton, N.J., 2001).

——, 'Spaces for Teaching in Late Antiquity', in *Alexandria: Auditoria of Kom El-Dikka and Late Antique Education. Journal of Juristic Papyrology Supplement 8*, Tomasz Derda, Tomasz Markiewicz, and Ewa Wipszycka eds. (Warsaw, 2007), 143–50.

Cumont, F., *Philonis De Aeternitate mundi* (Berlin, 1891).

Davies, Paul, *The Mind of God* (New York, 1992).

de Pretis, Anna, '"Insincerity," "Facts," and "Epistolarity": Approaches to Pliny's *Epistles* to Calpurnia', *Arethusa* 36 (2003), 127–45.

Derda, Tomasz, Tomasz Markiewicz, and Ewa Wipszycka, eds., *Alexandria: Auditoria of Kom el-Dikka and Late-Antique Education, Journal of Juristic Papyrology Supplement 8* (Warsaw, 2007).

Derrida, Jacques, *Of Grammatology* (Baltimore, Md., 1976).

——, *Dissemination* (London, 1981).

Devreesse, Robert, 'Chaines exégétiques grecques', in *Supplément au Dictionnaire de la Bible*, Vol. 1, Louis Pirot et al. eds. (Paris, 1928), 1084–1233.

Devros, Paul, 'Peter the Iberian and His Biographers. Extrait de the Journal of Ecclesiastical History 158–168', *Analecta Bollandia* 70 (1950), 385–88.

di Segni, Leah, 'The Church of Mary Theotokos on Mount Gerizim: The Inscriptions', in *Christian Archaeology in the Holy Land: New Discoveries. Essays in Honour of Virgilio C. Corbo, OFM*, Studium biblicum franciscanum, Collectio maior 36, G. C. Bottini, Leah di Segni, and E. Alliata eds. (Jerusalem, 1990a), 343–50.

——, 'The Life of Chariton', in *Ascetic Behavior in Greco-Roman Antiquity*, V. Wimbush ed. (Claremont, Calif., 1990b), 393–421.

——, 'The Territory of Gaza: Notes of Historical Geography', in *Christian Gaza in Late Antiquity. Jerusalem Studies in Religion and Culture*, Vol. 3, Arieh Kofsky and Bruria Bitton-Ashkelony eds. (Leiden, 2004), 41–60.

Dillon, John M., *The Middle Platonists: A Study of Platonism, 80 B.C. to A.D. 220* (London, 1977).

——, *The Middle Platonists: A Study of Platonism, 80 B.C. to A.D. 220*, Revised edition with new afterword (London, 1996).

——, 'Philosophy as a Profession in Late Antiquity' in *Approaching Late Antiquity*, Simon Swain and Mark Edwards eds. (Oxford, 2004), 401–18.

Dixneuf, D., 'Production et circulation des biens à Gaza durant l'antiquité tardive: Le Témoignage des amphores', in *Gaza dans l'antiquité tardive: Archéologie, rhétorique et histoire: Actes du colloque international de Poitiers, 6–7 Mai 2004*, Catherine Saliou ed. (Salerno, 2005), 41–50.

Dodds, E. R., 'Theurgy and its Relationship to Neoplatonism', *JRS* 37 (1947), 55–69.

——, *The Elements of Theology*, 2nd ed. (Oxford, 1963).

Dörrie, H., 'Kontroversen um die Seelenwanderung im kaiserzeitlichen Platonismus', *Hermes* 85.4 (1957), 414–35.

Dörrie, H., M. Baltes, et al., *Der Platonismus in der Antike*, Bd. I–VII (Stuttgart, 1987–2008).

Dougherty, Carol, and Leslie Kurke, 'Introduction: The Cultures within Greek Culture', in *The Cultures within Ancient Greek Culture: Contact, Conflict, Collaboration* (Cambridge, 2003), 1–19.

Downey, Glanville, 'The Christian Schools of Palestine: A Chapter in Literary History', *HLB* 12 (1958), 297–319.

——, *Gaza in the Early Sixth Century* (Norman, Okla., 1963).

Dräseke, J., 'Prokopios' von Gaza "Widerlegung des Proklos"', *ByzZ* 6 (1897), 55–91.

Edwards, M. J., *Neoplatonic Saints: The Lives of Plotinus and Proclus by their Students* (Liverpool, 2000).

——, *Origen against Plato*, Ashgate Studies in Philosophy and Theology in Late Antiquity (Aldershot, UK, 2002).

Elter, René, and Ayman Hassoune, 'Le Monastère de saint Hilarion: Les Vestiges archéologiques du site de Umm el-'Amr', in *Gaza dans l'antiquité tardive: Archéologie, rhétorique et histoire: Actes du colloque international de Poitiers, 6–7 Mai 2004*, Catherine Saliou ed. (Salerno, 2005), 13–40.

Elton, Hugh, 'Illus and the Imperial Aristocracy under Zeno', *Byzantion* 70.2 (2000), 393–407.

Emrich, Gerhard, 'Prokopios', in *Biographisch-Bibliographisches Kirchenlexikon*, Friedrich Wilhelm Bautz and Traugott Bautz eds. (Herzberg, Ger., 1994), 993–94.

Evans, G. R., ed., *The First Christian Theologians* (Oxford, 2004).

Evans, J. A. S., *Procopius* (New York, 1972).

Flusin, Bernard, 'Préface', in *Gaza dans l'antiquité tardive: Archéologie, rhétorique et histoire: Actes du colloque international de Poitiers, 6–7 Mai 2004*, Catherine Saliou ed. (Salerno, 2005), ix–xii.

Foster, M., 'The Christian Doctrine of Creation and the Rise of Modern Natural Science', *Mind* 43.172 (1934), 446–68.
——, 'Christian Theology and Modern Science of Nature (I)', *Mind* 44.176 (1935), 439–66.
——, 'Christian Theology and Modern Science of Nature (II)', *Mind* 45.177 (1936), 1–27.
Foucault, Michel, *The Order of Things: An Archaeology of the Human Sciences*, World of Man (London, 1970).
——, *The History of Sexuality*, trans. Robert Hurley (London, 1979).
——, *Discipline and Punish: The Birth of the Prison*, 2nd Vintage Books ed. (New York, 1995).
Foulkes, P., 'Where was Simplicius?' *JHS* 112 (1992), 143.
Fowden, G., 'The Pagan Holy Man in Late Antique Society', *JHS* 102 (1982), 33–59.
——, 'The Athenian Agora and the Progress of Christianity', *JRA* 3 (1990), 494–501.
Frankfurter, David, 'BMCR 95.02.15', Review of *Hellenic Religion and Hellenisation c. 370–529*. *Bryn Mawr Class Rev* 5.7 (1995), 640.
Frantz, A., *Late Antiquity, A.D. 267–700*, Vol. 24, *The Athenian Agora* (Princeton, N.J., 1988).
Frede, Michael, *Die stoische Logik* (Göttingen, 1974).
——, 'Monotheism and Pagan Philosophy in Later Antiquity', in *Pagan Monotheism in Late Antiquity*, Polymnia Athanassiadi and Michael Frede eds. (Oxford, 1999), 41–67.
Frend, W. H. C., *The Rise of the Monophysite Movement: Chapters in the History of the Church in the Fifth and Sixth Centuries* (Cambridge, 1972).
Gadamer, H.-G., *Truth and Method*, 2nd rev. ed. (New York, 1989).
Gallicet, E., 'Per una rilettura del Teofrasto di Enea di Gaza e dell'Ammonio di Zacaria Scolastico (Parte I e II)', *AAT* 112 (1978), 117–67.
Garitte, Gerard, 'Textes hagiographiques orientaux relatifs à saint Léonce de Tripoli. ii. L'Homélie copte de Sévère d'Antioche', *Le Muséon* 79 (1966), 335–86.
Gatti, M. L., 'Plotinus: The Platonic Tradition and the Foundation of Neoplatonism', in *The Cambridge Companion to Plotinus*, Lloyd P. Gerson ed. (Cambridge, 1996), 10–37.
Geertz, Clifford, *The Interpretation of Cultures: Selected Essays* (London, 1975).
——, *Local Knowledge: Further Essays in Interpretive Anthropology* (New York, 1983).
Geiger, Joseph, 'Aspects of Palestinian Paganism in Late Antiquity', in *Sharing the Sacred: Religious Contacts and Conflicts in the Holy Land, First–Fifteenth Centuries CE*, Arieh Kofsky and Guy G. Stroumsa eds. (Jerusalem, 1998), 3–18.
Gellner, E., *Nations and Nationalism* (Oxford, 1983).
Gersh, Stephen, *Kinêsis akinêtos: A Study of Spiritual Motion in the Philosophy of Proclus* (Leiden, 1973).
——, 'Proclus' *Commentary on the Timaeus*—the Prefatory Material', in *Ancient Approaches to Plato's Timaeus*, BICS Supplement 78, R. W. Sharples and Anne D. R. Sheppard eds. (London, 2003), 143–54.
Gerson, Lloyd P., ed., *The Cambridge Companion to Plotinus* (Cambridge, 1996).
——, *Aristotle and Other Platonists* (Ithaca, N.Y., 2005).
Glucker, Carol A. M., *The City of Gaza in the Roman and Byzantine Periods* (Oxford, 1987).
Goldhill, Simon, ed., *The End of Dialogue in Antiquity* (Cambridge, 2008).
Gould, G., *The Desert Fathers on Monastic Community* (Oxford, 1993).
Goulet, Richard, ed., *Dictionnaire de philosophes antiques* (Paris, 1989).
Grafton, Anthony, and Megan Williams, *Christianity and the Transformation of the Book: Origen, Eusebius and the Library of Caesarea* (Cambridge, Mass., 2006).
Greatrex, G., and J. Watt, 'One, Two or Three Feasts? The Brytae, the Maiuma, and the May Festival at Edessa', *OC* 83 (1999), 1–21.
Grice, H. P., *Studies in the Way of Words* (Cambridge, Mass., 1989).

Guillaumont, Antoine, *Les 'Képhalaia gnostica' d'Évagre le Pontique et l'histoire de l'origénisme chez les Grecs et chez les Syriens*, Patristica Sorbonensia 5 (Paris, 1962).
Gunton, Colin E., *The Cambridge Companion to Christian Doctrine*, Cambridge Companions to Religion (Cambridge, 1997).
Haarer, F. K., *Anastasius I: Politics and Empire in the Late Roman World*, ARCA Classical and Medieval Texts, Papers and Monographs 46 (Cambridge, 2006).
Haas, C., *Alexandria in Late Antiquity: Topography and Social Conflict* (Baltimore, Md., 1997).
Haas, Christopher, 'Kôm El-Dikka in Context: The Auditoria and the History of Late-Antique Alexandria', in *Alexandria: Auditoria of Kom El-Dikka and Late Antique Education. Journal of Juristic Papyrology Supplement 8*, Tomasz Derda, Tomasz Markiewicz, and Ewa Wipszycka eds. (Warsaw, 2007), 85–96.
Haas, Frans A. J. de, *John Philoponus' New Definition of Prime Matter: Aspects of its Background in Neoplatonism and the Ancient Commentary Tradition* (Leiden, 1997).
Hadot, Ilsetraut, *Le Problème du néo-platonisme alexandrin, Hiérocles et Simplicius* (Paris, 1978).
——, 'The Life and Work of Simplicius in Greek and Arabic Sources', in *Aristotle Transformed: The Ancient Commentators and Their Influence*, Richard Sorabji ed. (London, 1990), 275–303.
——, *Studies on the Neoplatonist Hierocles*, trans. from the French by Michael Chase, TAPhS 94.1 (Philadelphia, Pa., 2004).
Hadot, Pierre, 'Reflections on the Notion of the "Cultivation of the Self"', in *Michel Foucault, Philosopher: Essays Translated from the French and German*, Timothy J. Armstrong ed. (New York, 1992), 225–32.
——, *Philosophy as a Way of Life: Spiritual Exercises from Socrates to Foucault*, trans. Arnold Ira Davidson (Oxford, 1995).
Hägg, Tomas, Philip Rousseau, and Christian Høgel, *Greek Biography and Panegyric in Late Antiquity*, Transformation of the Classical Heritage 31 (Berkeley, Calif., 2000).
Hall, Linda Jones, *Roman Berytus: Beirut in Late Antiquity* (New York, 2004).
Hankinson, R. J., *Cause and Explanation in Ancient Greek Thought* (Oxford, 2001).
Hanson, R. P. C., 'The Transformation of Pagan Temples into Christian Churches in the Early Christian Centuries', *Journal of Semitic Studies* 23.2 (1978), 257–67.
Harl, K. W., 'Sacrifice and Pagan Belief in Fifth- and Sixth-Century Byzantium', *P&P* 128.1 (1990), 7–27.
Harris, Roy, *Saussure and his Interpreters*, 2nd ed. (Edinburgh, 2003).
Harrison, R. M., and John W. Hayes, *Excavations at Saraçhane in Istanbul* (Princeton, N.J., 1986).
Haupt, M., 'Excerpta ex Timothei Gazaei libris de animalibus', *Hermes* 3 (1869), 5–30.
Hayes, John W., *Excavations at Saraçhane in Istanbul*, Vol. 2: *Pottery* (Princeton, N.J., 1992).
Hevelone-Harper, Jennifer L., *Disciples of the Desert: Monks, Laity and Spiritual Authority in Sixth-Century Gaza* (Baltimore, Md., 2005).
Hirshfeld, Yizhar, 'The Monasteries of Gaza: An Archaeological Review', in *Christian Gaza in Late Antiquity*, Jerusalem Studies in Religion and Culture, Vol. 3, Arieh Kofsky and Bruria Bitton-Ashkelony eds. (Leiden, 2004), 61–88.
Hoffmann, P., 'Simplicius' Polemics', in *Philoponus and the Rejection of Aristotelian Science*, Richard Sorabji ed. (London, 1987), 57–83.
Hollum, K. G., 'Flavius Stephanus, Proconsul of Byzantine Palestine', *ZPE* 63 (1986), 231–39.
Hombergen, Daniel, *The Second Origenist Controversy: A New Perspective on Cyril of Scythopolis' Monastic Biographies as Historical Sources for Sixth-Century Origenism*, Studia Anselmiana 132 (Rome, 2001).

Honigmann, E., *Patristic Studies*, Studi e testi 173 (Città del Vaticano, 1953).

Horn, Cornelia B., *Asceticism and Christological Controversy in Fifth-Century Palestine: The Career of Peter the Iberian*, Oxford Early Christian Studies (Oxford, 2006).

Impellizzeri, Salvatore, *La letteratura bizantina de Costantino agli iconoclasti* (Bari, 1965).

Jackendoff, Ray, *Semantic Structures* (Cambridge, Mass., 1990).

Jenson, Robert W., *Unbaptized God: The Basic Flaw in Ecumenical Theology* (Minneapolis, Minn., 1992).

——, *Systematic Theology: The Triune God*, Vol. 1 (New York, 1997).

Judson, Lindsay, 'God or Nature? Philoponus on Generability and Perishability', in *Philoponus and the Rejection of Aristotelian Science*, Richard Sorabji ed. (London, 1987), 179–96.

Kahn, C. H., 'The Place of the Prime Mover in Aristotle's Teleology', in *Aristotle on Nature and Living Things*, Allan Gotthelf ed. (Bristol, 1985), 183–205.

Karamanolis, George E., 'Porphyry: The First Platonist Commentator on Aristotle', in *Philosophy, Science and Exegesis in Greek, Arabic & Latin Commentaries*, BICS Supplement 83.1, Peter Adamson, Hans Baltussen, and M. W. F. Stone eds. (London, 2004), 97–120.

——, *Plato and Aristotle in Agreement? Platonists on Aristotle from Antiochus to Porphyry*, Oxford Philosophical Monographs (Oxford, 2006).

Karivieri, A., 'The House of Proclus on the Southern Slopes of the Acropolis: A Contribution', in *Post-Herulian Athens*, Finnish Institute of Athens, Vol. 1, P. Castrén ed. (Athens, 1994), 115–40.

Kaster, Robert A., *Guardians of Language: The Grammarian and Society in Late Antiquity*, The Transformation of the Classical Heritage 11 (Berkeley, Calif., 1988).

Kelly, J. N. D., *Early Christian Creeds*, 3rd ed. (Harlow, UK, 1972).

——, *Early Christian Doctrines*, 5th rev. ed. (London, 1977).

——, *Golden Mouth: The Story of John Chrysostom: Ascetic, Preacher, Bishop* (Ithaca, N.Y., 1995).

Kennedy, George Alexander, *Greek Rhetoric under Christian Emperors* (Princeton, N.J., 1983).

Kennedy, Hugh, 'Syria, Palestine and Mesopotamia', in *Late Antiquity: Empire and Successors, AD 425–600, Cambridge Ancient History*, Vol. 14, Averil Cameron, B. Ward-Perkins, and M. Whitby eds. (Cambridge, 2000), 588–611.

Kofsky, Arieh, and Bruria Bitton-Ashkelony, *Christian Gaza in Late Antiquity*, Jerusalem Studies in Religion and Culture, Vol. 3 (Leiden, 2004).

Konstantinovsky, Julia, *Evagrius Ponticus: The Making of a Gnostic* (Farnham, UK, 2009).

Lampe, G. W. H., *A Patristic Greek Lexicon* (Oxford, 1961).

Lang, D. M., 'Peter the Iberian and His Biographers', *JEH* 2 (1951), 158–68.

Lee, A. D., 'The Eastern Empire: Theodosius to Anastasius', in *Late Antiquity: Empire and Successors, AD 425–600, Cambridge Ancient History*, Vol. 14, Averil Cameron, B. Ward-Perkins, and M. Whitby eds. (Cambridge, 2000), 33–62.

Lehmann, Clayton Miles, and Kenneth G. Holum, *The Greek and Latin Inscriptions of Caesarea Maritima* (Boston, Mass., 2000).

Lernould, Alain, *Physique et théologie: Lecture du Timée de Platon par Proclus*, Problématiques Philosophiques, Philosophie Ancienne (Villeneuve d'Ascq, 2001).

Lévi-Strauss, Claude, *The Savage Mind*, Nature of Human Society Series (London, 1966).

Levine, Joseph M., 'Intellectual History as History', *JHI* 66.2 (2005), 189–200.

Levine, Lee I., *Caesarea under Roman Rule*, Studies in Judaism in Late Antiquity 7 (Leiden, 1975).

Liebeschuetz, J. H. W. G., *The Decline and Fall of the Roman City* (Oxford, 2001).

Lieu, S. N. C., 'An Early Byzantine Formula for the Renunciation of Manichaeism—the Capita VII Contra Manichaeos of <Zacharias of Mitylene>', *JAC* 26 (1983), 152–219.

Lilla, Salvatore R. C., 'Neoplatonic Hypostases and the Christian Trinity', in *Studies in Plato and the Platonic Tradition: Essays Presented to John Whittaker*, Mark Joyal ed. (Aldershot, UK, 1997), 127–89.

Lim, Richard, 'Christians, Dialogues and Patterns of Sociability in Late Antiquity', in *The End of Dialogue in Antiquity*, Simon Goldhill ed. (Cambridge, 2008), 151–72.

Litsas, Fotios K., 'Choricius of Gaza: An Approach to His Work. Introduction, Translation and Commentary'. Ph.D. Dissertation, Department of History, The University of Chicago (1980).

Littlewood, Antony Robert, ed., *Originality in Byzantine Literature, Art and Music*, Oxbow Monograph 50 (Oxford, 1995).

Long, A. A., *Stoic Studies* (Berkeley, Calif., 1996).

Ma'oz, Zvi U., 'Comments on Jewish and Christian Communities in Byzantine Palestine', *PalEQ* 117 (1985), 59–68.

Maas, Michael, ed., *The Cambridge Companion to the Age of Justinian* (Cambridge; New York, 2005).

MacCormack, S., 'Christ and Empire, Time and Eternity', *Byzantion* 52 (1982), 287–309.

MacCoull, L. S. B., 'A New Look at the Career of John Philoponus', *JECS* 3.1 (1995), 47–60.

MacMullen, Ramsay, *Christianizing the Roman Empire A.D. 100–400* (New Haven, Conn.; London, 1984).

——, *Christianity and Paganism in the Fourth to Eighth Centuries* (New Haven, Conn.; London, 1997).

Mai, Angelo, ed., *Classicorum auctorum e vaticanis codicibus editorum tomus*, Vol. 4 (Vatican, 1831).

Majcherek, Grzegorz, 'The Late Roman Auditoria of Alexandria: An Archaeological Overview', in *Alexandria: Auditoria of Kom el-Dikka and Late-Antique Education. Journal of Juristic Papyrology Supplement 8*, Tomasz Derda, Tomasz Markiewicz, and Ewa Wipszycka eds. (Warsaw, 2007), 11–50.

Maltese, E. V., 'Un'epistola inedita di Procopio di Gaza', *Parola del passato* 39 (1984), 53–54.

Mansfeld, Jaap, 'Alcinous on Fate and Providence', in *Traditions of Platonism. Essays in Honour of John Dillon*, J. J. Cleary ed. (Aldershot, UK, 1999), 139–50.

Mansfeld, Jaap, and D. T. Runia, *Aëtiana: The Method and Intellectual Context of a Doxographer* (Leiden, 1996).

Maraval, Pierre, *Lieux saints et pélerinages d'Orient: Histoire et géographie des origines à la conquête arabe* (Paris, 2004).

Marinescu, C. A., 'Transformations: Classical Objects and Their Re-Use during Late Antiquity', in *Shifting Frontiers in Late Antiquity*, Ralph W. Mathisen and Hagith Sivan eds. (Aldershot, UK, 1996), 285–98.

Markowicz, W. A., 'Chrysostom's Sermons on Genesis: A Problem', *ThStud* 24 (1963), 652–64.

Martijn, Marije, 'Proclus on Nature: Philosophy of Nature and its Methods in Proclus' Commentary on Plato's Timaeus', Doctoral Dissertation, Leiden University. Chapter One—Introduction. Chapter Three—the Prooemium: The Geometrical Method of *Physiologia* (Leiden, 2006a).

——, 'Theology, Naturally. Proclus on Science of Nature as Theology and the Aristotelian Principle of Μετάβασις', in *Proklos: Methode, Seelenlehre, Metaphysik. Akten der Konferenz in Jena vom 18.–20. September 2003*, Philosophia Antiqua, Vol. 98, Matthias Perkams and Rosa Maria Piccione eds. (Leiden, 2006b), 49–70.

Martin, Dale B., and Patricia Cox Miller, *The Cultural Turn in Late Ancient Studies: Gender, Asceticism, and Historiography* (Durham, N.C., 2005).

Martinich, Aloysius, *The Philosophy of Language*, 5th ed. (Oxford, 2008).

Massa Positano, Lydia, ed., *Enea di Gaza. Epistole*, 2nd ed., Collana di studi greci, 19 (Naples, 1962).
Matthen, M., 'The Holistic Presuppositions of Aristotle's Cosmology', *OSAPh* 20 (2001), 171–200.
May, Gerhard, *Creatio Ex Nihilo: The Doctrine of Creation out of Nothing in Early Christian Thought* (Edinburgh, 1994).
Mayer, Wendy, and Pauline Allen, *John Chrysostom*, The Early Church Fathers. Selections from John Chrysostom (London, 1999).
Mayerson, Philip, 'Choricius of Gaza on the Watersupply System of Caesarea', *IEJ* 36.3–4 (1986), 269–72.
McKenzie, Judith S., 'The Place in Late Antique Alexandria "Where Alchemists and Scholars Sit (...) Was Like Stairs"', in *Alexandria: Auditoria of Kom el-Dikka and Late-Antique Education. Journal of Juristic Papyrology Supplement 8*, Tomasz Derda, Tomasz Markiewicz, and Ewa Wipszycka eds. (Warsaw, 2007), 53–83.
Mercati, G., *Notizie di Procoro e Demetrio Cidone, Manuele Caleca e Teodoro Meliteniota ed altri appunti per la storia della teologia e della letteratura bizantina del secolo XIV* (Vatican, 1931).
Merlan, Philip, 'Ammonius Hermiae, Zacharias Scholasticus and Boethius', *GRBS* 9 (1968), 193–203.
Millar, Fergus, *A Greek Roman Empire: Power and Belief under Theodosius II, 408–450*, Sather Classical Lectures, 64 (Berkeley, Calif., 2006).
Miller, Timothy S., *The Birth of the Hospital in the Byzantine Empire*, The Henry E. Sigerist Supplements to the Bulletin of the History of Medicine; New Ser., No. 10. (Baltimore, Md., 1985).
Minniti-Colonna, Maria, ed., ed., *Teofrasto* (Naples, 1958).
——, *Ammonio. Introduzione, Testo Critico, Traduzione, Commentario* (Naples, 1973).
Moore, Jerry D., *Visions of Culture: An Introduction to Anthropological Theories and Theorists*, 3rd ed. (Lanham, Md., 2008).
Moss, Cyril, 'Jacob of Serugh's Homilies on the Spectacles of the Theatre', *Le Muséon* 48 (1935), 87–112.
Most, Glen, ed., *Commentaries—Kommentare* (Göttingen, 1999).
Mouriki-Charalambous, D., *The Octateuch Miniatures of the Byzantine Manuscripts of Cosmas Indicopleustes* (Ann Arbor, Mich., 1970).
Mullett, M., 'Byzantium: A Friendly Society', *P&P* 118 (1988), 3–24.
Murdoch, Iris, *The Sovereignty of Good* (London, 2001).
Newman, Cardinal John Henry, *Two Essays on Biblical and on Ecclesiastical Miracles*. New Impression (London, 1901).
Neyt, François, 'A Form of Charismatic Authority', *Eastern Churches Review* 6 (1974), 52–65.
——, 'La Formation au monastère de L'abbé Séridos à Gaza', in *Christian Gaza in Late Antiquity*, Jerusalem Studies in Religion and Culture, Vol. 3, Arieh Kofsky and Bruria Bitton-Ashkelony eds. (Leiden, 2004), 151–63.
Nicks (= Haarer), Fiona, 'Literary Culture in the Age of Anastasius I', in *Ethnicity and Culture in Late Antiquity*, Stephen Mitchell and Geoffrey Greatrex eds. (London, 2000), 183–203.
Nietzsche, F., *The Twilight of the Idols and the Anti-Christ* (Harmondsworth, UK, 1968).
O'Brien, Denis, 'Plotinus on Matter and Evil', in *The Cambridge Companion to Plotinus* L. P. Gerson ed. (Cambridge, 1996), 171–95.

O'Meara, Dominic J., *Pythagoras Revived: Mathematics and Philosophy in Late Antiquity* (Oxford, 1989).
Olinder, Gunnar, 'The Letters of Jacob of Sarug. Comments on an Edition', *Lunds Universitets Årsskrift. N.F. Avd. 1.* 34.1 (1939), 1–140, and twenty pages of text for a letter erroneously ascribed to Jacob of Sarug.
O'Neill, J. C., 'How Early is the Doctrine of *Creatio Ex Nihilo*?' *JThS* 53.2 (2002), 449–65.
Opsomer, Jan, 'Proclus on Demiurgue and Procession: A Neoplatonic Reading of the *Timaeus*', in *Reason and Necessity: Essays on Plato's Timaeus*, R. M. Wright ed. (London, 2000), 113–43.
——, 'Who in Heaven is the demiurge? Proclus' Exegesis of Plato *Tim* 28c3–5', *AW* 32.1 (2001), 52–70.
——, 'La Démiurgie des jeunes dieux selon Proclus', *Études classiques* 71 (2003), 5–49.
Osborn, Eric, *Justin Martyr*, Beiträge zur historischen Theologie 47 (Tübingen, 1973).
——, *The Beginning of Christian Philosophy* (Cambridge, 1981).
——, 'Causality in Plato and Origen', *Origeniana Quarta* (1988), 362–364.
——, *The Emergence of Christian Theology* (Cambridge, 1993).
——, *Tertullian, First Theologian of the West* (Cambridge, 1997).
——, *Irenaeus of Lyons* (Cambridge, 2001).
——, 'Irenaeus: Rocks in the Road', *Expository Times* 114.8 (2003), 255–58.
——, 'Irenaeus', in *The First Christian Theologians*, G. R. Evans ed. (Oxford, 2004), 121–26.
Osler, Margaret J., 'The History of Philosophy and the History of *Philosophy*: A Plea for Textual History in Context', *JHPh* 40.4 (2002), 529–33.
Ovadiah, A., 'Excavations in the Area of the Ancient Synagogue at Gaza', *IEJ* 19 (1969), 193–98.
——, 'The Synagogue at Gaza', in *Ancient Synagogues Revealed*, Lee I. Levine ed. (Jerusalem, 1982), 129–32.
Pagels, Elaine, 'The Politics of Paradise: Augustine's Exegesis of Genesis 1–3 versus That of John Chrysostom', *HThR* 78 (1985), 67–99.
Papadoyannakis, Yannis, 'Instruction by Question and Answer: The Case of Late Antique and Byzantine *Erotapokriseis*', in *Greek Literature in Late Antiquity: Dynamism, Didacticism, Classicism*, Scott Fitzgerald Johnson ed. (Aldershot, UK, 2006), 91–106.
Papazian, Michael, 'The Ontological Argument of Diogenes of Babylon', *Phronesis* 52.2 (2007), 188–209.
Passmore, John, 'The Idea of a History of Philosophy', *H&T* 5 Beiheft 5: The Historiography of the History of Philosophy (1965), 1–32.
Peeters, Paul, 'La Vie géorgienne de Saint Porphyre de Gaza ', *AB* 59 (1941), 65–216.
Pelikan, Jaroslav J., *What Has Athens to Do with Jerusalem? Timaeus and Genesis in Counterpoint* (Ann Arbor, Mich., 1997).
Pembroke, S. G., 'Oikeiosis', in *Problems in Stoicism*, A. A. Long ed. (London, 1971), 114–49.
Penella, R., 'From the Muses to Eros: Choricius's Epithalamia for Student Bridegrooms', in *Gaza dans l'antiquité tardive: Archéologie, rhétorique et histoire: Actes du colloque international de Poitiers, 6–7 Mai 2004*, Catherine Saliou ed. (Salerno, 2005), 135–48.
Perrone, Lorenzo, 'The Necessity of Advice: Spiritual Direction as a School of Christianity in the Correspondence of Barsanuphius and John of Gaza', in *Christian Gaza in Late Antiquity*, Jerusalem Studies in Religion and Culture, Vol. 3, Arieh Kofsky and Bruria Bitton-Ashkelony eds. (Leiden, 2004), 131–49.
Peters, Ted, Robert J. Russell, and Michael Welker, eds., *Resurrection: Theological and Scientific Assessments* (Grand Rapids, Mich., 2002).
Peterson, Erik, *Heis Theos: Epigraphische, formgeschichtliche und religionsgeschichtliche Untersuchungen* (Göttingen, 1920).

Petit, Françoise, *La Chaîne sur la Genèse. Édition intégrale*, 4 vols., Vol. 1, Traditio exegetica graeca 1–4 (Leuven, 1991).
——, 'La Chaîne grecque sur la Genèse, miroir de l'exégèse ancienne', in *Stimuli: Exegese und ihre Hermeneutik in Antike und Christentum. Festschrift für Ernst Dassmann*, Jahrbuch für Antike und Christentum 23, Ernst Dassmann, Georg Schöllgen, and Clemens Scholten eds. (Münster Westfalen, 1996), 243–53.
Phillips, John F., 'Neoplatonic Exegeses of Plato's Cosmogony (*Timaeus* 27c–28c)', *JHPh* 35.2 (1997), 173–97.
Polkinghorne, J. C., *Belief in God in an Age of Science* (New Haven, Conn., 1998).
Praechter, K., 'Review of the *Commentaria in Aristotelem Graeca*', in *Aristotle Transformed: The Ancient Commentators and their Influence*, Richard Sorabji ed. (London, 1990), 31–54.
Raban, Avner, and Kenneth G. Holum, *Caesarea Maritima: A Retrospective after Two Millenia*, Documenta et Monumenta Orientis Antiqui 21 (Leiden, 1996).
Raban, Avner, M. Artzy, B. Goodman, and Z. Gal, *The Harbour of Sebastos (Caesarea Maritima) in its Roman Mediterranean Context*, BAR International Series 1930 (Oxford, 2009).
Rabe, Hugo, 'Aus Rhetoren-Handschriften', *RhM* 63 (1908), 512–30.
Rabinowitz, A., 'Choricius of Gaza's Description of Palestine', in *Commentationes Iudaico-Hellenisticae in Memoriam I. Lewy*, M. Schwabe and I. Gutman eds. (Jerusalem, 1949), 173–87.
Rapp, Claudia, *Holy Bishops in Late Antiquity: The Nature of Christian Leadership in an Age of Transition*, Transformation of the Classical Heritage 37 (Berkeley, Calif., 2005).
Rashed, Marwan, 'The Problem of the Composition of the Heavens (529–1610). A New Fragment of Philoponus and its Readers', in *Philosophy, Science and Exegesis in Greek, Arabic & Latin Commentaries*, BICS Supplement 83.2, Peter Adamson, Hans Baltussen, and M. W. F. Stone eds. (London, 2004), 35–58.
Regnault, Lucien, 'Moines et laïcs dans la région de Gaza au VIe siècle', in *Christian Gaza in Late Antiquity*, Jerusalem Studies in Religion and Culture, Vol. 3, Arieh Kofsky and Bruria Bitton-Ashkelony eds. (Leiden, 2004), 165–72.
Renault, Delphine, 'Les Déclamations d'*ekphraseis*: Une réalité vivante à Gaza au VIe siècle', in *Gaza dans l'antiquité tardive: Archéologie, rhétorique et histoire: Actes du colloque international de Poitiers, 6–7 Mai 2004*, Catherine Saliou ed. (Salerno, 2005), 171–95.
——, 'The Influence of Alexandria on the Intellectual Life of Gaza', in *Alexandria: Auditoria of Kom el-Dikka and Late Antique Education. Journal of Juristic Papyrology Supplement 8*, Tomasz Derda, Tomasz Markiewicz, and Ewa Wipszycka eds. (Warsaw, 2007), 11–50.
Reydams-Schils, Gretchen J., ed., *Plato's Timaeus as Cultural Icon* (Notre Dame, Ind., 2003).
Reynolds, P., 'Levantine Amphorae from Cilicia to Gaza: A Typology and Analysis of Regional Production Trends from the 2nd to the 6th Cent', in *Late Roman Coarse Wares 1: Cooking Wares and Amphorae in the Mediterranean Bar Is 1340*, J. M. Gurt, J. Buxed, and M. A. Cau eds. (Oxford, 2005), 563–611.
Richard, M., 'Apo Phones', *Byz* 20 (1950), 191–222.
Rist, John, *Plotinus: The Road to Reality* (Cambridge, 1967).
——, 'Basil's Neoplatonism: Its Background and Nature', in *Basil of Caesarea. Christian, Humanist, Ascetic*, P. J. Fedwick ed. (Toronto, 1981), 137–220.
——, 'Plotinus and Christian Philosophy', in *Cambridge Companion to Plotinus*, Lloyd P. Gerson ed. (Cambridge, 1996), 386–413.
——, 'Christian Theology and Secular Philosophy', in *The First Christian Theologians*, G. R. Evans ed. (Oxford, 2004), 105–14.
Rist, Josef, 'Zacharias Scholastikos', in *Biographisch-Bibliographisches Kirchenlexikon*, Friedrich Wilhelm Bautz and Traugott Bautz eds. (Herzberg, 1998), v. <3–23>.

——, 'Zacharias [5]', in *Der neue Pauly: Enzyklopädie der Antike*, von Hubert Cancik and Helmuth Schneider eds. (Stuttgart, 2003), 663.
Roberts, Michael, 'The Use of Myth in Latin Epithalamia from Statius to Venatius Fortunatus', *TAPhA* 119 (1989), 321–48.
Roisman, Joseph, 'Rhetoric, Manliness and Contest', in *A Companion to Greek Rhetoric. Blackwell Companions to the Ancient World. Literature and Culture*, Ian Worthington ed. (Oxford, 2007), 393–410.
Rorem, Paul E., 'Iamblichus and the Anagogical Method in Pseudo-Dionysian Liturgical Theology', *StudPat* 17 (1982), 453–60.
Roueché, Charlotte, and Joyce Maire Reynolds, *Aphrodisias in Late Antiquity: The Late Roman and Byzantine Inscriptions Including Texts from the Excavations at Aphrodisias Conducted by Kenan T. Erim* (London, 1989).
Rousseau, Philip, *Basil of Caesarea* (Berkeley, Calif., 1994).
Rubenson, Samuel, 'The Egyptian Relations of Early Palestinian Monasticism', in *The Christian Heritage in the Holy Land*, A. O'Mahony, G. Gunner, and Hintlian eds. (London, 1995), 35–46.
——, 'Origen in the Egyptian Monastic Tradition of the Fourth Century', *Origeniana Septima* (1999), 319–37.
——, 'Philosophy and Simplicity: The Problem of Classical Education in Early Christian Biography', in *Greek Biography and Panegyric in Late Antiquity*, Transformation of the Classical Heritage 31, Tomas Hägg, Philip Rousseau, and Christian Høgel eds. (Berkeley, Calif., 2000), 110–39.
Rubin, Miri, 'What is Cultural History Now?' in *What is History Now?* David Cannadine ed. (New York, 2002), 80–94.
Rubin, Zeev, 'The See of Caesarea in Conflict with Jerusalem from Nicaea (325) to Chalcedon (451)', in *Caesarea Maritima: A Retrospective after Two Millenia*, Documenta et Monumenta Orientis Antiqui 21, Avner Raban and Kenneth G. Holum eds. (Leiden, 1996), 559–74.
——, 'Porphyrius of Gaza and the Conflict between Christianity and Paganism in Southern Palestine', in *Sharing the Sacred: Religious Contacts and Conflicts in the Holy Land*, Arieh Kofsky and Guy G. Stroumsa eds. (Jerusalem, 1998), 31–66.
Runia, D. T., *Philo of Alexandria and the Timaeus of Plato* (Leiden, 1986).
——, *Philo in Early Christian Literature* (Leiden, 1994).
——, 'Caesarea Maritima and the Survival of Hellenistic-Jewish Literature', in, Documenta et Monumenta Orientis Antiqui 21, Avner Raban and Kenneth G. Holum eds. (Leiden, 1996), 476–95.
——, *On the Creation of the Cosmos According to Moses. Introduction, Translation and Commentary* (Leiden, 2001).
——, 'Plato's *Timaeus*, First Principle(s) and Creation in Philo and Early Christian Thought', in *Plato's Timaeus as Cultural Icon*, Gretchen J. Reydams-Schils ed. (Notre Dame, Ind., 2003), 133–51.
Russell, Robert J., 'Contingency in Physics and Cosmology: A Critique of the Theology of Wolfhart Pannenberg', *Zygon* 23.1 (1988), 23–43.
Russos, D., *Τρεῖς Γαζαῖοι* (Constantinople, 1893).
Sadek, M. M., 'Gaza', *Les Dossiers d'archéologie* 240 (1999), 46–67.
Saeed, John I., *Semantics*, 2nd ed., Introducing Linguistics, 2 (Malden, Mass., 2003).
Saffrey, H. D., 'Allusions antichrétiennes chez Proclus: Le Diadoque platonicien', *RSPhTh* 59 (1975), 553–63.
——, 'La Théurgie comme phénomène culturel chez les néoplatoniciens (IVe–Ve siècles)', *Koinoonia* 8.2 (1984), 161–71.

Said, Edward W., *Orientalism* (London, 1978).
Saliou, Catherine, 'L'Orateur et la ville: Réflexions sur l'apport de Chorikios à la connaissance du théâtre du VIe siècle', in *Gaza dans l'antiquité tardive: Archéologie, rhétorique et histoire: Actes du colloque international de Poitiers, 6–7 Mai 2004*, Catherine Saliou ed. (Salerno, 2005a), 171–95.
——, ed., *Gaza dans l'antiquité tardive: Archéologie, rhétorique et histoire: Actes du colloque international de Poitiers, 6–7 Mai 2004* (Salerno, 2005b).
Salles, Ricardo, *The Stoics on Determinism and Compatibilism* (Aldershot, UK, 2005).
Sambursky, Samuel, *The Concept of Time in Late Neoplatonism*, trans. Shlomo Pines (Jerusalem, 1971).
Sandwell, Isabella, *Religious Identity in Late Antiquity. Greeks, Jews and Christians in Antioch* (Cambridge, 2007).
Saradi, H., 'The Dissolution of the Urban Space in the Early Byzantine Centuries', *Symmeikta* 9 (1994), 295–308.
Saussure, Ferdinand de, *Course in General Linguistics*, ed. Charles Bally, Albert Sechehaye, Albert Riedlinger, and Roy Harris (London, 1983).
Schibli, Hermann Sadun, *Hierocles of Alexandria* (Oxford, 2002).
Schmid, Wilhelm, Wilhelm von Christ, and Otto Stählin, *Geschichte der griechischen Literatur*, Handbuch der Altertumswissenschaft 7 (Munich, 1920).
Schneewind, J. B., *The Invention of Autonomy: A History of Modern Moral Philosophy* (Cambridge, 1998).
Scholten, Clemens, *Antike Naturphilosophie und christliche Kosmologie in der Schrift 'De Opificio Mundi' des Johannes Philoponos*, Patristische Texte und Studien 45 (Berlin, 1996).
Scott, R. D., 'The Classical Tradition in Byzantine Historiography', in *Byzantium and the Classical Tradition*, M. Mullett and R. D. Scott eds. (Birmingham, UK, 1981), 61–74.
——, 'Malalas and His Contemporaries', in *Studies in John Malalas*, Byzantina Australiensia 6, Elizabeth Jeffreys, Brian Croke, and Roger Scott eds. (Sydney, 1990), 67–86.
Scotti Muth, N., *Proclo negli ultimi quarant' anni: Bibliografia ragionata della letteratura primaria e secondaria riguardante il pensiero procliano e i suoi influssi storici (anni 1949–1992)*, introduction by W. Beierwaltes (Milan, 1993).
Segonds, A., 'Ainéas de Gaza', in *Dictionnaire de philosophes antiques*, R. Goulet ed. (Paris, 1989), 82–87.
Seitz, Kilian, *Die Schule von Gaza: Eine litterargeschichtliche Untersuchung* (Heidelberg, 1892).
Sellers, R. V., 'Pseudo-Justin's *Expositio Rectae Fidei*: A Work of Theodoret of Cyrus?' *JThS* Old Series 46 (1945), 145–160.
Sewell, William, *Logics of History* (Chicago, 2005).
Shaw, David Gary, 'Happy in Our Chains? Agency and Language in the Postmodern Age', *H&T* 40.4 (2001), 1–9.
Sheppard, Anne D. R., 'Philosophy and Philosophical Schools', in *Cambridge Ancient History*, Vol. 14, Averil Cameron, B. Ward-Perkins, and M. Whitby eds. (Cambridge, 2000), 835–54.
Sikorski, Stephan, 'De Aenea Gazaeo', Dissertation, Breslau University, (Vratislaviae, 1909).
Siniossoglou, Niketas, *Platonism in Byzantium: Illumination and Utopia in Gemistos Plethon* (Cambridge, 2011).
Siorvanes, Lucas, *Proclus: Neo-Platonic Philosophy and Science* (Edinburgh, 1996).
Sivan, Hagith, *Palestine in Late Antiquity* (Oxford, 2008).
Skinner, Quentin, 'Conventions and the Understanding of Speech Acts', *PhilosQ* 20 (1970), 118–38.

——, 'The Idea of Negative Liberty: Philosophical and Historical Perspectives', in *Philosophy in History*, R. Rorty, J. B. Schneewind, and Quentin Skinner eds. (Cambridge, 1984), 193–221.
——, 'A Reply to My Critics', in *Meaning and Context: Quentin Skinner and his Critics*, James Tully ed. (Oxford, 1988a), 231–88.
——, 'Meaning and Understanding in the History of Ideas', in *Meaning and Context: Quentin Skinner and his Critics*, James Tully ed. (Oxford, 1988b), 29–67.
——, '"Social Meaning" and Social Action', in *Meaning and Context: Quentin Skinner and his Critics*, James Tully ed. (Oxford, 1988c), 79–96.
——, 'A Third Concept of Liberty', *PBA* 117 (2002), 237–68.
——, *Hobbes and Republican Liberty* (Cambridge, 2008).
Smith, Andrew, *Porphyry's Place in the Neoplatonic Tradition: A Study in Post-Plotinian Neoplatonism* (The Hague, 1974).
——, 'Did Porphyry Reject the Transmigration of Souls into Animals?' *RhM* 127 (1984), 276–84.
——, *The Philosopher and Society in Late Antiquity: Essays in Honour of Peter Brown* (Swansea, 2005).
Sorabji, Richard, *Time, Creation, and the Continuum: Theories in Antiquity and the Early Middle Ages* (Ithaca, N.Y., 1983).
——, 'Infinity and Creation', in *Philoponus and the Rejection of Aristotelian Science*, idem. eds. (London, 1987a), 164–78.
——, 'John Philoponus', in *Philoponus and the Rejection of Aristotelian Science*, idem. eds. (London, 1987b), 1–40.
——, ed., *Philoponus and the Rejection of Aristotelian Science* (London, 1987c).
——, ed., *Aristotle Transformed: The Ancient Commentators and Their Influence* (London, 1990).
——, 'Infinite Power Impressed: The Transformation of Aristotle's Physics and Theology', in *New Perspectives in Renaissance Thought: Essays in Memory of Charles B. Schmitt*, J. Henry and S. Hutton eds. (London, 1990a), 148–62.
——, *Animal Minds and Human Morals: The Origins of the Western Debate* (London, 1993).
——, 'Divine Names and Sordid Deals in Ammonius' Alexandria', in *The Philosopher and Society in Late Antiquity: Essays in Honour of Peter Brown*, Andrew Smith ed. (Swansea, 2005a), 203–14.
——, *The Philosophy of the Commentators, 200–600 AD: A Sourcebook*, 3 vols. (Ithaca, N.Y., 2005b).
Sotinel, Claire, 'La Disparition des lieux de culte paiens en occident: Enjeux et méthodes', in *Hellénisme et christianisme. Collection 'Mythes, imaginaires, religions'*, Michel Narcy and Eric Rebillard eds. (Villeneuve d'Ascq, 2004), 35–60.
Spiegel, Gabrielle M., *The Past as Text: The Theory and Practice of Medieval Historiography* (Baltimore, Md., 1997).
——, *Practicing History: New Directions in Historical Writing after the Linguistic Turn*, Rewriting Histories (New York, 2005).
Stanton, G. R., 'Sophists and Philosophers: Problems of Classification', *AJPh* 94.4 (1973), 350–64.
Stedman Jones, Gareth, 'The Determinist Fix: Some Obstacles to the Further Development of the Linguistic Approach to History in the 1990s', *History Workshop Journal* 42 (1996), 19–35.
Steel, C., 'Why Should We Prefer Plato's *Timaeus* to Aristotle's *Physics*? Proclus' Critique of Aristotle's Causal Explanation of the Physical World', in *Ancient Approaches to Plato's*

Timaeus, BICS Supplement; 78, R. W. Sharples and Anne D. R. Sheppard eds. (London, 2003), 175–88.

———, 'Proclus' Defence of the *Timaeus* against Aristotle's Objections', in *Platons Timaios als Grundtext der Kosmologie in Spätantike, Mittelalter und Renaissance = Plato's Timaeus and the Foundations of Cosmology in Late Antiquity, the Middle Ages and Renaissance*, Ancient and Medieval Philosophy, Series 1, 34, Thomas Leinkauf and Carlos G. Steel eds. (Leuven, 2005), 163–93.

Steel, Carlos, et al., 'Proclus' Influence', *Lustrum* 44 (2002/2005), 220–77.

Steel, Carlos G., et al., *Bibliography Proclus Covering the Years 1990–2008*, Plato Transformed team at the Katholieke Universiteit Leuven, accessed at http://www.hiw.kuleuven.be/dwmc/ancientphilosophy/proclus/proclusbiblio.html (Last accessed August 2013) (Leuven, 2013).

Stiglmayer, J., 'Die "Streitschrift des Prokopios von Gaza" gegen den Neuplatoniker Proklos', *ByzZ* 8 (1899), 263–301.

Striker, G., *Essays on Hellenistic Epistemology and Ethics* (Cambridge, 1996).

Swete, Henry Barclay, Richard Rusden Ottley, and H. St J. Thackeray, *An Introduction to the Old Testament in Greek* (Cambridge, 1914).

Szbat, Elzbieta, 'Teachers in the Eastern Roman Empire (Fifth–Seventh Centuries)', in *Alexandria: Auditoria of Kom el-Dikka and Late Antique Education. Journal of Juristic Papyrology Supplement 8*, Tomasz Derda, Tomasz Markiewicz, and Ewa Wipszycka eds. (Warsaw, 2007), 177–345.

Tanner, Kathryn, *Theories of Culture: A New Agenda for Theology* (Minneapolis, Minn., 1997).

Tarrant, H., 'The Date of Anonymous *in Theatetum*', *CQ* 33 (1983), 161–87.

Tarrant, Harold, 'Introduction to Book One', in *Proclus. Commentary on Plato's Timaeus Volume I. Book I: Proclus on the Socratic State and Atlantis.* Translated with an introduction and notes by Harold Tarrant, with a general introduction by Dirk Baltzly and Harold Tarrant (Cambridge, 2007), 21–84.

Taylor, C. C. W., *Plato, Protagoras: Translated with Introduction and Notes by C. C. W. Taylor*, Revised ed., Clarendon Plato Series (Oxford, 1991).

Taylor, Charles, 'What's Wrong with Negative Liberty?' in *The Idea of Freedom: Essays in Honour of Isaiah Berlin*, Alan Ryan ed. (Oxford, 1979), 175–93.

Ter Haar Romeny, R. B., 'Procopius of Gaza and His Library', in *From Rome to Constantinople: Studies in Honour of Averil Cameron*, Late Antique History and Religion 1, Averil Cameron, Hagit Amirav, and R. B. ter Haar Romeny eds. (Leuven, 2007), 173–90.

Torrance, A. J., '*Creatio ex nihilo* and the Spatio-Temporal Dimension with Special Reference to Jürgen Moltmann and D. C. Williams', in *The Doctrine of Creation*, Colin E. Gunton ed. (Edinburgh, 1997), 81–103.

Trapp, Michael B., *Greek and Latin Letters: An Anthology, with Translation*, Cambridge Greek and Latin Classics (Cambridge, 2003).

Trombley, Frank R., *Hellenic Religion and Christianization: C. 370–529*, 2 vols. (Leiden, 1993).

Tsafir, Yoram, 'The Fate of Pagan Cult Places in Palestine', in *Religious and Ethnic Communities in Later Roman Palestine*, Studies and Texts in Jewish History and Culture 5, Hayim Lapin ed. (Potomac, Md., 1998), 197–218.

Tully, James, ed., *Meaning and Context: Quentin Skinner and his Critics* (Cambridge, 1988).

Tuominen, Miira, *The Ancient Commentators on Plato and Aristotle*, Ancient Philosophies (Stocksfield, UK, 2009).

Turner, Victor, *The Ritual Process: Structure and Anti-Structure*, Lewis Henry Morgan Lectures (London, 1969).

Tyler, Stephen, 'Post-Modern Ethnography: From Documents of the Occult to Occult Documents', in *Writing Culture: The Poetics and Politics of Ethnography*, James Clifford and George E. Marcus eds. (Berkeley, Calif., 1986), 122–40.
Tzamalikos, P., *Origen: Cosmology and Ontology of Time*. Supplements to Vigiliae Christianae 77 (Leiden, 2006).
van Dam, Raymond, 'From Paganism to Christianity in Late Antique Gaza', *Viator* 16 (1985), 1–20.
van den Hoek, Annewies, 'The "Catechetical" School of Early Christian Alexandria and its Philonic Heritage', *HThR* 90.1 (1997), 59–87.
Verrycken, K., 'The Metaphysics of Ammonius son of Hermeias', in *Aristotle Transformed: The Ancient Commentators and their Influence*, Richard Sorabji ed. (London, 1990), 199–231.
——, 'La Métaphysique d'Ammonius chez Zacharie de Mytilène', *RSPhTh* 85 (2001), 241–66.
Volgers, Annelie, and Claudio Zamagni, *Erotapokriseis: Early Christian Question-and-Answer Literature in Context. Proceedings of the Utrecht Colloquium, 13–14 October 2003* (Leuven, 2005).
Vössing, Konrad, 'Scholae et bibliothecae. Überleungen zum Zusammenhang von Schulen und Bibliotheken im römischen Reich', in *Alexandria: Auditoria of Kom el-Dikka and Late Antique Education. Journal of Juristic Papyrology Supplement 8*, Tomasz Derda, Tomasz Markiewicz, and Ewa Wipszycka eds. (Warsaw, 2007), 157–68.
Wacht, Manfred, *Aeneas von Gaza als Apologet. Seine Kosmologie im Verhältnis zum Platonismus* (Bonn, 1969).
Watson, Richard A., 'What is the History of Philosophy and Why is it Important', *JHPh* 40.4 (2002), 525–28.
Watts, Edward, 'Justinian, Malalas and the End of Athenian Philosophical Teaching in AD 529', *JRS* 94 (2004a), 168–83.
——, 'Travel to Educational Centers: What Was the Attraction?' in *Travel, Communication and Geography in Late Antiquity*, Linda Ellis and Frank L. Kidner eds. (London, 2004b), 11–21.
——, 'An Alexandrian Christian Response to Fifth-Century Neoplatonic Influence', in *Philosophy and Society in Late Antiquity*, Andrew Smith ed. (Swansea, 2005a), 215–29.
——, 'The Student Self in Late Antiquity', in *Religion and the Self in Antiquity*, David Brakke, Michael L. Satlow, and Steven Weitzman eds. (Indianapolis, Ind., 2005b), 234–41.
——, 'Where to Live the Philosophical Life in the Sixth Century? Damascius, Simplicius, and the Return from Persia', *GRBS* 45.3 (2005c), 285–315.
——, 'Winning the Intracommunal Dialogues: Zacharias Scholasticus' *Life of Severus*', *JECS* 13.4 (2005d), 437–64.
——, *City and School in Late Antique Athens and Alexandria* (Berkeley, Calif., 2006).
——, 'Creating the Ascetic and Sophistic Mélange: Zacharias Scholasticus and the Intellectual Influence of Aeneas of Gaza and John Rufus', *Aram* 19 (2007), 153–64.
Webb, Ruth, *Demons and Dancers: Performance in Late Antiquity* (Cambridge, Mass., 2008).
Welch, Katherine E., 'Some Architectural Prototypes for the Auditoria at Kom el-Dikka and Three Late Antique (fifth century AD) Comparanda from Aphrodisias in Caria', in *Alexandria: Auditoria of Kom El-Dikka and Late Antique Education. Journal of Juristic Papyrology Supplement 8*, Tomasz Derda, Tomasz Markiewicz, and Ewa Wipszycka eds. (Warsaw, 2007), 115–33.
Wellmann, M., 'Timotheos von Gaza', *Hermes* 62 (1927), 179–204.
Westerink, L. G., 'Proclus, Procopius, Psellus', *Mnemosyne* Series 3: 10 (1942), 275–80.
——, 'Ein unbekannter Brief des Prokopios von Gaza', *ByzZ* 60 (1967), 1–2.

——, 'Anonymous Prolegomena to the Commentators', in *Aristotle Transformed: The Ancient Commentators and their Influence*, Richard Sorabji ed. (London, 1990), 325–48.

Whittaker, J., 'ΕΠΕΚΕΙΝΑ ΝΟΥ ΚΑΙ ΟΥΣΙΑΣ' *VChr* 23 (1969), 91-104.

——, 'Platonic Philosophy in the Early Centuries of the Empire', *ANRW* Band 2 36.1 (1987), 81–123.

Wilberding, James, *Plotinus' Cosmology: A Study of Ennead II.1 (40): Text, Translation, and Commentary* (Oxford, 2006).

Wildberg, Christian, 'Prolegomena to the Study of Philoponus' *Contra Aristotelem*', in *Philoponus and the Rejection of Aristotelian Science*, Richard Sorabji ed. (London, 1987), 197–209.

——, *John Philoponus' Criticism of Aristotle's Theory of Aether* (Berlin, 1988).

Williams, Raymond, *Keywords: A Vocabulary of Culture and Society*, Revised and expanded ed. (London, 1988).

Williams, Rowan, 'What Does Love Know? St Thomas on the Trinity. The Aquinas Lecture, Oxford Jan 24th 2001', *New Blackfriars* 82.964 (2001), 260–72.

——, 'Origen', in *The First Christian Theologians*, G. R. Evans ed. (Oxford, 2004), 132–42.

Wilson, N. G., 'A Chapter in the History of Scholia', *CQ* 17.2 (1967).

Wolfson, H. A., *Philo: Foundations of Religious Philosophy in Judaism, Christianity and Islam* (Cambridge, Mass., 1968).

Wolska, W., *Recherches sur la 'Topographie Chrétienne' de Cosmas Indicopleustès: Théologie et science au VIe siècle* (Paris, 1962).

Young, Frances M., *Biblical Exegesis and the Formation of Christian Culture* (Cambridge, 1997).

Index Locorum

General Index